TRAGIC SENECA

TRAGIC SENECA

An essay in the theatrical tradition

A. J. Boyle

London and New York

First published 1997
by Routledge
11 New Fetter Lane, London EC4P 4EE

Simultaneously published in the USA and Canada
by Routledge
29 West 35th Street, New York, NY 10001

© 1997 A. J. Boyle

Typeset in Garamond by RefineCatch Limited, Bungay, Suffolk

Printed and bound in Great Britain by
Creative Print and Design (Wales), Ebbw Vale

Brtitish Library Cataloguing in Publication Data
A catalogue record for this book is available from the British Library

Library of Congress Cataloging in Publication Data
Boyle, A. J. (Anthony James)
Tragic Seneca: an essay in the theatrical tradition / A. J. Boyle
Includes bibliographical references and index.
1. Seneca, Lucius Annaeus, *c.*4BC–65AD – Tragedies.
2. European drama – Renaissance, 1450–1600 – History and criticism.
3. Seneca, Lucius Annaeus, *c.*4BC–65AD – Influence.
4. Latin drama (Tragedy) – History and criticism.
5. European drama (Tragedy) – Roman influences.
6. Mythology, Greek, in literature.
I. Title.
PA6685.B69   1997
872'.01 – dc21   96–52766

ISBN 0–415–12495–6

For my brother
John Michael Boyle

TRAGEDY   I must haue passions that must moue the soule,
       Make the heart heaue, and throb within the bosome,
       Extorting teares out of the strictest eyes,
       To racke a thought and straine it to his forme,
       Untill I rap the sences from their course.
                     Anon. *A Warning for Fair Women* (1599)

CONTENTS

PREFACE

This book is the product of almost two decades of thinking about Seneca *tragicus*. I began to teach Senecan drama at both the graduate and the undergraduate level in Australia during the late 1970s, inspired by John Herington's seminal *Arion* article of 1966 and my own developing interest in Roman theatre. Dissatisfaction with the then current state of Senecan criticism and with Senecan tragedy's exclusion from both classics curricula and the modern canon was only intensified by the intellectual excitement experienced in the classroom and the dramatic power generated on stage. Productions of *Phaedra* at the Sydney Opera House in 1987 and of *Troades* at the Alexander Theatre, Melbourne, in 1988 testified to the tragic force and theatrical craftsmanship, indeed theatrical self-consciousness, of these plays. My previous work has focused primarily on individual plays: both through critical essays (1983 and 1985) and through editions, translations and commentaries on specific texts: *Phaedra* (1987) and *Troades* (1994). In 'Senecan tragedy: twelve propositions' (*The Imperial Muse I*, 1988) I attempted to make some larger statement about Senecan drama. This book develops some positions of that essay, incorporating and expanding my earlier work into a dramatic and cultural critique of Seneca's tragic corpus, and a new investigation of his seminal role in the formation of Renaissance drama.

My attention to Seneca *tragicus* has not been unique. No reader of this book will be unaware that it is part of an upsurge in Senecan studies (some even call it an 'industry') which has taken place especially over the last decade, embracing commentaries on specific texts, specialised monographs on dramaturgy, metrics, Ovidian influence, argumentative structure, spectacle, choruses, and the theatrical and textual traditions. The following revaluation of Senecan tragedy and its impact on the Renaissance is conscious of its status as part of this collaborative scholarship. Its aim is to further the canon revision implicit in recent work and to help restore Seneca to a position of centrality in the European literary and dramatic tradition.

It is a pleasure to acknowledge debts. To Francis Cairns Publications I am grateful for permission to reuse material from my editions of Seneca's *Phaedra* and *Troades*. To the National Endowment for the Humanities I am indebted for the award of a Senior Fellowship for the year 1994/5, which combined with a sabbatical leave from USC to give me a year's uninterrupted research time. I thank both the NEH and USC for their generous provision. An important part of my Fellowship year (February to May 1995) was spent as a Visiting Professor at King's College, Cambridge, where the hospitality and intellectual stimulus of the college and its classicists, Dr John Henderson and Dr Simon Goldhill, provided an ideal context for Senecan thinking. Several friends and colleagues read an earlier draft of the book and offered advice: Claire Campbell, Alan Heinrich, and Joseph Smith of USC; Peter Davis of the University of Tasmania; Ruth Morse of Cambridge University and the Sorbonne; and Marcus Wilson of the University of Auckland. I thank them. I state the truism that the responsibility for what follows is not theirs. I dedicate the book to my brother, John, as a token of my esteem for him. For over fifty years he has been both a brother and a friend. I hope this book is not unworthy.

A. J. B.
University of Southern California, Los Angeles
Hallowe'en 1996

TEXTUAL NOTE

For Seneca's *Phaedra* and *Troades* I have used the text contained in my editions of 1987 (Liverpool) and 1994 (Leeds) respectively. For Seneca's *Agamemnon* I have used Tarrant's 1976 edition, and for the remaining Senecan plays, unless otherwise indicated, the OCT of Zwierlein (1986). I have occasionally changed the punctuation of Tarrant's and Zwierlein's texts, and have not always adopted their capitalisation (or non-capitalisation) practices. The editions used for the text of Renaissance plays are listed in the bibliography on p. 240.

The translations throughout the book are my own. Those of verse are in verse. The translations of passages from *Phaedra* and *Troades* are from my editions cited above.

Prologue

1

THE ROMAN THEATRE

The theatre is a gift which has not been vouchsafed to every race, even of the highest culture. It has been given to the Hindus, the Japanese, the Greeks, the English, the French, and the Spanish, at moments; in less measure to the Teutons and Scandinavians. It was not given to the Romans, or generously to their successors the Italians.

T. S. Eliot, 'Seneca in Elizabethan Translation' (1927)

Eliot's judgement of the Roman aptitude for, and achievement in, 'theatre' (he means 'drama') could not have been more mistaken. Throughout the whole of the late republic (240–227 BCE) Roman tragedy and comedy were vital literary and cultural forces. Horace's account of the origins of Roman drama, in his *Epistle* to the first emperor Augustus, though as prejudicial in its own way as that of Eliot, underscores the civilising effect of Rome's theatrical arts:

> Graecia capta ferum uictorem cepit et artes
> intulit agresti Latio . . .
> serus enim Graecis admouit acumina chartis,
> et post Punica bella quietus quaerere coepit,
> quid Sophocles et Thespis et Aeschylus utile ferrent.
> temptauit quoque rem, si digne uertere posset,
> et placuit sibi, natura sublimis et acer;
> nam spirat tragicum satis et feliciter audet,
> sed turpem putat inscite metuitque lituram.
>
> (*Epistles* 2.1.156–67)

> Enslaved Greece enslaved her savage victor and brought
> The arts to rustic Latium . . .
> It was late when Romans attacked Greek scripts with wit,
> And in the peace after the Punic wars began to ask
> The uses of Sophocles, Thespis, and Aeschylus.
> They also tried to make worthy adaptations,

3

And, by nature lofty and vigorous, took pride;
For they've enough tragic spirit, and their boldness works,
But in ignorance they're ashamed and afraid to blot.

Horace is writing *c*.12 BCE, some 200 years after the events he describes, and he has his own axe to grind. He deplores the contemporary adulation of the older poets and dramatists, whom 'mighty Rome learns by heart and views packed in her narrow theatre' (*hos ediscit et hos arto stipata theatro | spectat Roma potens, Epistles.* 2.1.60f.) – to the neglect of a poet such as himself. He sees clearly, however, the theatre's contemporary cultural importance and its origins in the Hellenisation of Rome. The observations are causally related. During an extraordinarily creative period beginning in the middle of the third century BCE, Rome's competitive aristocrats, driven by the desire to surpass each other and by a collective craving for an enhancement of Rome's self-image, adopted, adapted, appropriated or stole Greek literary and artistic forms with creative energy and political zeal. The result was Rome's transformation within approximately a hundred years (240–*c*.150 BCE) from the Mediterranean's major politico-military power into a civilisation. From the second century BCE onwards into imperial times the Roman theatre, however complex and ambivalent its treatment by Roman writers, who sometimes represent it as a cesspool of foreign excess (Tacitus *Annals* 14.20), becomes a prime index of Roman social and cultural order and the paradoxes of the Roman self.[1]

The first drama known to have been written in Latin was the adaptation of a Greek play, probably a tragedy, by the early translator of Homer's *Odyssey*, the ex-slave, Livius Andronicus; it was performed at the *Ludi Romani* or 'Roman shows' of 240 BCE. Thence until the end of the republic the writing and the performance of Roman tragedy and comedy were active industries. Comedy has fared better historically, since many whole plays have survived, whereas not a single complete republican Roman tragedy is extant. The main figures in comedy were Naevius (d. *c*.200 BCE), Plautus (*c*.250–184 BCE), Caecilius Statius (d. 168 BCE) and Terence (185–159 BCE), all of them exponents of what became known as the *fabula palliata* (i.e. drama in which actors wore the *pallium* or Greek cloak), a Roman adaptation, indeed transformation, of the Greek New Comedy of manners. Their comedy was essentially domestic, bourgeois, generally concerned with the removal of barriers to young love, but in the hands of Plautus, the 'playmaker' *par excellence*, whose plays 'play' with their own dramatic conventions (see esp. *Miles Gloriosus, Pseudolus, Bacchides* and *Casina*), it achieved an almost precocious metatheatrical dimension.[2] Plautus' popularity was immense; less so that of Terence, whose plays were occasionally driven from the stage by the competing attractions of boxing or tightrope-acts, or by the prospect of a gladiatorial contest (see *Hecyra's* Prologues), and who always achieves a level of social criticism in his drama apparently at odds with audience expectation.

In Terence we also witness a telling signal of drama's centrality in Roman culture: sustained theatrical polemic. After the death of Terence no major writer of *palliatae* emerges, the Roman public being essentially content with replaying the works of the earlier writers. A different kind of comedy, however, now comes to the fore, the *fabula togata*, in which the Greek context is abandoned and the scene is set in identified Italian townships. Its leading and most prolific exponent, whose plays were performed even in imperial times (his *Incendium*, 'The Fire', was watched by Nero: Suetonius *Nero* 11.2ff.), was Lucius Afranius (born *c*.150 BCE). Just over 400 lines remain from Afranius' substantial *oeuvre*, of which we know the titles of some forty-four plays.

Most republican tragedy, like comedy, took its themes and plots from existing Greek plays (but, as with comedy, the process was nothing at all like 'translation'), and a new kind of tragedy also emerged, the historical drama or *fabula praetexta* (Horace *Ars Poetica* 288), which took its theme from Roman history but was always a secondary form. The *praetexta* was never as popular as its comedy counterpart, the *togata*, of which seventy titles survive from three writers alone. In republican tragedy four major figures stand out, whose works, however, exist only in fragments: Naevius and Ennius (239–*c*.169 BCE), both of whom also wrote comedies; Pacuvius (220–130 BCE), and Accius (170–*c*.85 BCE). The first of these to devote himself entirely to tragic drama was Pacuvius – erudite, allusive, Alexandrian, master of pathos and 'highly wrought verses' (*elaborati uersus*, Cicero *Orator* 36). But it was 'soaring' Accius (Horace *Epistles* 2.1.55), famed for his 'verbal violence' and rhetorical skills,[3] especially the emotive force of his speeches, who dominated the late republic. His output was huge, and contained forty-six plays whose titles are known (including two *praetextae*), works on stage history and stage practice, and a hexameter poem, *Annals*. His popularity was also huge, and not only in his lifetime. Revivals of Accius' plays – sometimes performed with contemporary political overtones (see Cicero *Pro Sestio* 123) – are attested for the years 57 BCE (*Eurysaces* and *Brutus*), 55 BCE (*Clytemestra*), 54 BCE (*Astyanax*), and 44 BCE (*Tereus*). Other second-century tragedians too had their work performed at this time, but Accius' popularity seems to have been unmatched. Even Cicero, who judged Pacuvius supreme in tragedy (*De Optimo Genere Oratorum* 1.2), admired him greatly (see e.g. *Pro Sestio* 119ff.).

Like that of Athens, Roman drama was constituent of a historical and social context. Many native Italian factors contributed to the birth of Roman drama: harvest festival games, Fescennine jesting (obscene jokes and abuse at harvest-time and during marital and triumphal processions), the 'Atellane farce' native to Campania, the Saturnalian festival in December, and even, if Livy is right at least in this (7.2), Etruscan dancing. Italo-Greek influences from southern Italy and Sicily also ensured an appetite for theatre. Indeed it was a Greek from Tarentum in the heel of Italy, Andronicus, who initiated the fusion of native Italian appetite with Greek form in 240 BCE. From that year onwards the *ludi*, 'games' or 'shows', marking the annual festivals held at

Rome in honour of Jupiter, Apollo, the Great Mother, Flora and Ceres,[4] began gradually to incorporate *ludi scaenici* or 'theatrical shows', including comedies, tragedies, Atellane farces, mime, music and dancing, into the carnivalesque atmosphere of the religious festivals. The *ludi* began with a sacrifice to the appropriate deity and a procession from the cult temple, but, when the play began, the actors had to compete with all kinds of circus-style entertainment. As Terence's prologues reveal, they sometimes failed.

By the first century BCE all the festivals mentioned above featured dramatic shows. Even by 190 BCE perhaps some seventeen official days each year were committed to *ludi scaenici*,[5] to which should be added an unknown number of days given over to the repetition of festivals which had been improperly conducted and to the performance of plays in other, less regular contexts: at the triumphs or funerals of distinguished citizens and at the consecration of temples, spectacular occasions which the spectacle of theatre appropriately enhanced. The *ludi scaenici* were organised by Roman magistrates, who used them (among other things) to impress their peers, clients and the citizen body as a whole, and (especially where the *praetexta* was concerned)[6] for specific political goals. Initially the bulk of the credit for a performance went to the magistrate who commissioned and arranged the *ludi*, often at great, sometimes ruinous personal expense. The early playwrights themselves were accorded little social status, being regarded as paid employees of the magistrate, if they were not his actual slaves. This situation began to change during the second century BCE, and by the first century the early writers of Roman tragedy were being regarded as the fathers of an important indigenous literature. They were sometimes even thought to excel their Greek counterparts (see Cicero *Tusculans* 2.49). Tragic and comic actors, however, became legally marginalised. Many of them were either slaves or non-citizens; but even those who were Roman citizens were legally classified as *infames*, 'infamous', banned apparently from the army and disenfranchised, liable in the late republic to be flogged by Roman magistrates anywhere, unable (by Augustan times) to marry freeborn citizens, and subject along with prostitutes and gladiators to a large range of other legal restrictions.[7] There were distinguished exceptions, including the great comic actor Roscius, raised to equestrian status by the dictator Sulla and regarded by Cicero as a friend (Macrobius *Saturnalia* 3.14.11ff.). But on the whole actors (*histriones*), like gladiators, were Rome's celebrities and its dregs. The guilds in which they organised themselves along with writers (*scribae*) seem to have had little power.

As to how early Roman drama was staged, much remains obscure. Clearly, however, Roman productions were more operatic than their Greek predecessors. Lyric sections, which are prominent in Plautine comedy and take up a far greater proportion of republican tragedy than of either Attic tragedy or Seneca, were accompanied by a piper or flute-player, *tibicen*, whose importance to the production is indicated by the practice (unknown in the Greek tradition) of recording his name in the play-notices. At least by the first century BCE actors were wearing the tragic or comic mask (Cicero *De Oratore* 3.221) and generically appropriate footwear, the *coturnus* or raised boot for tragedy, the *soccus* or slipper for comedy. From 56 BCE there is evidence of a stage-curtain (*aulaeum*), which was rolled down at the beginning of a performance and raised to conceal the stage at the end.[8] Elaborate costuming was normal in tragedy. In comedy those taking the roles of free men wore the 'Greek cloak' or *pallium* over a tunic, slave characters wore a sleeveless tunic, short cloak and red wig, and 'free-born women' a full-length tunic or gown beneath a woman's cloak or *palla*. Specialist comic roles (soldiers, sailors, travellers, etc.) required specialist costuming. All actors in tragedy and comedy seem to have been male. They were often the same persons; the dramatic forms were never the separate institutions they were in Greece. Acting itself was a virtuoso performance in a self-consciously 'grand' or 'comic' style, involving highly expressive movement, stance and gesture, as well as power and nuance of voice. What Roman audiences most wanted – at the theatre, amphitheatre or triumphal processions – was visual spectacle:

> si foret in terris, rideret Democritus, seu
> diuersum confusa genus panthera camelo
> siue elephans albus uulgi conuerteret ora;
> spectaret populum ludis attentius ipsis,
> ut sibi praebentem nimio spectacula plura;
> scriptores autem narrare putaret asello
> fabellam surdo. nam quae peruincere uoces
> eualuere sonum referunt quem nostra theatra?
> Garganum mugire putes nemus aut mare Tuscum,
> tanto cum strepitu ludi spectantur et artes,
> diuitiaeque peregrinae, quibus oblitus actor
> cum stetit in scaena, concurrit dextera laeuae.
> 'dixit adhuc aliquid?' 'nil sane.' 'quid placet ergo?'
> 'laena Tarentino uiolas imitata ueneno.'
> (Horace *Epistles* 2.1.194–207)

Were he on earth, Democritus would laugh, whether
Some mongrel breed of camel-crossed-with-panther
Or a white elephant enticed the crowd's eye;
He'd watch the people more keenly than the shows
As providing far the greater spectacle;
He'd think the playwrights were telling their tale
To a deaf ass. For what voices have prevailed
To drown the din echoing from our theatres?
You'd think the Garganus forest or Tuscan sea roared,
So great is the noise when they view shows, art-works
And foreign finery, plastered with which the actor

Steps on stage to the crashing of right hand with left.
'Has he said something yet?' 'Nothing.' 'Why the applause?'
'It's that violet-coloured cloak, Tarentum-dyed.'

The Horatian commentary is again prejudicial. But it corresponds to a consistently attested emphasis in Roman theatrical practice. Cicero tells his friend Marcus Marius that, at the opening of Pompey's theatre, the entrance of Agamemnon in Accius' *Clytemestra* was accompanied by 600 mules and in *Trojan Horse* (by Naevius?) 3,000 wine-bowls were used (*Ad Familiares* 7.1.2). The audience loved it. A generation later Livy writes of the theatre's 'mad extravagance', *insania*, 'scarcely able to be supported by opulent kingdoms' (*uix opulentis regnis tolerabilem*, 7.2.13).

Yet for almost two centuries, until 55 BCE, all plays were staged in Rome on temporary wooden structures, erected for the duration of the *ludi scaenici*. Both the long, raised stage and the stage-building with its roofing, its painted scenery-panels, and its three doorways, which could represent three houses and led conveniently to the actors' dressing-area, would have been of wood. Tiers of wooden seating would have been erected for the audience, some members of which might sit on the ground or watch the play standing. The wealthier Greek cities of southern Italy and Sicily had stone theatres dating from the fifth century (the theatre of Syracuse was dedicated *c.*460 BCE) and by the end of the second century several Italian towns had acquired their own permanent stone-built theatre (the large theatre of Pompeii, with seating for 5,000, dates from *c.*200 BCE). But Rome had to wait until the dying days of the republic for its 200-year theatrical tradition to receive a permanent base. The reasons are not difficult to divine. Theatres were places associated in the rigid ideology of Rome's aristocracy and in their public speech with immorality and idleness. Perhaps more to the point, they were places where 'the judgement and will of the Roman people in public matters' (Cicero *Pro Sestio* 106) could be, and often were, directly expressed. The membership of Rome's theatrical audience, unlike that of Athens, came from all sections of the community: patrician, plebeian, aristocratic, base, free-born, slave, male, female, seated hierarchically according to social status, with members of the senatorial and equestrian classes occupying the best seats. Laws were passed at different times restricting various sections of the theatre to particular social groups, the most famous being the Roscian Theatre Law of 67 BCE assigning the first fourteen rows in the theatre to members of the equestrian class. The theatre was where Rome's structures of power were visibly and vulnerably displayed. Hence the legal restrictions placed upon actors, whose lines often targeted prominent political figures, especially in the audience itself (Pompey, Julius Caesar, Nero), with powerful effect.[9] Hence too the successful baulking by conservative politicians of all attempts to provide the capital with a permanent stone theatre until the construction of the Theatre of Pompey in 55–52 BCE.[10] The wait was perhaps worthwhile. A revolutionary concrete and marble structure, in which stage-building, semicircular orchestra and tiered concave auditorium (for perhaps 17,500 *spectatores*) were united into a closed, holistic space, the Theatre of Pompey provided the model and the standard for the theatres of the capital and the empire to come. Even in the fourth century CE it was still heralded as one of the outstanding monuments of Rome (Ammianus Marcellinus *Res Gestae* 16.10.14).

But if the physical context of Roman drama improved after the death of Accius, the same cannot automatically be said about drama itself. Many maintain that Accius was the last great Roman dramatist, and that after his death all serious dramatic composition ceased and tragedy especially became the plaything of aristocratic litterateurs, composing for diversion, not for the stage. Cicero's brother, Quintus, for example, composed four tragedies in sixteen days; Julius Caesar wrote an *Oedipus* and Augustus attempted an *Ajax*.[11] But although the second half of the first century BCE seemed to produce no tragedian of the stature of an Accius, notable tragedies were written by Asinius Pollio, praised by Virgil (*Eclogues.* 8.9f.) and Horace (*Odes* 2.1.11f.), by Varius Rufus, whose *Thyestes* was performed at the Actian Games of 29 BCE, and by Ovid. Varius' *Thyestes* and Ovid's *Medea* were held in high esteem at least by Quintilian (*Institutio Oratoria* 10.1.98).[12] During the early empire (first century CE) the *ludi scaenici* became increasingly dominated by 'popular theatre', in the form of mime and pantomime. The former, despite its name, was not mute, but a lively, maskless farce or vaudeville, featuring women 'actresses' (*mimae*) in the female roles and uninhibited in its staging of sexual activity, generally obscene, often sententious, occasionally politically pointed (if not barbed).[13] The latter, pantomime, was little like its modern namesake, but a highly expressive 'ballet' by a single masked performer, based upon mythological, increasingly 'tragic' themes. But despite the emphatic popularity of these other theatrical forms (to which should also be added the Atellane farce), it is clear that both tragedy and comedy continued to be publicly performed (even if far less often) into the second century CE itself.[14] There is evidence too of 'political' tragedy during this period. Mamercus Aemilius Scaurus, for example, wrote a tragedy, *Atreus*, which angered Tiberius (Dio *Roman History* 58.24; Tacitus *Annals* 6.29). In Tacitus' *Dialogus* Curiatius Maternus is credited with a tragedy, *Cato*, which may have offended Vespasian (*princeps* 69–79 CE), and with another political tragedy, *Thyestes*. Maternus is also described as reciting his tragedies in public (Tacitus *Dialogus* 2.3, 11.2), but that tragedies were still being written for, as well as performed on, the stage in the mid-to-late first century CE is clear from the example of Seneca's contemporary Pomponius Secundus, a distinguished dramatist (Tacitus *Dialogus* 13.7) who, according to Quintilian, excelled in 'learning', *eruditio*, and 'brilliance', *nitor* (*Institutio Oratoria* 10.1.98), and who definitely wrote for the stage (*is carmina scaenae dabat*, Tacitus *Annals* 11.13).[15] Pomponius Secundus figured in fact in a celebrated argument with Seneca on tragic diction (Quint. *Institutio Oratoria* 8.3.31).[16] As for comedy, it was still not only being performed but written. Some forty years after Seneca's death the younger Pliny classed the comedies written by his friend Vergilius Romanus with those of Plautus and Terence (*Epistles* 6.21.4).

The following complex picture emerges of the theatrical conditions of Seneca's day. Although temporary wooden stages continue to be erected for occasional theatrical performances, throughout Italy and the empire stone theatres abound (three in Rome itself, providing over 38,000 seats): Roman theatres, not Greek. Their concrete structures, marble revetments, socially stratified seating (beneath a great linen awning), holistic design, their deep stages, on which all the action takes place (the small *orchestra* having been given over to senatorial seating), richly decorated stage curtains (including in Seneca's day the 'drop-curtain', raised at the beginning of a performance and lowered at the end), revolving scenery-stands, massive flying devices and collapsible sets, their baroque stage-buildings adorned with statues, scene-paintings, masks and garlands – index their *romanitas*. Spectacle informs spectacle. Mime and pantomime predominate, but comedy and high tragedy are still regularly performed in the theatre, and probably also in private houses (*intra domum*: a phenomenon even in Marius' day).[17] Tragedies too are often 'recited' (by a single speaker). The recitation takes place in a private house or recitation-hall, *auditorium* (both for its own sake and as a preliminary to theatrical performance or publication: see Pliny *Epistles* 7.17.11), or in the theatre itself as a virtuoso individual recital of a tragic speech, episode or monody. To the last category probably belong Nero's own performances (Suetonius *Nero* 21.3) of 'the tragedies of heroes and gods wearing the tragic mask (*personatus*)'.

But while an intricate but clear picture emerges of the continuing existence and developing complexity of Roman drama as both social institution and literary form, little is known of its dramaturgical practices and conventions, especially those of tragedy. Contemporary witnesses of republican tragedy mention such matters as the presence of the flute-player, the wearing of tragic masks and the predominance of spectacle, but provide little detailed dramaturgical information. The Augustan picture is a little clearer. Vitruvius' comments in *De Architectura* 5.6, although confined essentially to theatre design and construction, include important remarks on stage scenery and the different functions of the two stage-exits; and Horace in *Ars Poetica* (189–92) draws attention to the five-act rule, the three-actor rule (neither of which are adhered to strictly by Seneca) and the *deus ex machina*. The evidence, however, remains largely internal. And what the fragments of the early Roman tragedians suggest is that even in the republic there had been a fusion of classical and Hellenistic techniques. Certainly the tragedies of Seneca, while they reveal and exploit an obvious counterpoint with the plays of Aeschylus, Sophocles and Euripides, especially in respect of divergent treatments of the same myth, display dramaturgical features foreign to fifth-century Attic tragedy: the five-act structure (*Oedipus* and, possibly, *Phaedra* are exceptions here),[18] the use of extended asides, including entrance monologue-asides,[19] choral exit and re-entry, and various items of stage-business (withdrawing to plot future action, as at *Agamemnon* 308f., or surveying the stage for eavesdroppers, as at *Phaedra* 599ff.). These practices are derived in the main from the conventions of Hellenistic drama, particularly New Comedy of the fourth and third centuries BCE. Even the probably reduced size of the Senecan chorus (estimated by some to consist of between three and seven members) has Hellenistic precedent,[20] although the delivery of the choral odes from the stage itself, to which the chorus was confined at least by Vitruvius' day (*De Architectura* 5.6.2), seems something decidedly Roman.[21] Some of these non-Attic features can be found in Roman tragedy of the late republic. It is not unreasonable to suppose that by the Augustan period, when the Hellenistic influence on Roman poetry was at its height, most (if not all) were standard Roman practice. Seneca is certainly indebted to Augustan tragedians for their refinement of the crude iambic dialogue line (the *senarius* or 'sixer') of the earlier playwrights (Horace *Ars Poetica* 251ff.) and probably also for aspects of his tragic language. It seems likely that the debt extended to Augustan dramaturgy too, and to both Augustan and late republican tragedy's preoccupation with spectacle.

Not all would agree. Some scholars believe that Seneca was not much interested either in dramaturgy or in theatrical spectacle, arguing that he wrote his tragedies not for performance in the great theatres of Rome or a private house or villa, but rather to be read (privately) or recited.[22] The theatrical situation and practice of Seneca's day, as described above, were complex; and plays admitted differing forms of realisation. To assign Senecan tragedy, however, to the category of recitation drama or closet drama seems misdirected. It is not known and may never be known whether Seneca's tragedies were performed on stage or otherwise during their author's lifetime.[23] But it is certainly the case that they were and are performable: they have been and are performed.[24] The contemporary practice of *recitatio* clearly affected the form of Seneca's plays, which, appropriately edited, could have been used for selective theatrical recital or for a public 'reading' by the author prior to performance. Such was Pomponius Secundus' practice and that (occasionally) of Corneille.[25] But there is little possibility that either recitation or (even less) private reading was their intended primary mode of realisation. Not only do the 'reading' and the 'recitation' hypotheses generate more problems than those they seek to address,[26] but they are vitiated by the theatricality of Senecan tragedy, its concern with dramatic structure and effect and with the *minutiae* of stagecraft. Recent analyses of Seneca's stage techniques reveal theatrical mastery in the shaping of dramatic action, the structural unfolding of dramatic language and imagery, the blocking of scenes and acts, the disposition of roles, the handling of actors and of the chorus, the interrelationship of chorus and act, the use of ghosts, messengers, extras, mutes, the dramatic and thematic use of stage-setting and props, the employment of implicit stage directions in the text itself (especially entrance and exit cues, random but more substantial than often noted, identification cues, and implicit directions for stage business) – and in Senecan tragedy's manipulation of pace, movement, violence, spectacle and closure.[27] As Herington demonstrated in his foundational essay of 1966, the 'recitation' hypothesis self-destructs. If Seneca's tragedies were written for recitation *in toto*, they were undeniably written to be delivered by a number of voices playing separate parts, that is to say, for 'dramatic' performance.[28] Whether the performance envisaged was in the theatre or in a private house to a coterie audience (or both).[29] Indeed it was partly on the grounds of representational power (*rappresentatione*), i.e. theatrical effectiveness, that Giraldi Cinthio, a practical dramatist who 'never for a moment imagined that Seneca did not write for a stage performance', preferred Seneca to the Greeks.[30] The Elizabethan translators would have concurred.[31] Those who condemn Seneca's dramatic sense out of hand would do well to remember that even Eliot, whose essays on Seneca have been as injurious as any, thought that they might be regarded as 'practical models for . . . broadcasted drama'.[32] Senecan tragedy belongs, if anything does, to the category of Roman performance theatre.

Part I
SENECAN TRAGEDY

2

THE DECLAMATORY STYLE

oratio certam regulam non habet; consuetudo illam ciuitatis, quae num-
quam in eodem diu stetit, uersat.

Style has no fixed rules; the usage of society changes it, which never stays
still for long.

Seneca, *Epistle* 114.13

There are eight extant Senecan tragedies: *Hercules Furens, Troades, Medea,
Phaedra, Oedipus, Agamemnon, Thyestes, Phoenissae.*[1] Each of them is marked by
dramatic features which were to influence Renaissance drama: vivid and
powerful verse, psychological insight, highly effective staging, an intellectually
demanding verbal and conceptual framework, and a precocious preoccupation with theatricality and theatricalisation. Composed presumably in the
second half of Seneca's life, the precise dates of the plays are yet uncertain.
The earliest unambiguous reference to any of Seneca's plays is the *Agamemnon* graffito from Pompeii, of uncertain date but obviously before the catastrophe of 79 CE;[2] the next is by Quintilian (*Institutio Oratoria* 9.2.8), writing a
generation after Seneca's death. Seneca makes no mention of his tragedies in
his prose works. Many commentators allocate them to the period of exile on
Corsica (41–9 CE); others regard it as more likely that their composition, like
that of the prose works, was spread over a considerable period of time. A
recent stylometric study has attempted to break the plays into three chrono-
logically consecutive groups (1: *Agamemnon, Phaedra, Oedipus*; 2: *Hercules
Furens, Medea, Troades*; 3: *Thyestes, Phoenissae*),[3] but the groupings and implied
chronology are by no means agreed. Most contemporary scholars would
perhaps accept that on stylometric, dramatic and other grounds *Thyestes* and
the incomplete *Phoenissae* are Seneca's final (extant) tragedies.

But, if the chronology of Senecan tragedy is uncertain, its rhetoricity is
not. Indeed Senecan drama's rhetorical nature has been the target of much
adverse criticism and is frequently cited as an impediment to modern
appreciation. It is well to begin here. For the plays not only flaunt their

15

rhetoricity openly, but use it to articulate some of Seneca's most theatrical moments. Rhetoric structures Senecan tragedy through and through; and empowers it theatrically. Listen to Andromache's entrance speech in *Troades*, in which she reproves her fellow captives with a host of rhetorical techniques, even as she frames her own devastation with hyperbole, paradox and epigram:

> quid, maesta Phrygiae turba, laceratis comas
> miserumque tunsae pectus effuso genas
> fletu rigatis? leuia perpessae sumus
> si flenda patimur. Ilium uobis modo,
> mihi cecidit olim, cum ferus curru incito
> mea membra raperet et graui gemeret sono
> Peliacus axis pondere Hectoreo tremens.
> tunc obruta atque euersa quodcumque accidit
> torpens malis rigensque sine sensu fero.
> iam erepta Danais coniugem sequerer meum,
> nisi hic teneret. hic meos animos domat
> morique prohibet. cogit hic aliquid deos
> adhuc rogare. tempus aerumnae addidit.
> hic mihi malorum maximum fructum abstulit:
> nihil timere. prosperis rebus locus
> ereptus omnis, dira qua ueniant habent.
> miserrimum est timere, cum speres nihil.
>
> *(Troades* 409–25)

Wailing band of Phrygians, why tear your hair,
Beat sorrowing breasts and drench cheeks with floods
Of sobs? Our sufferings must be trivial
If tears suffice. For you Ilium fell just now,
For me long ago, when that brutal chariot
Ravaged my limbs and Pelian axle
Screamed aloud shuddering beneath Hector's weight.
That day crushed and wasted me. I endure
Events numb and stiff with pain, impervious.
I'd escape the Danai and follow my spouse
Now, if he *(points to Astyanax)* didn't hold me. He tames my pride
And prevents my death. He compels me still
To importune the gods. He prolongs my pain.
He's robbed me of suffering's finest fruit:
Fear of nothing. All chance of happiness
Is snatched away, horrors can still reach us.
Fear is its most painful when hope is dead.

Listen to Medea, as she builds upon a conventional interchange with her

Nurse, turning the latter's barrage of commonplaces and sententious epigram into a conceptual and verbal duel, in which the Nurse's words are
thrown back in her face,[4] and a rapid, at times stichomythic, exchange leads
to the linguistic annexation of the universe for a redefinition of 'Medea':

Nutrix	Sile, obsecro, questusque secreto abditos
	manda dolori. grauia quisquis uulnera
	patiente et aequo mutus animo pertulit,
	referre potuit: ira quae tegitur nocet;
	professa perdunt odia uindictae locum.
Medea	Leuis est dolor qui capere consilium potest
	et clepere sese: magna non latitant mala.
	libet ire contra.
Nutrix	Siste furialem impetum,
	alumna: uix te tacita defendit quies.
Medea	Fortuna fortes metuit, ignauos premit.
Nutrix	Tunc est probanda, si locum uirtus habet.
Medea	Numquam potest non esse uirtuti locus.
Nutrix	Spes nulla rebus monstrat adflictis uiam.
Medea	Qui nil potest sperare, desperet nihil.
Nutrix	Abiere Colchi, coniugis nulla est fides
	nihilque superest opibus e tantis tibi.
Medea	Medea superest: hic mare et terras uides
	ferrumque et ignes et deos et fulmina.

(*Medea* 150–67)

Nurse	Be silent, I beg you; bury complaints
	In secret pain. Whoever bears grievous blows
	Quietly with calm, enduring spirit
	Can repay them. Anger stabs when concealed;
	Displays of hate destroy the chance for vengeance.
Medea	A trivial pain can accept advice
	And stay concealed: great wrongs do not lie hid.
	I rejoice to face him.
Nurse	Stop this mad impulse,
	My child; even still silence may not shield you.
Medea	Fortune fears the brave and crushes cowards.
Nurse	Courage is applauded when the time is right.
Medea	Never for courage can the time be wrong.
Nurse	No hope shows a way through our calamity.
Medea	Who hopes for nothing, despairs of nothing.
Nurse	The Colchians are gone; your husband's vows are nothing;
	Nothing is left of all your wondrous wealth.
Medea	Medea's left. Here you see ocean and land,
	Iron and fire, gods and thunderbolts.

Or listen to Theseus declaim his agony with all the force of Senecan bombast, a deluge of balanced cadences and clauses, alliterated consonants, sonal and syntactic repetition, violent imagery, portentous diction, uniting with a 'steady rhythmic punch'[5] and an architected crescendo structure, which climaxes in pith and epigram, to overwhelm the audience with verbal power:

> pallidi fauces Auerni, uosque, Taenarii specus,
> unda miseris grata Lethes, uosque, torpentes lacus,
> impium rapite atque mersum premite perpetuis malis.
> nunc adeste, saeua ponti monstra, nunc uastum mare,
> ultimo quodcumque Proteus aequorum abscondit sinu,
> meque ouantem scelere tanto rapite in altos gurgites,
> tuque, semper, genitor, irae facilis assensor meae.
> morte facili dignus haud sum qui noua natum nece
> segregem sparsi per agros quique, dum falsum nefas
> exsequor uindex seuerus, incidi in uerum scelus.
> sidera et manes et undas scelere compleui meo.
> amplius sors nulla restat: regna me norunt tria.
>
> (*Phaedra* 1201–12)

> Jaws of pallid death and you, caverns of Taenarus,
> Balm of the damned, Lethe's stream, and you, the stagnant pools,
> Ravage this impious man, sink him in ceaseless pain.
> Come, savage monsters of the deep, come, endless sea,
> And all that Proteus hides in ocean's furthest womb,
> For my evil triumph snatch me to your deep abyss,
> And help them, father, ever compliant with my wrath.
> I deserve no easy end, creator of new death
> Scattering dismembered son afield, stern avenger
> Who hunting fictitious sin committed the true crime.
> Stars, shades and ocean I have sated with my sins.
> No region now remains: all three kingdoms know me.

Faced with bombast it is always well to remember Eliot's dictum that 'the art of dramatic language ... is as near to oratory as to ordinary speech or to other poetry',[6] and that other times and other places have responded fully to the sonorous weight of Seneca's verse.[7] But what should also be noted is that rhetoric not only structures and empowers Senecan tragedy, it gives it contemporary accessibility. A playwright operates in a public medium, which, if he is to communicate anything, must be shaped by contemporary idiom. Seneca's astonishing fusion of spectacle, bombast, paradox, epigram, brevity, plenitude, abstraction, grandeur, violence, disjunction, allusion, sensuousness is no arbitrarily chosen mode; it is product of a baroque, post-classical sensibility and grounded in the semiotic forms of contemporary Roman life.

It is index of an age: the age of fourth-style Roman painting, the baroque in Roman architecture and sculpture, the 'pointed', declamatory style in poetry. It was a spectacular, histrionic age. It was a world of grandiose, almost strident aesthetics: in the theatre where spectacle predominated; in imperial villas and palaces; in private houses; in the recitation halls and the arena; in political, military and religious display. Tiberius' summer retreat at Sperlonga on the coast of Latium, where the grotto is lavishly decorated with brilliant glass wall mosaics and with colossal pieces of baroque sculpture depicting scenes from Homer's *Odyssey*, intensely dramatic in their twisted torsos, strained musculature, writhing compositional lines, deeply cut drapery, and tortured, expressive faces, signalled the tenor of the times. Tiberius' main architectural energies were devoted to his villas on Capri, especially the *Villa Iouis*. But in Rome itself on the Palatine he constructed the first imperial palace, the *Domus Tiberiana*, which Caligula planned to remodel and enlarge in the most fantastic way and which Nero succeeded in transforming first into the incomplete *Domus Transitoria*, built to join the *Domus Tiberiana* to the imperial properties on the Esquiline, and then, after the great fire of 64 CE, into the *Domus Aurea* or Golden House. Both the Neronian palaces are architectural revolutions, baroque in their preoccupation with curvilinear and polygonal form, visual surprise, stridency, even shock. Architectural restlessness, mystery and paradox predominate, together with a theatrical exploitation of contrast and light. Theatrical motifs also feature as design elements in the palaces, most conspicuously perhaps in the nymphaeum of the *Domus Transitoria*, where the fountain is modelled to represent the *scaenae frons* of an imperial theatre. What is also important to emphasise is the scale, the grandiosity, of both Caligula's and Nero's schemes; for scale and grandiosity are defining features of the Senecan tragic mode. To accommodate the Golden House the whole central area of Rome between the Palatine, Caelian and Esquiline hills was transformed into a huge parkland, adorned with fountains, porticoes, pavilions and tempietti and prefaced by a huge vestibule framing a colossal gilt statue of the emperor a hundred and twenty feet high. 'At last', Nero proclaimed, 'I begin to be housed like a human being!' (*quasi hominem tandem habitare coepisse*, Suetonius *Nero* 31.2).

Perhaps also emanating from the Neronian court (the first datable instance is to be found in the earlier of the two palaces) is what became known as fourth-style Romano-Campanian wall-painting, which combines the architectural illusionism and colour experimentation of earlier styles into a theatrical, even surrealistic design. The Ixion and Pentheus rooms of the House of the Vettii in Pompeii – with their violent colour contrasts and precisely delineated architectural fantasies, juxtaposed with large-scale paintings of imminent bestiality, human strength, violence and torture – reflect the essence of the style. The theatrical masks and elusive spectators of the Ixion room underscore the theatricality of the design. Many of the late painting schemes of Herculaneum and Pompeii were overtly theatrical in focus, none more so than the famous architectural fresco from Herculaneum now in the Museo Archeologico Nazionale in Naples, which seems to depict a baroque stage-set, crammed with fantasising architecture and featuring a central porch capped by dolphins, pegasi, hippocamps and, in the middle of its broken pediment, a tragic mask. Above hangs a drop curtain advertising the theatricality of its design. Like the early imperial theatre it displays itself self-consciously.

Within this iconosphere Senecan tragedy was created, structured by, even as it re*presents*, the late Julio-Claudian world. That world and its cultural modes are not always understood, especially its literary forms, which are often castigated as the forms of literary decadence or at least decline.[8] The change which took place in Roman poetry between the early Augustan period and that of Nero, between the 'classicism' of Virgil and Horace and the 'post-classicism' of Seneca and Lucan, is conventionally described as the movement from Golden to Silver Latin. The description misleads on many counts, not least because it misconstrues a change in literary and poetic sensibility, in the mental sets of reader and audience, and in the political environment of writing itself, as a change in literary value. What happened awaits adequate description, but it seems clear that the change began with Ovid (43 BCE to 17 CE), whose rejection of Augustan classicism (especially its concept of *decorum* or 'appropriateness'), cultivation of generic disorder and experimentation (see, e.g., *Ars Amatoria* and *Metamorphoses*), love of paradox, absurdity, incongruity, hyperbole, wit, and focus on extreme emotional states, influenced everything that followed. Ovid also witnessed and suffered from the increasing political repression of the principate; he was banished for (among other things) his words, *carmen*. And political repression seems to have been a signal factor, if difficult to evaluate, in the formation of the post-classical style.

After Ovid political and literary repression accelerated. The trial and suicide of the historian Cremutius Cordus and the burning of his books in 25 CE showed what could and did happen (Tacitus *Annals* 4.34ff.).[9] And no major Roman poet emerges before Seneca and the Neronians. During the reigns of Tiberius and Caligula, though occasional tragedies, for example, are written, poetry is confined essentially to such literary kinds as fable (Phaedrus, himself a victim of Tiberius' minister, Sejanus, *Fabulae* 3, Prologue 41 ff.) and scientific didactic (Manilius and possibly the author of *Aetna*), or else occupies the attention of aristocratic amateurs like Germanicus and Tiberius himself. The middle of the first century (primarily the Neronian era) witnessed a literary renaissance. Epic (Lucan), satire (Persius), pastoral (Calpurnius), the prose-verse novel (Petronius) erupted on to the scene – together with renascent tragedy (Seneca) – saturated with the imagery, diction, commonplaces, narratology and character-analysis of Augustan literature, indebted above all to the triad of Virgil, Horace and Ovid (*Aeneid* and *Metamorphoses* especially inform Neronian texts), but operating in a post-Ovidian, non-Augustan manner. Augustan literary forms returned but subject to new energies and new stylistic modes. Individual styles varied, but what specifically characterised this new post-classical mode was the cultivation of paradox, discontinuity, antithesis and point, the adoption of declamatory structures and techniques, and the striking mixture of compression, elaboration, epigram and hyperbole.

Several factors seem involved in the evolution of this style. One was Ovid. Another was the emphasis on rhetoric in the schools. During the early empire training in *declamatio* in a school run by a professional declaimer or *rhetor* was the final and indispensable constituent of a young Roman's formal education. This was in itself nothing new. What, however, had occurred from the early Augustan period onwards was a rise in the number of such schools, and (more significantly) an increasing focus in them on the skills of declamation and rhetorical role-play as ends in themselves and an increasing detachment of the declamatory exercises from any obvious practical function. Another important innovation was the 'display' declamation of a practising *rhetor*. Public declamations by rival professors and declamatory 'debates' between them became a social institution and a regular form of public and imperial entertainment. The *Controuersiae* and *Suasoriae* of Seneca's father, which were probably written in the 30s CE, and must have had a profound impact on Seneca himself, document such declamations and indicate the kind of training the schools provided.

There were essentially two kinds of speech in which students were practised: deliberative (*suasoriae*) and disputatious (*controuersiae*). In the former students purported to 'advise' mythological or historical characters at critical points in their lives ('Agamemnon deliberates whether to sacrifice Iphigenia'; 'Cicero deliberates whether to beg Antony's pardon', *Suasoriae* 3 and 6); in the latter they played the role of litigants or advocates in imaginary law suits, debating intricate and generally far-fetched moral and legal issues. An armoury of rhetorical techniques was the progeny of such training. Students were taught the declamatory employment of antitheses and conceits, of descriptive set-pieces and historical *exempla*, of moralising commonplaces (*loci communes*) and rhetorical flourishes. They were taught the use of apostrophe, alliteration, assonance, tricolon, anaphora, asyndeton, homoeoteleuton, polyptoton, *figura etymologica*, *commutatio*; the use of synonyms, antonyms, oxymora, paradox, innuendo (*suspicio*), epigram, point; above all, declamatory structure. The watchwords of the new rhetoric, as proclaimed by Marcus Aper at Tacitus *Dialogus* 20ff., give the essence of the instruction: *nitor*, 'brilliance'; *cultus*, 'elegance'; *altitudo*, 'elevation'; *color*, 'colour'; *laetitia*, 'luxuriance'; *aliquid inlustre*, 'splendour'; *dignum memoria*, 'memorability'; *sententia*, 'epigram'. The schools were later much criticised, for the unreality of the declamatory themes and the unsuitability of the 'education' they provided for the rigours of law-court life. So Seneca's contemporary Petronius has Encolpius declaim at the opening of the fragments of *Satyricon*:

et ideo ego adulescentulos existimo in scholis stultissimos fieri, quia nihil ex his, quae in usu habemus, aut audiunt aut uident, sed piratas cum catenis in litore stantes, sed tyrannos edicta scribentes quibus imperent filiis ut patrum suorum capita praecidant, sed responsa in pestilentiam data ut uirgines tres aut plures immolentur, sed mellitos uerborum globulos et omnia dicta factaque quasi papauere et sesamo sparsa.

(*Satyricon* 1)

I maintain that the schools make total idiots of young men, because they neither hear nor see anything of real life, but pirates standing with chains on the shore, tyrants writing orders for sons to decapitate their fathers, oracles in time of plague to sacrifice three or more virgins, honeyed blobs of words, and every word and gesture sprinkled with poppy-seed and sesame.

So too more soberly Quintilian:

eo quidem res ista culpa docentium reccidit, ut inter praecipuas quae corrumperent eloquentiam causas licentia atque inscitia declamantium fuerit.

(*Institutio Oratoria* 2.10.3)

The practice (of declamation) has degenerated to such an extent through the fault of the teachers as to rank among the leading causes of the corruption of eloquence thanks to the licence and ignorance of the declaimers.

To this the earlier testimony of Seneca's father (Seneca Rhetor *Controuersiae* 3 Preface, 9 Preface) and the later of Tacitus (*Dialogus* 35) lend support. But it should be noted that Quintilian argues for a reformation of declamation, not its removal; and Encolpius, despite his criticisms, reproduces the very rhetoric he denounces. The declamatory mode was ubiquitous; its popularity incontestable, as was that of the virtuoso public declamations of the *rhetores* themselves. To the readers and audiences of early imperial Rome rhetoric taught and was structure. Senecan theatre accorded with the contemporary passion for rhetoric and contemporary fullness of response to rhetoric, to declamation, dialectic, verbal brilliance and ingenuity. Witness Phaedra's Nurse begin what the schools of rhetoric labelled a *suasoria:*

> deum esse amorem turpis et uitio fauens
> finxit libido . . .

> That love is god is a fiction of vile
> And sinful lust, which for greater freedom
> Assigned a false deity's name to passion.
> Erycina, I think, sends her son roaming

Through every land; he, flying through heaven,
Works wanton weapons with delicate hands
And tiniest of gods holds sovereign sway.
Demented minds adopted these conceits,
Invented Venus' power and the god's bow.

(*Phaedra* 195–203)

To mislabel this as 'non-theatrical' is to ignore not only Eliot's observation on the proximity of oratory and dramatic language (Mercutio's 'Queen Mab' speech, *Romeo and Juliet* 1.4.53ff., is an excellent analogue to the Nurse's *suasoria*), but Senecan rhetoric's contemporary cultural force.

Another social practice sustained the imperial passion for declamation: *recitatio* or the public reading of poetry. A prominent feature of Roman literary and social life from the beginning, it became *de rigueur* in the early empire, often carried out at great expense, and, like declamation, was not without its critics.[10] And, whatever the new rhetoric's success in preparing pupils for public careers (and Seneca's own life indicates that not all pupils failed), it taught verbal strategy, psychic mobility and public role-play, and substantially altered the mental sets of the Roman reader and audience, and the Roman world's verbal and literary modes. The new rhetoric's structuring of Senecan tragedy quickened its theatrical force, even as it gave it contemporary accessibility and furnished the opportunity for something other than display. For Seneca's declamatory style is not simply the rhetoric of surface. Observe Thyestes denounce the life of luxury and wealth, a conventional topic of the declamatory schools:

mihi crede, falsis magna nominibus placent,
frustra timentur dura . . .

Believe me, false titles give greatness charm;
Fear of poverty's groundless. While I stood high,
My terror never ceased; even the sword
At my side brought panic. O, how good it is
To block no one's path, to enjoy carefree
Banquets on the earth! Crime avoids cottages,
One eats with safety at a poor man's table;
Poisoned cups are golden. I speak from knowledge:
Bad fortune, not good, is preferable.
No house of mine imposing on its high
Mountain peak makes the citizen below tremble;
No high ceiling flashes resplendent ivory;
No guard protects my sleep. I have no fleet
Of ships for fishing, no breakwater
To drive back the sea, no tribute of nations
To feed my vile belly, no harvest fields

Beyond the Getae and the Parthians;
No incense burns in my worship, no shrines
Of mine are decked to Jove's neglect; no grove
Waves planted on my towers, no heated
Pools steam; my day is not given to sleep
Nor my night conjoined with wakeful Bacchus.
But I'm not feared: unarmed my house is safe,
And to my little life great peace is given.
Great kingship is strength to endure without kingship.

(Thyestes 446–70)

The castigation of the false world of wealth and power was a regular theme of Roman literature, derived apparently from Hellenistic popular philosophy, and a standard subject for declamation in the schools.[11] Here, as elsewhere in Seneca (see especially the speech of Hippolytus at *Phaedra* 483ff.), it is used as pointer to a mind. Thyestes' address is to his son Tantalus, whose appetite for the world Thyestes denounces is reflected in his inherited name. It is a reply to the son's question (445), 'Who would choose misery to happiness?' (*miser esse mauult esse qui felix potest?*), and reaches logical completion at 454 with the climactic epigram, *malam bonae praeferre fortunam licet* ('Bad fortune, not good, is preferable'). Thyestes however continues, and, though he is praising the life of hardship and obscurity, he does so in strongly negative terms, which shift the focus not only to the life of power but to those aspects of the life in virtue of which it is normally desired. Even the climactic *sententia* of line 470 rings hollow:

immane regnum est posse sine regno pati.

Great kingship is strength to endure without kingship.

A life of endurance (*pati*) seems a less than exalted alternative to the life of power.[12] Thyestes is fascinated by the life he decries and drawn irresistibly to it. 'To praise the humble life and to speak of peace and sleep' (*laudare modica et otium ac somnum loqui, Oedipus* 683) can be a mark, as Oedipus observes, of one who desires power. In Thyestes' case it almost certainly is. Tantalid hunger, the *fames infixa* of this play's prologue (97), burgeons beneath the surface of Thyestes' declamation, the knowledge that constitutes that declamation impotent before the imperatives of appetite. Almost immediately Thyestes will accept a crown he knows should fill him with terror, eat without fear where he knew fear to be appropriate, and succumb to a world he has proclaimed as deluding. His 'capitulation' in Act 3's concluding verbal duel (*cape, capesse, capitis, recipit, accipis, accipio, capiti,* 525–45) – with literally only 'token' pressure to do so – signals his desire.

In an age which revelled in exteriority and display Seneca writes tragedy that focuses on the soul. Senecan rhetoricity is no mere verbal ornament; bombast, *suasoriae*, stichomythic exchanges, word-play, *sententiae* are used in the creation of tragic character and the revelation of states of mind. One of the most conspicuous devices employed in Senecan tragedy is the aside, a device common in Hellenistic drama, but foreign to the more public world of Attic tragedy.[13] Seneca's frequent use of it is a function of his drama's pervasive concern with psychological interiority – a concern most particularly and clearly exhibited in Seneca's predilection for self-presentational soliloquies or monologues,[14] in which the focus is on the inner workings of the human mind, on the mind as *locus* of emotional conflict, incalculable suffering, insatiable appetite, manic joy, cognitive vulnerability, self-deception, irrational guilt. The dramatisation of the emotions seems to have been central to Roman tragedy in a way that it was not to Greek.[15] Seneca inherits this concern and gives it impressive realisation. Consider Oedipus' opening soliloquy, its presentation of a mind racked by fear of unspeakable iniquities, *infanda*, at the same time intuitively aware of its own terrible guilt:

> iam iam aliquid in nos fata moliri parant . . .

> Now, even now fate fashions something for me.
> What else can I think when this plague that fouls
> Cadmus' folk, dealing universal death,
> Spares me alone? For what evil am I kept?
> Amid the city's ruin, the endless funerals,
> The unceasing sobs, this massacre of men,
> I stand apart untouched – damned by Phoebus.
> Can one expect sin like mine to receive
> A healthy realm? I have made the air guilty.
> (*fecimus caelum nocens*)
> (*Oedipus* 28–36)

Or consider Helen's opening soliloquy, as she enters *Troades* at the beginning of Act 4, the presentation of a mind struggling with its own scripted history, full of self-knowledge, self-disgust, compassion, shame, and of moral weakness – before the new murderous role written by the Greeks:

> quicumque hymen funestus, inlaetabilis
> lamenta caedes sanguinem gemitus habet,
> est auspice Helena dignus . . .

> Every marriage fraught with death and sorrow,
> With murder, lamentation, blood and sobs,
> Merits Helen's blessing. Even in their ruin
> I'm forced to harm the Phrygians. I'm ordered
> To report Pyrrhus' false marriage and provide
> Greek jewellery and dress. By my deceit
> Paris' sister will be caught, by my skill killed.
> Make her deceived: far easier for her, I think.

25

Ideal death is to die without death's fear.
Why delay your orders? Compelled crime returns
The guilt to its author.

(Troades 861–71)

Consider too the psychological complexities of Cassandra in *Agamemnon* (especially 695ff., 791ff., 867ff., 1004ff.,), of Hippolytus in *Phaedra* (1ff., 483ff., 566ff., 671ff.), of Medea in *Medea* (esp. 1ff., 893ff.),[16] and the intensity of personal agony that resonates in Senecan tragedy with a force beyond that normally presented by the Greeks. Seneca's focus on human subjectivity is such that in several plays, *Phaedra, Medea* and *Thyestes*, for example, it does not so much punctuate as structure the dramatic action itself.

It needs immediately to be said that this psychological focus is never simply ideological. The human mind is not dramatised by Seneca to exemplify abstract ideas or philosophical (especially Stoic) concepts, with little concern for the intricacies of human psychology, for psychological credibility and realism.[17] The presentation of the human figures of Senecan drama is of course part of the intellectual design, the ideological structure of each play. But what it is important to realise is that Seneca's presentation of figures such as Oedipus, Cassandra, Thyestes, Medea, Hercules, Hippolytus, Phaedra reveals a concern with the complexities of human psychology and behaviour and their intelligible dramatisation, a concern with making his tragic world not simply symbol or emblem of a world outside itself but an image of that world, an involving, psychological, intelligible image. Consider Phaedra, in whose dramatisation Seneca's concern with the presentation of humanly intelligible psychology is especially revealed.[18] Her opening speech (85–128) is both index and harbinger of Seneca's overall treatment of her.

> o magna uasti Creta dominatrix freti,
> cuius per omne litus innumerae rates
> tenuere pontum, quicquid Assyria tenus
> tellure Nereus peruium rostris secat,
> cur me in penates obsidem inuisos datam
> hostique nuptam degere aetatem in malis
> lacrimisque cogis? . . .

> O mighty Crete, mistress of endless sea,
> Whose countless ships along every coast
> Grip the deep, where even to Assyria's
> Land Nereus cuts a passageway for prows,
> Why compel me, hostage to a hated house,
> Married to my foe, to consume a life
> In pain and tears? My fugitive lord is gone;
> Theseus shows his wife his usual faith:
> Brave he walks the dense darkness of the lake

That none recross, a bold suitor's henchman,
To drag torn from hell's royal throne a bride.
Proceeds this soldier of passion. No fear
Or shame gripped him. Debauch and illicit beds
Deep in Acheron Hippolytus' father seeks.
    Yet other, greater pain broods in my distress.
Not the night's tranquillity, not deep sleep
Release me from care. Evil feeds and grows
And burns within like the billowing heat
In Etna's cave. Pallas' loom stands idle
And the day's wool even slips from my hands.
I have no heart to deck shrines with votive gifts,
Or to join Attic women at the altars
Torch-bearing in witness of the silent rites,
Or to approach with chaste prayer and pious vow
The guardian goddess granted this land.
My joy's to follow startled beasts in the chase
And to hurl stiff javelins with tender hand.
    Where to, my soul? Why this raging love for glades?
I recognise poor mother's fateful evil:
Her love and mine are skilled in forest sin.
Mother, I pity you. Unspeakable evil
Seized you when bold you loved that savage herd's
Wild leader; fierce, intolerant of the yoke,
Adulterous leader of an untamed herd –
Yet at least he loved. For my wretchedness
What god or Daedalus could ease the flames?
Not if that master of Attic arts returned,
Who immured our monster in his blind house,
Could he offer help to our misfortune.
Hating the despised Sun's offspring, Venus
Through us claims redress for her Mars' fetters
And her own, loads all Phoebus' stock with guilt
Unspeakable. No daughter of Minos
Has found love light; it is always joined to sin.

(Phaedra 85–128)

The speech immediately establishes Phaedra's tragic stature. Long, intro-spective, and brooding, portentous in language, majestic in rhythm, it con-trasts sharply with Hippolytus' immediately preceding energetic monody, which with its rapid series of external instructions and constantly shifting focus of interest is full of verve, vitality, apparent freedom and power. Phaedra's speech has the impact of a monolithic dirge, exhibiting herself as tragic victim. The very formality of the speech, its scale, structure, language, tone, rhythm generate dramatic stature. Notice, for example, the rhetorical format of the opening question: the formal, impassioned *O* followed by a parallel arrangement of adjectives and nouns (abAB), a threefold address to Crete with increasing length of clauses, initial relatives, alliteration, resonant nomenclature and language (85–8), the sudden focus on *me* (89) and the suspension of the main verb of compulsion governing it until the end of the sentence two lines later (91); and how the format places Phaedra at the helpless centre of a range of forces both domestic and political, whose power is suggested by the grandiloquence of the language and the rhetorical and poetic structures used to describe them. Or consider the end of the speech (124–8):

> stirpem perosa Solis inuisi Venus
> per nos catenas uindicat Martis sui
> suasque, probris omne Phoebeum genus
> onerat nefandis. nulla Minois leui
> defuncta amore est: iungitur semper nefas.

> Hating the despised Sun's offspring, Venus
> Through us claims redress for her Mars' fetters
> And her own, loads all Phoebus' stock with guilt
> Unspeakable. No daughter of Minos
> Has found love light; it is always joined to sin.
>
> (*Phaedra* 124–8)

– with its alliteration and verbal play, simple syntax and prosaic language, culminating in the finality and apparent factuality of its ringing climax: *iungitur semper nefas*. Phaedra's stature in the play is secured.

A precise aspect of that stature is a consequence of the interiority of the speech, its revelation of a mind. The realistic chain of thought in the speech is noteworthy: Crete – the sea – Theseus – the shamelessness and faithlessness of this father of Hippolytus (*Hippolyti pater*, 98) – then (at mention of Hippolytus) her own emotional chaos – suspension of normal domestic activities – withdrawal from chaste religious rites – the mysterious passion for the woods and the wild – her mother's fateful and fatal passion (*fatale malum*, 113) – the bull – Daedalus – the impossibility of a cure – the divine curse (*Venus uindex*). This is no series of debating markers dragged from the schools; the nodal points of Phaedra's declamation signal the dramatisation of a mind. The speech is redolent with emotive, moral language: *pudor*, 'shame', 97; *malum*, 'evil', 101, 113; *castis*, 'chaste'; *pio*, 'pious', 108; *peccare*, 'sin', 114; *infando malo*, 'unspeakable evil', 115; *probis nefandis*, 'unspeakable guilt', 126f.; *nefas*, 'sin', 128 (the speech's final word) – moral language used not as ingredient of a philosophical debate but as register of a human psychology. Phaedra is presented, amid condemnation of husband and self, driven by shame (not simply reputation, for none as yet know) to absent herself from

28

the Attic women's rites, finding herself fantasising about the hunt, caught up in an evil that bound her mother, moving headlong towards a love which repulses her, which seems to her unspeakable, *infandum*.[19] At the heart of the speech is an awareness of a normal world from which she is barred.[20] What is dramatised is moral torment and helplessness as felt, as experienced.

What is dramatised also, here and elsewhere, is moral and psychological shock. Seneca's declamatory style is almost necessarily one of shock, product of a world which screamed its aesthetic and moral structures, which imaged through hyperbole in the arts, in the arena and in political and social behaviour the vacuum and appetitive excess of aristocratic Roman life. Phaedra's entrance speech is as much a function of this 'style of shock' as the nightmarish images and scenes that to many define Senecan tragedy: the apparition of Laius' ghost in *Oedipus* (619–58), the monstrous bull from the sea in *Phaedra* (1035–49), the preparation, cooking and eating of human flesh in *Thyestes* (759–82), Medea's black mass (*Medea* 740–842). So too the often praised 'cosmic imagery' of Seneca, from which the Elizabethans took so much, the capacity of his characters to appropriate the universe in their process of self-dramatisation. Sometimes this 'cosmic' imagery takes the form of a geographical or astronomic catalogue, in which the immensity of the world is proclaimed even as its itemisation vainly attempts to control it (e.g. *Phaedra* 54–72, *Troades* 814–57, *Thyestes* 844–74). At other times it is to be found in the enigmatic proclamation of a Medea. Her climactic riposte to the Nurse (*Medea* 166f.) was noted above. Observe too her speech prior to the entrance of Jason in Act 3, in which once more she purloins the universe for the construction of her self and unleashes that self and its passion in a rhetorical avalanche of turbulence and 'psychic aggression'.[21] The object of Medea's address is herself.

> si quaeris odio, misera, quem statuas modum,
> imitare amorem. regias egone ut faces
> inulta patiar? segnis hic ibit dies,
> tanto petitus ambitu, tanto datus?
> dum terra caelum media libratum feret
> nitidusque certas mundus euoluet uices
> numerusque harenis derit et solem dies,
> noctem sequentur astra, dum siccas polus
> uersabit Arctos, flumina in pontum cadent,
> numquam meus cessabit in poenas furor
> crescetque semper. quae ferarum immanitas,
> quae Scylla, quae Charybdis Ausonium mare
> Siculumque sorbens quaeue anhelantem premens
> Titana tantis Aetna feruebit minis?
> non rapidus amnis, non procellosum mare
> Pontusue Coro saeuus aut uis ignium

adiuta flatu possit inhibere impetum
irasque nostras: sternam et euertam omnia.
(*Medea* 397–414)

If you seek, wretch, how to limit hatred,
Copy love. Shall I endure royal weddings
Unavenged? Will this day pass idly by,
So protestingly petitioned, so granted?
While earth balances the circling heavens
And the shining world rolls its settled rounds,
While sands lack number, days pursue the sun
And stars the night, while the pole turns the thirsting
Bears and rivers descend to the ocean,
My rage will never recoil from vengeance,
And ever will increase. What bestial savagery,
What Scylla, what Charybdis sucking Ausonian,
Sicilian sea, what Etna as it crushes
The breathless Titan will burn with such threats?
No swirling river, no storm-racked ocean
Or Pontus filled with Corus' rage, or fire's might
Fanned by the winds could inhibit my force
And wrath: I'll prostrate and overturn all.

Observe also Hippolytus' transcendent rage in Act 3 of *Phaedra* upon Phaedra's confession of her love:

magne regnator deum,
tam lentus audis scelera? tam lentus uides?
et quando saeua fulmen emittes manu,
si nunc serenum est? omnis impulsus ruat
aether et atris nubibus condat diem,
ac uersa retro sidera obliquos agant
retorta cursus. tuque, sidereum caput,
radiate Titan, tu nefas stirpis tuae
speculare? lucem merge et in tenebras fuge.
(*Phaedra* 671–9)

Great monarch of gods,
Hear these crimes and not act? See and not act?
When will your savage hand impel its bolts
If the sky is cloudless now? All heaven
Collapse in ruin, black clouds bury day,
Let stars run back and wrenched from course turn all
Into confusion. You too, lord of stars,
Titan radiate, see your daughter's sin?
Submerge your light and flee into the dark.

30

The sound-pattern of the Latin of both speeches impresses: harsh gutterals, alliterated labials, palatals, dentals, sibilants, nasals: a veritable network of sound bound by consonantal interrelationships and the controlling cadences of the verse. Variation in caesura and verse-pause, enjambment, elision combine with repeated letter, repeated phrase, repeated sound, repeated syntax and with imagery that annexes the cosmos to suggest the accents of psychological and moral rage. C. J. Herington commented on the 'superb speakability' of Senecan verse.[22] I refer to its ability to re*present* and to cause 'shock', and to do it, here and often elsewhere, through a self-dramatising rhetoric of cosmic and psychic violence, in which the speaker does not so much express as construct him-or-herself out of the very language used. Seneca's declamatory style was and remains a powerful, shocking mode; but also a psychological one. As the author of *Titus Andronicus* (4.1.81f.) saw, for the tragedian who had something compelling to say, it could expand the agony of an individual soul into a fractured world.

3

IDEAS MADE FLESH

I doubt whether there bee any amonge all the Catalogue of Heathen wryters, that with more grauity of Philosophicall sentences, more waightynes of sappy words, or greater authority of sound matter beateth down sinne, loose lyfe, dissolute dealinge, and unbrydled sensuality; or that more sensibly, pithily, and bytingly layeth downe the guerdon of filthy lust, cloaked dissimulation and odious treachery; which is the dryft, whereunto he leueleth the whole yssue of ech one of his Tragedies.

Thomas Newton, *Seneca His Tenne Tragedies* (1581)

Seneca *had* something compelling to say.[1] Born under Augustus and committing suicide three years before Nero's similar fate, he lived in and through interesting times. After his entry into the senate, especially from the late thirties onwards, he moved in the circle of princes, among 'that tiny group of men on which there bore down, night and day, the concentric pressure of a monstrous weight, the post-Augustan empire'.[2] He survived the final years of Tiberius, the brief principate of the vicious Caligula, exile on Corsica engineered by Messalina, to find himself tutor and then chief minister of Nero, for whose matricide he wrote a *post factum* justification, but whose 'excesses' he and the praetorian prefect eventually became unable to control.[3] He witnessed at first hand and participated in the corrupting power, hypocrisy, self-abasement and abnormal cruelty defining (or so the ancient historians, especially Tacitus, will have us believe) the early imperial court. The declamatory themes of the schools – vengeance, rage, power-lust, incest, hideous death, fortune's savagery – were the stuff of his life. His literary response was twofold: the consolatory discourse of Stoic moral philosophy, reflected in his prose works, and the tragedies, which articulate a world quite different from that of the dialogues and epistles. The tragedies abound in Stoic moral ideas (many traceable to the *Epistulae Morales*) and their preoccupation with emotional pathology and with the destructive consequences of passion, especially anger, is deeply indebted to the Stoic tradition (see especially *De Ira*). But such Stoicism is no outer ideological clothing but part

32

of the dramatic texture of the plays, in which the world-view is generally unStoic, even a negation of Stoicism,[4] central principles of which are critically exhibited within a quite different vision.

Among the themes and ideas the tragedies make flesh: the determinism of history; the genealogy and competitive cyclicity of evil; the fragility of social and religious forms; the fragility of epistemological forms; the failure of reason; civilisation as moral contradiction; man as appetite, as beast, as existential victim; power, impotence, delusion, self-deception; the futility of compassion; the freedom, desirability, and value-paradox of death; man, god, nature, guilt, unmerited suffering; the certainty of human pain, the terror of experienced evil; the inexorable, paradoxical, amoral – even morally perverse – order of things; the triumph of evil; in one play (*Hercules Furens*), the possibility of human redemption; in all, the gap between language and the world.

But if the world of the tragedies is not simply Stoic, it is not simple either. There are conspicuous ideological differences between play and play.[5] On moral order, for example. In *Agamemnon, Hercules Furens, Phaedra, Medea* crime (*scelus*) is punished; gods, nature, fate, fortune seem in quasi-moral control; prayer (though not necessarily to gods) sometimes seems answered. Electra's prayer to Strophius (*Agamemnon* 929–31), Amphitryon's to Jupiter and Hercules (*Hercules Furens* 205ff., 516ff.), the Nurse's to Diana (*Phaedra* 406–23), Theseus' to Neptune (*Phaedra* 945–58), Medea's to Sol and to Hecate (*Medea* 32–6, 817–42), all appear answered, even if, as in the case of the Nurse in *Phaedra*, in a way that was not foreseen. But neither *Phaedra* nor *Medea* asserts the moral order implied in *Agamemnon* or the redemptive possibilities of *Hercules Furens*; nor is nature's order as presented in *Phaedra*, where all suffer and human impotence seems total, identical with the cosmic order of *Medea*, in which one of the human figures, working with the divine forces of the cosmos, triumphs. *Thyestes* differs radically from all four plays. Here nature, the gods are reduced to shocked, impotent observers of human bestiality and sin. There is no life-destroying storm to punish *scelus* as in *Agamemnon* (465ff.); no monster from the sea as in *Phaedra* (1007ff.); no Hecate-generated fire that feeds on its natural antagonist water, as in *Medea* (885ff.). *Scelus* is unpunished and prayers unfulfilled. 'The gods are fled', cries Thyestes, *fugere superi* (*Thyestes* 1021). And he is right. As is Oedipus in asserting the existence of mendacious gods (*Oedipus* 1042ff.) in a world where those who use reason to escape crime and guilt compound them both. Senecan moral and metaphysical tragedy investigates distinct and distinctive worlds. The world of *Oedipus* is not that of *Thyestes*. Nor is it that of *Troades* or *Medea*.

Examination of *Agamemnon* and *Thyestes* will prove instructive.[6] Devoted to the same mythological saga (the history of the house of Tantalus), the two plays are united too by a prominent dramaturgical feature, the ghost-prologue, not shared by the other extant Senecan tragedies, by similar

33

thematic imagery (both plays climax in a feast-sacrifice), and by an abundance of themes, *topoi* and motifs: revenge, the family cycle of evil, the contest of evil, fortune's revolutions, birth as destiny, power and illusion, true kingship, the desirability of death, the relationship between humankind, gods, nature, history.[7] But just as formal similarity between the plays coexists with substantial stylistic and dramaturgical differences,[8] the thematic continuities underscore defining ideological distinctness. Even the similar and central emphasis of both plays on structures, patterns – patterns of behaviour, crime, retribution, history – informs quite different worlds.

AGAMEMNON

Agamemnon is probably the earlier play.[9] In it, as in *Phaedra, Medea, Troades*,[10] the repetition of history is paramount. Past becomes present. References to the past at crucial moments of the play imply this;[11] the ghost of Thyestes in the prologue makes it overt. He moves from Tantalus' feast (21) to his own Thyestean feast (11, 26f.), to the approaching feast of Agamemnon's blood:

> iam iam natabit sanguine alterno domus.
> enses secures tela, diuisum graui
> ictu bipennis regium uideo caput.
> iam scelera prope sunt, iam dolus caedes cruor –
> parantur epulae.[12]
>
> (*Agamemnon* 44–8)

Now, now the house'll swim in blood answering blood.[13]
I see swords, axes, spears, a king's head split
By the heavy fall of double-bladed axe.
Now crime draws near, now treachery, slaughter, blood –
A feast is prepared.

Scelus to *scelus* to *scelus*: evil to evil to evil (25ff.); an alternating cycle of blood. An alternating cycle borne out in the play, as the *scelus alternum* theme of the opening chorus is taken up by Clytemnestra in her outburst to the Nurse to link Iphigenia's sacrifice with the Pelopian past (165ff.) and to foreshadow Clytemnestra's *scelus* to come. The murder of Agamemnon, both sacrifice and feast (898ff., 875ff.), as the imagery of the prologue had proclaimed (43, 48), re-enacts both Thyestes' banquet (testified by the sun itself, 908f.) and Agamemnon's own slaughter of kin (162ff.). It ends one cycle, begins another. Vengeance continues: from Thyestes to Clytemnestra and Aegisthus, from the latter to Electra and Orestes. Hell's tortuous repetitions, lavishly described in the ghost-prologue, seem paradigm not only for the world of the dead.

Cyclic, history is also determinant. The past's self-repetition is product of fortune/fate, *fortuna/fatum* (28ff., 33). From Thyestes' most recent inversion of nature (28ff.), through the storm of Clytemnestra's turmoil (109, 138ff.) and the wreck of the Greek fleet (415, etc.),[14] to Cassandra's appearance before the palace (698) and Agamemnon's death (758, 885), fortune's storm (57ff.),[15] fate, drives the action. The instruments of destruction, Clytemnestra and Aegisthus, are creatures fashioned by the past, doomed to recreate it as the future. Aegisthus is only too aware of the *causa natalis* (48), the imperatives of his birth (*sic nato*, 233); he trembles before the past's injunctions (226ff.). No less is Clytemnestra defined by the past: by Agamemnon's slaughter of Iphigenia and his Trojan lusts (162ff.). Feelings for her lover – 'base lust' notwithstanding (135) – she has none; she manipulates him until he is ready for the deed.[16] The deed done generates its own repetition. The future is preformed.

But there is more to the past's repetition than Tantalid crime. The Trojan model elicits attention.[17] Analogies between Aegisthus and Paris, Clytemnestra and Helen, Agamemnon and Priam, Argos and Troy, the Argive chorus and deluded Trojan 'youth' and their 'festive mothers',[18] present the murder of Agamemnon as re-enactment of and revenge for Priam's death and the fall of Troy. The circumstances of the latter – treachery and guile, festal day or feast, adultery, fatal gift – repeat themselves as the circumstances of Agamemnon's death.[19] Brilliantly the staccato half-lines or *antilabai* exchanged between Cassandra and Agamemnon in the finale to Act 4 focus the analogy:

Agamemnon	Festus dies est.
Cassandra	Festus et Troiae fuit.
Ag.	Veneremur aras.
Cass.	Cecidit ante aras pater.
Ag.	Iouem precemur pariter.
Cass.	Herceum Iouem?
Ag.	Credis uidere te Ilium?
Cass.	Et Priamum simul.
Ag.	Hic Troia non est.
Cass.	Helena ubi est, Troiam puto.

(*Agamemnon* 791–5)

Agamemnon	It's a feast-day.
Cassandra	It was a feast-day at Troy.
Ag.	Let's revere the altars.
Cass.	By altars father fell.
Ag.	Let's pray to Jove together.
Cass.	Hercean Jove?
Ag.	Think you see Ilium?
Cass.	And Priam too.
Ag.	Troy's not here.
Cass.	Where Helen is, I think is Troy.

35

Cassandra's and the play's final words, spat triumphantly in the face of Clytemnestra, drive the analogy home: 'To you too will rage come', *ueniet et uobis furor* (1012). In the sacrificial killing of Agamemnon are recreated not only Atrean butchery, Thyestean banquet and Agamemnon's own sacrifice of kin, but the slaughter of Priam at the altar of Hercean Jove (448) and the fall of Troy itself. The present is dramatised as product of many pasts and their re*presentation*, a re*presentation* as morally obscure as it is inevitable: *uenere fata*, 'fate has come' (885). The altars of the gods provide few answers.

Rather, they provide questions. The questions concern the moral structure of *Agamemnon*'s world. The divine altars on the stage, the *arae caelitum*, are a conspicuous ingredient of the theatrical setting. They are addressed by Eurybates (392aff.), drawn attention to by Clytemnestra (585), approached and venerated by Agamemnon (778ff.), clung to and left by Electra (951, 972). They imply a concept of divine–human interrelationship which aspects of the play's action seem to undermine. Put bluntly, in *Agamemnon* prayers to the gods are unfulfilled. The elaborate prayer of the Argive chorus to Phoebus, Juno, Pallas, Diana and Jupiter (310–407), the matching prayer of the victorious Agamemnon to the Father and Argolic Juno (802–07), prove as futile as the futile prayer of the storm-tossed Greeks (519ff.). Indeed each prayer proves dramatic prelude to the kind of disaster it seeks to avert. Eurybates' pious narrative (421–578) undercuts the theological optimism of the Argive chorus; Cassandra's reported vision (867–909) exposes her conqueror's religious illusions. Like the prayers of Theseus in *Phaedra*, those of Agamemnon 'move no gods' (*Phaedra* 1242). Not that events are uncontrolled. Control there is; even divine control. Phoebus especially seems interwoven with the play's events: Thyestes' oracle (28ff.), Aegisthus' birth (294), the Argive prayer (310ff.), the storm at sea (577), Cassandra-Phoebas (588,710), catalyst of doom. In retrospect the ghost's parting remark – *Phoebum moramur* ('we delay Phoebus', 56) – seems double-edged. But to the participants in the drama this governance of events seems savage, unjust or at least amoral, even perverse. So Aegisthus:

> crede perniciem tibi
> et dira saeuos fata moliri deos.
> (*Agamemnon* 229f.)

> Be sure savage gods
> Fashion your destruction and dreadful fate.

So Cassandra:

> uicere nostra iam metus omnes mala.
> equidem nec ulla caelites placo prece
> nec si uelint saeuire quo noceant habent:
> fortuna uires ipsa consumpsit suas.

quae patria restat, quis pater, quae iam soror?
bibere tumuli sanguinem atque arae meum.
> (*Agamemnon* 695–700)

Our sufferings now have conquered every fear.
No prayer comes from me to placate the gods –
If they wish to rage, they cannot harm me:
For even fortune has spent her powers.
What homeland is there, what father, what sister now?
Burial mounds and altars have drunk my blood.

The Trojan women's remarks on the 'unjust Thunderer' (594f.) and 'fickle gods' (606), and Electra's doubt even of the gods' existence (930), seem in accord.

And yet the structure of events, the network of cause and effect, seems less perverse than the *dramatis personae* on the whole seem to recognise. History is no irrational cyclicity. The inversion of nature, for example, which Phoebus commanded (34), seems to counterbalance and to respond to the earlier inversion of nature which drove Phoebus from the sky (295–7). Principles of balance and atonement permeate the play's action. Agamemnon's death is presented as atonement for crime at three levels:[20] ancestral crime (the Thyestean *cena*); national crime (the Greek sack of Troy, the burning of the temples, the murder of Priam); personal crime (the sacrifice of Iphigenia, the leadership of the Greek expedition, offences against Phoebus at Troy).[21] At each level Phoebus is involved. Of course Agamemnon's own murder is itself a crime, and is described as such: 'Each in this great crime (*tanto scelere*) answers to his kin' (906). It is a crime which generates social as well as moral disorder (884, 912), and will be followed by the appropriate redress.

Interwoven with the pattern of crime and punishment is that of fortune's rise and fall:

> ut praecipites regum casus
> fortuna rotat.
>> (*Agamemnon* 71f.)

> As the headlong fates of kings
> Fortune rolls.

> quidquid in altum
> fortuna tulit, ruitura leuat.
>> (*Agamemnon* 100f.)

> Whatever fortune
> Raises high, she lifts to cast down.

Again the paradigm-case is Agamemnon, the returning victorious *imperator*,[22] whose movement from victor to vanquished is anticipated (412ff., 738ff.,

754, 799), underscored (869ff.), and reflected upon (1007–9). Again the
corollary is Clytemnestra, the new victor, *cruenta uictrix* (947), awaiting in turn
her defeat. Again moral issues seem involved. The opening chorus displays
fortuna as a quasi-moral force that punishes excess and the vices that attend
power and wealth:

> quas non arces scelus alternum
> dedit in praeceps? impia quas non
> arma fatigant? iura pudorque
> et coniugii sacrata fides
> fugiunt aulas.
>
> (*Agamemnon* 77–81)

> What palace has crime answering crime
> Not hurled headlong? Which do impious
> Arms not oppress? Right and shame
> And the hallowed pledge of marriage
> Shun the court.

This seems obvious preface to the second act's focus not only on
Clytemnestra's lack of 'morality, right, honour, duty, loyalty' and 'shame' or
'self-respect' (*mores, ius, decus, pietas, fides . . . pudor*, 112f.), but on the collapse of
those virtues in Agamemnon's past (158f., 164ff.). Similarly Eurybates'
speech exhibits fortune's storm as atonement for Greek success and as
divine punishment for the sack of Troy (524f., 528): 'Atonement was made
for Ilium' (*postquam litatum est Ilio*, 577; cf. 1005ff.). His narrative not only
foreshadows the devastation to come but places that devastation within a
context of crime, punishment and retribution.

The play's final act confirms this moral reading. Indeed the crudely
handled Strophius scene (918ff.) seems expressly fashioned to stress the
issue of moral order. A veritable *uir ex machina*, Strophius, equipped with
the palm of victory around which the whole scene revolves, responds to
Electra's prayer with courage and 'loyalty', *fides*, and, handing the palm, 'gift
of Pisaean Jove', to Orestes as veil and *omen* (938f.), prefigures Orestes'
triumph and the regicides' defeat. The Strophius scene not only underscores
the pattern of crime and retribution, but, associating with the foreshadowed
victory the *pietas* (931) and *fides* which the Mycenaean house has debased or
lost (285ff., 307, 882; 112, 159, 164ff., 900, 957), seems to offer the possibility of (ambiguous) moral hope.[23]

> condisce, Pylade, patris exemplo fidem.
>
> (*Agamemnon* 941)

> Learn, Pylades, from your father's example,
> Loyalty.

The act's final scene does nothing to dissipate this promise. Cassandra springs from the altars rejoicing to witness the atonement for Troy's suffering and predicts Clytemnestra's suffering to come (1004ff.). *Fortuna* seems far from blind.

Paradox ensues. History's moral order entails human responsibility for history's crimes, even as it precludes it. The play's climactic *scelus*, product of history's unimpedable cycle, is *scelus* committed by human agents acting deliberately and in accordance with character. Clytemnestra and Aegisthus are 'morally' responsible and guilty. But in reality they determine nothing. Both intention and character in *Agamemnon*'s world, as in orthodox Stoicism,[24] are as much the determined products of history,[25] as the events to which they give rise. 'Morally' responsible for history's cycle, the human denizens of *Agamemnon*'s world are yet simply that through which history's cycle of crime and punishment takes place. As the structures and patterns of the play reveal, fate, fortune, Phoebus, Jupiter, the moral order of history, shape all.[26]

But if *Agamemnon* dramatises human impotence, it dramatises human delusion:

> at te pater, qui saeua torques fulmina
> pellisque nubes, sidera et terras regis,
> ad quem triumphi spolia uictores ferunt,
> et te, sororem cuncta pollentis uiri,
> Argolica Iuno, pecore uotiuo libens
> Arabumque donis supplici et fibra colam.
> >> (*Agamemnon* 802–7)

> You, father, who hurl savage thunderbolts,
> Impel the clouds, and govern stars and earth,
> To whom victors bring the spoils of triumph,
> And you, sister of an almighty lord,
> Argive Juno, with votive flocks, Arabia's gifts
> And suppliant entrails I'll gladly adore.

So Agamemnon prays, only to be sacrificed himself – immediately. The returning *imperator*, king of kings (39, 291), leader of leaders (39, 1007), conqueror of Asia and avenger of Europe (204f.), is as deluded about his own ability to control and to effect either through action or through prayer as were the people he had conquered about theirs:

> secura metus Troica pubes
> sacros gaudet tangere funes . . .
> festae matres uotiua ferunt munera diuis,
> festi patres adeunt aras.
> >> (*Agamemnon* 638f., 644f.)

> Careless of fear Trojan youth
> Rejoices to touch sacred ropes . . .

Festive mothers bring votive gifts to gods,
Festive fathers approach altars.

Experience generates illusions of power, safety, success. *Fortuna fallax*. So
Agamemnon; so 'Trojan youth' and 'festive mothers'. So too the Argive
chorus, it also 'youthful' and 'festive' (*pubes . . . festa*, 310f.), whose victory ode
not only assumes divine protection where none exists but assumes it of gods
actively hostile to the Greek cause.[27] So too Eurybates, whose narrative
demonstration of human powerlessness before fate evidences the pointlessness of the narrator's piety and prayers (392aff., 406aff.). His ironic anticipation of the doom he seeks strenuously to avoid only underlines this (412,
448, 514). Nor are the play's chief instruments of fate exempt. As their
discussion of Agamemnon's power (244–83) proves preface to the revelation of his powerlessness, so Clytemnestra's and Aegisthus' possession of
the kingdom is prefaced and concluded by pointers to its vanity (932–43,
1012). Signally Aegisthus' initial insight into history's intolerable cycle (226–
33) vanishes as the wheel turns. *Fortuna rotat*.

But the turning is not everything. Ironically history's ineluctable cycle and
the human powerlessness it entails are context for tragic splendour.

> solus inuictus malis
> luctatur Aiax.
> > (*Agamemnon* 532f.)

> Alone unvanquished by disaster
> Ajax fights.

In his defiant struggle, refusal to be subdued, heroic resistance, courage and
challenge in the face of hostile, apparently perverse gods (532–56), Ajax of
Locris – like Phaedra, Hippolytus, Astyanax and Polyxena – dramatises the
spectacular paradox of the greatness of impotent humanity. He pre-
exemplifies the Trojan chorus' ideal of human freedom, the 'contemner of
fickle gods' (*contemptor leuium deorum*, 606). It is an ideal exemplified too by
Cassandra, like Ajax characterised by *furor* (720, 724, etc.; cf. 544, 552), like
Ajax contemner of gods (cf. 550ff.):

> uicere nostra iam metus omnes mala.
> equidem nec ulla caelites placo prece
> nec si uelint saeuire quo noceant habent:
> fortuna uires ipsa consumpsit suas.
> > (*Agamemnon* 695–8)

> Our sufferings now have conquered every fear.
> No prayer comes from me to placate the gods –
> If they wish to rage, they cannot harm me:
> For even fortune has spent her powers.

Alone among the leading characters of the play Cassandra has no illusions about her power. Powerless she sees. Defeated she conquers. She does not follow, as in Aeschylus' play, her conqueror on to the stage. In accordance with Roman triumphal practice,[28] she precedes him, but, like Agamemnon in the scene to come, crowned with laurel. She is both captive and victor; enslaved she is free.

In Cassandra freedom and victory conjoin – with death. In freedom lies her victory; in death and its acceptance lies her freedom.

> heu quam dulce malum mortalibus additum
> uitae dirus amor, cum pateat malis
> effugium et miseros libera mors uocet
> portus aeterna placidus quiete.
> (*Agamemnon* 589–92)

> Ah, how alluring a vice for mortals is
> Perverse love of life, though a refuge from ills
> Lies open and death's freedom summons wretches
> To a peaceful port of eternal rest.

Thus the Trojan women,[29] whose narrative, tears and suffering (612ff.), however, betray an involvement with life at odds with the full realisation of death's freedom. It is not the chorus but Cassandra who dramatises the truth of these sentiments. Devastated by fortune, with nothing to fear because she has nothing to lose ('For even fortune has spent her powers', 698), she demonstrates death's freedom in words:

Agamemnon	Ne metue dominam famula.
Cassandra	Libertas adest.
Ag.	Secura uiue.
Cass.	Mihi mori est securitas.

> (*Agamemnon* 796f.)

Agamemnon	Fear no mistress, slave.
Cassandra	Freedom is at hand.
Ag.	Live secure.
Cass.	Death is my security.

And in deeds:

> ne trahite, uestros ipsa praecedam gradus.
> perferre prima nuntium Phrygibus meis
> propero: repletum ratibus euersis mare,
> captas Mycenas, mille ductorem ducum,
> ut paria fata Troicis lueret malis,
> perisse dono, feminae stupro, dolo.

41

nihil moramur, rapite; quin grates ago.
iam iam iuuat uixisse post Troiam, iuuat.
(*Agamemnon* 1004–11)

No need to drag me. I will precede you.
I rush to be the first to take the news
To my Phrygians: that the sea's filled with wrecked ships,
Mycenae's taken, a thousand kings' own king –
To atone for Troy's pain with matching fate –
Destroyed by gifts, female lust, treachery.
I cannot wait, take me; I owe you thanks.
Now, now it's sweet to have outlived Troy – sweet.

The dramatic power of Cassandra's words and the personal triumph which they display need no demonstration. Dramatic power and thematic importance coalesce. From the moment of her entry at 586–8 Cassandra dominates the play, providing a model of triumphal human behaviour. She conquers adversity not by altering it but by rejoicing in the freedom devastation offers, in the dissolution it can provide of the very attachment to life which generates delusion, suffering, fear. In contrast the Trojan women, Agamemnon, Clytemnestra, reveal in their verbal exchanges with the Trojan princess precisely that delusive attachment to life productive of pain and terror. Their estimate of the value of life, evidenced by their grief, anxiety, striving, jealousy, vengefulness and ambition, is exhibited by the play as false.

The final scene focuses on this issue. Electra, after her final tie with the living (Orestes) has been removed, willingly offers herself to death (946), and, joining Cassandra at the altars, shows in her exchange with the 'bloody husband-slayer' (947) Cassandra-like freedom and strength. Comprehending little, Clytemnestra threatens Electra with death, according a value to life which Electra actively rejects. Electra dwells with satisfaction on her end:

recedo ab aris. siue te iugulo iuuat
mersisse ferrum, praebeo iugulum uolens;
seu more pecudum colla resecari placet,
intenta ceruix uulnus expectat tuum.
scelus paratum est; caede respersam uiri
atque obsoletam sanguine hoc dextram ablue.
(*Agamemnon* 972–7)

I leave the altars. If you wish to plunge
Steel in my throat, I offer my throat gladly;
Or if you're resolved to sever my neck
Like a beast's, a bent neck awaits your stroke.
The crime is ready; cleanse your filthy hand,
Stained with a husband's murder, in my blood.

Aegisthus, however, knows the value of death and punishes Electra with life, depriving her of death's freedom (988ff.).[30] She will be bound, enclosed, imprisoned. Clytemnestra is unimpressed. She demands the death of the *captiua coniunx*, whose behaviour she cannot understand:

Cassandra	Nihil moramur, rapite; quin grates ago.
	iam iam iuuat uixisse post Troiam, iuuat.
Clytemnestra	Furiosa morere.[31]
Cassandra	Veniet et uobis furor.
	(*Agamemnon* 1010–12)

Cassandra	I cannot wait, take me; I owe you thanks.
	Now, now it's sweet to have outlived Troy – sweet.
Clytemnestra	Die raging.
Cassandra	To you also rage will come.

Retribution will come. But so too will what Clytemnestra sees as Cassandra's *furor*, the longing for the freedom of death.[32] The play began with Thyestes' desertion of hell and his desire to return there (*libet reuerti*, 12); it ends, as the Trojan princess is taken from the stage, with the focus on Cassandra's death-wish, her desire to die, and on her prophecy of Clytemnestra's and Aegisthus' death-longing to come. The present delusion of Clytemnestra is complete. The victim has the last word and wins. This is in a curious way a moral world, if one both problematic and generative of little comfort.[33]

THYESTES

If the world of *Agamemnon* has little comfort, that of *Thyestes* has none. In *Thyestes* the victorious *tyrannus*, Atreus, speaks last:

Thyestes	Vindices aderunt dei;
	his puniendum uota te tradunt mea.
Atreus	Te puniendum liberis trado tuis.
	(*Thyestes* 1110–12)

Thyestes	The gods of vengeance shall come;
	To them my prayers deliver you for punishment.
Atreus	You I deliver for punishment to your children.

The play's focus is not the moral order of things nor even death's refuge, but man as appetite, as beast, as eternal hunger and thirst (149f.). The prologue makes this clear.

> quid famem infixam intimis
> agitas medullis? flagrat incensum siti

cor et perustis flamma uisceribus micat.
sequor.

(*Thyestes* 97–100)

> Why do you stir the hunger
> Fixed deep in my marrow? Scorching thirst burns
> My heart; the flame darts as my intestines blaze.
> I follow.

Released from the accursed underworld where hunger and thirst torture him for ever, the ghost of Tantalus in a transparently symbolic scene is driven – despite his resistance (68ff.) – to infect the 'beast-hearts' (*ferum pectus*, 85f.) of his descendants with the gaping hunger and parching thirst (2–6, etc.),[34] the lust for power, slaughter and familial sin, the *libido*, emptiness and *furor* (23–67, 101–3), which he represents both as ancestor of the Tantalid house and as emblematic human *nefas*, as mythic prototype of man.[35] Commanded by the Fury to 'fill the whole house with Tantalus' (*imple Tantalo totam domum*, 53), he does so. The physical environment withers (107ff.); the spiritual environment likewise (176ff.). The world of the play is filled with emptiness. The prologue structurally, imagistically and thematically integrates with the play. It not only predicts the horror to come (especially 56–67), but its structure (resistance to hunger/*furor*, followed by subservience to hunger/*furor*) and even its formula for submission ('I follow', *sequor*, 100, 489) prove model for the dramatic and tragic turning-point: Thyestes' capitulation to the new Tantalus. The central ideas of the prologue (blood-lust, familial crime, craving for power, slaughter, vengeance) and their associated imagery and motifs anticipate precisely those of the action to come.

Applied to the motivational forces of the play, these images and motifs (hunger, thirst, eating, drinking, feasting, filling, emptying, satiety, limit, unlimit) index man as appetite, his essential status as beast. This is underscored even in the first choral ode, in which the Argive nobles, fearing a return of the 'inveterate thirst' (119), pray for an end to the 'bestial impulses' (136) of the impious offspring of 'dry' Tantalus, whose 'bestial feast' (150) was fittingly punished with 'eternal hunger' and 'eternal thirst' (*aeterna fames*, 149, *aeterna sitis*, 150). Their concluding picture of dry Tantalus with 'empty gullet' (152), reduced to 'yawning chasm' (157) before fleeing prey, driven by burning hunger, by burning thirst, to grasp vainly for food (165–8), to chase water that turns into dust (171–5), reflects brilliantly on to the opening of Act 2, in which Atreus exhibits himself immediately as raging appetite for vengeance. The focus in Act 2 on Atreus' appetitive emptiness, his almost insatiable lust for revenge (245–79), his need to be 'filled' with 'greater monstrosity', *maiore monstro* (253f.), is undisguised:

> non satis magno meum
> ardet furore pectus.
>> (*Thyestes* 252f.)

> My heart blazes with rage
> Insufficiently vast.

> nullum relinquam facinus et nullum est satis.
>> (*Thyestes* 256)

> I'll leave no crime undone and no crime's enough.

The motif permeates the play into the final act itself, where Atreus' unfilled void, his apparent inability to be satisfied, is drawn attention to not only by Atreus' own frenzied words (889ff., 907, 1053ff.), but by the irony of his having filled Thyestes in the attempt to satisfy himself (890, 979f.).

Acts 3 and 4 make the dramatisation of Atreus not simply as appetite, but as beast explicit. Thus Atreus, as he views the returned Thyestes, the beast in the trap (*plagis . . . fera*, 491):

> uix tempero animo, uix dolor frenos capit.
> sic, cum feras uestigat et longo sagax
> loro tenetur Vmber ac presso uias
> scrutatur ore, dum procul lento suem
> odore sentit, paret et tacito locum
> rostro pererrat; praeda cum proprior fuit,
> ceruice tota pugnat et gemitu uocat
> dominum morantem seque retinenti eripit.
>> (*Thyestes* 496–503)

> It's hard to keep control, hard to bridle hate.
> So when a sharp-nosed Umbrian tracks wild beasts
> Held on a long leash, and with muzzle pressed down
> Sniffs out the trail – while the boar is distant
> And the scent weak, he obeys and scours the field
> In silence; but when the prey draws nearer,
> He fights with all his neck, noisily protests
> His master's delay and breaks from his restraint.

Two further extended animal similes follow in the Messenger's account of Act 4. His narrative of the slaughter of the first child images Atreus as famine-driven tigress (*ieiuna tigris*, 707f.), uncertain where to set her fangs, keeping her hunger waiting (707–13); as he strikes, he is simply *ferus*, 'a beast' (721, cf. 546). Then the 'savage' (*saeuus*, 726) slaughter of Plisthenes, after which, before the final death, Atreus is gore-drenched Armenian lion, whose 'banished hunger' brings no satisfaction; the lust for blood rages (732–41). Not that the trapped Thyestes is exempt from the beast paradigm: 'the net is spread, the beast entrapped' (491); indeed the play will end on his Tantalid hunger. It is Atreus, however, who primarily exemplifies beast. And unlike in *Agamemnon*, in which the lion is killed (*uictor ferarum . . . leo*, 738f.) and the beast that slays him (740) will be slain, in *Thyestes* the beast (*leo . . . uictor*, 732ff.) triumphs and lives. Indeed Atreus outbestialises the beasts. So the Messenger and the Chorus:

Chorus	Quid ultra potuit? obiecit feris
	lanianda forsan corpora atque igne arcuit?
Nuntius	Vtinam arcuisset! ne tegat functos humus
	nec soluat ignis! auibus epulandos licet
	ferisque triste pabulum saeuis trahat –
	uotum est sub hoc quod esse supplicium solet:
	pater insepultos spectet!

(Thyestes 747–53)

Chorus	What more could he do? Throw out
	Their bodies for beasts to tear and deny them fire?
Messenger	Would he had denied it! Let earth not cover
	Nor fire consume the dead. Let them be dragged out
	To feast the birds, ghastly food for savage beasts.
	What most think punishment is now our prayer:
	Would their father could view them unburied!

So Thyestes and Atreus:

Thyestes	Vtrumne saeuis pabulum alitibus iacent,
	an beluis seruantur,[36] an pascunt feras?
Atreus	Epulatus ipse es impia natos dape.

(Thyestes 1032–4)

Thyestes	Do they lie out as food for savage birds,
	Kept for wild animals, nourishment for beasts?
Atreus	*You* feasted impiously on your sons.

And Atreus outbestialises the beasts by inverting the kinds of institution which make human civilised life possible: kingship, sacrifice, feast. The beast Atreus triumphs through civilisation's controlling forms.

The final three acts are structured around three separate institutions of civilised life – political, religious, social – in order dramatically to express this. Act 3 is concerned with political authority, power, kingship. It climaxes theatrically in the ritual of coronation, as Atreus, who has divested Thyestes of his beggar's robes and put royal garments upon him (524–6), places on Thyestes' head the crown that imprisons him and turns his sons into dead men:

> imposita capiti uincla uenerando gere;
> ego destinatas uictimas superis dabo.

(Thyestes 544f.)

> Wear the band placed on your reverend head.
> I'll offer appointed victims to the gods.

Act 5 focuses on the ritual of the feast, on the laws of hospitality and the serving of food; it presents the transformation of a social ritual that should foster the values of human harmony, gratitude, generosity, into an instrument of torture, horror, sickness. Act 4 focuses on sacrifice, a ritual which, like the feast, sustains the ordered distinctions of life: god, man, beast.[37] Although the sacrificial murders of Act 4 have been prepared for (by the dead Tantalus' admonition against the defiling of altars, 93–5, by the first chorus' attention to Tantalus' own sacrificial history, 146–8, by Atreus' implied sacrificial intent, 545), Atreus' meticulous attention to sacrificial procedure has not.[38] The rules, the rite, the proper order of things, seem almost as important as the vengeance they exact:

Nuntius	Seruatur omnis ordo, ne tantum nefas
	non rite fiat.
Chorus	Quis manum ferro admouet?
Nuntius	Ipse est sacerdos, ipse funesta prece
	letale carmen ore uiolento canit.
	stat ipse ad aras, ipse deuotos neci
	contrectat et componit et ferro admouet;
	attendit ipse: nulla pars sacri perit.

(Thyestes 689–95)

Messenger	Every ritual's observed, lest the monstrous act
	Be improperly performed.
Chorus	Who puts hand to knife?
Messenger	He himself is the priest, *his* roaring voice
	Intones the death-chant and funeral prayers.
	He stands at the altars, *he* feels the victims,
	Arranges them and draws them to the knife.
	He attends to all: no part of the rite's ignored.

The emphasis on ritual draws attention to its inversion. The *sacerdos* is beast; the beast-victim is human. The distinctions the sacrifice implies are dissolved. Indeed in Acts 3 to 5 central rituals of political, religious and social life, emblematic of civilisation's controlling forms, are used not to promote community, not to confirm socio-religious realities, not to harness individual differences and instinctual energies into a larger, more stable entity, but to implement savagery. In Acts 4 and 5 especially the dissolution of the distinctions of ordered society which its social and religious institutions imply is emphatic: Atreus is god (911), man and beast; he has replaced the gods, the stars, the sun (885ff.); he is both sacrificer and recipient of sacrifice. The structures of civilisation dissolve into man the beast-god, the beast-king, the beast-sacrificer, the beast-sacrificed and eaten.[39] The death of a culture, the inversion and perversion of its civilising forms and practices – prominent in Seneca's brilliant contemporary, Petronius, narrated and analysed in the Neronian *Annals* of Tacitus – seems unequivocally denoted.

As does the power of the beast. In contrast with *Agamemnon* it is conventional morality, *sanctitas, pietas, fides* (216f.; cf. 507ff., 717f., 972, 1024, and 139ff.), which proves illusory, not the power of the beast-king. And yet paradoxically the play foregrounds the deluding and deluded nature of the world of power, of the *rex* and the *tyrannus:*

> nescitis, cupidi arcium,
> regnum quo iaceat loco.
> regem non faciunt opes,
> non uestis Tyriae color,
> non frontis nota regia
> non auro nitidae trabes:
> rex est qui posuit metus
> et diri mala pectoris.
> > (*Thyestes* 342–9)

> Palace-hungry you ignore
> The place where kingship lies.
> Wealth doesn't create a king,
> Nor dye of Tyrian cloth,
> Nor forehead's royal mark,
> Nor gleaming beams of gold:
> He's a king who's banished fear
> And dreadful heart's distress.

The kingship chorus, tranquil, analytic, reflective, offers an alternative paradigm of power to that illustrated in the preceding act. It locates power not in the false trappings and splendour of the terror-filled world of conventional kingship – 'O ceremony, show me but thy worth' (*Henry V* 4.1.241) – but in the kingdom of the mind (*mens bona*, 380). Self-control, self-possession, self-sufficiency, self-knowledge, absence of the fear of death (342–403): this is what kingship is. Highlighted of course by the contrast with the preceding act's discussion of tyrannical power and its emphasis on power through fear (204ff., 334f.),[40] this quasi-Stoic vision is further underscored by Thyestes' apparent exemplification of it in the opening scene of the following act. Standing before the sacred towers of Argos and the visible symbols of its power (404–10), Thyestes remonstrates with himself:

> clarus hic regni nitor
> fulgore non est quod oculos falso auferat
> > (*Thyestes* 414f.)

> This gleaming splendour of kingship
> Should not deceive your eyes with its false show.

And then with his son:

> mihi crede, falsis magna nominibus placent,
> frustra timentur dura. dum excelsus steti,
> numquam pauere destiti atque ipsum mei
> ferrum timere lateris. o quantum bonum est
> obstare nulli, capere securas dapes
> humi iacentem! . . .
> immane regnum est posse sine regno pati.
>
> *(Thyestes* 446–51, 470)

> Believe me, false titles give greatness charm,
> Fear of poverty's groundless. While I stood high,
> My terror never ceased; even the sword
> At my side brought panic. O, how good it is
> To block no one's path, to enjoy carefree
> Banquets on the earth! . . .
> Great kingship is strength to endure without kingship.

Ironically in the second half of Act 3 Thyestes himself demonstrates the naivety and impotence of this vision. Succumbing to a world he has castigated as deluding, he accepts a crown which he knows should fill him with fear and the love of a brother whose hatred of him he knows to be boundless. The 'persuasion' scene is conspicuous for its absence of persuasiveness. Thyestes refuses the crown (531–4); Atreus objects:

Atreus	Recipit hoc regnum duos.
Thyestes	Meum esse credo quidquid est, frater, tuum.
At.	Quis influentis dona fortunae abnuit?
Thy.	Expertus est quicumque quam facile effluant.
At.	Fratrem potiri gloria ingenti uetas?
Thy.	Tua iam peracta gloria est, restat mea:
	respuere certum est regna consilium mihi.
At.	Meam relinquam, nisi tuam partem accipis.
Thy.	Accipio: regni nomen imposti feram,
	sed iura et arma seruient mecum tibi.
At.	Imposita capiti uincla uenerando gere;
	ego destinatas uictimas superis dabo.

(Thyestes 534–45)

Atreus	This kingdom has room for two.
Thyestes	What is yours, brother, I hold to be mine.
At.	What man denies the influx of fortune's gifts?
Thy.	The man who knows how easily they ebb.

At.	Do you forbid your brother great glory?
Thy.	Your glory's already won; mine remains.
	To reject the crown is my fixed intent.
At.	I'll resign my share, unless you accept yours.
Thy.	I accept; I'll bear a king's title on me,
	But laws and arms shall serve – with me – yourself.
At.	Wear the band placed on your reverend head.
	I'll offer appointed victims to the gods.

Heralded immediately (546ff.) by the deluded chorus as a triumph of 'true piety' (*uera pietas*) and 'true love' (*uerus amor*), the scene intentionally intrigues. Despite the objections he himself articulated earlier in the act, Thyestes accepts the crown with only token pressure to do so. Act 3's opening soliloquy explains why. As he gazes on 'the longed-for buildings' (404) of his homeland, 'the wealth of Argos' (404), 'the sacred towers of the Cyclops, glory (*decus*) surpassing human effort' (407f.), 'the race-course thronged with youth' (409), where 'more than once' he 'won the palm (*palmam*) of victory and fame' (409f.), Thyestes dreams of the people's acclaim:

> occurret Argos, populus occurret frequens.
> *(Thyestes* 411)

> Argos will rush to meet me, throngs will rush out.

Thyestes clearly longs for the world of fame and power.[41] Knowledge of that world, born of experience and suffering, may have qualified that desire; it has not removed it. Like old Tantalus' 'ingrained hunger' (97), it lies within, able to be rekindled when the prospect of 'wealth', *diuitiae*, draws near (162ff.). It was observed above how Thyestes' extensive but negative eulogy of the simple life betrayed one who desired power.[42] Atreus' evaluation of his brother (*regna nunc sperat mea*, 'even now he hopes for my kingdom', 289) proves as veridical as the dead Tantalus' capitulation proves predictive. Note how Thyestes not only confesses immediately to all Atreus has believed of him (512–14),[43] but, without any prompting, hands over as 'pledges of his trust' (520) the children for whose safety he had feared (485f.). It is as if, as soon as Thyestes' longing for his old life starts to manifest itself and resistance to it ends, the intellect is subverted and moral priorities reversed. Hence the neglect in the very area where previously he was so concerned: his sons. Dissidence between personal appetite on the one hand and moral knowledge and moral responsibility on the other seems central to Thyestes' dramatisation.

Thyestes seems to exemplify, as the ghost of Tantalus in the prologue had done, the contra-rational nature and the compulsive power of appetite. Caught in a net similar to that in which Agamemnon is ensnared, Thyestes yet differs from the self-confident returning *impostor* of the other play in his delusion. Thyestes knows the falsenesses of power and the true nature of his brother; unlike Agamemnon, who seems to know very little, he moves from knowledge to blindness. Significantly, he recreates the movement of the prologue, on which his progression in Act 3 is clearly modelled (*sequor*, 'I follow', 100, 489), from knowledge and resistance to appetite, to submission to it. He thus stands as pointer to a contra-rational view of man, exhibiting the impotence of knowledge, practical idealism, even Stoic vision (important here is the connection between Thyestes' opening attitudes and those of the kingship chorus) against the constraints of appetite.[44] The ironies of Act 3 underline this. Thyestes leaves a life among beasts (412–14), the advantages of which he sees, to live with a beast who kills his children; he leaves a situation where food is eaten without fear (449ff.) to eat without fear where he knew fear to be appropriate; he is deluded by a world he castigated as deluding, by a crown which frees him from poverty and binds him (*uincla*, 544) for Atreus' lust. Hunger triumphs in Thyestes as it does in Atreus; and disgusts. The repulsive descriptions in Acts 4 and 5 of 'satiate' Thyestes[45] – dripping and glistening with oil (780, 948), groggy with wine (781, 910), sprawled on purple and gold (909–11), belching (*eructat*, 911) or choking on his food (781f.) – evidence both appetite's triumph and its value. But while hunger triumphs in both brothers, Thyestes alone it blinds.

Nor only once. It is apparent in the play's concluding lines that even Thyestes' movement from delusion to knowledge in the final act, his post-revelation passion for death, his disgust with life, his tortured awareness both of divine impotence and his own self-deception, generate but another delusion:

> uindices aderunt dei;
> his puniendum uota te tradunt mea.
> (*Thyestes* 1110f.)

> The gods of vengeance shall come;
> To them my prayers deliver you for punishment.

The prophecy is specific; *te*, 'you', is Atreus. But Atreus will not be punished. Thyestes' hunger for vengeance has spawned a similar delusion to that engendered by the appetite for power. As in *Agamemnon*, however, not all are deluded. As the 'seeing' Cassandra ends *Agamemnon*, the 'seeing' Atreus ends *Thyestes*:

> te puniendum liberis trado tuis.
> (*Thyestes* 1112)

> You I deliver for punishment to your children.

Unlike Thyestes, Atreus predicts the truth. Thyestes will be forced by his own passion for revenge to commit further monstrosities, *nefas*, upon his children, subvert nature once more, confound the distinctions between

51

father and husband, and make all his family an abomination (cf. *Agamemnon* 28–36). In *Thyestes* it is not the victim but the beast who sees – and triumphs:

> nunc meas laudo manus,
> nunc parta uera est palma.
> (*Thyestes* 1096f.)

> Now I praise my hands' work,
> Now the true palm is won.

Atreus is victor; the palm of victory is his.[46] At the end of *Agamemnon* the palm went to Orestes, signalling his future triumph and the play's moral order. In *Thyestes* the *uera palma*, 'true palm', goes to Atreus, signalling his present triumph and the play's moral void. The second choral ode was wrong. The beast is the true king; to him the true palm belongs. And like all true kings, Atreus is satisfied. The hunger goes elsewhere – to the victim. *Aeterna fames.*

The moral blackness of *Thyestes* seems absolute. Seneca's other tragedies similarly discomfort in the kinds of moral worlds they imply. But those worlds, morally perplexing, hostile, paradoxical, generally involve retribution for *scelus* and sometimes the apparent (though ironic) answering of prayer. In *Thyestes scelus* is unpunished; the gods dictate nothing; no prayers are fulfilled. The anxious prayer of the opening chorus – if any god loves Argos (122ff.),

> aduertat placidum numen et arceat,
> alternae scelerum ne redeant uices.[47]
> (*Thyestes* 132f.)

> Let him look kindly here and stop
> Alternating cycles of crime.

– and the agonised prayers of the feasted Thyestes (1006–19, 1077–92) receive no response from the gods they address. They are uttered in a moral void. Indictments of the gods and their alleged moral guardianship of man are of course frequent in Senecan tragedy. So, for example, Jason in the final two lines of *Medea*:

> per alta uade spatia sublimi aetheris,[48]
> testare nullos esse, qua ueheris, deos.
> (*Medea* 1026f.)

> Journey through high heaven's soaring spaces;
> Bear witness, where you ride, there are no gods.

So Theseus in the final act of *Phaedra*:

> non mouent diuos preces;
> at, si rogarem scelera, quam proni forent.
> (*Phaedra* 1242f.)

My prayers move no gods.
But, if I prayed for sin, how prompt they'd be.

So too Cassandra in *Agamemnon* (695ff.). But Jason is wrong;[49] Theseus admits divine power (he simply argues for its perversity); Cassandra lives to witness the 'morality' of things. *Thyestes'* indictment is less retrievable. In *Thyestes* direct promulgation of the gods' withdrawal from man's world is accompanied by the dramatisation of their impotence. 'The gods are fled', cries Thyestes: *fugere superi* (1021). The truth is sometimes screamed.

The issue of the gods' existence and moral function pervades the play from the prologue's opening lines to the final act's concluding ones. Importantly it is a central issue in the *volte-face* of Act 3. A conspicuous feature of that *volte-face* is how, under the impact of his son's acceptance of the gods' moral supervision of human affairs ('god will respect your prudence', 489f.; cf. 471) and his own reawakened desire for wealth and power, Thyestes' theological position changes from scepticism (407) to belief, and belief not only in the existence of gods but in their concern for morality and justice (530f.). It is clear how this reversal is to be judged. Atreus' successful perversion of the values attributed to the gods' protection (especially of *pietas* and *fides*)[50] combines with young Tantalus' dying attitude ('he did not allow prayers to perish pointlessly', 720f.) to point up the naivety of Thyestes' transformed conviction. As does the chorus' own transformation. The Argive nobles' movement from prayerful solicitude in their appeal for divine aid in the Tantalid ode (122–75), through emotional tranquillity and moral confidence in the kingship ode (336–403), through joyful acceptance of the brothers' reconciliation, subsequent apprehension and assertion of divine power in the *pietas* ode (546–622), into the climactic terror of the star ode, with its dramatised fear of *deforme chaos* (789–884), underscores not only *their* initial naivety. In the star chorus' stunning climax to the play's cosmic imagery,[51] all previous assumptions or assertions of divine power and guardianship seem rescinded by choric terror, terror of the imminent dissolution of the world and its gods, the collapse of the cosmos, its order, its distinctions:

> trepidant, trepidant pectora magno
> > percussa metu:
> ne fatali cuncta ruina
> quassata labent, iterumque deos
> hominesque premat deforme chaos,
> iterum terras et mare et ignes[52]
> et uaga picti sidera mundi
> > natura tegat.
> > > (*Thyestes* 828–35)

Our hearts tremble, tremble
> Struck with terror:

53

Lest all things fall shattered
In fatal ruin, and once more gods
And men sink in formless chaos,
Once more lands and ocean and fire
And a spangled world's wandering stars
Nature entomb.

Ironically both the star chorus and the Messenger's preceding account of the Sun's flight (637f., 776f.) demonstrate in part the kind of interpenetration between man, nature and god which the assumption of divine guardianship implies.[53] Atreus' unnatural act dislocates nature; the sun disappears, night is confused with day. But whereas in *Agamemnon* (as in *Phaedra* and *Medea*) nature punishes as well as reacts, in *Thyestes* nature reacts, is revolted; but then nothing happens.[54] Divine observation, divine shock, divine impotence. The gods have become the helpless audience of Atreus' bestial play.

Fugere superi (1021; cf. 893, 1070). The impressive theatrics of the opening of Act 5 show Atreus not only unpunished for his *scelera* against nature, the firmament, *pietas* and the gods. He has replaced them:

aequalis astris gradior et cunctos super
altum superbo uertice attingens polum.
nunc decora regni teneo, nunc solium patris.
dimitto superos: summa uotorum attigi.
                                        (*Thyestes* 885–8)

Equal to stars I move; supreme over all
My exalted head touches heaven's height.
Now I grasp kingship's glory, now father's throne.
I dismiss the gods; my prayers' summit is reached.

He is king of kings, most exalted of the gods (911f.); he is the sun and the light (896ff.). His ghoulish ironies and control of meaning ('Think of your sons in their father's embrace', 976, 'Take [*cape*] this family cup [*poculum gentile*] filled with wine', 982f., etc.)[55] index the inverted world and his supremacy. Even his initial, proclaimed insatiateness (890ff., 907, 1053ff.) dissolves in the witnessed agonies of his victim (1096–9). Atreus is pre-eminently fulfilled.

And yet Tantalus dominates Act 5. He has dominated the play. Not only was his behaviour in the prologue a precursor to that of Thyestes in Act 3, but the Tantalus images or motifs of hunger, thirst, eating, drinking, feasting, filling, emptying, satiety, limit, unlimit have so interlaced the dramatic action that Atreus' crime against Thyestes appears as consequence and re-enactment of Tantalus' original sin. When the *satelles* counsels Atreus against entrusting the false message of reconciliation to his sons, Atreus replies:

> ne mali fiant times?
> nascuntur.
>
> > (*Thyestes* 313f.)

> Do you fear they may become evil?
> They are born so.

The past dictates all. As in *Agamemnon*,[56] it is the model and the mould; it preshapes the present.

> quid stupes? tandem incipe
> animosque sume: Tantalum et Pelopem aspice;
> ad haec manus exempla poscuntur meae.
>
> > (*Thyestes* 241–3)

> Why no action? At last begin,
> Steel yourself; look on Tantalus and Pelops.
> To their example my hands are summoned.

Even the Messenger of Act 4, though overwhelmed by the horror of the present, draws attention to the relevance of the past (625f.). The scale of crime of course increases,[57] but the pattern never changes, as the chorus' opening prayer and its non-fulfilment show.

It is in Act 5 especially that the past's tyranny and its consequences are revealed. Not only is Tantalus' original banquet re*incarnated*, but the insatiable appetite which is Tantalus (*imple Tantalo totam domum*, 'fill the whole house with Tantalus', 53) is dramatised in Atreus' initial emptiness. It is dramatised too in Thyestes' final state. The *tumultus* or swelling turmoil which the Fury had commanded Tantalus to cast into the beast-hearts of his descendants (85f.), and which drives Atreus in Act 2 to new dimensions of *scelus* (260ff.), burgeons at the beginning of Act 5 within Thyestes himself (961, 999). It erupts in the imaging of Tantalus in Thyestes, as the former's longing for the punishments of hell (68ff.) and subsequent thirst for blood (97ff.) are re-enacted in Thyestes' agonised prayers (1006ff.) and demand for vengeance (1110f.). Past becomes present; becomes future. Ironically it is Thyestes who adverts to the Tantalus paradigm:

> stare circa Tantalum
> uterque iam debuimus.
>
> > (*Thyestes* 1011f.)

> Each of us should long since
> Have stood with Tantalus.

He recognises the Tantalus in Atreus, but – despite *uterque*, 'Each of us' – only a little of the Tantalus in himself. He sees fortune's revolutions, not his position on the wheel. He ends the play 'self-deceived', *ignotus sibi* (403).

But not Atreus. He is far from deluded. What most disquiets about the play's finale is neither the manner in which Atreus exacts his revenge, nor the consequences of that manner for the ordered distinctions of things, but that Atreus' hunger is satisfied, and satisfied by the observed suffering of his brother:

> nunc meas laudo manus,
> nunc parta uera est palma.
> (*Thyestes* 1096f.)

> Now I praise my hands' work,
> Now the true palm is won.

Past determines present, determines future. But the beast may triumph and survive. The tyranny of the past is the tyranny of man as beast; and the beast may be fulfilled. The doctrine of fortune's revolutions as articulated by the *pietas* chorus (615ff.) needs demoralising. There is neither moral promise nor moral completeness about the end of *Thyestes*. Tantalid hunger continues but the beast Atreus survives his own appetitive emptiness. The victim does not. The play in fact does not end; it stops. It stops at the precise moment of the beast's satisfaction. And to Thyestes' deluded prayer (1110f.) the beast's retort is predictive. Punishment awaits the victim, not the satisfied beast.[58]

4

THE BODY OF THE PLAY

Senecan tragedy, on unprejudiced inspection, proves to possess many of
the qualities that we still associate with the greatest drama: speakability;
actability; powerful theatrical situations; conflict both between minds and
within minds; and what we may describe . . . as an unrestricted symbolic
use of the concrete universe for the abstract, which gives his text, rightly
read, the immediate impact of nightmare.

C. J. Herington, 'Senecan Tragedy' (1966)

The theatrically effective realisation of ideas evident in Seneca's *Agamemnon*
and *Thyestes* is product in part (a substantial part) of dramatic structure.
Seneca's tragedies display painstaking attention to dramatic structure and
form, and to density of verbal and ideological texture. The first word of
Medea, for example, is *di*, 'gods'; the last word (1027) is *deos*, 'gods'. Within
this verbal circle prayers, appeals, statements, questions to and concerning
gods permeate the play's actions and chorus.[1] Similarly imagery and motifs
of birth, law, power, cosmos, sun, fire, sacrifice and serpent dominate the
prologue (1–55), texture the play,[2] and climax in the play's finale (esp. 983ff.),
when the Colchian princess annexes the powers of the cosmos, gives birth to
death, sacrifices her sons, consumes Corinth with fire, removes the final
vestige of law from herself, and climbs to freedom in the serpent-drawn
chariot of the sun. *Medea*'s finale is the imagery of its prologue realised.

Phaedra is analogously textured. The opening commands of Hippolytus,
with which the play begins (17ff., 31ff., 48ff.), are echoed by the closing
commands of Theseus, with which the play ends (1277f.): both are instructions for the hunt, addressed to the same huntsmen. The object of the hunt
has changed. Hunting in fact is the play's main image. It is used with structurally pervasive and ironic effect. Associated with Diana (esp. 54ff., 70ff.),
Venus (esp. 274ff.) and 'nature', *natura* (esp. 352, 777ff.), and with the issues
of control, dominance and power, it is associated too with each of the play's
human figures. It articulates their attempt in fantasy or in fact to control the
shaping forces of their lives. It articulates too the failure of that attempt.

Hippolytus, the confident hunter of the first scene (1–84), becomes hunted beast and prey (1077ff., 1105ff., 1277f.); Phaedra and the Nurse, partners in the erotic hunt for Hippolytus (233ff., 240f., 271f., 387ff., 406ff.), reveal themselves instruments of a larger, more sinister hunt; Theseus, the great male hero, returned alive from the world of the dead, initiates too a Hippolytan hunt (938ff.), only to be manifest instrument and victim of the huntress *par excellence, natura.*

The hunt is not the only structuring image in *Phaedra.* Imagery of sex, pregnancy and procreation pervade the play from Hippolytus' initial sexualisation of the landscape at 54ff., to his rape and castration in the Messenger's speech by the nature he thought he controlled (1093ff.), thence to Phaedra's fusion of sexual consummation and death in the final act (1159ff.). Images and motifs of heaviness, oppression, sea, fire, planet, star, animal, wildness, woods, sceptre, sword, are similarly and structurally important.[3]

Although *Medea* and *Phaedra* are two of Seneca's most crafted plays, their exhibited verbal and ideological texture are typically Senecan. *Troades,* for example, is pervaded with and structured by a whole syntax of polarities which the play itself dissolves.[4] *Thyestes* has one of the richest of Senecan imagistic patterns, especially important and pervasive being the Tantalid images of hunger, thirst, eating, drinking, emptiness, fullness, feast.[5] In *Oedipus* legal imagery and the fate/fortune motif are important;[6] in *Agamemnon* storm, feast, sacrifice and wound,[7] although *Agamemnon* is one of the less well crafted plays in this regard.[8] In *Hercules Furens,* also less well crafted, the most permeating motif is that of the hero's hand, *manus.*[9] All the plays are textured through and through with the Senecan moral vocabulary of *pudor, furor, scelus* and *nefas,* 'shame', 'passion', 'crime' and 'evil'.

In most plays too the dramatic action is textured with and structured by analogies with the past.[10] *Troades, Medea, Phaedra, Agamemnon* and *Thyestes* are particularly important in this regard. *Agamemnon* and *Thyestes* were examined above. In *Medea* the Argonautic expedition, to which the long central odes of the chorus are dedicated (301–79, 579–669) and which pervades *Medea's* thoughts,[11] sits like an incubus on the play, encapsulating a series of events which proves model for and cause of the events of the play itself. The unloosing of nature's bonds and breach of nature's covenants (*foedera,* 335, 606) by the crew of the *Argo,* the fear generated (*metus,* 338; *timores,* 341) and the death and destruction which ensued as 'penalty' for the breach (esp. 616ff.), are mirrored in Jason's breach of marital 'faith', *fides* (see esp. 434ff.), in exhibited Corinthian fear,[12] and in the chaos and destruction of the finale, where Medea's past actions on behalf of Jason and his comrades (her breaking of familial bonds, murder of kin and flight into exile)[13] are re-enacted in her dissolution of all familial ties, the murder of her children, and her climactic serpentine flight.[14] The determinant nature of Medea's past is unconcealed. In the final act itself the appearance of the ghost of Absyrtus (963ff.) just before the first child is slain, Medea's subsequent intoxicated reverie on the erasure of her post-Jasonic past (982ff.), and her final acerbic question –

> coniugem agnoscis tuam?
> sic fugere soleo.
>
> *(Medea* 1021f.)

> Don't you recognise your wife?
> This is how I usually escape.

– underscore the relationship between the play's denouement and Medea's earlier history.[15]

Like *Medea*, *Phaedra* and *Troades* are studded with analogies with the past, articulating a compelling sense of history and nature's cyclicity, of *semper idem*. *Troades'* concentric structure seems itself to suggest the circles of history, even as its action is structured to re*present* the past. The delay or *mora* of the Greek fleet at Aulis at the beginning of the war, which was ended by the sacrifice of Agamemnon's virgin daughter, Iphigenia, and her alleged 'marriage' to Achilles (see *Agamemnon* 162ff.), authorised by Calchas and vainly opposed by Agamemnon, is re-enacted in another *mora* for the fleet, ended by the sacrifice of Priam's virgin daughter, Polyxena, and her 'marriage' to Achilles' ghost. The sacrifice is again authorised by Calchas and vainly opposed by Agamemnon (esp. *Troades* 164ff., 246ff., 287ff., 331, 353ff., 360ff.). Notable also in the play is the way Achilles' wrath and demand for compensation are visited a second time on the Greeks (*Troades* 193f.), and once again the demand is for a girl-prize; while the concluding 'marriage' between Greek and Trojan (Achilles and Polyxena) recalls the earlier 'marriage' between Greek and Trojan (Helen and Paris), heralding once again the departure of a fleet and both Greek and Trojan loss. In *Phaedra* analogies between Phaedra and her mother, Pasiphae, between Hippolytus and the bull that Pasiphae loved, and between the Minotaur and the bull from the sea,[16] the latter product of Phaedra's love as the former was product of her mother's love (note especially the pregnancy imagery of 1016 and 1019f.), and other analogies too (e.g., between Hippolytus and the Minotaur) seem to assert the imperatives of history, the dispassionate cyclic order of things, the circle of fate, fortune, nature. Time past becomes time present; time present becomes time future. The world changes to remain the same:

> constat inferno numerus tyranno.
>
> *(Phaedra* 1153)

> For hell's king the numbers tally.

Always. Even the delusion of human power recycles to stay constant, as the Roman analogies of *Phaedra's* opening act and *Medea's* first Argonautic chorus show. To *natura*, fate or history belong the power and the glory.

But verbal and ideological texture is not everything. Without consummate theatrical structuring Senecan tragedy's intellectual force would be as naught. Consider two of his finest and most structured plays, *Phaedra* and *Troades*, which merit performance today not because of their verbal or ideological texture, nor even because of the importance of the issues which they explore and present. They merit performance because they make great drama of those issues, because they turn issues such as cultural dissolution, death, nature, history and suffering into dramatically moving form.

PHAEDRA

Phaedra is a play which meditates on 'nature'. Enshrined on stage is Diana, the play's emblematic and central divinity, mistress of forest, mountain, beast and hunt, goddess of the moon. Associated both with the movement of the planets and stars (309ff., 410ff., 785ff.) and with that part of earth's domain still free of man's 'civilising' hand (55ff., 406f.), she appears 'nature's' goddess *par excellence*; she is paradoxically conjoined, as will be seen, with the goddess of sexual love, in turn associated directly with *natura* (352). The play's main image is the hunt, activity of Diana, Venus, *natura*; it both structures and permeates the drama. But other images too – images of fire, sea, storm, winter, summer, planets, stars, images of 'nature's' violence, order, beauty – reflect the concern with *natura*. The action of the play, the dramatisation of its major figures, and (often the index in Senecan tragedy of where a play's attention lies) the preoccupations of the chorus sustain the focus on 'nature' and its relationship to the human world.

The play begins in the murky half-light of dawn with an address by Hippolytus – lively, energetic, full of vital feeling (1–84) – to his huntsmen and his goddess. The monody heralds much. The contradictory aspects of Diana's kingdom, nature's uncivilised realm, are barely concealed: order, beauty, perceptual richness and life (1–30); destruction, fear, violence and death (31–53). The ambivalence of Hippolytus' attitude is patent. Evidencing a deep, emotional response to the countryside and the wild, a felt sense of its beauty, grandeur, its aesthetic richness and variety (1–30), Hippolytus is yet far from Wordsworth's 'priest'. As the instructions for the hunt (31–53) especially reveal – with their emphasis on the controlled manipulation of violence, reaching vigorous climax in the final 'victory' (*victor*, 52), the knifing of the innards from the prey (52f.) – Hippolytus, unlike the primitives of Seneca's *Epistles* who receive 'nature's' gifts (*Epistle* 90.36–8), seeks to control the world he inhabits, seeks to attack, ensnare, kill, plunder. Important in this regard is the prayer to the huntsman's own goddess:

> ades en comiti, diua uirago,
> cuius regno pars terrarum
> secreta uacat, cuius certis

petitur telis fera quae gelidum
potat Araxen et quae stanti
ludit in Histro. tua Gaetulos
dextra leones, tua Cretaeas
sequitur ceruas; nunc ueloces
figis dammas leuiore manu.
tibi dant uariae pectora tigres,
tibi uillosi terga bisontes
latisque feri cornibus uri.
quicquid solis pascitur aruis,
siue illud Arabs diuite silua
siue illud inops nouit Garamans
uacuisque uagus Sarmata campis,
siue ferocis iuga Pyrenes
siue Hyrcani celant saltus,
arcus metuit, Diana, tuos.
    Tua si gratus numina cultor
tulit in saltus, retia uinctas
tenuere feras, nulli laqueum
rupere pedes; fertur plaustro
praeda gementi; tum rostra canes
sanguine multo rubicunda gerunt
repetitque casas rustica longo
      turba triumpho.
                (*Phaedra* 54–80)

Come to your comrade, man goddess,
For whose kingdom earth's secret parts
Lie open, whose shafts seek out
Unerringly the beast that drinks
The cold Araxes' stream or plays
On frozen Hister. Yours the hand
That hunts Gaetulian lions,
Yours the Cretan hind; now you prick
With lighter touch the quick gazelle.
You receive the striped tiger's
Breast, the shaggy bison's back,
The spine of spreading-horned wild ox.
No creature feeds in lonely fields,
In rich Arabia's groves,
Or in poor Garamantia
And Sarmatian nomad's desert,
Hidden on wild Pyrene's
Ridge or in Hyrcanian ravines,

But fears, Diana, your bow.
    If the worshipper favoured takes
Your power into the glades, nets
Grip fast entangled beasts, no feet
Break the snares; spoils are carried
On groaning cart; the hounds
Sport muzzles red with blood,
And a rustic band heads home
    Long-lined in triumph.

Diana, to whom Hippolytus prays, is exhibited by her worshipper as a goddess of death, not of life. The kingdom she rules is one of fear (esp. 72); the
beasts who owe her allegiance she terrifies and kills (54–72). Mistress of
'earth's secret parts' (55), she appears to connote something in *natura* of
irresistible power and irresistible violence, a power and a violence
unconsciously (and ironically) sexualised in Hippolytus' description (55ff.),
and which Diana's worshipper imagines can be transferred to himself (73–
80). The military imagery of the monody is overt and telling – the victor (52),
the spoils (*praeda*, 77), the triumph (*triumpho*, 80) – imagery which creates an
analogy between Hippolytus' confident aggression, his urge to control, to
dominate, his worship of destructive power and that of Rome's triumphant
military, emphasising the former and intimating its contemporary relevance.
Signally, the geographical bounds of Diana's kingdom (67–71) suggest those
of Rome itself. Not only in the case of Hippolytus is the issue of human power
and its reality or illusion paramount.

Conspicuous in Senecan tragedy at large, the *potentia* theme, the issue of
man's desire to assert control over the universe he inhabits, over his destiny,
his life, is especially prominent in *Phaedra*. Its presence in the opening monody and its association there with imagery of hunting, pursuit, snares,
entrapment, violence, preface theme, action and imagery to come. Certainly
the issue of human power and its relationship to 'nature' pervades the following scene between Phaedra and the Nurse (85ff.), as Phaedra, self-
exhibited victim of forces political, domestic, moral, emotional, biological,
historical, divine, shows herself driven towards a love which repulses her
(112ff.), which seems as unnatural and as monstrous as her mother's monstrous love. The Nurse's abstract moralising and interrogatory rhetoric
(129ff., 195ff.) serve only to allow Phaedra to become more confirmed in her
sense of helplessness, until she moves into wish-fulfilment (Theseus will not
return, 219–21) and fantasy (Theseus will pardon her, 225), as the urge for
the hunt, described with alarm in her opening soliloquy (110–12), explodes
into a fantasy image of an erotic hunt for Hippolytus in the wild (233ff.),
Phaedra seeking to take control, if only in fantasy, of her life. When Phaedra's fragile optimism, her fantasies and delusions founder on the Nurse's
emotional appeal (246–9), her talk of shame, honour and death (250ff.) only

succeeds in drawing the Nurse into the fantasy of a successful Hippolytan hunt.

The choral ode on sexual passion which follows at 274ff., the first choral ode of the play, is crucial. It serves to place in a larger metaphysical framework not only Phaedra's dilemma and the inevitability of her destruction but Hippolytus' sex-excluding commitment to Diana and its deluded basis. Delineating the universality of love's power, its irresistibility, its devastation, its violence, the ode confirms Phaedra's position as to her own impotence (cf. esp. 186–94 and 294ff.) and suggests an analogy between Venus and Cupid, on the one hand, and Diana, on the other, the huntsman's own goddess. The analogy seems less than casual, linked as the divinities are by identity of weapons (the bow, 72, 278), analogous destructive power and violence, analogous universality, analogous irresistibility (cf. esp. *certis telis*, 'unerring shafts', 56f., *certo arcu*, 'unerring bow', 278). The chorus' description of love's kingdom (285–90) echoes that of Diana in Hippolytus' monody (66–72), confirming the relationship between the divinities. Indeed Diana's kingdom of deer, tiger, lion and forest, like Diana herself, who left the heavens for love of Endymion (309–16), is subject to the power of love (341–50). The divinities of sexual love and the goddess of the moon, wilderness and the hunt seem to represent complementary aspects of nature's power, savagery and violence; for it is with *natura* that the ode seems concerned. Controlling gods (294ff.), animals (338ff.) and humankind (290ff.), sea (335ff., 351f.) and land (285ff.) and sky (294ff., 338), directing the movements of the planets themselves (309ff.), imaged in terms of nature's element *par excellence*, fire,[17] sexual passion is presented as a manifestation of *natura* itself:

> amat insani
> belua ponti Lucaeque boues.
> uindicat omnes natura sibi.
> (*Phaedra* 350–2)

> Raging ocean's
> Beast and Luca-bulls love.
> Nature for itself claims all.

Venus' 'claims' (*Venus uindex*, 124f.) have become nature's 'claims' (*natura uindex*, 352)[18] with pointed paradox. In Phaedra's initial, perceptive analysis and the Nurse's subsequent rejoinder the Cretan princess' love for Hippolytus was presented as monstrous passion, a perversion of nature (esp. 173–7); from the perspective of the first choral ode it is *natura* itself, which claims its victims like the goddess of the hunt. Ironically the ode's opening address to the 'daughter of the ungentle sea' (274) has foreshadowed whence nature's 'vindication' will come. The realm which Cretan might thought its own (85) will prove instrument of a higher and more enduring power.

In Act 3 the hunt for Hippolytus begins, preceded appropriately by a picture of the deranged huntress, Phaedra, attempting to make her fantasy world reality (387–403), and by a prayer from the Nurse to Diana to assist in the ensnaring of her hunter (406–23). Significantly the prayer to Diana is to her in her dual 'nature' role as goddess of the moon (410–12, 418–22) and of the wild (406–9). Diana will indeed ensnare her hunter, but not in the way the Nurse prays for. In the ensuing confrontation with Hippolytus (431–582), in fact, the Nurse's cunning rhetoric fails to ensnare despite its general position (that Hippolytus' mode of life is essentially a violation of the code he claims to follow, namely *natura*: see esp. 481) being, as the first chorus had under-lined, in an important sense correct. Hippolytus' asexual idealisation of the wild (483ff.), contradicted by the exhibited and latently sexual violence of the monody, is made to seem in context less the product of noble vision than of a deranged psychology. Connected with a ferocious misogyny (556–64f.), the irrationality of which is virtually acknowledged by Hippolytus himself (566–8f.), Hippolytus' golden age vision leads inevitably to a condemnation of Phaedra as unnatural monstrosity, when the revelation of her love and appeal for compassion are made (671–97). The climax of the revelation scene at 704ff. as Hippolytus, the hunter, sword in one hand, Phaedra's hair twisted back in the other, about to plunge the steel in her throat, turns to ask the enshrined Diana, 'goddess of the bow' (*arquitenens dea*, 709), to accept the just sacrifice of Phaedra as if hunted beast, is not only brilliant theatrics, but, reinforcing the helplessness of Phaedra and the delusion of Hippolytus, focuses once more on the issue of the larger framework of things in which the human scene is set. The delusion of Hippolytus, the hunter hunted, and hunted not only by Phaedra, is cardinal. Diana, as the first choral ode revealed, has felt love's pangs and, as the next ode will disclose, is enamoured of and watching Hippolytus himself. The world of 'forests' and 'beasts' to which the young prince flees at 718 is more ambiguous and more complex than he thinks.

Little doubt is expressed on this matter by the chorus which follows (736–823), concerned as it is with and for Hippolytus, concerned too with that larger scheme of things, *natura*, to which Hippolytus seems blind. Uniting diverse aspects of nature's operation – the movement of the planets and stars (736–52), the ravaging process of summer (764ff.), the ravishing of beauty by time (770ff.), the fragility and ambiguity of beauty itself, the moral imperative that enjoins (774), the treachery and violence of the wild (777–84), the blush and delay of the moon (785–94), Diana's Hippolytan and amatory gaze (785, 793f.) – the ode creates an atmosphere of foreboding and menace embracing Diana's 'favourite'. The atmosphere is not diminished by recollection of the first choral ode's attention to the 'ravages' (*populante*, 280) of *amor/natura*. Hippolytus' neurotic fantasy of innocent communion with the wild is specifically undermined by this chorus (cf. esp. 519–21 and 777–84), whose lyrics expose his ignorance of the sexual entrapment of the wilderness, of nature's sexual imperative, and of himself as object of Diana's erotic gaze (785–94). The son of Theseus seems destined prey to the wilderness, Diana and *natura*. Ironically Hippolytus' deathly skill as hunter, his surrogate embodiment of Diana's violence and power, are recalled (812–19) just prior to the final hunt, in which the world he thought he controlled rips the flesh from his limbs and the limbs from his body.

A final party needs to be embroiled in nature's 'vindicatory' hunt before the denouement itself: the deserter of Ariadne (245, 665, 760), the murderer of Hippolytus' mother Antiope (226ff., 926ff.), the despised husband of Phaedra (89ff.), the violator of covenants moral and natural (89ff., 835ff.), Theseus. The short fourth act (835–958) serves to give Theseus the dubious privilege of accelerating the movement towards nature's vindication, intensifies too the concern with human impotence and delusion. Falling victim to Phaedra's deceptive ambiguities (891ff.), trapped too by his own self-image, appealing (903–14) to the covenants of morality and nature of which he is singularly in breach (910, 914), Theseus joins the hunt for Hippolytus (see esp. 929ff.). It is little wonder that the ode to *natura* which follows at 959, parading Hippolytus as test-case for the moral machinery of the universe, is one of unrelieved despair. Drawing an explicit contrast between, on the one hand, the physical order of the cosmos governed by *natura* and, on the other, the moral chaos of man's experience governed by blind *fortuna*, the third chorus sees the world of human affairs, *res humanae*, not simply as amoral, but as morally perverse. But what this third choral ode ignores in this severe contrast between the cosmic order of *natura* and blind *fortuna* are those aspects of *natura* to which the first two choral odes drew attention: the violent, destructive, transformational aspects of *natura*, the violence of the wild, the universal tyranny and ravage of love, forces intrinsic to the world of this play, and not only the world of this play. They are forces which, albeit morally perplexing and perhaps from man's point of view amoral *simpliciter*, may yet be far from blind, but may be closely linked, in a way the chorus will later acknowledge, to the very cosmic order it sees as paradigm. *Natura* and the world of human action and history are not so easily separated. There is *natura* in the fall of a sparrow.

There is certainly *natura* in the fall of Hippolytus and the collapse of the Athenian royal house, as Acts 5 and 6 exhibit. With devastating speed and finality Phaedra's closing scenes show *natura uindex* in triumphant and irresistible operation, as Theseus' curse, Phaedra's monstrous love and Hippolytus' denial of Venus' covenant and nature's rule generate a monster from Venus' native realm, the sea (cf. 274), and Hippolytus, ensnared by his own instruments of control (1085–7), is 'ravaged' (*populatur*, 1095) by the *natura* he had worshipped, just as Phaedra was earlier 'ravaged' (*populatur*, 377) by love. The chorus' earlier pronouncements on the 'ravages' of Cupid/Venus/ *natura* (274ff.; esp. *populante*, 280), on nature's plunder of beauty and the sexual violence and entrapment of the wild (761ff., 777ff.), prove tragically veridical in Hippolytus' gruesome death, as the hunter of the play's first scene, confident then with his armoury of snares, nets, spears and dogs, falls victim to the 'gripping snares' and 'clinging knots' of a far more powerful huntress (1086f.), and Diana's kingdom of field, rock, bramble, bush and tree tears his flesh and his body apart in a grotesque and unambiguous orgy of sexual violence (1093ff.). The irresistibility and destructiveness of Diana's erotic gaze (785ff.) and of Venus/*natura uindex* receive dreadful confirmation. The goddess and the landscape he had unwittingly sexualised in *Phaedra*'s opening act (esp. 55ff.) now works its sexual violence on him. One final irony awaits. Hunted by Phaedra, the Nurse, Theseus and the bull from the sea (1077ff.), hunted by Diana, Venus, *natura* to his death, Hippolytus becomes victim of an even more macabre hunt, as the Messenger describes how Hippolytus' own hunting dogs and servants track the remnants of their master's body (1105ff.).

Theseus cannot be indifferent. *Natura* binds as well as separates. It involves Theseus in the catastrophe he has in part caused:

> o nimium potens,
> quanto parentes sanguinis uinclo tenes,
> natura, quam te colimus inuiti quoque.
> (*Phaedra* 1114–16)

> O too potent
> Nature, with what bond of blood you tether
> Parents; we serve you even against our will.

Endeavouring to make sense of all this the final chorus on human reversals (1123–53) dissolves the *natura-fortuna* contrast of the preceding ode and presents fortune's operations in Theseus' case as evidencing an ironic cosmic justice, a paradoxical pattern and order reflective of, and by implication originating from, the order of nature itself. Hippolytus' death is seen as payment for the debt incurred by Theseus' breach of natural law in returning from the world of death (1150ff.). The numbers now tally (1153) and Pluto's 'greed' (1152) seems but an instance of the rapacity of *natura* itself (764ff.), great mother of gods, *natura parens deum* (959).

There is no comfort in this. Phaedra, burdened with guilt, shame and a life bereft of purpose, suicides (1159–98) and Theseus is left (1199ff.) not only with the experience of catastrophic reversal but with the unendurable knowledge of his own role in the perversion and irreversible dismemberment of his world (esp. 1208ff., 1249ff.). Ironically his final description of Hippolytus –

> haecne illa facies igne sidereo nitens,
> inimica flectens lumina? huc cecidit decor?
> (*Phaedra* 1269f.)

> Is this the face that shone with starry fire,
> Turned hostile eyes aside? This that beauty set?

echoes earlier cosmic imagery associated with his son (736ff., 1111f., 1173f.) and presents the spectacle of Hippolytus' downfall as part of nature's inexorable processes. The play ends in ritual and order (1275–80), as Hippolytus' opening instructions to his fellow-hunters are echoed in those of Theseus to the same huntsmen (1277–9). The framework, the structure of things, *rerum natura*, remains constant.

TROADES

Inverting *Phaedra*'s examination of the bonds of nature, *Troades* dramatises human dissolution. Among its major concerns: human power, human impotence, human knowledge, human delusion, language, fate, death, compassion, freedom and captivity, history's determined and dissolving cycle. The themes of death and dissolution pervade and unite the play, from queen Hecuba's opening presentation of the dissolution of her kingdom and the death of her children, her husband and her world (1–56), to the bitter, quasi-erotic summoning of death with which she almost closes the drama (1171–5). Imagery and motifs of dust, ashes, tomb, smoke, loosing, tearing, burning, ravaging, scattering, dismembering, bursting, collapsing,[19] sustain the play's preoccupation with death and dissolution. So too does the dramatic action itself. The main body of the drama – Acts 2, 3, 4 and 5 – concerns itself with the tearing of a child from its mother (Astyanax from Andromache, Polyxena from Hecuba; their deaths are required if the Greek fleet is to sail) and the dissolving of the bond that ties mother to life. For Andromache, widow of the Trojan warrior Hector, her son Astyanax is what holds her to life:

> iam erepta Danais coniugem sequerer meum,
> nisi hic teneret. hic meos animos domat
> morique prohibet. cogit hic aliquid deos
> adhuc rogare. tempus aerumnae addidit.
> hic mihi malorum maximum fructum abstulit:
> nihil timere.
>
> *(Troades 418–23)*

> I'd escape the Danai and follow my spouse
> Now, if he [*points to Astyanax*] didn't hold me. He tames my pride
> And prevents my death. He compels me still
> To importune the gods. He prolongs my pain.
> He's robbed me of suffering's finest fruit:
> Fear of nothing.

67

In the Messenger's report of Act 5 the dissolution of the bond between mother and son finds dramatic expression in Astyanax' dismembered body (1110–17).

The play's preoccupation with dissolution is apparent too in the choral odes. The chorus of Trojan women enter the play to find Hecuba locked in grief and their joint lamentation (67–141) for the death of Troy, its chief warrior Hector, and its king Priam, realises itself in imagery of dissolution and dismemberment, in dust, ashes, the untying of hair, the opening of dresses, the rending of flesh – in Priam's headless trunk on the beach. The chorus' nudity itself dissolves earlier values. Later odes focus even more sharply on dissolution. The second choral ode (371–408) presents death as personal dissolution absolute: 'it kills | The body, spares not the soul' (*noxia corpori* | *nec parcens animae*, 401f.). The third and fourth odes (814–60, 1009–55) focus on social dissolution: the scattering of Trojan women through every part of Greece, the dissolving of their union and their land. Thus the final lines of the final ode proclaimed with pain, anger and despair:

> soluet hunc coetum lacrimasque nostras
> sparget huc illuc agitata classis,
> cum tuba iussi dare uela nautae
> et simul uentis properante remo
> prenderint altum fugietque litus.
> quis status mentis miseris, ubi omnis
> terra decrescet pelagusque crescet,
> celsa cum longe latitabat Ide?
> tum puer matri genetrixque nato,
> Troia qua iaceat regione monstrans,
> dicet et longe digito notabit:
> 'Ilium est illic, ubi fumus alte
> serpit in caelum nebulaeque turpes.'
> Troes hoc signo patriam uidebunt.
>
> *(Troades 1042–55)*

> The fleet will dissolve our union,
> Will scatter our tears as it drives,
> When trumpet blasts bid crews spread sail
> And the winds and speeding oars grip
> The deep, and the shoreline retreats.
> What will we wretches feel as all
> Land shrinks and ocean looms large
> And Ida's summit fades away?
> Son will tell mother, and mother
> Tell son, showing where Troy now lies,
> Pointing to it in the distance:
> 'There is Ilium, where smoke snakes

High to heaven and clouds hang foul.'
So the Trojans shall view their land.

It is a mark of the intricacy of the verbal and imagistic texture of this play that the image of smoke in this final choral ode picks up not only Hecuba's description of the death and fall of Troy in the prologue (19–21) but the pointed use of the same image to describe the soul's dissolution in the death chorus (392–5).

Troades' study of dissolution impresses. Especially important is the play's focus on the conceptual and linguistic dissolution that attends the death of a culture. Categories, linguistic and behavioural forms, devised to order and control the world, dissolve. The mother of children is the mother of corpses (32f.); the king of kings is the slave of fate (352ff.); the free and victorious are as helpless as the conquered and captive (256ff., 524ff.); the marriage-breaker is a marriage-broker (861ff.). Time and moral values implode. Truth is falsehood (599ff., 871ff.), past is present (164ff., 360ff.); honour is indistinguishable from dishonour, justice from injustice, piety from unspeakable sin (203ff.). Rites and rituals manifest the same contradictions. A dirge is a laudation; a wedding is a funeral; a burial is salvation; a sacrifice is a bloody murder.[20] The forms of civilisation are employed to implement barbarism, as in *Thyestes*, but ironically they accord with nature's laws: Polyxena's death is the setting of a sun (1139–42).

Death itself in the tragedy is the ultimate unresolved contradiction. The dead themselves are an absent presence. To the chorus (371ff.) and perhaps to Polyxena (945ff., 1148ff.)),[21] death is annihilation; to Andromache, Hecuba, perhaps Astyanax, it is freedom and Elysian bliss (142ff., 790f., 1102f., 1171ff.). At all events, as elsewhere in Senecan tragedy – and in Seneca's own life – it is at death that human greatness shines, as Astyanax and Polyxena show.

But if the conceptual categories with which human beings attempt to make sense of their world seem confused and the modalities of life to which they give rise ill-based, some aspects of the play's presentation of the human condition seem without ambiguity. As in *Phaedra*, *Oedipus* and *Medea*, human power is dramatised as illusion:

> quicumque regno fidit et magna potens
> dominatur aula nec leues metuit deos
> animumque rebus credulum laetis dedit,
> me uideat – et te, Troia. non umquam tulit
> documenta fors maiora quam fragili loco
> starent superbi.
>
> *(Troades 1–6)*

Whoever trusts power and plays potent lord
In princely court unafraid of fickle gods

Lending a credulous heart to happiness
Look on me – and on you, Troy. Fortune brings
No greater proof of the fragile basis
Of pride.

Such are the play's opening lines, delivered by the captive Hecuba, queen of fallen Troy. They are echoed in Act 2 not by a fellow captive but the victorious king of kings, the conqueror of Troy, lord Agamemnon:

> quoque fortuna altius
> euexit ac leuauit humanas opes,
> hoc se magis supprimere felicem decet
> uariosque casus tremere metuentem deos
> nimium fauentes. magna momento obrui
> uincendo didici. Troia nos tumidos facit
> nimium ac feroces? stamus hoc Danai loco
> unde illa cecidit.
>
> (*Troades* 259–66)

> The higher fortune
> Has raised and exalted human power,
> The more her favourites should check themselves,
> Shiver at changing circumstance and fear
> Too generous gods. Victory has taught me
> Greatness falls at a touch. Does Troy make us
> Arrogant and brutal? We Danai stand
> From where she fell.

Agamemnon's words have dramatic point. Among the conceptual distinctions which *Troades* dissolves are precisely those between Greek and Trojan, victor and vanquished, conqueror and captive in respect of the commonality of human suffering and human impotence: impotence before gods, fate, fortune, history, which to Seneca are the same (*De Beneficiis* 4.7f.). One of the many ironies surrounding the fierce moral debate between Agamemnon and Achilles' son, Pyrrhus, in Act 2 of *Troades* (203–348) is its conspicuous inability to affect history. It proves itself irrelevant to what transpires. The priest Calchas, spokesman of fate and dissolver *par excellence*, who broke the bonds of the Greek fleet at Aulis and will break them again at Troy, ignores the intricacies of Agamemnon's and Pyrrhus' positions and simply decrees what fate demands. And what fate demands (significantly) is the repetition of history – with increasing, dissolving savagery. Thus Calchas' only words in the play:

> dant fata Danais quo solent pretio uiam:
> mactanda uirgo est Thessali busto ducis –
> sed quo iugari Thessalae cultu solent

Ionidesue uel Mycenaeae nurus.
Pyrrhus parenti coniugem tradat suo.
sic rite dabitur. non tamen nostras tenet
haec una puppes causa: nobilior tuo,
Polyxene, cruore debetur cruor.
quem fata quaerunt, turre de summa cadat
Priami nepos Hectoreus et letum oppetat.
tum mille uelis impleat classis freta.

(*Troades* 360–70)

Fate grants Danaans passage at the usual price:
A virgin must be sacrificed on the tomb
Of Thessaly's chief – but dressed like a bride
In Thessaly, Ionia or Mycenae.
Pyrrhus is to hand his father his wife.
She will thus be duly wed. This cause alone
Does not detain our ships: more noble blood,
Polyxena, than your blood is required.
Whom fate demands must fall from beetling tower –
Priam's grandson, Hector's son – to his death.
Then let the fleet's thousand sails fill the sea.

This response of the seer and priest of the Greek army concludes Act 2 and is the motor of the play's ensuing action. Its statements are crucial to both dramatic action and dramatic theme. Central rituals devised by man to structure and control his world (in this instance sacrifice and marriage) are to be conjoined with the slaughter of the innocent to fulfil history's cycle: fate is exacting 'the usual price' (360) – and more. Fate and the unimpedable revolutions of history dictate all. Past becomes present, becomes future by means of human action; but the cycle is its own power and its own law.

The recycling of past as present, it was noted above, is a permeating theme of *Troades*, as of several other Senecan plays. The whole of the second act realises the theme in detail. Talthybius' focus on the earlier delay of the Greek fleet at Aulis and on the return of Achilles' wrath underscores the past's repetition (164–202), as does the ensuing altercation between Pyrrhus and Agamemnon over Polyxena (203–359), which is an undisguised re*presentation* of Achilles' quarrel with Agamemnon in *Iliad* 1. The altercation repre*sents* too the debate over the sacrifice of Iphigenia to end the earlier delay of the Greek fleet at Aulis, which similarly achieved resolution in the 'authority' of Calchas. The wedding-sacrifice motif of the final two acts confirms and sharpens this analogy with the past: Polyxena's 'sacrificial marriage' to Achilles re-enacts that of Iphigenia. Appropriately it is Helen, the 'plague, holocaust, blight|Of both nations' (as Andromache calls her, 892), who arranges Polyxena's marriage (861ff.) and acts as bride's attendant at the

wedding-sacrifice itself (1132ff.). To Act 3 the theme of history's determinant force adds both texture and irony. At one level, and an important one, the
long third act is an attempt by the Greeks to stop the cycle of history by
preventing Andromache's son, Astyanax, from becoming another Hector.
'One great thing daunts the Danai', proclaims Ulysses, 'A future Hector'
(550f.). The third act is also an attempt by Andromache to reverse history's
dissolution by saving Astyanax so that he may live to resurrect Troy. Her
address to Astyanax before Ulysses enters focuses on this:

> eritne tempus illud ac felix dies
> quo Troici defensor et uindex soli
> recidiua ponas Pergama et sparsos fuga
> ciues reducas, nomen et patriae suum
> Phrygibusque reddas?
>
> (*Troades* 470–4)

> Will that time come and blessed day
> When you Troy's champion and avenger
> Set up Pergamum restored, bring her scattered
> People home and return to our country
> And the Phrygians their name?

What results from the interaction of Andromache and Ulysses in Act 3 is
that neither have their way. Astyanax is found, taken and killed, but Ulysses'
success serves only to make of Astyanax another dismembered Hector (see
esp. 1117) and to achieve the release of the Greek fleet, which the audience
knows will implement history's cycle by scattering and destroying the victors
as its earlier release scattered and destroyed Troy. The fulfilment of fate's
demands revealed by Calchas ensures history's cycle.

History's cyclic structure seems mirrored in the play's dramatic circle.
Tragic form indexes tragic meaning. Hecuba, for example, begins and ends
the play, and the ritual lamentation for the death of Troy, Hector and Priam,
with which the play opens, is echoed in the mourning for the death of
Hector's son and Priam's daughter and for 'the final act of Troy's collapse',
with which the play closes. Hecuba's invocation to death in her last and
perhaps most moving speech pinpoints this circle:

> quo meas lacrimas feram?
> ubi hanc anilis expuam leti moram?
> natam an nepotem, coniugem an patriam fleam?
> an omnia an me?
>   sola mors uotum meum,
> infantibus uiolenta, uirginibus uenis,
> ubique properas saeua. me solam times
> uitasque. gladios inter ac tela et faces
> quaesita tota nocte cupientem fugis.

non hostis aut ruina, non ignis meos
absumpsit artus. quam prope a Priamo steti.
(*Troades* 1168–77)

> Where can I take my old tears
> And spit out death's delay? Should I weep for
> Daughter or grandson, husband or country,
> The world or myself?
>   Death, my only prayer,
> You visit with violence virgins and babes,
> Savage in your speed. You fear and shun me
> Alone. I chased you that whole night amid swords
> And spears and torches. You flee your lover.
> No foe or devastation, no fire consumed
> My limbs. Yet how near I stood to Priam.

The final act is designed to highlight the play's cyclic structure. And within the dramatic circle formed by Acts 1 and 5 is another circle formed by Acts 2 and 4, focusing on Polyxena and her sacrificial wedding. At the centre of the two circles is Act 3, itself structured concentrically to complete a triad of circles.[22] Concentricity is the principle also structuring Acts 2 through to 5, transforming the separate fates of Astyanax and Polyxena into a closed dramatic unit.

This imprisonment of form binds the allusions to the past into an imprisonment of events. What results in *Troades*, as in other great Senecan plays, *Phaedra*, for example, or *Medea*, is the sense of an ironic universe, where the patterns of history repeat themselves through and by means of human agents unable to impede their own world's cyclic processes. The physical, moral and societal creations of the human species – empires, cities, civilisations, philosophies, moral systems, moral values, social institutions, rituals and practices, conceptual and linguistic categories, human relationships – are dissolved by history's degenerative cycle. Their fragility is emphatic. And Seneca's own civilisation, it should be noted, was self-conscious product of history's cycle. Rome was Troy reborn: the house of Assaracus, which burns in the prologue of *Troades* (17), resurrected in Italy.

THEATRICAL POWER

Especial attention should be given to the theatrical power of these two plays, their ability to engage an audience in the representation before it. Particularly important in *Troades* is the dramatisation of the great female figures of the play, Hecuba, Andromache, Helen, and the focus on their distinct psychologies, their emotions, their individual suffering. Seneca's predilection for the self-presentational soliloquy or monologue and the extended aside was discussed above,[23] where it was noted that his use of these devices gives his drama a far greater degree of interiority than is to be found in Attic tragedy, in which the aside is unknown. He deploys these devices to the full in his dramatisation of the principal Trojan women. The theatrical and psychological force of the entrance monologues of Andromache (409ff.) and Helen (861ff.) were observed above.[24] The male figures too in *Troades*, especially Agamemnon, Ulysses and the Messenger of Act 5, are given impressive psychological realisation. Seneca refuses to yield to stereotypical portraits. Inverting inherited types (especially Euripidean types) he presents a series of tired, self-critical warriors, endeavouring to break free of their pre-scripted roles, yet half-aware of their own impotence before the forces both of history and the literary tradition.[25] It is worth noting too that, though there are more male figures in the play than in Euripides' *Troades* or *Hecuba*, each figure speaks in only one scene, giving the play a discrete, episodic structure but one which paradoxically proves subject to a controlling concentric design – like disparate human events subject to a controlling ironic world.

Other aspects of the play's design deserve notice: its pervasive imagery of death and dissolution, which fuses in Act 3 with the dramatic action itself, as Andromache tries to preserve her son's life by burying him in her husband's tomb; the structuring of the play around theatrical 'high-spots', such as the semi-naked violent dirge of the opening (67ff.), the fateful pronouncement of Calchas at the end of Act 2 (360ff.), Andromache's lyrical supplication in Act 3 (705ff.), the collapse of Hecuba in Act 4 as her daughter, Polyxena, tries on the fatal bridal dress (945ff.); the play's bold employment of silent characters in the fourth act, especially the pathetic Polyxena, whose silence speaks more poignantly than all the words Euripides gives her in *Hecuba*; the play's use of choral lyric (often accompanied by music in modern performance, always in ancient performance) not only for thematic development but to shift dramatic mood – from sorrow and defiance in the opening dirge (67ff.), through aggressive determination in the death chorus (371ff.), to anxiety in the destination chorus (841ff.), to despair and a most bitter acceptance of dissolution in the final chorus (1009ff.) – each of these shifts in dramatic mood priming the audience for the act to come and contributing signally to the pace and energy of the play. Especially effective is the death chorus at the end of Act 2, with its dramatic shifts in tone and speed, yet its 'steady rhythmic punch',[26] and pervading it an insistent and incisive rhetoric, an intense imagistic power. It deserves quotation in full (at least in English), although its dramatic effect can only be realised through the allocation of different lines to different voices:

> Is it truth or a mind-drugging myth
> That a ghost survives the buried corpse
> When the wife has sealed her husband's eyes,
> The final day blotted out the suns,
> And the dismal urn confined the dust?

Is it useless to hand death our souls,
But must the wretched keep on living?
Or do we die whole, no part of us
Persist when breath has fled and spirit
Mingling with mists vanishes in air
And the flamed torch touches naked flesh?

All that sees the rising sun, all that
Sees it set, all that's washed by Ocean's
Ebbing tide and feels its blue return,
Time will snatch up with Pegasus' speed.

Fast as the twelve stars fly on the winds,
Fast as the star-king spins the rolling
Ages, fast as Hecate hurtles
Her chariot down its slanting course,
We seek our fated end; who has touched
The lake sacred to gods no longer
Exists at all. As smoke from hot fires
Fades, staining the air for a moment,
As pregnant clouds we ourselves have seen
Yield to arctic Boreas' assault,
The spirit that rules us will dissolve.

After death is nothing; death itself
Is nothing, swift race's final post.
Let greed lose hope, anxiety fear.
Time's greed and chaos devour us.

Death is indivisible: it kills
The body, spares not the soul. Taenarus,
The pitiless king's realm, Cerberus –
Threshold guardian of no easy gate,
These are hollow rumours, empty words,
Myth that resembles an anxious dream.
Wish to know where you lie after death?
    Where the unborn are.
              (*Troades* 371–408)

Thirty lines later (438ff.) Andromache recounts to the old servant her vision of the dead Hector appearing to her in her dreams. Such ironic interchange between chorus and act is a regular Senecan dramatic mode.[27] So too is what the death chorus conspicuously exemplifies: the naked power of poetic verse. For Senecan tragedy is poetic tragedy. Brilliant exploitation of poetic language, poetic rhythms, poetic structures quickens the great odes and speeches of the play, informs the baroque fusion of spectacle, bombast, lyricism and sensuousness which in part constitutes *Troades'* irresistible force.

Not that *Troades* is a typical Senecan play. In many respects it is an innovative play, and its innovation adds to its dramatic interest and power. The play has the most individualised chorus of any Senecan play[28] and the largest number of characters, including two quite separate messengers, the first terrified (168ff.), the second compassionate and self-critical (1056ff.). The play's dissolution of the dialogue of the opening act into lyric interchange is unique in Senecan tragedy, as is the impressive second act, which is split into two separate scenes (164–202, 203–370), involving entirely different characters and a change in dramatic setting. In the opening acts Seneca seems to be playing against the imperatives of the five-act structure, dissolving the first act into the opening chorus and the latter into the second act, and then creating a severe disjunction within the second act itself. This principle of disjunction is important to the play and governs the appearance of its male figures, none of whom, as was mentioned above, speaks in more than one scene. But this principle of disjunction is itself subordinate to the play's intricate concentric structure. Dramatic experimentation seems involved in the closure of this structure in a messenger scene, in which the distance of reported narrative stills the passions and energies of the play by giving verbal shape and finality to inexpressible suffering. *Troades* alone among Seneca's tragedies makes of a messenger's report and its reception the play's final and climactic act, as if only thus could the pathos of this play be stopped. And then there is the extraordinary third act, thought by John Dryden to be 'the masterpiece of Seneca' and 'the nearest resemblance of anything in the tragedies of the ancients to the excellent scenes of passion in Shakespeare or Fletcher' (*Of Dramatic Poesy*). The third act introduces the play's leading figure, Andromache, and with her opening words –

> quid, maesta Phrygiae turba, laceratis comas
> miserumque tunsae pectus effuso genas
> fletu rigatis? leuia perpessae sumus
> si flenda patimur.
>
> (*Troades* 409–12)

> Wailing bands of Phrygians, why tear your hair,
> Beat sorrowing breasts and drench cheeks with floods
> Of sobs? Our sufferings must be trivial
> If tears suffice.

– Andromache inaugurates one of the most tense and harrowing acts in ancient drama and the longest act (409–813) in Senecan tragedy.[29] Act 3 of *Troades* is virtually a tragedy within a tragedy and its intricate concentric structure reflects the concentric structure of the drama as a whole. The third act has the symmetry of a tombstone, as Andromache's refusal to mourn in the act's opening lines (409ff.) gives way to ritual lamentation for her son, Astyanax, at its close (766ff.), and the message from Hector which she receives in her dream (443ff.) finds concluding response in the message to Hector which she sends with her son to the land of the dead (799ff.). There is an oppressiveness about the structure of *Troades* and of its third act; it is the oppressiveness of the circle: the circle of events, motif, theme, language, the unbreakable bonds of dramatic structure indexing the unbreakable bonds of history's cycle. Fittingly perhaps the play's most brilliant move occurs at the centre of the play's circles, in the third act itself, the shift to lyric in Andromache's song of supplication (705–35), as the mother of Astyanax attempts with all the resources of music, song, voice, language, spectacle and feeling to break the bonds of history. The attempt fails.

The attempt to resist history's determinant cycle fails too in *Phaedra*, where again the play's structure is part of both its meaning and its force. The ironies and paradoxes of the play's action and structure, its dramatic reversals and cycles, suggest not only the revolutions of fate, nature and fortune, their power, irresistibility and apparent perversity, but the ironies and paradoxes constitutive of and indicative of human impotence and the human world. Other aspects of the bonding of the play, the close thematic and linguistic interrelation between chorus and act,[30] the tightly woven serial effect of repeated language, imagery, analogies, connecting action with action, thought with thought, speech with speech, event with event, seem also related to the concern with *natura* and fate, the inexorable order of things, the unbreakable chain of cause and effect. As with *Troades*, there is an oppressiveness about *Phaedra*, which comes in part from its unbreakable form, an oppressiveness as theatrically effective as it is emblematic of the world of the play. The asymmetry and dramatic pace of *Phaedra* similarly discomfort: lengthy opening song, long second act and chorus, followed by even longer third act and chorus, followed by short fourth act and minuscule chorus. The effect is of speed and devastating finality. The complex issues of the play and the positions of its human figures, laid out and played out at considerable dramatic length, are resolved suddenly, finally, violently. Prayer to Neptune, short ode of despair, Hippolytus' dismemberment as history. No time for reflection; inexorable swiftness.

As with *Troades* impressive theatrics drive the drama home. The power–impotence, freedom–incarceration issue is boldly realised in the stark juxtaposition of the crowded scene of the opening, with its energy, life, animation, action, openness, and the monolithic, brooding, introspective speech of the cabined Phaedra. Similarly the terror of acknowledged delusion, impotence, futility, and of nature's dismembering finality is enacted in a climactic scene of horror, as Theseus attempts to piece together the bloody remnants of Hippolytus' body (1247ff.). Like Diana in Hippolytus' opening song, *natura* terrifies and it kills. The cardinal confrontation scene between Phaedra and Hippolytus dramatises its central issues through theatrical spectacle. The whole scene is organised around a series of theatrical 'high-spots': Phaedra's entrance after the Antiope pronouncement (578f.), her fainting into Hippolytus' arms (585ff.), her prayer for compassion (671), Hippolytus' demand for cosmic reversal (671ff.), and the latter's manic prayer to Diana, sword in one hand, Phaedra's hair twisted back in the other, to accept the sacrifice of Phaedra as if hunted beast (706ff.). These 'high-spots' theatrically underscore major themes of both scene and play: the determinism of the past; spiritual struggle and its futility; delusion, impotence, humanity's ordained status as victim; the alleged 'morality' of nature, reality's disquieting, cynical smile. Theatrical punctuation sharpens the intellectual focus of the play.

Much of *Phaedra*'s performed force derives, as with *Troades*, from Seneca's dramatisation of psychological interiority, his presentation of the main figures of the drama, their psychology and behaviour, as humanly involving, as in important senses humanly intelligible. The dramatisation of Hippolytus' self-deception is especially noteworthy because of its particularising and percipient blend of moral rejectionism, psychological trauma, and the human aspiration towards freedom, self-sufficiency, power over self. The scene with the Nurse in Act 3 is telling in this regard. Hippolytus' golden age reverie (483ff.), conspicuous for the contradictions it exposes between vision and personal practice,[31] and conjoined as it is with the most neurotic, frenetic misogyny (555–79), seems product not of primeval innocence or Stoic wisdom but of self-deceived, pathological idealism. This idealism, the play suggests, has its origins in Theseus' murder of Hippolytus' mother, Antiope (578f.; cf. 226f., 926–9), whose life-style Hippolytus has adopted, and whose replacement, Phaedra, he loathes and, through her, womankind (238f., 558). Phaedra's dramatic entrance after Hippolytus' Antiope pronouncement –

> solamen unum matris amissae fero,
> odisse quod iam feminas omnes licet.
> (*Phaedra* 578f.)

> I've one consolation for my mother's loss:
> That I may now detest all womankind.

– signals the complex nexus of circumstances from which Hippolytus' self-validating fantasy derives. Seneca's concern with human psychology and intelligibility is evident too in the dramatisation of Theseus: the deluded, unthinking, self-confident and self-deceived man of action, psychological as well as biological father of Hippolytus, like Hippolytus incarcerated by his own self-image (see esp. 903ff.). The dramatic focus in the final act (1199ff.) on Theseus' personal suffering (he demands 'no easy end', 1208), on mental anguish, on the humanly involving and intelligible, exemplifies Seneca's dramatic mode.

But it is in the dramatisation of Phaedra that Seneca's concern with the presentation of humanly intelligible psychology and action is especially revealed. Often unobserved, the subtlety and depth of her characterisation deserve close attention. The psychological intricacies of Phaedra's entrance monologue were discussed above.[32] The psychological focus continues into the scene as a whole, as the vacillating Phaedra becomes more confirmed in her sense of helplessness, starts to give in to the passion, rationalises rather than analyses (179–94), indulges in wish-fulfilment and fantasy (219–45), falling from fantasy to depressed talk of suicide (250–66), until the Nurse joins her in the fantasy world she has created. The movement into fantasy (esp. 233ff.) has particular psychological import; it seems a corollary of Phaedra's impotence. Victim of political, domestic, moral, hereditary and other forces, Phaedra moves into a fantasy world of delusion – a fantasy world both fragile and, paradoxically, irresistible (250ff.) – to seize the control over her life so conspicuously absent in reality. In the following act Phaedra's mental and emotional state is dramatically to the fore throughout both the dressing scene (387–403) and the revelation scene, where Phaedra's actions and words (see esp. the soliloquy at 592–9) reveal psychological and moral discomfort. The revelation itself is handled in a masterly way: Hippolytus' observance of both courtesy and duty, his naivety and the words which seem to fall by accident from his lips, drawing from the increasingly committed Phaedra the disclosure of her love. The grand machine of the universe, fate, fortune, *natura,* is shown moving through and by means of human psychologies and behaviour in ironic (and tragic) interaction. Observe, for example, how Hippolytus' address to Phaedra as *mater*, 'mother', at 608 proves starting point for Phaedra's self-revelation, while his blithe promise of filling his father's place (633) and reference to love of Theseus (645) enable Phaedra to carry through the declaration of her love, to exhibit her sensuous and physical passion for Hippolytus, and endeavour to make fantasy and reality one. On Hippolytus' violent and contemptuous rejection (671–97) Phaedra's fantasy world once more (and this time irrevocably) shatters, returning her to the realism of her opening speech in the play, awareness of the monstrosity of her passion, its irresistibility, mindlessness, futility (698–703). The prospect of dying by Hippolytus' hand – madness cured, honour saved, sexual desire vicariously satisfied – seems a consummation devoutly to be wished (710–12). It is little wonder that Hippolytus fails to cope.

In the act which follows the complexities of Phaedra's psychology are again evident in the dialogue with Theseus, as Phaedra, desperate to preserve her honour, her reputation, even to save Hippolytus, hides her true feelings behind a barrage of cryptic replies and *sententiae* in response to Theseus' questions. Noticeably Seneca sexualises Theseus' interrogation of his wife with imagery of opening and concealment (859ff.) and a scenic structure designed to highlight the movement from female refusal through male violence to female surrender (870–85). Especially effective and almost precocious is the dramatist's use of Hippolytus' sword, which, if held by Phaedra

79

in performance close to her body as she faces Theseus during the interrogation scene, focuses brilliantly the sexual issues of the play. The scene is presented as an act of verbal rape, a variation on the Lucretia paradigm, with Theseus as both Tarquin and Collatinus, and Phaedra as a failed Lucretia.[33] But a Lucretia none the less. Note that even when driven by Theseus' assault on the Nurse to carry out the original plan, the denunciation of Hippolytus, she delivers no open accusation of rape, but a series of ambiguities, ironies and innuendoes:

> temptata precibus restiti; ferro ac minis
> non cessit animus; uim tamen corpus tulit.
> labem hanc pudoris eluet noster cruor.
>
> (*Phaedra* 891–3)

> Attacked by prayers, I resisted; steel and threats
> My mind repelled; my body suffered violence.
> This stain on honour shall my blood wash out.

Phaedra was 'attacked by prayers', 'threatened by sword', and her body did 'suffer violence'. And beneath the public sense of the last line, 'suicide will wash away the stain of rape', lies for Phaedra a private sense, 'suicide will wash away the stain of sin'. Even the final accusation is left to the sword (896f.) and the slaves (901ff.). It is all as if, in the midst of the accusation itself, Phaedra is trying to preserve a sense of honesty, integrity, self-respect. For, despite all, Phaedra remains an intensely moral creature.

Her behaviour in Act 6 (1159–98) exemplifies. Echoing the opening words of her first speech in the opening words of her last (cf. 85 and 1159), Phaedra turns verbal echo into psychological cycle and manifests the moral consciousness displayed at her first appearance. Rebuking Theseus but acknowledging too her own guilt (1164–9), even placing herself in the company of death-dealing monsters slain in turn by Theseus (1169–73), Phaedra in language and deed enacts a suicide of atonement. Unrestrained by either shame or fear she addresses the mangled pieces of Hippolytus' body in words that would make the winds weep:

> heu me, quo tuus fugit decor
> oculique nostrum sidus? exanimis iaces?
> ades parumper, uerbaque exaudi mea.
>
> (*Phaedra* 1173–5)

> O, where has your beauty fled
> And eyes that were my stars? Do you lie dead?
> Come back a little while and hear my words.

Her aim: a suicide of atonement for monstrous deeds, freeing her from both life and sin (1178). After a momentary movement into fantasy, the ritual of placation and of offerings to the dead asserts control, enabling Phaedra to wrest from failure, suffering and sin a momentary triumph: union with Hippolytus in death (1179–84). Variations of a moral fugue follow, as Phaedra's concern with shame, integrity, honour, reputation plays itself out and culminates in a prayer to death, balm of *malus amor* and ornament of blighted shame, to spread wide his merciful arms (1184–90). Phaedra is now in full control and with careful, balanced diction confesses her guilt to the citizens of Athens, restores Hippolytus' reputation and character, and puts meaning into her death, which she was unable to put into her life (1191–8). Her supreme and only moment of control over her life resides in the ending of it.

The dramatic architecture of *Troades* and *Phaedra* is no exception. *Medea* and *Thyestes*, most especially, evidence the same degree of dramatic crafts-manship. Important to notice in *Thyestes* is how Seneca again organises the dramatic action around a series of theatrical 'high spots': the Fury's coercion of the ghost of Tantalus in Act 1 (96ff.), the appearance of the ragged Thyestes before the palace at the beginning of Act 3 (404 ff.), the coronation of Thyestes at the end of that act (544ff.), the star chorus after the messen-ger scene (789ff.), and the opening of Act 5 as Atreus enters walking among the stars (885ff.) – he has himself replaced the stars, he is king of kings and most exalted of gods, he is the sun and the light. Important too is the forceful way in which the imagery of the play fuses with the dramatic action, as Tantalus' hunger and thirst of the prologue, the *fames infixa* and *sitis* which can never be quenched (97f.), become the hunger and thirst of Atreus' lust for vengeance, paradoxically exemplified in his getting Thyestes to eat and drink. Notice also how, as often in Seneca, the action has a carefully archi-tected crescendo movement beginning at the end of the third chorus (622), as its image of fortune's whirl is taken up by the Messenger, whose descrip-tion of Atrean bestiality is structured not only to build to its own stunning climax but to lead, via the cosmic note on which it ends, straight into the star chorus' terror of the imminent collapse of the zodiac – thence to Atreus the new sun (896f.).

Ironically much of *Thyestes'* power comes from Seneca's brilliant handling of the chorus, 'ironically', because Seneca's choruses have so often been the object of misguided contempt.[34] Particularly strong in *Thyestes*, as in several other Senecan plays, is the imagistic linking between chorus and act. The opening Tantalid chorus (122–75) takes up the god motif of the first lines of the prologue, develops the prologue's main images, and ends with the image of insatiable Tantalid thirst (174f.) – enter Atreus thirsting for vengeance (176). The second choral ode, the kingship chorus (336–403), contrasts sharply with Act 2, taking over its theme of kingship but outlining another quite different ideal, in fact a Stoic ideal, focusing on the advantages of poverty and obscurity – enter Thyestes dressed in rags (404), a visual embodiment of the ideal. The third choral ode on *pietas* and fortune (546–622) takes up the appearance–reality theme of Act 3 together with its animal imagery (cf. 491, 546), and ends on the whirl of fortune (*turbine*, 622), which, picked up immediately (*turbo*, 623) by the entering Messenger of Act 4, begins the crescendo movement of the play to which the star chorus (789–884) contributes most effectively. The shifting emotional tone of the choruses also contributes to *Thyestes'* dramatic impetus: the movement from prayerful solicitude, through tranquil reflection, joy and apprehension, to horror and terror, a movement intensified by the way the star chorus brings the play's cosmic imagery to an imploding climax.

Medea also merits notice in this context as one of Seneca's most finely structured plays. Variety and functional contrast in scenic composition, the fusion of imagery and dramatic action, consummate formal design, chorus–act interlinking, the use of choral odes to control dramatic speed, tone, atmosphere and to manipulate audience sympathy, mark *Medea* also. And, like *Phaedra* and *Thyestes*, the play makes use of a crescendo structure in the building of the dramatic action, which is punctuated once again by theatrical 'high spots' designed to serve as the structural and semiotic nodes of a performance.

What also merits notice is the dramatic and thematic use of stage-setting in all of the plays considered, and indeed in Seneca's plays as a whole. Consider the use made of Hector's tomb in the central act of *Troades* (409–813), or of the Cyclopean walls of Argos in *Thyestes* (404ff.), or of the city of Corinth, emblem of civilised order and control, throughout *Medea*. Also to be noted are the sometimes quite brilliant uses of stage-props: the crown in *Thyestes*, for example, or the altar and the sword in *Phaedra*.[35] And then there is the Senecan ending and its overt and powerful theatricality. Atreus' reply to Thyestes has already been noted.[36] So too has Cassandra's predictive retort at the end of *Agamemnon*, and Jason's atheistic outburst, which closes *Medea* and stirred Eliot to rare praise: 'No other . . . play reserves such a shock for the last word.'[37] For once Eliot's instincts were right. Seneca's mastery of theatrical closure impresses.

As does Seneca's diversity. Among the conventional misjudgements of his tragedies few have been as widespread or as damaging to Seneca's dramatic reputation as the classification of him as a monolithic playwright, simplistic, even formulaic in dramatic composition, structure and technique. What will be apparent from the foregoing analyses is that the central issue of a Senecan tragedy is always handled from a multiplicity and variety of perspectives. In *Agamemnon* Clytemnestra, Aegisthus, Cassandra, Electra conceptualise differently the tragic action. So in *Thyestes* do Atreus, Thyestes, Argos, the Messenger; in *Medea* Creon, Jason, Medea, Corinth; in *Troades* Pyrrhus, Agamemnon, Ulysses, Helen, the Trojan women, the final Messenger. In *Phaedra* one of the chorus' principal effects is to shift audience sympathy from Phaedra (first ode), to Hippolytus (second and third odes), to Theseus (final ode), complicating, even problematising the response elicited by the dramatic events. Multiplicity and variety are evident at the dramaturgic level too. Senecan dramaturgic inflexibility is a myth.[38] Prologue-design and integration vary;[39] choral length and sequence vary;[40] techniques of choral identification vary,[41] as does the number of choruses and actors. *Agamemnon*, for example, has two identified choruses, neither of which (at least in the text) is identified until the second ode, and has four speaking parts in its final scene (Aegisthus, Electra, Clytemnestra, Cassandra: 981–1012). *Oedipus* similarly requires four speaking actors on stage for its second act (201–402). *Thyestes* is virtually a two-actor play; it has a single chorus, whose *persona* is established immediately.[42] Seneca's treatment of the messenger's speech varies considerably. The long, unbroken messenger's speech is restricted to three plays: *Phaedra* (1000–114), *Oedipus* and *Agamemnon* (421ff.);[43] and in *Oedipus* there are two such speeches: Creon's in Act 3 (530ff.), the Messenger's in Act 5 (951ff.: the penultimate act, as in *Phaedra*). In *Troades* (Act 5, 1068ff.) and *Thyestes* (Act 4, 641ff.), the Messenger provides a discontinuous account broken up by questions; in *Phoenissae* (387ff.) and *Medea* (Act 5, 879ff.) his report is extremely brief and, in the latter, interleaved with questions. In *Troades* too there is a secondary messenger's speech at the beginning of the second act (168ff.). In *Hercules Furens* there is no messenger's speech at all, although Theseus' long and discontinuous account of the underworld in Act 3 (658ff.) might be said to replace it. It should be noted too that the Messenger may appear in Acts 3, 4 or 5, and even, in the case of *Troades*, in Act 2.

Senecan dramaturgical variety exhibits itself also in verse-dialogue composition[44] and dialogic interaction (contrast the psychological and dramatic development of *Phaedra* 602ff. with the combative staticity of *Troades* 203ff.), in choral lyric (polymetric *cantica* only in *Oedipus* and *Agamemnon*), in dramatic movement and tempo, and in overall dramatic structure. Variations in dramatic structure are particularly interesting. *Agamemnon*, for example, has a diptych structure, is episodic and discontinuous; *Troades* is episodic and discontinuous, but within an encompassing concentric design; *Phaedra*, *Medea* and *Thyestes* reveal a continuous dramatic movement with a crescendo effect beginning after the third chorus. Even the division of the play into five acts is not always adhered to. *Oedipus* certainly has six acts. *Phaedra* too can be considered a six-act play. Its lyric opening at any rate dissolves the conventional five-act division.[45] *Phoenissae* of course dissolves the five-act division even further by removing the chorus entirely. The common and probably accurate assumption is that *Phoenissae* is unfinished; but, even so, it is perhaps just possible that it was an intentionally unchorused play.[46] For the more the tragedies are examined, the more they reveal a dramatist not only interested in drama but in dramatic experimentation, even perhaps innovation. The use of the sword in *Phaedra*, for example, is very likely an innovative move,[47] as indeed perhaps is Seneca's most unvarying dramaturgical device, the dialogue-ending. Each Senecan play ends in dialogue uttered by one of the *dramatis personae*. Attic tragedy ends more frequently than not (it becomes the rule in the received texts of Euripides)[48] with a short ode or lyric utterance from the chorus, as do the non-Senecan plays of the corpus, *Hercules Oetaeus* and *Octavia*. No extant Senecan play does this. Those famous Senecan endings exhibit not only dramatic power, but a considerable departure, it seems, from standard tragic practice. Tradition is reconfigured for theatrical effect.

5

THE PALIMPSESTIC CODE

> No poet, no artist of any art, has his complete meaning alone. His significance, his appreciation is the appreciation of his relation to the dead poets and artists.
>
> T. S. Eliot, 'Tradition and the Individual Talent' (1919)

Verbal and ideological interplay between Seneca's plays shapes and clarifies their meanings. *Agamemnon* and *Thyestes* are again a paradigm case. Witness the following motifs or images common to both plays: the cycle of crime, *alternum scelus*; the contest of crime; fortune's wheel; the 'freedom of death', *mors libera*; 'perverse love of life', *uitae dirus amor*; birth as destiny; the beast in the net; clothing that brings catastrophe; Tantalid auspices; bloody decapitation; fear of universal chaos; Thyestean eclipse; Thyestean crime against children; *rex regum*, 'king of kings'; mingling of blood and wine; the underworld's criminal triad; the lion, *uictor ferarum*, 'vanquisher of beasts'; *festus dies*, 'feast-day'; the palm of victory; the sacrifice and the feast; the incompatibility of morality and power; true kingship and the absence of fear; the ship-oar-waves analogy for psychological struggle and compulsion; advice against staining altars with impious blood.[1] The list is not exhaustive and many of these motifs occur in other Senecan tragedies. But, given that, as was noted above, *Agamemnon* and *Thyestes* are already connected through subject-matter (the Tantalid saga), ghost-prologues and the figure of Thyestes himself, these common images and motifs seem clear pointers to a designed interplay between the two works; they are indices of intertextual intent.

The intent is semiotic. The contrast between the qualified moral stance of *Agamemnon* and the absolute blackness of *Thyestes* is reflected in and sharpened by the transformed ideological use of image and motif. On the feast-day of *Agamemnon*, the lion, Agamemnon, king of kings, *uictor ferarum*, is sacrificed, but the palm of victory goes not to the beast that slays him but to the avenger, Orestes, who will slay that beast and restore, if problematically, 'loyalty', 'duty', 'righteousness', *fides* and *pietas*, to the Argive world. On the feast-day of *Thyestes*, the lion, Atreus, *uictor*, is not sacrificed but sacrificially slays; he is true beast, god and king of kings. Dissolving the distinctions on which civilisation depends, he receives the true palm, *uera palma*, emblem of his victory and his truth. *Agamemnon*'s ambiguous moral order gives way, if *Agamemnon* is the earlier play, to *Thyestes*' cultural death.

The *Agamemnon* and *Thyestes* intertextuality is by no means exceptional. Analogous intertextuality seems to govern *Agamemnon*'s relationship to *Troades* and *Phoenissae*'s relationship to *Oedipus*;[2] while the entire Senecan dramatic corpus is itself intertexted with recurrent themes, ideas, images and motifs. And this is to leave aside the complex – and generally misunderstood – intertextual relationship between Seneca's dramatic and philosophical works.[3]

There is another kind of intertextuality too – one which concerns the relationship between Seneca's dramatic texts and the dramatic and poetic tradition which they inherit and rewrite. *Phaedra*, for example, fairly obviously alludes to and rewrites (*inter alios*) Virgil, Ovid and Euripides, most especially the latter two. *Heroides* 4 is alluded to pervasively, and is expressly remodelled in *Phaedra*'s revelation speech at 652ff.[4] *Phaedra*'s rewriting of Euripides' second *Hippolytus* (the one we have) is even more conspicuous.[5] Observe the following. Euripides separates Aphrodite and Artemis; Seneca fuses Venus and Diana. Hippolytus' outburst of misogyny follows the revelation of Phaedra's love in Euripides (*Hippolytus* 616ff.), precedes it in Seneca (*Phaedra* 559ff.). Euripides' Theseus curses his bastard son with the first prayer granted him by Poseidon (*Hippolytus* 887ff.); Seneca's with the last one (*Phaedra* 942ff.), and the son is now an 'assured heir' (*certus heres*, 1112). Phaedra hangs herself (*Hippolytus* 764ff.) and accuses Hippolytus by means of a written tablet (856ff.) in the Greek play; in the Roman play she kills herself (*Phaedra* 1197f.) with the very sword she had used as proof of Hippolytus' guilt (896f.), and with which she had asked Hippolytus to enter her (710ff.). And the accusation itself, plain and unadorned in Euripides (*Hippolytus* 885f.), in Seneca is ambiguous and encrusted with irony (*Phaedra* 891–3). As for Phaedra's inherited family curse and the determinism of the past made so much of by Seneca,[6] they have virtually no role to play in Euripides' drama, which makes but a single brief reference to Pasiphae and the bull (*Hippolytus* 337f.) and none to the Minotaur. Significantly, Hippolytus' mother, unnamed in Euripides, is named (*Phaedra* 226ff., 926ff.) and dramatically exploited (see esp. 578f.) in Seneca. Both dramatists have choruses on sexual desire (*Hippolytus* 525ff., *Phaedra* 274ff.): Euripides limits its operation to humankind, Seneca, rewriting also Virgil's *Georgics*,[7] extends its operation to the gods and all sentient life, and identifies it crucially with *natura* (*Phaedra* 352).[8] The two messenger's speeches (*Hippolytus* 1173–254, *Phaedra* 1000–114) have much in common and much not. Seneca's phantasmagoric monster (*Phaedra* 1035ff.) is not in Euripides; nor is the Senecan contrast between the effect of the bull on Hippolytus' companions and the countryside at large and its effect on Hippolytus himself (*Phaedra* 1050–6). And Seneca, unlike Euripides (*Hip-*

polytus 1218ff.) and Ovid (*Metamorphoses* 15.514ff.), in accord with his own thematic design gives Hippolytus an *aristeia* of controlling power (*Phaedra* 1054ff.). He was to be followed in this to some extent by Racine (*Phèdre* 1527–34).[9] It goes without saying, perhaps, that Seneca's hunting imagery (see esp. *Phaedra* 1085–7) and the sexualisation of Hippolytus' death (1098f.) are not in Euripides. Nor is Seneca's rewriting of Euripides in *Phaedra* limited to Euripides' *Hippolytus*. The final scene, for example, as Theseus attempts to piece together the dismembered limbs of his son's body, conflates Euripides' *Hippolytus* and *Bacchae*.[10]

Intertextuality of this order has complex effects. Some of these are clearly thematic or relate to differences in the dramatisation of the main figures of the play. Some are cultural signals. In the final scene of *Phaedra*, even as Euripides' *Hippolytus* and *Bacchae* are almost brought together, Seneca asserts a distinctly Roman world through a spectacular theatricalisation of the Roman ritual of *concinnatio corporis*, the gathering of the body parts and remaking of the body, owed to the dead (see Statius *Thebaid* 3.131f., Apuleius *Metamorphoses* 7.26). The last lines of the play make reference to Athens and derive from Rome.

> patefacite acerbam caede funesta domum.
> Mopsopia claris tota lamentis sonet.
> uos apparate regii flammam rogi;
> at uos per agros corporis partes uagas
> inquirite. istam terra defossam premat,
> grauisque tellus impio capiti incubet.
> (*Phaedra* 1275–80)

> Open the dismal palace sour with death.
> All Attica resound with loud lament.
> You prepare the flames of the royal pyre;
> You search the fields for parts of the body
> Astray. [*Points to Phaedra*] This one – earth press deep upon her,
> And soil lie heavy on her impious head.

Theseus' curse on Phaedra in the play's final line not only employs the social distinctions inherent in Roman funerary practices (aristocratic cremation for his son, ignoble inhumation for his wife), but reformulates the standard grave-formula, *sit tibi terra leuis* ('may earth lie gently on you'), into a command of spite. Differences from Euripides here, as elsewhere, are markers of a different world.

Let one more scene suffice. It was remarked above that Phaedra's accusation of Hippolytus is more ambiguous and contextually ironic in Seneca. That ambiguity and irony were examined in the last chapter, where Seneca's Romanising of the whole interrogation scene through allusion to one of the city's foundational myths (Tarquin and Lucretia) was observed.[11] What needs to be noted here is how the accusation itself is preceded in Seneca by a verbal exchange of extraordinary dramatic power which not only (obviously) has no counterpart in Euripides' extant *Hippolytus* but also cannot plausibly be derived from Euripides' other Hippolytan play. It signals a distinctly non-Euripidean world. Towards the end of his interrogation of Phaedra on her intended suicide, Theseus asks:

> quod sit luendum morte delictum indica.
> > (*Phaedra* 879)

> Tell me what sin is to be purged by death.

Phaedra replies:

> quod uiuo.
> (*Phaedra* 880)

> That I live.

Theseus, of course, ignores Phaedra's reply, construing it, if at all, along the lines of the aristocratic tradition represented by Lucretia of death before sexual dishonour. For the audience 'that I live', *quod uiuo*, has other meanings. To Phaedra, who has lost both Hippolytus and honour, life is intolerable, valueless. More important, to Phaedra, for whom nature's ordinances and nature's inversion, life and monstrous love, existence and guilt, moral consciousness and the violation of integrity, of honour, of 'shame', *pudor*, are inextricably interwoven, living is itself a sin, an obscenity, a *delictum*.

> fatale miserae matris agnosco malum.
> > (*Phaedra* 113)

> I recognise poor mother's fateful evil.

> et ipsa nostrae fata cognosco domus:
> fugienda petimus.
> > (*Phaedra* 698f.)

> I too recognise the fate of our house:
> What we should shun, we seek.

> quod sit luendum morte delictum indica.
> quod uiuo.
> > (*Phaedra* 879f.)

> Tell me what sin is to be purged by death.
> That I live.

The timing of *quod uiuo* is dramatically important. Just before Phaedra is forced to accuse Hippolytus, the dramatic focus falls on the profoundly tragic nature of Phaedra's life, and simplistic moral judgements are averted.

Her comment has more than theatrical force. Inevitable corollary of Seneca's presentment of life as sin, as obscenity, as *delictum* and *monstrum*, as unbreakable circle of suffering, as entrapment in catastrophic revolutions and reversals (1123ff.), Phaedra's death-wish (see also 710ff., 868ff., 1188ff.), like that of Theseus (1238–42), seems mirror of an age.

Phaedra is a palimpsestic text. That is to say, it is like a palimpsest or document written upon several times, with traces of earlier writing visible beneath. Nor is *Phaedra* the only Senecan dramatic text of this kind. Beneath each Senecan tragedy are a host of subtexts – Greek and Roman, Attic, Hellenistic, republican, Augustan and early imperial – clarifying and informing their discourse. In *Troades*, for example, almost as a pointer to the play's concern with the recycling of history, Seneca rewrites and recycles many texts: most obviously, Homer's *Iliad*, the cyclic epics, Sophocles' *Polyxena*, Euripides' *Andromache*, *Hecuba*, *Troades* and *Iphigenia at Aulis*, Naevius' *Andromacha*, Ennius' *Iphigenia*, *Hecuba* and *Andromacha*, Accius' *Astyanax* and *Hecuba*, Lucretius' *De Rerum Natura* 3, Catullus' *Peleus and Thetis*, Horace's *Odes* 3.30, Virgil's *Aeneid*, Ovid's *Metamorphoses*, and (possibly) his own *Agamemnon*. And *Troades* rewrites and recycles these texts self-consciously. Overt textual allusion and metaliterary language make of *Troades* a self-reflective, multi-referential text, which engages in a constant and pervasive counterpoint with the dramatic and poetic tradition. The play's concept of 'fate', *fatum* (lit. 'what has been said'), seems itself at times to signal this tradition,[12] as the dramatic figures struggle against not only the determinism of history but the determinism of the literary past and of their own literary pedigrees.

The rewriting of Euripides is again instructive. In Euripides the deaths of Astyanax and Polyxena are the dramatic focus of two separate plays (*Troades* and *Hecuba*), and both are announced by the Greek herald Talthybius. Seneca gives the two deaths equal and conjoined dramatic focus in one play, does not have Talthybius announce either, and unlike Euripides connects both deaths with the delay of the Greek fleet. Euripides' plays begin with gods or ghosts, Seneca's play with a paradigm of human suffering, the *mater dolorosa*, Hecuba; it climaxes, unlike either of Euripides' plays, in the wedding-sacrifice of Polyxena. For Euripides Polyxena's death is in essence simply sacrifice.[13] Female conflict and relationships are realised differently by each playwright. Euripides' conflict between Helen and Hecuba is replaced by one between Helen and Andromache, and Hecuba, who demands Helen's death in the Greek *Troades* and is equally hostile in *Hecuba* itself, appears sympathetic towards Helen in Seneca's play, taking upon herself much of the responsibility for Troy's fall. The figure of Ulysses too deserves mention. In Euripides' *Troades* it is Ulysses or Odysseus who proposes Astyanax' death; in Seneca it is Calchas, spokesman of fate and index of history's cycle. Seneca's Ulysses plays the more sympathetic role, played by Talthybius in Euripides, of reluctant executor of the army's will. He pointedly does not play the role assigned him in Euripides' *Hecuba*, the removal of Polyxena from her mother. Seneca's inversion of Euripidean figures extends to Polyxena, who speaks at length in *Hecuba* but remains silent in Seneca's play, and most noticeably to Helen, who is far from being the *femme fatale* of Euripides' *Troades*, but rather reflective, self-critical, compassionate and desirous of the comfort of shared grief. Other differences – and not only from Euripides – abound. They are differences with point. Seneca's rewriting of earlier texts, including Euripidean ones, is itself model of one of his play's central themes: the recycling and rewriting of history. Seneca's palimpsestic play differs from all the works it rewrites; its main figures, for example, are more humane, compassion is a more prominent value. But Astyanax and Polyxena are again killed; Ulysses and Helen play against but fulfil their inscribed selves;[14] the Trojan women, enslaved and allotted, head 'once more' (*repetite*, 1178) to the sea; the Greek fleet departs (*classis mouet*, 1179). The pattern of the tragic myth, like the pattern of history, remains constant. Like the past, the myth changes to remain the same. Seneca's *Troades* is not merely palimpsestic; it images a palimpsestic world.

The palimpsestic world imaged is the world of the play. But it is not only the world of the play. Late Julio-Claudian Rome, especially (but not only) the Rome of the last Julio-Claudian emperor, Nero, was itself a palimpsestic world. A world dominated by the forms of its past, political, social, religious, legal, which it attempted to re*present*. According to the Roman historian Suetonius (*Nero* 10.1), Nero at the start of his reign proclaimed his intention to rule *ex Augusti praescripto*, that is, in accordance with the prescription of the founder of the dynasty, the first emperor, Augustus; his professed aim was to realise Augustus' *pre*text. Ironically he fulfilled this aim in ways he never comprehended. For what Nero succeeded in doing was to recycle the tyranny of his predecessors (including that of Augustus) together with the political, social, religious and legal forms of the Roman world emptied of their substance. It was a palimpsestic world on the verge of dissolution, and portrayed as such by the great writers of the period, Lucan, Petronius, Seneca, all of whom dissolved themselves through suicide before Nero's reign ended. It was a palimpsestic world on the verge of dissolution, in which death was a source of aesthetic pleasure (Seneca *Naturales Quaestiones* 3.18) and the death-wish, *libido moriendi* (Seneca *Epistle* 24.25), a paradigm emotion, as individuals sought the empowerment they lacked in life through the controlled artistry of death. It is left to Seneca's Phaedra (*Phaedra* 880) or Petronius' withered Sibyl to articulate the appropriate response: *apothanein thelō*, 'I want to die' (*Satyricon* 48). It was a palimpsestic world on the verge of dissolution, in which the modalities of life had become perversely and irredeemably confused. Nero was a fratricide, matricide, sororicide, uxoricide; most relevantly for *Troades* he was a political murderer of children (Britannicus) and of brides (Octavia). Relevant too to *Troades* is the way the social and religious rituals of the state were used by Nero to implement bloody savagery – something the Roman historian Tacitus particularly focuses upon in his account of Nero's reign (*Annals* 14–16). Indeed Tacitus refers to the same conflation of wedding and funeral in the brutal murder of Nero's wife, Octavia (*Annals* 14.63), as Seneca does – pervasively – in the dramatisation of Polyxena's death.

What should be recognised too is that, though perhaps most appropriately dated to the Neronian principate (its actual date is unknown), *Troades* in no sense depends upon such dating for its relevance to late Julio-Claudian Rome. Nero simply realised in sharp and telling form the palimpsestic dimension and modality confusion of this 'new' imperial world – an imperial world for which the Trojan myth itself furnished an apposite and easily cognisable grammar. The cultural semiotics of the Trojan myth were laid out and played out in political (and artistic) word and fact throughout the whole of Seneca's lifetime. Imperial Rome was Troy rewritten and reborn. After Virgil's *Aeneid*, Ovid's *Metamorphoses* and *Fasti*, and the 'Trojan' imagery of the Augustan monuments (especially the Ara Pacis and Augustan Forum), no writer, reader, *spectator* or emperor could forget it. The Julio-Claudian dynasty, of which Nero was the final member, traced its ancestry back to the Trojan Aeneas and the house of Assaracus blazing in the opening lines of Seneca's play (*Troades* 17). Virgil's *Aeneid*, a school text in Seneca's day, makes this claimed ancestry the basic datum of the epic and pointedly refers to the connection between the house of Assaracus and the Julian family in Jupiter's great prophecy of Augustus' birth in *Aeneid* 1 (1.284).[15] To underscore Rome's Trojan past Augustus established the 'Troy Game', *Troiae lusus* (referred to by Andromache at *Troades* 778), as a regular state event, and the tradition was continued by both Caligula and Claudius.[16] Neronian writers – Calpurnius Siculus (*Eclogue* 1.44f.), Persius (*Satire* 1.4), Lucan (*Bellum Ciuile* 9.961–99), Petronius (*Satyricon* 89) – conspicuously exploited the connection with Troy.[17] So too did Nero himself. He participated in the Trojan Games of 47 CE (together with Claudius' son, Britannicus: Tacitus *Annals* 11.11) at the age of 9; he delivered an oration on behalf of the contemporary city of Ilium (*Annals* 12.58) in 53 CE at the age of 16, 'setting out at length', according to Tacitus, 'the origins of the Roman people in Troy, Aeneas the founder of the Julian house'; and during his maturity (if one may call it that) he wrote an epic, *Troica*, from which his detractors claim he sang during the great fire of Rome in 64 CE.[18] *Troades* thus exploits a myth of immediate contemporary import. The death of a civilisation, the dissolution of a culture, dramatised in *Troades*, has patent ramifications for the palimpsestic, dissolving world of late Julio-Claudian Rome. Its ramifications were realised in history. Three years after Seneca killed himself at Nero's command history's cycle dissolved Nero's world. The Julio-Claudian dynasty came to an end as abrupt as that of the royal house of Troy.

OEDIPVS

But if the palimpsestic mode of *Phaedra* and, most especially, *Troades* reflects upon the early imperial world, so too does that of Seneca's *Oedipus*. And this time the Greek tragedian reconstituted for Rome is Sophocles – the play perhaps the most famous of antiquity, *Oedipus Tyrannus*. The reconstitution is substantial. The Sophoclean focus on Oedipus' identity, on the search for and the revelation of the truth, and the attendant and extensive concern with plot-development and the creation of dramatic suspense are removed from Seneca's play, in which Oedipus' 'impieties' are confirmed in Acts 2 and 3 by dramatised supernatural events, and the Sophoclean dialogue leading to the determination of Oedipus' origins is tersely confined to the short fourth act (764–881). The dialogue is treated in a dramatically perfunctory fashion. Notably Seneca's choral odes are less concentrated on Oedipus and the specifics of plot than the stasima of *Oedipus Tyrannus*. His play's attention lies elsewhere. Similarly, the Greek tragedian's preoccupation with character, with the demonstration of Oedipus' human greatness in intelligence, compassion and moral strength, and with the gradual display of his moral and emotional weaknesses, is not repeated by Seneca, who produces a play in which Oedipus is intuitively aware from the start of his guilt and suffers little change of fortune. The ending of Seneca's *Oedipus* plays out externally the moral situation internally experienced by its protagonist in the drama's opening lines.

In stark contrast to the presentation of Sophocles' strong, caring king, confident in the loyalty and respect he commands, engaged in sympathetic converse with the people of Thebes and the priest of Zeus, Seneca begins his play with an Oedipus alone on stage at dawn before an 'uncertain sun', preoccupied with power's deceitful allure (6ff.), riddled with anxiety, guilt, and, most of all, fear. Confronted by the havoc of the 'ravenous' Theban plague (*auida peste*, 4), he fears everything, especially the 'unspeakable' (*infanda*, 15): patricide and incest with his mother.

> pro misera pietas (eloqui fatum pudet),
> thalamos parentis Phoebus et diros toros
> gnato minatur impia incestos face.
> hic me paternis expulit regnis timor,
> hoc ego penates profugus excessi meos.
> parum ipse fidens mihimet in tuto tua,
> natura, posui iura. cum magna horreas,
> quod posse fieri non putes metuas tamen:
> cuncta expauesco meque non credo mihi.
>
> iam iam aliquid in nos fata moliri parant.
> nam quid rear quod ista Cadmeae lues
> infesta genti strage tam late edita
> mihi parcit uni? cui reseruamur malo?

inter ruinas urbis et semper nouis
deflenda lacrimis funera ac populi struem
incolumis asto – scilicet Phoebi reus.
sperare poteras sceleribus tantis dari
regnum salubre? fecimus caelum nocens.
                              (*Oedipus* 19–36)

Wretched filial love! My fate shames me.
Phoebus threatens the son with his sire's bed
And unholy sheets stained by impious marriage.
This fear drove me from my ancestral realm,
Made me flee my own home a fugitive.
Distrusting my own self I moved your laws,
Nature, to safety. When terror is great,
You dread even that you think impossible.
I fear all things and have no faith in me.
    Now, even now fate fashions something for me.
What else can I think when this plague that fouls
Cadmus' folk, dealing universal death,
Spares me alone? For what evil am I kept?
Amid the city's ruin, the endless funerals,
The unceasing sobs, this massacre of men,
I stand apart untouched – damned by Phoebus.
Can one expect sin like mine to receive
A healthy realm? I have made the air guilty.

Prostrate at the altar (71ff.), he demands the hastening of his fate (*matura fata*, 72), immediate death. Death is refused. The only recourse is to depart the kingdom he has 'infected with his deathly hand' (77f.). Jocasta intervenes. In Sophocles' play she makes her initial appearance late, during the quarrel between Oedipus and Creon (*Oedipus Tyrannus* 634). Here she appears immediately in dramatic and ironic response to Oedipus' concluding self-injunction ('flee . . . even to your parents', *profuge . . . vel ad parentes*, 80f.), and lectures her husband on the responsibilities of power (81–6). Her Romano-Stoic homily affects Oedipus' frame of mind but little. His wish is still for death, if now too late (103f.). The prologue's concluding reference to the need to consult Phoebus (109), the *dubius*, 'uncertain', god of the play's opening line, fails to reassure, and is but lip-service to the Sophoclean script. The emphasis remains on guilt, fate, human impotence, and the concomitant pointlessness of prayer. These latter motifs are especially prominent in the ensuing plague chorus (110–201), which reinforces the atmosphere of nightmare and horror with a concentrated description of the physical effects of the pestilence, derived in part from Virgil. The chorus' visualisation of the plague-infested land of Thebes rings the negative changes on the Stoic doctrine of *sympatheia* or universal interaction to present a world where nature has been inverted, the barriers between life and death have dissolved, and the living and the dead conjoin (149–79). The theological optimism of Sophocles' parodos, especially of its climactic appeal to Zeus, Apollo, Artemis and Bacchus (*Oedipus Tyrannus* 200–15), is decidedly absent from the hell on earth which is the Senecan Oedipus' kingdom.

The next two acts completely change the inherited script. The superbly crafted 'episode' in which Tiresias is forced to identify Oedipus as the killer of Laius (*Oedipus Tyrannus* 216–462) and the subsequent one, in which Oedipus accuses Creon of conspiracy to seize the throne and Jocasta intervenes and discusses with Oedipus the circumstances of Laius' death (513–862), are replaced with extraordinary dramatisations of supernatural events, in which through oracular revelation, sacrifice, extispicy, and the raising of the dead, Oedipus' premonitions of his own guilt are not revealed as much as verified. In Act 2 Creon's eerie narrative of the Delphic oracle and its specific reference to both murder and incest lead to Oedipus' curse on Laius' murderer and a lengthy scene (291–402), in which the blind Tiresias supervises his daughter Manto in a ritual sacrifice of bull and heifer and inspection of their entrails for 'fate-revealing' signs (in Roman religion an *extispicium* or 'extispicy'). Wine changes to blood (324), dense smoke enshrouds Oedipus' head (325ff.), and the extispicy reveals abominations and perversions of nature (353ff.), including a twitching foetus in an unmated heifer, filling its mother in an unnatural place (*alieno in loco*, 374). The irony of Manto's double-headed cry –

> mutatus ordo est, sede nil propria iacet.
> (*Oedipus* 366)

The order's awry, nothing's in its right place.

> natura uersa est; nulla lex utero manet.
> (*Oedipus* 371)

Nature's perverted; the womb preserves no law.

– underscores the meaning of this ritual nightmare, which will be replayed less symbolically by a blind man and his female kin in the play's final act.[19] The audience understands much; but for the *dramatis personae* there has been a marked increase in fear, little in knowledge. Still lacking is the name, the *nomen* (392), of Laius' killer. While the audience waits for the final supernatural event, a dithyrambic laudation of Bacchus (403–508), punctuated with imagery of brightness, energy, abundance and power and with fantastic, even grotesque scenes of transformation, creates an ambiguous, frenetic light between two acts of horror. The Sophoclean choral 'model' is the ironic dance-invocation of Dionysus towards the end of *Antigone* (1115–54) just before the catastrophe is revealed. Similar irony governs this ode. Its final litany of worship in a world now out of joint points only to the cosmic and moral order which pestilential Thebes lacks (503–8). In Act 3 the necro-mancy of Tiresias confirms all. This time it is the dead father who speaks, Laius, 'a thing of horror, limbs streaming with blood, half hidden by hair matted with foul filth' (624–25); his denunciation of his son, the bloody king (*rex cruentus*, 634), is unambiguous. Though he recognises the truth of what he has long feared (659–60) and had himself forced Creon with threats of violence to speak (518ff.), Oedipus returns to the Sophoclean plot and accuses Creon of political conspiracy. The latter advises Oedipus to give up the throne and is hurled into prison.

After a choral ode in which disbelief is expressed concerning Oedipus' guilt, a short fourth act (764–881) plays out a syncopated version of the Sophoclean search for the identity of the killer and Oedipus' own origins. The conclusion of this act, Oedipus' appeal for self-destruction, is pure Seneca (cf. *Phaedra* 1238ff.):

> dehisce tellus, tuque tenebrarum potens,
> in Tartara ima, rector umbrarum, rape
> retro reuersas generis ac stirpis uices.
> congerite, ciues, saxa in infandum caput,
> mactate telis: me petat ferro parens,
> me gnatus, in me coniuges arment manus
> fratresque, et aeger populus ereptos rogis
> iaculetur ignes. saeculi crimen uagor,
> odium deorum, iuris exitium sacri,
> qua luce primum spiritus hausi rudes
> iam morte dignus.
>
> (*Oedipus* 868–78)

> Gape earth, and you emperor of darkness,
> Lord of the shadows, fling into hell's pit
> This perverse mutation of race and stock.
> Citizens, pile stones on my impious head,
> Kill me with your spears. Let father and son
> Attack me with steel, husbands and brothers
> Grip their swords, and the plague-ridden people
> Thrust their funeral brands in me. I wander
> The age's crime, the gods' odium, holy law's
> Devastation, since first I drank virgin air
> Already deserving death.

The chorus can only respond by withdrawing into a eulogy of the *media uia*, the unambitious life (882–910; cf. *Hercules Furens* 192ff., *Medea* 603ff., *Thyestes* 391ff.).

The final two acts rewrite the Sophoclean ending. In the Greek play the Messenger describes how Oedipus blinds himself with the pins of Jocasta's dress which he snatches from her hanging corpse. Seneca's Messenger emphasises the blinding as an act of self-punishment carried out with Oedipus' bare hands and spurred on not by Jocasta's death (she is still alive) but by his own moral horror and shame. It is a deed to match his fate (*suis fatis simile*, 926), a 'living death', *mors longa* (949), the *diu mori* of the *Epistles* (*Epistle* 101.13f.), the only atonement possible for one in whom *natura* had 'perverted her own established laws' (942f.). The penalty is paid (976). The briefest of odes articulates the irresistible power of fate and the resulting impotence of the participants in this or any human event, and makes way for a sixth and final act in which Jocasta confronts her blinded son, proclaims the guilt of fate (1019), and suicides by plunging Oedipus' sword into her womb. Oedipus is left to upbraid the 'lying Phoebus' (for he has 'surpassed his impious fates', 1046) and to leave the stage accompanied by 'Ravaging Fates, Disease's dreadful tremor, | Wasting, black Pestilence, and rabid Pain' (1059f.). The pathos of Oedipus' farewell to his daughters that marks the end of Sophocles' drama is not to be found in Seneca's stark conclusion. Oedipus is as alone at the end as he was at the beginning. The reversal of fortune that defines the Greek tragedy is not an issue in Seneca. It is a strangely unpitying sight.[20]

There were many dramatisations of the Oedipus saga between Sophocles and Seneca. And as with his other plays Seneca's *Oedipus* rewrites a multitude of texts, many of them now lost. Both Aeschylus and Euripides produced an *Oedipus*, and the subject was popular with later Greek and Hellenistic dramatists. Although the topic was apparently avoided by the great tragedians of republican Rome,[21] it surfaced again in a youthful work of Julius Caesar, who is credited by Suetonius with writing a 'tragedy, *Oedipus*' (Suetonius *Iulius* 56.7). In imperial Rome (see below) the subject had particular force. The main palimpsestic counterpoint, however, is with Sophocles' famous play, which would have been well known to the educated elite of imperial Rome. And what the rewriting of Sophocles presents is a distinct and distinctively Roman world. Jocasta's opening speech is both Stoic and Roman:

> quid iuuat, coniunx, mala
> grauare questu? regium hoc ipsum reor:
> aduersa capere, quoque sit dubius magis
> status et cadentis imperi moles labet,
> hoc stare certo pressius fortem gradu:
> haud est uirile terga fortunae dare.
>
> (*Oedipus* 81–6)

> How does it help, husband,
> To load distress with complaint? A king I think
> Should seize adversity; the more doubtful
> His position and imminent his empire's fall,
> The firmer he should stand brave and steadfast.
> He is no man who turns his back on fortune.

The issue of man's epistemological status and that status' relationship to the possibilities for human achievement, moral fulfilment, even 'happiness', is at the centre of Sophocles' play. Seneca is concerned with power, its ideology and its rhetoric. Oedipus begins by talking about its false allure, and in his interviews with Creon in Act 3 and the herdsmen in Act 4 he uses his power in the form of threatened violence (or actual imprisonment) to bring about his own destruction. What the audience witnesses in Acts 2 and 3 is not simply the universe's reaction or 'sympathy' at the divine, earthly and infernal levels; what it witnesses quite specifically are empowerment mechanisms of the Roman state – divine consultation, sacrifice, extispicy – major institutionalised Roman practices, disintegrating, as the whole state has, under the impact of Oedipus' perversion. Their disintegration leads almost inevitably to necromancy, for explicit confirmation of the truth. Note how at the end of Act 2 the Roman nature of the processes dramatised is signalled. When Oedipus is expressly told that it is 'taboo' or *nefas* for him to have direct contact with the dead (398f.), the Roman model behind his presentation, the emperor as *pontifex maximus* or chief priest, to whom such taboo applied, is clearly visible.

The presentation of Oedipus in fact has more in common with a Tacitean portrait of a Julio-Claudian emperor than with Sophocles' protagonist. Oedipus is self-consciously guilty from the start, driven by a mixture of negative emotions, primarily by fear. Here is Tacitus' account of Nero after the murder of his mother:

> sed a Caesare perfecto demum scelere magnitudo eius intellecta est. reliquo noctis modo per silentium defixus, saepius pauore exsurgens et mentis inops lucem opperiebatur tamquam exitium adlaturam.
>
> (*Annals* 14.10.1)

> But Caesar, when the crime was finally accomplished, understood its magnitude. For the rest of the night, sometimes dumb and stupefied, more often starting up in panic and out of his mind, he awaited the daylight as if it would bring his doom.

The world Oedipus rules is consumed by plague. Land, animals, citizens of Thebes, even and especially the air,[22] are infected with Oedipus' contagion. Nor in Seneca does either the world or the contagion seem able to be controlled. Though humbling, the demonstration of the limits of human knowledge and power in *Oedipus Tyrannus* does not preclude some hope and the possibility of human order. Seneca's play offers little consolation at the end that the plague-ridden world will be cured by Oedipus' departure. What the Roman *Oedipus* insists upon is the irresistible force of fate and the absoluteness of human passivity before its ordinances:[23]

> fatis agimur: cedite fatis.
> non sollicitae possunt curae

mutare rati stamina fusi.
quidquid patimur mortale genus,
quidquid facimus uenit ex alto,
seruatque suae decreta colus
Lachesis dura reuoluta manu.
omnia certo tramite uadunt
primusque dies dedit extremum:
non illa deo uertisse licet
quae nexa suis currunt causis.
it cuique ratus prece non ulla
    mobilis ordo:
multis ipsum metuisse nocet,
multi ad fatum uenere suum
    dum fata timent.
              (*Oedipus* 980–94)

Fate drives us: yield to fate.
Anxiety cannot change
The destined spindle's threads.
What we mortals suffer,
What we do comes from high,
And Lachesis keeps the distaff's
Decrees her stern hand unwinds.
All moves on the appointed path;
The first day fixed the last.
No god can change these things
Speeding on their causal web.
For all, a fixed order proceeds
    Immune to prayer.
Fear itself unfixes many;
Many come to their fate
    Dreading fate.

This play's chorus dwell pervasively on fate, from their first to their final ode, exploiting to the full the semiotic ambiguities of *fatum*, 'what is said', 'death', and 'destiny'.[24] The unique fifth ode, given in its brief entirety above, brings choric preoccupation to a definitive and defining climax. No Stoic providence, *fatum* here is the 'fixed order' (*ratus ordo*) of things, the unimpedable mechanism of history, a causal patterning unaffected by divine or human intervention, which generates event upon event indifferent to issues of morality, justice or desert – the very mechanism of history which produced Rome and its civilisation, the great republic and the empire, the ideology of the Camilli, Scipios, and the Gracchi, and the Julio-Claudian monarchy.

arma uirumque cano, Troiae qui primus ab oris
Italiam *fato* profugus Lauiniaque uenit
litora . . .

(Virgil *Aeneid* 1.1–3)

Arms I sing and a man, who first from Troy's shores
By *fate* came exiled to Italy and Lavinian
Coasts . . .

Identified in the philosophical works (*De Beneficiis* 4.8) with 'fortune', 'nature' and 'divine reason' (*diuina ratio*), fate or *fatum* is morally more ambiguous throughout the tragedies, where its association with death is especially emphasised and its control over the human and natural worlds often more malignant than providential. In almost all the tragedies too fate or history is cyclic, and this cyclicity clarifies and underscores its determinism. So in *Oedipus*, where the chorus' Bacchic ode (435ff.), the necromancy scene (615ff.) and the play's subsequent dialogue (933, 1004ff.) present the prot-agonist's 'crimes' as a continuation of the impious history of the house of Cadmus. It is a continuation which the play also shows – through Apollo's oracle (237), Manto's extispicy (321ff., 360ff.), Laius' ghost (646) and the prescripts of the myth – has not yet ended.

Within this cycle of sin Oedipus' 'guilt' is notoriously problematic. It is also central to the play's dramatisation of imperial impotence. Oedipus is and is not guilty.

fati ista culpa est: nemo fit fato nocens.
(*Oedipus* 1019)

Fate is to blame: fate makes no one guilty.

Jocasta's one line utterance has the climactic force of any such statement in a play's final act. But yet Oedipus has felt his guilt from the start (28ff.) and later only vainly protests his innocence (661ff., 766f.) in an attempt to avoid the confirmation provided by supernatural signs, which themselves signal the inescapable nature of his guilt. Oedipus' self-punishment is climax to his own acknowledgement of this guilt. Legal language abounds in Oedipus' self-descriptions and in the play as a whole:

incolumis asto – scilicet Phoebi reus.
sperare poteras sceleribus tantis dari
regnum salubre? fecimus caelum nocens.
(*Oedipus* 34–6)

I stand apart untouched – damned by Phoebus.
Can one expect sin like mine to receive
A healthy realm? I have made the air guilty.

99

natura uersa est; nulla lex utero manet.
(Oedipus 371)

Nature's perverted; the womb preserves no law.

saeculi crimen uagor,
odium deorum, iuris exitium sacri,
qua luce primum spiritus hausi rudes
iam morte dignus.
(Oedipus 875–8)

I wander
The age's crime, the gods' odium, holy law's
Devastation, since first I drank virgin air
Already deserving death.

praedicta postquam fata et infandum genus
deprendit ac se scelere conuictum Oedipus
damnauit ipse . . .
(Oedipus 915–17)

When Oedipus saw his predicted fate
And unspeakable nature, and condemned himself
Convicted of the crime . . .

iam iusta feci, debitas poenas tuli.
(Oedipus 976)

Now justice is done; I've paid due penalty.

In fact the whole of Oedipus' reported speech of self-condemnation in Act 5 is redolent with the language of crime, punishment and law (see also 926f., 936–47). Jocasta too, despite her *fati ista culpa* declaration, condemns herself with the force and language of law:

omne confusum perit,
incesta, per te iuris humani decus.
(Oedipus 1025f.)

Through you, incestuous woman,
All glory of human law confounded dies.

All this takes place within a causal framework asserting the determinism of history. The result is that law itself, Rome's prime institution of social order, is as severely problematised in this play as the concept of moral guilt, perhaps reduced to a verbal nullity. So too are the conceptual concomitants of law: moral responsibility, justice, punishment, crime – and reason. What value reason in a world where Oedipus' rational attempt to avoid patricide and incest actually generates them? What value virtue in a world where virtuous intent produces a moral monstrosity and almost unbearable guilt?[25] What value humanity when its boundaries so easily dissolve and personal identity becomes as obscure as the play's 'uncertain sun' (*Titan dubius*, 1)? This is no Stoic world, but one irremediably diseased.

And what of imperial Rome? The date of *Oedipus*, like that of the other plays, is unknown. Both Suetonius and Dio mention 'Oedipus' as one of Nero's favourite tragic roles,[26] and rumours of his incest with his mother Agrippina, whom he later had killed, were widespread. What is particularly striking about the ending of Seneca's *Oedipus* in this regard is the manner of Jocasta's death. She does not hang herself as in the Sophoclean play, but plays the true Roman by suiciding with a sword. It is Oedipus' sword, as with Phaedra it was Hippolytus' sword, and she plunges it in her womb:

> hunc, dextra, hunc pete
> uterum capacem, qui uirum et gnatos tulit.
> > (*Oedipus* 1038f.)

> Strike here, my hand, here,
> This teeming womb which bore sons and husband.

In Seneca's other 'Oedipus' play, *Phoenissae*, Jocasta demands of her sons Eteocles and Polynices:

> hunc petite uentrem, qui dedit fratres uiro.
> > (*Phoenissae* 447)

> Strike this belly which gave a husband brothers.

Here is how the dramatist of the pseudo-Senecan *Octavia*, probably written shortly after Nero's death,[27] describes the murder of Nero's mother Agrippina:

> caedis moriens illa ministrum
> > rogat infelix,
> utero dirum condat ut ensem:
> 'hic est, hic est fodiendus' ait
> 'ferro, monstrum qui tale tulit.'
> > (*Octavia* 368–72)

> Dying, the poor woman asks
> > Death's minister
> To sink his foul sword in her womb:
> 'Here, here stab with your steel
> The place which bore such a monster.'

Tacitus describes the same death thus:

circumsistunt lectum percussores et prior trierarchus fusti caput eius adflixit. iam in mortem centurioni ferrum destringenti protendens uterum 'uentrem feri' exclamauit multisque uulneribus confecta est.

(*Annals* 14.8.4)

The assassins surround her couch, and first the trireme captain struck her head with a club. Then, as the centurion drew his sword for the death-blow, thrusting forward her womb she shouted, 'Strike the belly', and was despatched with many wounds.

The coincidence of phraseology is remarkable. If *Oedipus* is a late play, it is possible that Seneca is alluding to some story concerning Agrippina's death, to which *Octavia*'s author and Tacitus also allude. Or perhaps both authors saw in Seneca's presentation of Jocasta a suitable model for their account of Nero's mother, one which carried implications of incest and moral perversion at the heart of the late Julio-Claudian court. Tacitus indeed seems to combine quite specifically both *Oedipus* and *Phoenissae* in his narrative, and draws attention to the theatrical quality of Agrippina's death not only by such allusion but by inverting natural speech. Agrippina does not thrust forward her belly and say strike the womb; she does the opposite. Whatever the precise ramifications of Seneca's extraordinary play, his *Oedipus* has rewritten Sophocles to present a Roman world.[28]

ROME INSCRIBED: *PHOENISSAE* AND *HERCVLES FVRENS*

Two other plays may be mentioned in connection with Seneca's inscription of Rome on and in Greek texts: *Phoenissae* and *Hercules Furens*. The former, titled *Thebais* in the A MS tradition, is Seneca's dramatisation of the conflict between the sons of Oedipus, Eteocles and Polynices, over the throne of Thebes. Discussion of the play is complicated by its evidently incomplete nature. *Phoenissae* lacks choral odes, possibly intentionally. The suggestion that Seneca devised the play as an experimental, unchorused drama is not unattractive.[29] Since, however, the action breaks off abruptly at line 664 without any resolution of the play's issues or any signs of the dramatic closure evident in the remaining seven plays, what we have seems clearly unfinished. Even so, it is apparent that, although Seneca alludes to several plays (including Aeschylus' *Seven against Thebes*, Sophocles' *Oedipus Tyrannus* and *Oedipus at Colonus*, Ennius' *Sabinae*, Accius' *Phoenissae* and, if it is the earlier play, his own *Oedipus*), his primary text is Euripides' *Phoenissae*, which he has rewritten, even 'lacerated',[30] to throw a distinctly Roman emphasis on fratricide and civil war, on power, and on the ineffectuality of *pietas* before ambition and the drive to dominate. The attempt of Jocasta to mediate between her warring sons (*Phoenissae* 443–664) conspicuously echoes such exemplary scenes from Roman history as those of Veturia and Coriolanus, and of the Sabine women and their warring menfolk (Livy 1.13, 2.40; also cf. Ennius *Sabinae* fr. 370 Vahlen[3] and *Phoenissae* 571). Such scenes showed the triumph of *pietas* over the naked lust for power, and were inscribed in the Roman self, foundational to its justification of empire. Jocasta shows the failure of *pietas*, and she does so in the dramatisation of a myth which had become conspicuously politicised in the Roman tradition. From the first century BCE onwards, the Eteocles–Polynices fratricidal conflict became established as a mythic paradigm of the fratricidal realities of the Roman world. It is debatable whether the Theban saga lurks as a paradigm behind Catullus' amalgam of fratricide, filicide and incest which functions for him as a metaphor for the social and moral distemper of late republican Rome (64.397ff.). It was certainly on people's minds and lips. Cicero in a discussion of the inseparability of expediency and moral good (*De Officiis* 3.82) refers to Julius Caesar's habit of quoting the famous Euripidean lines (*Phoenissae* 524f.) in which Eteocles justifies power at the cost of moral right and advocates the confinement of *pietas* (in Greek *eusebia*) to private life. Propertius summarises the subject-matter of his friend Ponticus' *Thebaid* with words – *armaque frater-nae tristia militiae*, 'and the grim arms of brothers fighting' (1.7.2) – that seem intentionally to double for the Roman civil wars of his youth. Two generations later in the reign of Tiberius the tragedian Mamercus Aemilius Scaurus was sentenced to death because of his *Atreus*, which rather unwisely made use of Euripides' *Phoenissae* 393: 'The folly of princes has to be endured' (Dio *Roman History* 58.24.4). If Thebes was a model of 'the other' for Athens, a *cacotopia* in which the boundaries of family and the city are dissolved,[31] for Rome it was, as Statius later demonstrated, a model of itself.

This is why Seneca's *Phoenissae* throws into prominence the issue of incest. In Euripides' play, in which Oedipus is still at Thebes, incest seems deliberately underplayed, in striking contrast with the moral horror its revelation causes in Sophocles' *Oedipus Tyrannus*, whose messenger can say 'parricide' but has no words for Oedipus' sexual engagement with his mother (*Oedipus Tyrannus* 1288f.). Seneca reverts to the Sophoclean treatment and amplifies it.[32] Parricide is played down; in his *Oedipus*, but most especially in *Phoenissae*, incest becomes both the 'major crime', *maius scelus* (*Oedipus* 17, *Phoenissae* 269), and the major motif. The reason for this is caught up paradoxically with the Roman treatment of death. Romans attached enormous importance to the dead, whose innumerable monuments, often expensive and ostentatious, adorned the highways leading to the city of Rome, and whose exemplary deeds imposed upon the present with the force of a religious imperative (*mos maiorum*). Romans revered their ancestors as deified spirits. Two major religious festivals were held annually for the care and commemoration of the dead: the twelve-day *Parentalia* in February, which dealt specifically with the spirits of one's dead parents, and the older festival of the *Lemuria* in May, which embraced the spirits of all members of the household. In addition at the *Rosalia* in May and June roses were sprinkled on the tombs and funerary portraits of the deceased. In the atrium of the houses of the Roman nobility were kept (sometimes within a wooden shrine) the *imagines*, the ancestral portrait-busts and painted funeral masks, which were paraded in family funeral processions and at public sacrifices both for display and to inspire. At the ancestral tomb itself, whether individual or collective, an annual banquet was normally held (often on the anniversary of the deceased's birthday) in which both the living and the dead participated.[33] Romans lived in a world peopled by their dead ancestors, whose presence confirmed not only 'core civic values',[34] but the importance of the family line, its integrity and continuance in defining Roman order and success. The purity of the blood-line, especially the male blood-line, essential to maintaining that integrity, was sacrosanct.

Hence the extraordinary preoccupation with adultery in *Thyestes*, which climaxes in vindication of the purity of Atreid blood: 'Now the true palm is won . . . Now I believe the children | Mine, now chastity restored to my bed' (*Thyestes* 1097ff.). Like adultery, incest implodes this cornerstone of Roman identity. In *Phaedra* the outburst of Hippolytus (688ff.) focuses on monstrous offspring, that of Theseus on the contamination of blood (*generis infandi lues*, 'foul infection of our race', 905). In Seneca's (but not Sophocles') *Oedipus* the ancestor himself appears (*Oedipus* 624ff.), and hurls at his son 'the greatest crime at Thebes', incest or 'mother love', *maternus amor* (630), railing against his 'impious progeny' (626ff.). Laius appears again (at least to Oedipus' mind) in *Phoenissae* (39ff.), and again the object of prime attention is not parricide. Incest becomes even more than in *Oedipus* the main issue, dominating the long, controversial opening 'act' (319 lines in length), in which Seneca replaces the Euripidean Jocasta's expositional prologue with a 'return to origins' scene, exhibiting 'the blind Oedipus' (*Oedipus excaecatus*: according to Suetonius one of Nero's favourite roles, *Nero* 21.3) as paradigm and as spectacle. Before Mount Cithaeron, where Oedipus was exposed as an infant, Oedipus discusses with his daughter Antigone his crimes against kin and his need for punishment and death, focusing most of all on incest, which has overturned nature's laws and generated a *nefanda domus*, an 'unspeakable house' (80). 'Grandfather's son-in-law and father's rival, | His children's brother and brothers' father' (134–5), he has become a riddle more inextricable than that of the Sphinx which he had solved; his incest is 'a crime, unknown, bestial, unprecedented . . . which puts even a parricide to shame' (264ff.): *nullum crimen hoc maius potest | natura ferre*, 'nature can endure no greater crime than this' (272f.). The substance of the rest of this dramatic 'fragment' is Jocasta's attempt to prevent the fraticidal duel. Recent analyses, however, plausibly suggest an ending to the play (based on Euripides' *Phoenissae*), in which the Theban brothers' mutual slaughter is followed by Jocasta's suicide with the sword of one of her dead or dying sons (possibly the sword with which Oedipus had killed his father, 106f.) plunged into her womb (in Euripides it is the throat: *Phoenissae* 1457).[35] Oedipus' command for a horror greater than fratricide, an incestuous union between his sons and Jocasta (*date arma matri*, 'give mother your weapons', 358), would thus at least be symbolically fulfilled.[36] Such an ending would not only continue the motif of symbolically incestuous matricide/suicide dramatised by Jocasta in *Oedipus*' final act, but also complete (in a typically Senecan mode of closure) *Phoenissae*'s own circle of incestuous parricidal horror. Such climactic treatment of 'incestuous' death over the bodies of fratricidal sons would be more than structurally appropriate. For what is dramatised most singularly in *Phoenissae* is not only civil war, the corruption of power, and the inseparable conjunction of political and social malaise, but the conjunction of all of them with the degeneracy and moral implosion of a ruling family.

It is on the issue of power that this fragmentary drama ends. And it does so with conspicuous echoes of Accius' famous apothegm put in the mouth of Atreus: *oderint dum metuant*, 'let them hate, provided they fear' (fr. 168 Warmington). Jocasta debates with Eteocles the desirability of power:

> *Iocasta* Regna, dummodo inuisus tuis.
> *Eteocles* Regnare non uult esse qui inuisus timet.
>   simul ista mundi conditor posuit deus,
>   odium atque regnum: regis hoc magni reor,
>   odia ipsa premere. multa dominantem uetat
>   amor suorum; plus in iratos licet.
>   qui uult amari, languida regnat manu.
> *Io.*   Inuisa numquam imperia retinentur diu.
> *Et.*   Praecepta melius imperi reges dabunt;
>   exilia tu dispone.[37] pro regno uelim –
> *Io.*   Patriam penates coniugem flammis dare?
> *Et.*   Imperia pretio quolibet constant bene.
>   (*Phoenissae* 653–64)

> *Jocasta* Rule, but hated by your people.
> *Eteocles* The man who fears hate has no desire to rule.
>   God who created the world joined these two:
>   Hate and sovereignty. Great kings define themselves
>   By crushing hate. The people's love inhibits
>   A monarch greatly; against their rage he's free.
>   The man who desires love rules with a weak hand.
> *Jo.*   Hated power is never maintained long.
> *Et.*   The rules of power are given by kings;
>   Exile is your domain. For sovereignty I'd –
> *Jo.*   Hand your country, gods, and wife to the flames?
> *Et.*   Power is well bought whatever the price.

Here *Phoenissae*, as we have it, ends. According to Suetonius (*Gaius* 30.1), Caligula often quoted the Accian text behind this dialogue. Seneca too quotes it in his prose works when handling the issue of tyranny (see, e.g., *De Clementia* 1.12.4, 2.2.2, *De Ira* 1.20.4). At the ending of *Phoenissae* Seneca has taken the preoccupation with power and tyranny which late republican tragedy and his own tragedies (with *Phoenissae* 660, cf. *Medea* 196, *Thyestes* 215ff.) and philosophical 'dialogues' addressed, and wedded it to the main mythic paradigm of civic and individual disorder. He has done so to continue his dramatisation of the social, political and moral implosion defining early imperial Rome.

In *Hercules Furens*, the longest of the extant Senecan plays, Euripides is again the tragedian inscribed with Rome. Although some Hellenistic or Augustan treatments may have influenced Seneca,[38] dramas dealing with Hercules' madness seem to have been comparatively rare and there is little doubt that Seneca's primary dramatic subtext is Euripides' *Heracles*. Euripides' dramatisation of Heracles' triumphant return from the underworld, his slaughter of the usurping tyrant Lycus, descent into madness and murder of his wife and children becomes the basis in Seneca of a dramatic critique of the central Roman value, *uirtus*. Divided by the Stoics into moderation, bravery, prudence and justice (*temperantia, fortitudo, prudentia, iustitia*, Seneca *Epistle* 120.11), and aligned by them with *ratio* or 'reason', *uirtus* is dramatised pervasively in this play as 'manliness' or 'valour' in its crudest and most popular sense, namely physical prowess and power, independent of any intellectual or moral quality. Even the poor man's Hercules, Lycus, claims *uirtus* (340). It is at the centre of his dialogue with Megara:

> *Lycus* Obici feris monstrisque uirtutem putas?
> *Megara* Virtutis est domare quae cuncti pauent.
> (Hercules Furens 434f.)

> *Lycus* Think it 'valour' to fight beasts and monsters?
> *Megara* It's 'valour' to master what all men dread.

Hercules' wife is soon to feel the effects of that 'valour' gone mad. Indeed for Hercules, who identifies and even addresses himself as *uirtus* (1157; see also 1315),[39] *uirtus* is intimately bound to physical force, to what his 'hands' can do. The words *manus*, 'hand', and *dextra*, 'right hand', dominate the linguistic texture of this play as of no other, and pervade most especially both Hercules' own dialogue and the descriptions by others of Hercules' power.[40] The chorus, who provide ambivalent, at times critical presentation of Hercules' *uirtus animosa* ('spirited valour') throughout the play, voices also ironically the most ringing laudation of this power at the moment of Hercules' triumphant return from the killing of the tyrant:

> pax est Herculea manu
> Auroram inter et Hesperum,

et qua sol medium tenens
umbras corporibus negat.
(*Hercules Furens* 882–5)

Peace has come from Hercules' hand
From the Dawn to Hesperus,
And where the sun in mid-heaven
Denies bodies their shadows.

This 'hand', however, is also the instrument of anger, violent aggression and narcissistic, megalomaniacal ambition, an amalgam of passions or *affectus* which move easily into madness and genocide. The Euripidean gods, Iris and Lyssa (*Heracles* 822ff.), are not required to make Hercules mad; this play dramatises a 'continuity between the sane and insane mind',[41] even as it directs its bloody theatricalisation of the underside of *uirtus* at the early imperial world. The resonances of *pax Romana* in the chorus' proclamation of universal peace (in Euripides the chorus' laudation at this juncture is only for the deliverance of Thebes: *Heracles* 763–814)[42] are no isolated signals, but index of the text as Roman rescript.

The whole drama is saturated with Roman imagery and motifs. Euripides begins his *Heracles* with dialogue between Amphitryon and Megara (Act 2 in Seneca); Seneca recasts Virgil's (and Ovid's) Juno to provide from the start a Roman frame,[43] and confirms that frame not only through continuing Virgilian and Ovidian allusion, but through triumphal, military, legal and imperial imagery permeating both prologue (see esp. 46ff., 57ff.) and play (military and legal motifs compete for dominance in Act 5), and through motifs and language of religion, sacrifice (see esp. 634ff., 895–939), theatre and amphitheatre (esp. 838f., 939ff.)[44] especially potent to a Roman audience. Striking in its appeal to Roman structures is a scene such as the moment of Hercules' return from his slaughter of Lycus when the motifs of triumph and sacrifice combine:

nunc sacra patri uictor et superis feram
caesisque meritas uictimis aras colam.
(*Hercules Furens* 898f.)

Now my victor's offerings to father and the gods;
I'll honour his altar with victims duly slain.

Or when the ceremonial language of sacrifice is used to describe insane murder:

tibi hunc dicatum, maximi coniunx Iouis,
gregem cecidi; uota persolui libens
te digna, et Argos uictimas alias dabit.
(*Hercules Furens* 1036–8)

For thee, wife of almighty Jove, I've slain
This consecrated herd; I gladly paid vows
Worthy of you. Argos will give more victims.

So the deranged Hercules on the murder of his children. Interesting is the phrase *te digna*, 'worthy of you'. *Dignus* with the ablative is used elsewhere in this play, often by Hercules in heavily ironic contexts; at 927 he conceives prayers 'worthy of Jove and himself', *Ioue meque dignas*, just before the onset of madness; when madness descends he desires to assault the heavens, 'a task worthy of Alcides', *dignus Alcide labor* (957). Suetonius claims to quote an imperial rescript of Nero, during his infamous tour of Greece 66–7 CE, suggesting that the advice from Rome should be that he 'return worthy of Nero' (*ut Nerone dignus reuertar, Nero* 23.1). This may well have been a mannerism of Nero's. Similarly Hercules' competition with Jove may have reminded the audience of Caligula's insane attempt to replace Jupiter (Suetonius *Gaius* 22). What is clear is that from the late republic onwards politicians and emperors, most notably Augustus and Nero, had associated themselves with Hercules;[45] and, like Seneca's Hercules (926ff.), Augustus and Nero claimed to inaugurate a new Golden Age.[46] In Nero's case the association seems especially developed. Not only did the emperor have coins minted inscribed with the legend 'To Hercules Augustus' (*Herculi Augusto*), but Suetonius reports (*Nero* 21.3; see also Dio *Roman History* 63.9.4) that one of the tragic parts Nero particularly liked 'to sing' was that of *Hercules insanus*, 'Hercules Mad'.[47] The criticism in Juno's prologue of Hercules' being 'storied as a god on earth' (39f.) and of his own desire for Olympus (74) rewrites Euripides' underplaying of Heracles' destined divinity to frame the drama with contemporary imperial fictions. Recollection of Ovid's similar criticisms ('where you can, humankind, you aim for the heavens too: Romulus has his temple, and Bacchus and Hercules and now Caesar [*modo Caesar*]', *Amores* 3.8.51f.) makes the code overt. And this is not to mention Theseus' exclusive focus on princes in his non-Euripidean (and non-Virgilian)[48] account of the judgement of the dead:

> quod quisque fecit, patitur; auctorem scelus
> repetit suoque premitur exemplo nocens.
> uidi cruentos carcere includi duces
> et impotentis terga plebeia manu
> scindi tyranni. quisquis est placide potens
> dominusque uitae seruat innocuas manus
> et incruentum mitis imperium regit
> animoque parcit, longa permensus diu
> felicis aeui spatia uel caelum petit
> uel laeta felix nemoris Elysii loca,
> iudex futurus. sanguine humano abstine

quicumque regnas: scelera taxantur modo
maiore uestro.

(Hercules Furens 735–47)

Each suffers his own deeds; to its author crime
Returns, the guilty crushed by his example.
I saw blood-stained leaders incarcerated
And the raging tyrant's flesh ripped from his back
By the people's hand. The gentle monarch
And life's master who keeps his hands guiltless
And rules his empire mildly without blood,
Restraining his spirit, measures out long tracts
Of fruitful life and makes for the heavens,
Or for the joyful site of Elysium's grove,
Blessed – there to judge. Abstain from human blood
All you who rule: your crimes, they are assessed
One hundredfold.

The Roman political and social term, *plebeia*, 'belonging to the people' (738), intensifies the contemporary force of this description. So too does Theseus' concluding address (745–7), dramatically arresting as it is inappropriate. It's as if the character has stepped out of the play and is haranguing the audience (or certain members in it). Seneca could not be less opaque.

Other contemporary modes pervade this drama: Stoic ones. In the Greek and Roman literary traditions Hercules was an ambivalent figure: a wielder of just force and civiliser on the one hand, a hybristic, brutish thug on the other.[49] Stoic moral theory focused on the former image, and cast him regularly as a model of the Stoic *sapiens* or 'sage' and of the *uirtus* which defined him, especially the sage's ability to endure adversity. He was also paraded by the Stoics as a benefactor of mankind, a 'pacifier of land and sea', *terrarum marisque pacator*, as Seneca calls him in *De Beneficiis* (1.13.3). The latter 'title' belonged also to the emperor's image.[50] And while *Hercules Furens* exhibits the gap between this image (*pacis auctorem*, 250; cf. 441ff.), especially self-image (926ff.), and the manic violence which is the reality and which problematises the whole concept of *uirtus*, it comes closer than any of the surviving plays to promoting a Stoic value. One of Seneca's most extraordinary innovations in this play is its ending, which not only secures the connection to the contemporary intellectual and political world but is quite unlike anything else in Senecan drama.[51] In Euripides Heracles' suicidal state of mind is changed perhaps rather easily by Theseus' offer of refuge in Athens (*Heracles* 1311ff.). In Seneca Hercules' decision not to kill himself requires a dramatically arresting scene, Amphitryon's suicide attempt, in which Amphitryon makes it clear that his own death will be Hercules' responsibility and 'sane' crime: *aut uiuis aut occidis* ('your choice is life or murder', 1308). Hercules responds as follows to this attempt and to Amphitryon as father:

109

iam parce, genitor, parce, iam reuoca manum.
succumbe, uirtus, perfer imperium patris.
eat ad labores hic quoque Herculeos labor:
uiuamus.

(Hercules Furens 1314–17)

Now hold, father, hold, now withdraw your hand.
Yield, valour, endure a father's command.
To Hercules' labours add one labour more:
Let us live.

'It is the mark of a mighty heart to remain alive for another's sake', wrote
Seneca in *Epistle* 104. Hercules complies. Gone is the Lucretia paradigm: 'If I
live, I committed sin; if I die, I suffered it', *si uiuo, feci scelera; si morior, tuli*
(1278). Gone is the Aeneas paradigm and its conflation of *uirtus* and *arma*.
Victim of Juno's *furor*, Hercules yet resists the impulse to violence which
marks the end of Rome's great epic. Gone too, perhaps most importantly,
are the claims of divine paternity and status (1157ff., 1202ff.). Indifferent
earlier to the emotional suffering of his family (the Euripidean Heracles'
speech of affection for wife and children, *Her.* 621–36, is omitted by Seneca),
Hercules responds with recognition of his all too obvious humanity and of
the importance of the ties of kin. The *pietas uirtusque* for which the chorus
earlier prayed (1093f.) return to Hercules but in an unexpected, and (in part)
Stoic form. *Pietas* is dramatised as a human virtue displayed in the behaviour
of men to men, *uirtus* as the ability to resist violence, even to submit. The
values perverted by, and the self-knowledge absent from, the Julio-Claudian
court are affirmed as the basis of human salvation. But that salvation will not
come easily, as Hercules' agony reveals in words which the Renaissance did
not forget:

quis Tanais aut quis Nilus aut quis Persica
uiolentus unda Tigris aut Rhenus ferox
Tagusue Hibera turbidus gaza fluens
abluere dextram poterit? Arctoum licet
Maeotis in me gelida transfundat mare
et tota Tethys per meas currat manus,
haerebit altum facinus.

(Hercules Furens 1323–9)

What Tanais, what Nile or what Tigris
Raging with Persian flood or frenzied Rhine
Or Tagus whirling torrents of Spanish gold
Can cleanse this hand? Let icy Maeotis
Pour its arctic sea upon me, and Tethys
Stream across my hands with all her waters,
The crime will stick unmoved.

The hand which murdered his children (1192f.) and was to murder the 'impious monstrosity', *monstrum impium* (1280), he had become is also the hand which his father clasps (1319). It can be cleansed. The loyal comradeship of Theseus, tolerant towards the 'guilty' (*nocentes*, 1337), will ensure that. This play belongs with *Agamemnon* as offering the possibility of human hope. But it is a hope patently qualified for the world of imperial Rome.

> ubique notus perdidi exilio locum.
> (*Hercules Furens* 1331)

> Known everywhere I've destroyed a place for exile.

Echoing Juno's opening complaint that her place, *locus* (4), has been usurped, Hercules, 'Juno's glory' (= Greek *Herakles*), not only loses his place at Thebes, but laments that no place remains in which he may even hide. The great transgressor of bounded spaces and recent polluter of his own home believes he has destroyed all places, even place itself. He is wrong. For him, as for his great descendant Coriolanus, 'There is a world elsewhere' (*Coriolanus* 3.3.135). Another place 'awaits' (*manet*, 1341), Athens, a place however not for revenge, but for purification, one which can make even gods innocent (1344). To Euripides' Athenian audience the transference of Heracles from Thebes to Athens was a fact of civic history and ideology. The irony for imperial Rome, whose boundaries were coextensive with the civilised world, was that there was no place to go to. Rome was place. The purification of Rome's god (1342f.) predated the existence of Rome. No alternate world now awaited where the *impius* could be cleansed.

6

THE THEATRICALISED
WOR(L)D

Last of all Nero himself came on the stage, scrupulously tuning his lyre
and trying out his voice with his trainers beside him. A company of
soldiers had been added to the audience, centurions and tribunes, and
Burrus, who grieved – and applauded. Then were first enrolled the
Roman knights known as *Augustiani*, visibly strong young men, natural
troublemakers or hungry for power. Day and night they thundered
applause, showering on the emperor's appearance and voice epithets of
the gods.

Tacitus, *Annals* 14.15.3f. (on 59 CE)

Senecan tragedy contains its own autobiography: past and future. The analogies with the past which structure the majority of Senecan plays underscore
Senecan tragedy's relationship to its own past, which it cites and recycles.
The 'anxiety of influence' (to use Bloom's terminology)[1] which dominates
the behaviour of characters such as Phaedra, Hippolytus, Atreus, Thyestes,
Aegisthus, Oedipus, Jocasta, Agamemnon, Helen, Medea mirrors Seneca's
own anxiety before the determining literary past and prescriptive parental
figures of the Graeco-Roman poetic tradition. Dramatic action and dramatic
focus signal properties of the works themselves. It seems no accident, for
example, that Theseus' attempt to put together the separated fragments of
his dismembered son in the final act of *Phaedra* is the construct of a scene
which is itself an attempt by Seneca to put together the separated fragments
of the dismembered *oeuvre* of Euripides – as the Roman dramatist
endeavours to bring together fragments of Euripides' *Hippolytus* and *Bacchae*
into a new, harmonious whole. Appropriate ramifications of Theseus' failure
for the poetics of Senecan tragedy are at hand. What seems involved is not
only Seneca's sense of the impossibility of recreating the Attic form in a
post-classical age, but also his location of discord at the centre of the new
style.[2] Seneca's failed re*membering* articulates his theatrical world. Similarly
introspective is Seneca's preoccupation with the death-from-life paradox –
what creates destroys, the origin of life *is* the origin of death – a paradox

which he pursues dramatically in figures such as Hercules, Thyestes, Theseus and most particularly Medea, and which in *Medea* itself he enlarges into the socio-moral thesis, that what creates civilisation destroys it. Seneca's preoccupation with this paradox reflects critically on his own created work. Literary form gives life; it also gives death. The post-classical declamatory mode, the 'pointed', antithetic, epigrammatic style, which animates Senecan tragedy and gives it moral urgency and life, is the form too which at notorious moments in the history of European scholarship and taste killed it.[3]

Importantly the self-reflection of Senecan tragedy extends to its status as theatre.[4] The dithyrambic chorus of *Oedipus* (403–508), unique to Seneca's plays, images the god of drama, Bacchus, as an unpredictable and ambivalent god of fantastic, even grotesque, transformative power. It takes little imagination to see the ode's bearing on Seneca's theatrical craft. But relevant too, and more profoundly so, is the association in the preceding choral ode of Bacchus and the Theban plague:

> occidis, Cadmi generosa proles,
> urbe cum tota. uiduas colonis
> respicis terras, miseranda Thebe.
> carpitur leto tuus ille, Bacche,
> miles, extremos comes usque ad Indos,
> ausus Eois equitare campis
> figere et mundo tua signa primo.
> (*Oedipus* 110–16)

> You are dying, Cadmus' noble line,
> With all the city. You watch the land
> Widowed of its tillers, pitiable Thebes.
> Death plucks your soldiers, Bacchus,
> Comrades to the farthest Indies,
> Who dared to ride on Eastern plains
> And plant your standards at the world's edge.

Little adjustment is required to see these verses' relevance to imperial Rome. But there is a suggestion too that the transformative process of plague itself, its grotesqueries, violence and carnage, its production of the 'dreadful face of novel death, more grievous than death' (*dira noui facies leti, | grauior leto,* *Oedipus* 180f.; cf. Andromache at *Troades* 783), its metamorphosis of human behaviour, are essentially Bacchic and belong to Seneca's ideology of theatre. Nor only to Seneca's:

> L'action du théâtre, comme celle de la peste, est bienfaisante, car poussant les hommes à se voir tels qu'ils sont, elle fait tomber le masque, elle découvre le mensonge, la veulerie, la bassesse, la tartuferie.
> (Antonin Artaud, *Le Théâtre et la Peste*)[5]

113

The action of the theatre, like that of the plague, is redemptive, because it impels us to see ourselves as we are. It makes the mask fall; it uncovers the lie, the apathy, the contemptibility, the two-facedness.

Seneca's plague, however, strips theatre itself, exposing its 'two-facedness', its own masking, unmasking, and spectatorial constructedness. The recurrent dramatisation of role-playing – in which characters become actors before other characters as audience: Phaedra before Theseus (*Phaedra* 864ff.), Medea before Jason (*Medea* 551ff.), Clytemnestra before Aegisthus (*Agamemnon* 239ff.), Atreus before Thyestes (*Thyestes* 491ff.) – underscores Senecan tragedy's own conventions and artifice. So too the related focus on characters as audience, on action as spectacle,[6] on human behaviour as self-dramatisation; or the staging in *Medea* and *Thyestes* of a character's own staging as character, actor and dramaturge of the climactic evil itself. Such features reveal an overt metatheatrical dimension to Senecan tragedy, a concern to draw attention to its own theatricality.[7] In Seneca theatrical form self-consciously structures the presentation of human action. His tragedies point to themselves as verbal and performative constructs of the theatrical imagination. They are language theatricalised.

The theatricalised word has ramifications beyond itself. Early imperial Rome was emphasised above as a palimpsestic world on the verge of dissolution. It was also most obviously a histrionic one. Augustus' death-bed request (as reported by Suetonius: *Augustus* 99.1) to be applauded from the 'stage' of life for the part he had acted in 'life's drama/farce' (*mimus uitae*) indexes the tenor of the times. Imperial and non-imperial role-playing dominates Tacitus' extant account of the Augustan, Tiberian and Claudian principates (*Annals* 1–6, 11–12). In the narrative of Nero's reign (13–16) and its immediate aftermath 'acting' is elevated into the emblematic metaphor of the age. The distinction between play and public reality disappears. The play literally is the thing. The young emperor's initial 'mimicries of sorrow' (*tristiae imitamentis, Annals* 13.4) at the funeral of his stepfather Claudius lead into insistent attention not only to Nero's appearances on the stage but to the political and social imperatives of role-playing in the theatricalised world of imperial Rome, where citizens mourn what they welcome (16.7), applaud what they grieve (14.15), offer thanksgivings for monstrous murder (14.59, 64), and celebrate triumphs for national humiliation (15.18) or horrendous and impious sin (14.12f.). Tacitus' account of the mass executions attending the Pisonian conspiracy of 65 CE culminates in the ugly theatre of Roman servility:

sed compleri interim urbs funeribus, Capitolium uictimis; alius filio, fratre alius aut propinquo aut amico interfectis, agere grates deis, ornare lauru domum, genua ipsius aduolui et dextram osculis fatigare.

(*Annals* 15.71)

Funerals abounded in the city, thank-offerings on the Capitol. Men who had lost a son or brother or relative or friend gave thanks to the gods, bedecked their houses with laurel and fell at the feet of Nero, kissing his hand incessantly.

To be noted too is the people's reaction to Otho's conspiracy four years later, 69 CE:

> uniuersa iam plebs Palatium implebat, mixtis seruitiis et dissono clamore caedem Othonis et coniuratorum exitium poscentium ut si in circo aut theatro ludicrum aliquod postularent. neque illis iudicium aut ueritas, quippe eodem die diuersa pari certamine postulaturis, sed tradito more quemcumque principem adulandi licentia adclamationum et studiis inanibus.

> (Tacitus Histories 1.32)

The whole populace together with slaves now filled the palace, demanding with raucous cries the death of Otho and the destruction of the conspirators as if they were calling for some show in the circus or theatre. They had neither sense nor sincerity (for on the same day they would clamour for the opposite with equal passion), but followed the convention of flattering whoever was emperor with unlimited applause and empty enthusiasm.

And the response of the same people later in the year to the battle between the Vitellian and Flavian armies in the streets of Rome:

> aderat pugnantibus spectator populus, utque in ludicro certamine hos rursus illos clamore et plausu fouebat . . . alibi proelia et uulnera, alibi balneae popinaeque; simul cruor et strues corporum, iuxta scorta et scortis similes; quantum in luxurioso otio libidinum, quidquid in acerbissima captiuitate scelerum, prorsus ut eandem ciuitatem et furere crederes et lasciuire.

> (Tacitus Histories 3.83)

The people attended the fighting as the audience for a show, and, as with a stage battle, supported now this side, now that, with shouts and applause . . . on one side battles and wounds, on the other bath-houses and snack-bars; blood and heaps of corpses alongside prostitutes and their kind; all the lusts to be found in dissolute peace, all the crimes of a city's most bitter capture, so that in fact you would have believed the same city to be in uproar and frolicking simultaneously.

Seneca in the prose works offers similar representations: Cato is paraded as moral *spectaculum* (*Providentia* 2.9ff.), Lucilius is exhorted to do everything 'as if before a spectator (*tamquam spectet aliquis*)' (*Epistle* 25.5; cf. *Epistle* 11.8ff.), and 'human life' is declared 'a mime-drama, which assigns parts for us to play badly' (*hic humanae uitae mimus, qui nobis partes quas male agamus adsignat, Epistle* 80.7). Though the Stoic goal is the single part, 'we continually change our mask (*personam*) and put on one the very opposite of that we have discarded' (*Epistle* 120.22). Indeed Stoicism as a philosophy abounds in theatrical tropes, as both Greek Stoic writings and Seneca's own *Epistles to Lucilius* testify,[8] demanding from its heroes a capacity for dramatic display and exemplary performance.

Few educated Romans would have found either theatrical self-display or a multiplicity of *personae* difficult. On the contrary, training in *declamatio*, most especially mastery of the *suasoria*, which required diverse and sustained role-playing, gave to contemporary Romans not only the ability to enter into the psychic structure of another, i.e. 'psychic mobility' or 'empathy',[9] but a sub-stantial range of improvisational skills to create a *persona* at will. As works such as Petronius' *Satyricon* exhibit, the cultural and educative system had generated a world of actors. So too had the political system. The younger Pliny's depiction of Nero as 'stage-emperor', *scaenicus imperator* (*Panegyricus* 46.4), catches only one aspect of the theatricality of the times. Nero's public appearances on stage made not only himself but the audience actors, equal objects of spectatorial attention.[10] The rhetorical education of most mem-bers of that audience fitted them well for the required role of approving *spectator*, as for many others. Indeed it is arguable that in early imperial Rome's confounding culture personal identity began to be constructed from the performance of a plurality of politically and socially determined roles, thus collapsing the distinction between *persona* and person. Certainly the dis-tinction between 'reality' and 'theatre' dissolves conspicuously within the theatre-amphitheatre itself, where buildings burn, actors bleed, spectators are thrust into the arena, human and animal bodies dismembered, and pain, suffering, death become objects of the theatrical gaze and of theatrical pleasure.[11] Emperors like Vitellius seek popular support by joining 'the audi-ence at the theatre, supporters at the circus' (*in theatro ut spectator, in circo ut fautor*, Tacitus *Histories* 2.91) only to become later the spectacle itself.

It seems fitting that in this theatricalised world Senecan tragedy draws attention to its own theatricality. *Troades* and *Thyestes* deserve especial notice in this regard. As does *Medea*. In *Thyestes* the metatheatrical note is struck right from the start of the play, when the Fury instructs the 'transcribed' (13) ghost of Tantalus to 'watch' his descendants' cannibalistic drama:

> liberum dedimus diem
> tuamque ad istas soluimus mensas famem:
> ieiunia exple, mixtus in Bacchum cruor
> spectante te potetur.
>
> (*Thyestes* 63–6)

> Today we made you free
> And have unleashed your hunger for this feast.

Fill your famine, watch the blood mixed with wine
Being drunk.

Spectare, 'to watch', is also the term used specifically for theatrical viewing, *spectatores* being the Latin word for 'audience' (*spectatores, plaudite*, 'audience, your applause', Plautus *Curculio* 729).[12] And what the Fury is commanding at the climax of her opening speech in *Thyestes'* prologue is that Tantalus become audience to the very play or plays whose script(s) she elaborated a few lines earlier (25–51), as soon as his prologue performance has achieved its effect: *actum est abunde*, 'Your part has played itself out' (105). Her injunctions display a preoccupation with action as theatre which is to pervade the play.[13] It manifests itself most obviously throughout Acts 2 and 3 in Atreus' mode or even mannerism of self-dramatisation, which begins at his entry into the play with the rejection of the role of 'Atreus Enraged', *iratus Atreus* (180), and continues into his 'plotting' with his script-adviser or minister and his metadramatic inspiration (esp. 250ff.), and into his role-playing before his deluded brother. Noticeable is not only how Atreus acts out the ironic role of loving, forgiving brother, but how through soliloquy he creates a status for himself as audience to his brother's misery and joins with the audience of the play to watch Thyestes' downfall.

> aspice ut multo grauis
> squalore uultus obruat maestos coma,
> quam foeda iaceat barba. praestetur fides.
> fratrem iuuat uidere.
>
> (*Thyestes* 505–8)

> See how matted
> Filthy hair overwhelms his gloomy face,
> How foul his drooping beard. Now for a show of faith.
> It's a joy to view my brother.

So Atreus invites the audience to 'view' with him the unfolding torture, and to appreciate the verbal ironies which he cannot resist. The obvious *coup de théâtre* with which *Thyestes'* central act closes, the coronation of the 'power-resistant' brother with the crown that binds, adds 'dramaturge' and 'director' to Atreus' growing list of credits.

The self-conscious theatricality of Act 3 carries over into the messenger scene which follows, where the adoption of a five 'act' crescendo structure for the narrative of horror (641ff.) signals its dramatic artifice. The play's theatricality reaches both its climax and most overt display in the final act itself, in which Atreus plays again (this time pervasively) character, actor, audience and dramaturge, and controls the most minute details (even the lighting, for the sun has disappeared) of the play's dramatic climax. His main anxiety, when he appears, is that his crime will lack an audience. He has dismissed the gods; it gives him pause:

utinam quidem tenere fugientes deos
possem, et coactos trahere, ut ultricem dapem
omnes uiderent! quod sat est, uideat pater.
(Thyestes 893–5)

O that I could check the fugitive gods
And drag them all against their will to view
My vengeance-feast! Enough – if the father view it.

In the stage-managing of the subsequent horror, the abundant ghoulish ironies, the two stages of revelation, Thyestes' absolute humiliation and pain, Atrean theatricality is unconcealed. Atreus' need of Thyestes not simply as victim but as audience, as spectator to his revenge, structures the revelation itself:

<table>
<tr><td>Atreus</td><td>Expedi amplexus, pater:</td></tr>
<tr><td></td><td>uenere. – natos ecquid agnoscis tuos?</td></tr>
<tr><td>Thyestes</td><td>Agnosco fratrem.</td></tr>
</table>
(Thyestes 1004–6)

<table>
<tr><td>Atreus</td><td>Spread wide your arms, father:</td></tr>
<tr><td></td><td>They have come. – Do you recognise your sons?</td></tr>
<tr><td>Thyestes</td><td>I recognise my brother.</td></tr>
</table>

Indeed Atreus is so concerned with Thyestes as spectator that the revelation of pedophagy yields initially not to Atreus' satisfaction, but to regret that Thyestes and the children themselves were not knowing audience to Thyestes' 'impious feast':

omnia haec melius pater
fecisse potuit, cecidit in cassum dolor.
scidit ore natos impio, sed nesciens,
sed nescientes.
(Thyestes 1065–8)

The father could have done
All this better; his suffering was pointless.
He chewed his sons impiously, but he didn't know,
But they didn't know.

The ensuing *Schreirede* of his brother expresses the most inexpressible pain, and the director, satisfied at last with his theatrical production, awards himself victory's palm. Atreus ends the play by defeating his brother in verbal exchange ('I deliver you to your children's punishment', 1112). He knows the scripts of plays to come.

Troades too advertises itself as theatre. It features extensive scenes of role-playing, in which characters play actors before other characters as audience:

118

Andromache before Ulysses (556–691), Ulysses before Andromache (627–704), Helen before the Trojan women (871ff.). Metatheatrical language and motifs – 'viewing', ' recognition', 'myth/drama', 'self-dramatisation', 'playing', 'author', 'unlearning', 'presentation', 'spectator', (audience) 'assembly' and 'response'[14] – project and exhibit the play as dramatic artefact and spectacle. From the beginning, as in *Thyestes*, indeed from the play's opening lines onward, attention is given to the dramatic action as object of viewing, as spectacle.

> quicumque regno fidit et magna potens
> dominatur aula nec leues metuit deos
> animumque rebus credulum laetis dedit,
> me uideat – et te, Troia.
>> (*Troades* 1–4)

> Whoever trusts power and plays potent lord
> In princely court unafraid of fickle gods
> Lending a credulous heart to happiness
> Look on me – and on you, Troy.

So Hecuba, who trains the chorus of Trojan women to play their prescripted roles ('I recognise a Trojan band', 95), and, when she re-enters the play at the beginning of Act 4, does so as proleptic spectacle (*uidendam*, 859). Notably the concept of fate in this play seems to embrace the literary and theatrical as well as mythical past.[15] Even the play's final lines suggest completion of a theatrical circle:

> repetite celeri maria, captiuae, gradu.
> iam uela puppis laxat et classis mouet.
>> (*Troades* 1178f.)

> *Once more* head quickly to the sea, prisoners.
> Now sails unfurl on the ships. The fleet moves.

In the final act the metaphor of the amphitheatre and theatre pervades the whole reported action. The Messenger is not only the narrator, but the 'producer/presenter', the *editor* (1067),[16] of spectacle. The analogy of the amphitheatre underlying the description of the gathering and positioning of the crowd to watch the death of Astyanax is powerful and unambiguous:

> haec nota quondam turris et muri decus,
> nunc saeua cautes, undique adfusa ducum
> plebisque turba cingitur. totum coit
> ratibus relictis uulgus. his collis procul
> aciem patenti liberam praebet loco,
> his alta rupes, cuius in cacumine
> erecta summos turba librauit pedes.

119

hunc pinus, illum laurus, hunc fagus gerit;
et tota populo silua suspenso tremit.
extrema montis ille praerupti petit,
semusta at ille tecta uel saxum imminens
muri cadentis pressit atque aliquis – nefas! –
tumulo ferus spectator Hectoreo sedet.
(*Troades* 1075–87)

This once famous tower and pride of the walls,
Now a savage crag, is circled by a milling
Crowd of chiefs and people. The whole host left
The ships and assemble. A distant hill
Gives some a clear view of the open space,
A tall cliff others: on its top the crowd
Stood poised on tiptoe straining for a view.
Some climb pine-trees, some laurels, some beeches;
The whole forest shivers with hanging men.
One chooses the edge of a beetling rock,
Others burden half-burnt roofs or stonework
Jutting from fallen walls and – most horrible! –
A callous spectator sits on Hector's tomb.

The *ferus spectator*, 'callous spectator', provides a critical paradigm for the play's own audience, as does the behaviour of the crowd itself, stirred to impotent tears by the courage of the boy, who, like a gladiator in the arena or the Stoic sage (for whom elsewhere in Seneca the gladiator is often a model),[17] himself does not weep, but achieves heroic stature through voluntary death. For the death of Polyxena the amphitheatre is transformed into the theatre itself:

praeceps ut altis cecidit e muris puer
fleuitque Achiuum turba quod fecit nefas,
idem ille populus aliud ad facinus redit
tumulumque Achillis. cuius extremum latus
Rhoetea leni uerberant fluctu uada;
aduersa cingit campus et cliuo leui
erecta medium uallis includens locum
crescit theatri more. concursus frequens
impleuit omne litus. hi classis moram
hac morte solui rentur; hi stirpem hostium
gaudent recidi. magna pars uulgi leuis
odit scelus spectatque. nec Troes minus
suum frequentant funus et pauidi metu
partem ruentis ultimam Trolae uident.
(*Troades* 1118–31)

When the boy fell sheer from the lofty walls
And the Achaean crowd wept their own sin,
The same people turned to another crime
And Achilles' tomb. The tomb's far side is lashed
By the soft waves of Rhoeteum's waters;
Its near side faces a plain where a high
Vale's gentle slopes enclose a central space
And rise like a theatre. The thronging mass
Filled the whole shore. Some think this death dissolves
The fleet's delay; others are glad to have
The foe's seedling pruned. Most of the fickle mob
Hate the crime and watch it. The Trojans too
Attend their own funeral. Quaking with fear
They view the final act of Troy's collapse.

Theatri more, 'like a theatre'; *partem ultimam*, the 'final act'. And *spectare* again: the crowd hate the crime, but they watch it (*spectat*, 1129). There is nothing in Euripides' *Hecuba* (521ff.) like this. Initial spectatorial revulsion and addiction dissolve into the prescribed, Aristotelian tragic emotions of fear and pity, and the quintessentially Roman response, the marvelling reception of death's spectacle.[18] Corneille was later to separate admiration from tragic pity.[19] Seneca achieves a more complex, more Roman and an overtly self-reflective effect through their conjunction:

> stupet omne uulgus – et fere cuncti magis
> peritura laudant. hos mouet formae decus,
> hos mollis aetas, hos uagae rerum uices.
> mouet animus omnes fortis et leto obuius.
> Pyrrhum antecedit. omnium mentes tremunt,
> mirantur ac miserantur.
>
> (*Troades* 1143–8)

The whole crowd is numbed – mankind admires more
What's doomed. Some respond to beauty's glory,
Some to tender youth, some to life's shifting course.
All respond to a brave heart meeting death.
She walks before Pyrrhus. All souls tremble,
Marvel and pity.

This is almost pure metatheatre. The final act of *Troades* 'presents' (*ede*, 1067) the final act of Troy's collapse, complete with audience response (admiration, fear, pity) – the whole suffused with what Racine called 'cette tristesse majestueuse qui fait tout le plaisir de la tragédie'[20] – as the play draws attention to its status both as theatre and as *imago uitae*, as image of life. Hamlet's metatheatrical homily to the acting troupe at Elsinore seems realised:[21]

[The] end, both at the first and now, was and is, to hold, as 'twere, the mirror up to nature; to show virtue her own feature, scorn her own image, and the very age and body of the time his form and pressure.

(*Hamlet* 3.2.21 ff.)

The allure of Seneca *tragicus* to later theatrical ages was neither superficial nor able to be stopped.

MEDEA

The last of Seneca's plays to be considered in detail joins *Phaedra, Troades* and *Thyestes* as a masterwork.[22] Aspects of *Medea*'s dramatic form and of the density of its ideological and verbal texture were touched upon above.[23] From the play's first word to that word's repetition as the last, the tragedy is almost flawlessly structured by an intricate network of imagistic and linguistic signals, of motifs announced, fulfilled or inverted. The tightness and strength of *Medea*'s form operates in paradoxical counterpoint to its matter; for the play problematises the stability of social order, indeed the morality and durability of civilisation itself. As in Senecan tragedy at large, the palimpsestic code is telling, even though much of this code is beyond reach. Only fragments survive of several Greek and early Latin *Medeas*, including Ennius' *Medea Exul*, evidently modelled on Euripides, and Accius' *Medea* or *Argonautae*, which dramatises the murder of Absyrtus related in Apollonius *Argonautica* 4 (303ff.). Even more unfortunate is the loss of all but two lines of Ovid's *Medea*, which was praised by Quintilian (*Institutio Oratoria* 10.1.98) and may well have exerted a greater impact on Seneca's play than the Ovidian treatment of Medea in *Metamorphoses* 7 (1–403) and *Heroides* 12. The influence of the latter works on Seneca's *Medea* is discernibly substantial. Discernible and substantial too is the interplay between Seneca's dramatic version and the epic treatment of Apollonius, and again the rewriting of Euripides.

The remodelling of Euripides is evident from the play's opening lines and presses for analysis. Replacing the Nurse-prologue of the Euripidean play (and of Ennius' *Medea Exul*), Seneca begins his *Medea* with Medea herself alone on stage, already exiled (in Euripides she receives the sentence of exile at 271ff.), personally rejected, socially excluded, praying to gods for vengeance (1–55). He follows this short prologue with a stirring exhibition of Corinthian social order (56–115): a hymenaeal chorus without counterpart in Euripides' play,[24] in which a chorus of Corinthians enter in a wedding procession, bearing ritual torches and singing the *hymenaeus* or processional hymn, while the bride is escorted in the Roman ritual of *deductio*, complete with 'Fescennine jesting' (113), to her husband's home. The chorus's elaborate prayer to the protecting deities of Corinth echoes Medea's prayer in the prologue (1ff.), but ignores the deities of darkness whom the Colchian princess addressed (6ff.). Images of light and brightness govern their prayer to the gods of marriage and of social prosperity and peace (56–74). They sing the praises of groom and bride, Jason and Creusa (75ff.). The former's marriage to Medea is dismissively treated as outside the social order: 'bedchambers of barbaric Phasis', 'an unbridled wife', Jason's 'hand unwilling' (102–4). Medea is not named, but it is on her that the chorus conclude with their excluding and exclusive command:

> tacitis eat illa tenebris,
> si qua peregrino nubit fugitiua[25] marito.
> *(Medea* 114f.)

> Let her depart in silent darkness –
> The runaway who weds a foreign husband.

In Ovid's *Heroides* Medea complains to Jason that he is now treating her as a 'barbarian' *(nunc denique barbara, Heroides* 12.105).[26] In the hymenaeal chorus of Seneca's *Medea* the whole city is doing so.

What becomes clear in Act 2 is that the city needs Jason. The royal house of Corinth needs heirs; Creon a royal son-in-law. The city's social stability is dependent on a problematic marriage, involving the nullification of a previous marriage pledge – a pledge given to a woman who saved Jason's life. Corinth's attempt to deal with this is by means of exclusion: Medea is exiled and classified as 'other'. 'Noxious progeny of Colchian Aeetes', is how Creon initially addresses her (179). But Medea will not be so easily excluded. By appealing to Creon's self-image and his need for heirs, she manipulates the Corinthian king to give her time for vengeance. And, after a final, failed attempt in Act 3 to win back Jason, for whom she traded all previous human relationships and whose desertion dissolves her human world, Medea moves to control both the dramatic action and Corinth. Her ascendancy is reflected in the choral odes, which move from exclusion (114f.), through the brief mention of her name (362), to a developed expression of panic, which occupies the opening four stanzas of the third ode (579–94) and begins a crescendo movement dominated and controlled by Medea. The play is now all hers. Euripides played down the tradition of Medea as sorceress; Seneca, like Ovid *(Metamorphoses* 7.179–293), to whom he is here especially indebted, enlarges upon it, and devotes an entire act to a display of Medea's magic powers and her unleashing of the forces of darkness which the light of Corinthian order ignored. The final choral ode which follows is entirely concerned with Medea, her anger, rage, violence, force, her barbarity and, paradoxically to the chorus, her breach of the bonds of social exclusion put upon her by Corinth:

> quonam cruenta maenas
> praeceps amore saeuo
> rapitur? quod impotenti
> facinus parat furore?

uultus citatus ira
riget et caput feroci
quatiens superba motu
regi minatur ultro.
quis credat exulem?
flagrant genae rubentes,
pallor fugat ruborem.
nullum uagante forma
seruat diu colorem.
huc fert pedes et illuc,
ut tigris orba natis
cursu furente lustrat
Gangeticum nemus.
frenare nescit iras
Medea, nec amores;
nunc ira amorque causam
iunxere: quid sequetur?
quando efferet Pelasgis
nefanda Colchis aruis
gressum metuque soluet
regnum simulque reges?
nunc, Phoebe, mitte currus
nullo morante loro,
nox condat alma lucem,
mergat diem timendum
dux noctis Hesperus.
          (*Medea* 849–78)

Where's that bloody maenad
Hurled headlong by savage
Love? What crime stirs
Beneath her mad fury?
Distressed face stiff
With anger, head shaking
Wild but proud,
She threatens the king.
Who'd think her an exile?
Red cheeks blaze,
Pallor banishes red.
Her appearance shifts,
Always changing colour.
She dashes around
Like a tigress bereft
Of young pacing furiously

124

Through groves of Ganges.
Medea cannot bridle
Anger or love;
Now anger and love
Join cause: what will follow?
When will the monstrous
Colchian leave Pelasgian
Fields and free from fear
Kingdom and kings?
Now, Phoebus, release
Your chariot, let go the reins;
Gentle night bury the light,
And night-lord Hesperus
Sink the fearful day.

The Corinthian world is reversed. The motifs of the chorus' optimistic wedding song are here inverted by the reality of Medea's presence and power. Creusa's blush (*rubuit*, 100) and snowy complexion (99) become the red fire of Medea's anger (*rubentes . . . rubor*, 858f.) and the *pallor* (859) of her rage, the controlled tigers of Bacchus' chariot (85) transformed into a tigress ready for blood (863–5). The fragile ideology of the chorus' excluding social vision is shattered by Medea's power. Ironically the chorus' earlier *fugitiua* ('runaway') is recalled in an expression of their own astonishment: 'Who'd think her an exile (*exulem*)?' (857). She does eventually 'flee' (1022). But not until the Corinthian king and his daughter have been destroyed, her own and Jason's sons killed, and the whole city is on the verge of being engulfed by unquenchable fire. Jason concludes the play with his famous, anguished address to the departing Medea:

> per alta uade spatia sublimi aetheris,
> testare nullos esse, qua ueheris, deos.
> (*Medea* 1026f.)

> Journey through high heaven's soaring spaces;
> Bear witness, where you ride, there are no gods.

The Elizabethan translator, Studley, was so shocked by Jason's atheistic cry that he subjected the lines to a Christian appropriation:

> Goe through the ample spaces wyde, infect the poysoned Ayre,
> Beare witnesse, grace of God is none in place of thy repayre.

He would have been more horrified, had he realised that Jason is mistaken. Medea's vengeance was implemented with the powers of Hecate. She is taken away in the chariot of the Sun. Her prayers of the prologue to both deities are realised. The gods are there. They are simply not Jason's; nor are they those of Corinth. The world is a larger and more uncontrollable place than Corinthian society thinks. There is structure and order but they are not man-made, nor subject to human models of morality and sense.

The *potentia* theme, the questioning of human power and control, pervades Seneca's plays.[27] In *Medea* it not only embraces the issue of social order and stability, but that of civilisation itself. The two great central odes of the play direct themselves to the voyage of the *Argo*, which is mentioned in the opening line and elsewhere in Euripides' play, but given no choral ode. What Seneca is building on does not derive from Greece. Beneath his text is the specific deployment of the Argonautic expedition in the Roman literary tradition. From Catullus 64 onwards major Roman poets – Virgil (*Georgic* 1.136ff.), Tibullus (1.3.35ff.), Horace (*Odes* 1.3), Ovid (*Metamorphoses* 1.89ff.) – had treated the invention of navigation as a sign of the end of the fabled Golden Age of pristine harmony between nature, man and god, the consequences of which were the loss of human innocence, the dissolution of familial bonds, the accelerated technological abuse of nature, the onset of greed, war, moral decadence and human suffering, the development of cities and the growth of civilisation. Several of these poets had used the voyage of the *Argo* as paradigm of the initial stage of post-lapsarian decline,[28] even creating the incoherent fiction of the Argonautic expedition as the first sea-voyage. Virgil explicitly connects the voyage with the 'original sin', *prisca fraus*, of Prometheus (*Eclogue* 4.31, 6.42), who made technology possible by stealing fire from the gods; and in both Virgil (*Eclogue* 4.12) and Catullus (64.399) the voyage is presented as emblem of the spiritual *malaise* which resulted in the social and moral collapse of the Roman world. The Argonautic and related myths were thus inherited by Seneca already encrusted with the semiotics of a negative critique of the development of civilisation. These myths had become a grammar of imperial Rome.

It is a grammar Seneca uses well. Navigation is mentioned by Hippolytus at *Phaedra* 530 as a sign of the fall from the Golden Age. But there is nothing elsewhere in Seneca to match the great lyric outbursts of *Medea*'s two Argonautic odes (301–79, 579–669), which frame the problem of Corinthian social order with the problem of civilisation itself. In the first Argonautic ode emphasis is upon the voyage as one which generated knowledge and control: knowledge of the stars (309–17), control over the winds, for whom the helmsman Tiphys 'dared to write new laws' (*ausus . . . legesque nouas scribere*, 318–20), mastery of such monsters of the deep as the Siren through the power of Orphic song – mastery of the sea itself, apparently:

> bene dissaepti foedera mundi
> traxit in unum Thessala pinus
> iussitque pati uerbera pontum
> partemque metus fieri nostri
> mare sepositum.
>
> (*Medea* 335–9)

> The covenants of a well-fenced world
> Thessalian pine dragged together,
> Ordered ocean to endure the lash
> And our terror to include
> The inviolate sea.

The legal imagery here is important. Central to the movement from the Golden Age described in the lines before this (329–34) to the post-Golden Age of cities and civilisation (369ff.) is the breach of the 'covenant' which kept sea and land separate. The imposition of new laws on the winds or the ocean itself ('Now ocean has yielded, endures | All laws': *omnes | patitur leges*, 364f.) is itself based on broken natural law. Ironically the choral ode articulates a sequence – breach of covenant to fear to penalty (335–49) – which, like its description of Medea herself (*merces prima digna carina*, 'Payment worthy of that first voyage', 363), is to have far greater impact than they realise.

This greater impact looms large in the second Argonautic ode (579ff.), in which the notion of 'Medea as payment' is beginning to be understood, and fear is the pervading emotion. The premature deaths suffered by Argonauts are listed as penalty for violating the laws of the world.

> uade qua tutum populo priori,
> rumpe nec sacro uiolente sancta
>   foedera mundi.
> Quisquis audacis tetigit carinae . . .
> raptor externi rediturus auri,
> exitu diro temerata ponti
>   iura piauit.
>   (*Medea* 604–15)

> Go where others went safely,
> Don't burst with force a world's
>   Sacrosanct covenants.
> Whoever touched that bold ship . . .
> To return thief of foreign gold,
> With dreadful death atoned for ocean's
>   Outraged laws.

Tiphys, Orpheus, Hercules, Ancaeus, Hylas, Idmon, Peleus, Pelias, even sons and wives, suffer for this crime; the myth of their power implodes. The chorus' plea for Jason to be excluded from ocean's vengeance displays little confidence (595f., 668f.). This and the previous ode have articulated a causal sequence – breach of covenant to fear to death and destruction – which is to be mirrored in the dramatic action itself: breach of marital *fides* or 'pledge', to fear, to death and destruction. Medea is not only the payment for civilisation's birth; she is the instrument and reminder of its unnatural character and its fragility. She signals its birth from a primal sin. The undisguised reference to Rome's control of the world at the end of the first Argonautic ode brings these issues home:

> terminus omnis motus et urbes
> muros terra posuere noua,
> nil qua fuerat sede reliquit
> > peruius orbis:
> Indus gelidum potat Araxen,
> Albin Persae Rhenumque bibunt –
> uenient annis saecula seris,
> quibus Oceanus uincula rerum
> laxet et ingens pateat tellus
> Tethysque nouos detegat orbes
> nec sit terris ultima Thule.
> > (*Medea* 369–79)

> Every boundary has gone, cities
> Have set their walls in new lands,
> Nothing in its former place left
> > By an open world:
> Indians drink the cold Araxes,
> Persians the Elbe and the Rhine –
> A time will come in future years
> When Ocean will loose the bonds
> Of things, the great earth lie open,
> Tethys uncover new worlds,
> And Thule will not be Land's End.

Echoes here of Jupiter's proclamation of 'boundless' Roman *imperium* in Virgil's *Aeneid* (1.278f.) combine with allusions to Virgil's first *Eclogue* (61f.) to inscribe the Argonautic myth with memories of the inherited imperial image and the recent reality of Rome's social collapse.

Medea thus dramatises issues at the heart of imperial Rome. And like imperial Rome it is self-consciously theatrical. The play not only ends on a theatrical 'high spot', it begins on one, with a virtuoso linguistic display by Medea (1–55), who summons gods of all three realms, heaven, ocean, and the underworld, to witness her injustice and to heed her prayer for revenge. In an extraordinary display of verbal power, bombast and self-dramatisation, she threatens to strike the light from the heavens, even to embroil her ancestor the Sun-god in her vengeance:

> non ibo in hostes? manibus excutiam faces
> caeloque lucem – spectat hoc nostri sator
> Sol generis, et spectatur, et curru insidens
> per solita puri spatia decurrit poli?

non redit in ortus et remetitur diem?
da, da per auras curribus patriis uehi,
committe habenas, genitor, et flagrantibus
ignifera loris tribue moderari iuga:
gemino Corinthos litore[29] opponens moras
cremata flammis maria committat duo.

(Medea 27–36)

Not attack my foes? I'll strike torches from hands,
Light from heaven – Is the Sun our progenitor
Watching, and is he watched in turn pursuing
His chariot's normal path through pure sky?
Does he not return to dawn and retrace the day?
Let, let ancestral chariots take me through air,
Give me reins, father, and hand me fire-breathing
Horses to control with their blazing straps:
Let twin-shored Corinth, obstacle to ships,
Consumed by flames confound the double sea.

Recognition of herself as 'spectatorial' object (*spectat*, 28) incites Medea not only to bring her divine ancestor into the action of the play but to reveal the script she and her ancestor will follow at the play's denouement. Anticipation of the play's ending is not unique to *Medea*. In both *Agamemnon* and *Thyestes* the script is rehearsed, but not by one of the participants in it. Medea is taking on the role of actor-dramaturge right from the beginning of this play. 'Diese Medea hat Euripides gelesen', Wilamowitz remarked.[30] She certainly has. She has also pre-written Seneca.

Medea's self-theatricalisation resumes immediately after the hymenaeal chorus, when the audience witnesses her rehearsing her dramatic and literary pedigree (esp. 129–36) and craving the promontory of Malea as audience for her vengeance (*uidebit . . . Malea*, 'Malea shall see . . . ', 148f.). Then follows the famous interchange, in which Medea uses the Nurse's fearful *sententiae* and common sense to redefine herself in entirely elemental terms:

Nutrix	Abiere Colchi, coniugis nulla est fides
	nihilque superest opibus e tantis tibi.
Medea	Medea superest: hic mare et terras uides
	ferrumque et ignes et deos et fulmina.

(Medea 164–7)

Nurse	The Colchians are gone; your husband's vows are nothing;
	Nothing is left of all your wondrous wealth.
Medea	Medea's left. Here you see ocean and land,
	Iron and fire, gods and thunderbolts.

The redefinition accords with the descent from the Sun and the script

129

enunciated in the prologue. In the scene with Creon which follows Medea returns to the rehearsal of her past (203ff.) to keep her theatrical or mythic self in view. In Acts 3 and 4 this is left in part to another, the Nurse, who opens two successive acts in an identical fashion virtually unique in Seneca with extensive descriptions of the protagonist's behaviour and psychological state: the *ira* and *furor* of Medea, her anger and rage, narrativised.[31] The speech of Act 3 (382–96) focuses on the physical manifestations of rage: burning face, panting, tears, grimaces: *uultum furoris cerno*, 'I see the face of fury' (396). The seventy-line narrative which begins Act 4 relates Medea's rage in action, her elaborate preparation of the deadly poisons which will consume her enemies (670–739). Each of these descriptions distances both the Nurse and the audience from Medea, transforming the Nurse herself into an audience to Medea's theatre of magic. This theatrical isolation and objectification of Medea was accelerated by Medea herself in Act 3 through her continuing self-dramatisation, manifested both in extraordinary pro-clamations of power ('I'll overturn and flatten all', 414, 'I'll attack the gods | And shake the universe', 424f.) and, towards the end of the scene with Jason, in her self-referential use of the third person ('There's a greater fear: | Medea', 516f., 'Medea compels', 524). As she prepares herself for the crime to come, she has already objectified herself:

> perge nunc, aude, incipe
> quidquid potest Medea, quidquid non potest.
> (*Medea* 566f.)

> On now, be brave, begin
> All Medea can, all that she cannot.

What the Nurse presents at the opening of Act 4 (670–739) is a mini-recital drama, *Medea Parans* (see 674f.), employing both narrative and dialogue (690–704), in which Medea gathers the deadliest poisons in the universe and invokes the serpents of the cosmos and of legend. The fusion of images of life and death, creativity, horror and destruction, constructs a framework of generative perversion in anticipation of a spectacle of perverted power. When Medea enters at 740 the audience is not disappointed. What follows is a Black Mass, an incantation scene unique in extant Graeco-Roman tragedy, directed to the Queen of Hell. The mixture of music, incantation and sing-ing, the summoning of the most famous sinners of hell (740–51), the rehearsal of past powers (752–70), the offerings to Hecate (771–86), Hecate's arrival and the final ritual itself, including the shedding of Medea's own blood on the altar (787–839), the baying of Hecate's approval (840–2) constitute a *bravura* theatrical display. Three different lyric metres are involved as well as music and the iambic of dialogue. Medea has now become her own play. And as token of this her Black Mass is followed by a brief choral ode (849–78), in which, like the Nurse earlier, the chorus of

Corinthians are reduced to observers of Medea. Their failed attempt to create a world without her is underscored by the ode's ironic inversion, observed above, of the motifs of the chorus' opening song.

The final act is almost self-indulgently theatrical. Everything is stage-managed by Medea. The Messenger enters, delivers with unique brevity the news of Creusa's and Creon's death and the unstoppable fire in the palace (879–90), but, before he can launch into the predictable Euripidean narrative, Medea's entrance drives him from the stage (891), and instead of a messenger's speech the audience receives the longest soliloquy in Senecan tragedy, as Medea incites herself to slay her children and realise her own dramatic myth (893–977): *Medea nunc sum*, 'Now I am Medea' (910). In the end it is the appearance of the Furies, of Megaera, and most especially of the dismembered Absyrtus, which drives her to filicide, redefined at the moment of execution as sacrifice to her dead brother:[32]

> discedere a me, frater, ultrices deas
> manesque ad imos ire securas iube.
> mihi me relinque et utere hac, frater, manu
> quae strinxit ensem. – uictima manes tuos
> placamus ista.
>
> *(Medea 967–71)*

> Tell the avenging goddesses to leave me,
> Brother, to go in peace to the dead below.
> Leave me to myself and use this hand, brother,
> Its sword drawn. – With this victim we placate
> Your spirit.

She slays one child. Requiring an audience ('Your "manliness" [*uirtus*] is not to be squandered in secret', 976f.), she takes the other son and the dead child's body to the roof of the palace, where she revels in the triumph of the moment before the eyes of Jason, who has just entered:

> iam iam recepi sceptra, germanum, patrem,
> spoliumque Colchi pecudis auratae tenent.
> rediere regna, rapta uirginitas redit.
> o placida tandem numina! o festum diem!
> o nuptialem!
>
> *(Medea 982–6)*

> Now, now I've restored throne, brother, father,
> And Colchians keep the golden fleece's prize.
> Realms return, stolen virginity returns.
> O gods at last propitious! O festal,
> Wedding day!

The power of Medea's language has dominated the play. The chorus, Creon,

Jason (113f., 189, 530), have all tried to silence her, fearing that language's power. Their fear was justified. Medea's language is used in the play not only to evoke the powers of darkness but to realise Medea's own dramatic myth. As Medea's power in the play has grown, so has her domination of the play's language. Domination of the theatrical world and word are the same. In the linguistic reverie above the power of theatrical language to rewrite reality is openly displayed. Its ability to satisfy, however, is truncated, when Medea realises that her vengeance is incomplete. In Euripides' play both children are dead before Jason arrives (1293). In Seneca one child is left to be slain before its own internal audience. To Medea the lack of audience nullifies revenge. Oscillating between shame, remorse and pleasure, Medea is transfixed by desire for Jason as *spectator*.

> derat hoc unum mihi,
> spectator iste. nil adhuc facti reor:
> quidquid sine isto fecimus sceleris perit.
> *(Medea* 992–4)

> This one thing was missing,
> Him as audience. Nothing is yet achieved:
> What sin we performed in his absence dies.

In this most theatrical of all Seneca's finales, involving armed crowds, roof-top dialogue, child-slaying, and the arrival/departure of the serpent-drawn chariot of the Sun, Medea plays to and with her audience Jason, whose son will be given to death while Jason watches (*te uidente*, 1001). She kills the second child both as gladiatorial theatre before her spectator husband – *bene est, peractum est*, 'It's home, it's done' *(Medea* 1019)[33] – and as sacrificial spectacle before her own internal 'hurt' *(dolor*, 1019). She then implements the script which she announced in the prologue, mounting her ancestral chariot to be carried through air. She feigns surprise at Jason's failure to predict this ending:

> coniugem agnoscis tuam?
> sic fugere soleo.
> *(Medea* 1021f.)

> Don't you recognise your wife?
> This is how I usually escape.

One sense is that, as Medea has been at pains to rehearse in this play (129ff., 276ff., 471ff.), her flights in the past have been accompanied by social chaos, suffering and the murder of kin. The metatheatrical sense (here irresistible) is that this is how Medea always leaves her play. Failure on her part to repeat what are Medea's self-constituting acts would be to lose her theatrical identity. If 'this Medea has read Euripides', this Jason has not. Nor has he read his Ovid (*Metamorphoses* 7.394–99). Further evidence follows. Euripides'

Medea concludes with Medea's serpentine flight followed by the chorus' justification of the ways of gods to men (1415ff.).[34] Jason's atheistic proclamation in the final distich of Seneca's play is not only Eliot's famed *coup de
théâtre*,[35] but confirmation of how little Jason has either understood or read.
Neither gods nor previous scripts are on his side. They are all with Medea.
Jason rewrites Euripides' ending into a theatrical display of failed reading
both of literature and the world. The palimpsestic and the theatricalised
world and the world of delusion and failed power become one. In the late
Julio-Claudian era that world was Rome.

THEATRICALISED DEATH

One aspect of Seneca's tragic world prominent in *Medea* cannot be left
without comment: the representation of violent death on the stage. Here are
Horace's prescriptions about the staging of tragic violence and fantasy:

> aut agitur res in scaenis aut acta refertur.
> segnius irritant animos demissa per aurem,
> quam quae sunt oculis subiecta fidelibus et quae
> ipse sibi tradit spectator. non tamen intus
> digna geri promes in scaenam, multaque tolles
> ex oculis quae mox narret facundia praesens;
> ne pueros coram populo Medea trucidet,
> aut humana palam coquat exta nefarius Atreus,
> aut in auem Procne uertatur, Cadmus in anguem.
> quodcumque ostendis mihi sic, incredulus odi.
>
> (*Ars Poetica* 179–88)

> An event is either staged or reported.
> The mind is stirred less vividly through the ear
> Than by what's cast before reliable eyes and which
> The audience sees for itself. But don't produce on stage
> What should be performed behind the scenes, and keep
> From sight much which will soon be eloquently told.
> Don't let Medea butcher her children in public,
> Nor monstrous Atreus cook human flesh on stage,
> Nor Procne turn into a bird, and Cadmus a snake.
> All such displays I disbelieve and loathe.

Seneca's *Medea* breaks these prescriptions, and stages not only the filicide but
the shedding of Medea's own blood during the Black Mass. Perhaps *Thyestes*
is also in breach, for, although a messenger narrates the cooking of the
children's flesh, their severed heads are displayed in the final act. Neither
Oedipus nor *Phaedra* would have met with Horace's approval, since Jocasta
commits sexual suicide at the end of the former, as does Phaedra at the end

133

of the latter, where the final act is particularly bloody as Theseus tries to assemble Hippolytus' corpse. The incomplete *Phoenissae* too probably would have climaxed in a scene of sexual suicide.[36] The other three plays exhibit either no violent deaths on stage, or possibly one, if Hercules has not already left the stage when he slays the first child at *Hercules Furens* 992ff.[37] Such violence and bloodshed could have been 'vividly' represented through the use of artificial blood-bags, attested for the Roman stage from the time of Caligula.[38] Much violence too is narrated in Senecan tragedy in accordance with the purest of Hellenic modes and standard Roman republican practice. In all but *Medea* and *Phoenissae* the narration of such violence is extensive. The bloody deaths of Agamemnon, of Hercules' wife and children, of Astyanax and Polyxena, of Thyestes' children, of Hippolytus, Oedipus' act of self-blinding, are conveyed to the audience aurally (*per aurem, Ars Poetica* 180) by messengers or eye-witnesses (in Cassandra's case a clairvoyant one). In these narrations there is a focus on the body, its inner and outer parts, their penetration and dismemberment, entirely in accord with Roman dramatic practice from its inception and with Roman poetic practice from Ovid.[39]

> quos enim praeceps locus
> reliquit artus? ossa disiecta et graui
> elisa casu. signa clari corporis
> et ora et illas nobiles patris notas
> confudit imam pondus ad terram datum.
> soluta ceruix silicis impulsu; caput
> ruptum cerebro penitus expresso. iacet
> deforme corpus.
>
> (*Troades* 110–17)

> What body
> Survives that steep place? His heavy fall crushed
> And scattered the bones. That bright form's features,
> That face, those noble traces of his sire,
> Were pulped by the body's weight dropped to earth.
> The neck unhinged as he struck the flint rock.
> His head split and the brain squeezed out. He lies
> A shapeless corpse.

Stoicism is relevant here too. Stoic physics, which regarded the entire universe as material, made the body and the language of the body the defining constituents of its discourse.[40] Attention to the body punctuates Senecan drama, and is notable in scenes other than mutilation.[41] The extispicy of *Oedipus*, with its gruesome attention to bodily organs, their disease, ectopia and monstrosity, reflects an emphasis on body and physicality in Senecan drama both ideological and pervasive.

The violence of Senecan tragedy should be neither underestimated nor exaggerated. Much has been made of its relationship to the spectatorial cruelty of the era, the 'murderous games' and bloodshed of the arena,[42] where the public killing of gladiators and condemned criminals was frequently conducted on a massive scale for the pleasure of Roman *spectatores*. The construction of this relationship as an attempt by Senecan tragedy to cater to contemporary *Blutdurst* misconstrues. What is often ignored in such hypotheses, even apart from what may be inferred from tragedies such as *Troades* (see *Troades* 1087), is Seneca's own testimony in the prose works on the degrading effect of the butchery of the arena on the spectators:

> nihil uero tam damnosum bonis moribus quam in aliquo spectaculo desidere. tunc enim per uoluptatem facilius uitia subrepunt. quid me existimas dicere? auarior redeo, ambitiosior, luxuriosior? immo uero crudelior et inhumanior, quia inter homines fui ... mane leonibus et ursis homines, meridie spectatoribus suis obiciuntur. interfectores interfecturis iubent obici et uictorem in aliam detinent caedem; exitus pugnantium mors est. ferro et igne res geritur. haec fiunt dum uacat arena. 'sed latrocinium fecit aliquis, occidit hominem.' quid ergo? quia occidit, ille meruit ut hoc pateretur; tu quid meruisti miser ut hoc spectes.
>
> (*Epistle* 7.2–5)

Nothing is so injurious to morals as sitting at the games. Then vices more easily steal upon one through the medium of pleasure. What do you think I mean? I return from the games more greedy, more ambitious, more self-indulgent? Yes, and far more cruel and inhuman – for being among humans ... In the morning they hurl men to lions and bears, at noon to the spectators. They demand that killers be killed in turn and reserve the victor for another slaughter. The outcome for fighters is death; sword and fire keep the show going. It goes on while the arena is empty. 'But he committed robbery; he killed a man.' What of it? Because he killed, he has deserved to suffer this. But what have you done, wretch, to deserve to watch it?

In his *History of the Decline and Fall of the Roman Empire* Edward Gibbon commented on this letter that 'Seneca shews the feelings of a man'.[43] They were the feelings of a remarkable man, who expresses similar sentiments elsewhere (*De Brevitate Vitae* 13.6f.). They are sentiments not normally entertained by members of the Roman aristocracy. Seneca's theatrical violence seems in no sense an attempt (far less a 'calculated' one) to cater to what he depicts in his prose works as a decadent appetite, as if theatricalised death could possibly compete with the actual blood of the arena. By describing violent death verbally and representing it and the reaction to it theatrically Seneca is able to control the perception and evaluation of death in a way that the arena could not do. Every *spectator* at the games saw different things. Seneca controls what they see and how they see it in the theatre, and furnishes them with a conceptual framework with which to judge it. Theatricalised suffering evokes responses different from, sometimes even more powerful than, those generated by suffering itself.[44]

Theatricalised death is also part of Senecan drama's reflection of and on 'the very age and body of the time'. The theatrical nature of Agrippina's death was noted above; its theatricality is not unique. Both Suetonius' Nero and Tacitus' Lucan theatricalise their deaths, the former quoting Homer's *Iliad* in Greek before the knife is plunged through his throat (*Nero* 49), the latter quoting self-referential verses from his own epic describing a soldier's death (*Annals* 15.70). For the death of Seneca, constrained to suicide by Nero, Tacitus creates one of his most extensive, theatricalised narratives:

> Undisturbed, Seneca demanded the tablets containing his will. On the centurion's refusal, he turned to his friends to witness that, since he was prevented from requiting them for their services, he bequeathed them his one remaining possession and his finest, the image of his life (*imaginem uitae suae*); if they remained mindful of it, their loyal friendship would bring a reputation for virtue ... When he had made this and similar speeches as if to the world, he embraced his wife ... Paulina assured him that she too had decided on death, and demanded the assassin's stroke. Seneca, not opposed to her glory, and motivated by love to protect the unique object of his affection from outrage, said: 'I had shown you the solaces of life; you prefer the glory of death. I shall not begrudge your example. May the fortitude of this brave exit be shared between us, but greater honour attend your end.' Then with the same stroke they cut their arms ... Since even at the last moment his eloquence did not fail, he summoned his scribes and dictated much to them, which, since it has been published *verbatim*, I think it needless to paraphrase ... Seneca meanwhile, as death's protracted slowness lingered, begged Statius Annaeus, long valued for his loyal friendship and medical skill, to produce the poison which he had long prepared and which was used to execute those condemned by the public tribunal of Athens. It was brought, he drank – to no purpose. His limbs were already cold and his body closed to the poison's power. Finally he entered a pool of heated water, and sprinkling some on the slaves nearby he remarked that he poured the liquid as libation to Jove the Liberator. He was then lifted into the bath, suffocated by its vapour, and cremated without death-rites. He had given this instruction in his will, when, even at the height of wealth and power, he gave thought to his end.
>
> (*Annals* 15.62–4)

As the Stoic philosopher, tragedian and Nero's minister plays Socrates in his own theatre of death, Tacitus' moving and ironic account leaves little doubt that the *imago uitae*, 'image of his life', which Seneca leaves to his friends and posterity, is in part the image of his death. To the imperial historian and the imperial tragedian theatricalised death was both 'mirror' and emblem of Rome's world of players.

Part II

SENECA AND RENAISSANCE DRAMA

7

SENECA INSCRIPTVS

Yet English *Seneca* read by candle light yeeldes manie good sentences, as *Bloud is a begger*, and so foorth; and, if you intreate him faire in a frostie morning, he will affoord you whole *Hamlets*, I should say handfulls of tragical speaches. But ô griefe! *tempus edax rerum*, what's that will last alwaies? The sea exhaled by droppes will in continuance be drie, and *Seneca* let blood line by line and page by page, at length needes die to our stage.

Thomas Nash, 'Preface to Greene's *Menaphon*' (1589)

Ecerinis, Albertino Mussato's *irata tragoedia,* written in Padua in 1315, where it was publicly recited each Christmas, is the first known Renaissance tragedy. It models itself in theme, style and metre on Seneca. The neo-Latin tragic tradition which Mussato founded continued until the seventeenth century,[1] and, though it was soon to be marginalised by a complex, evolving vernacular drama, from that point onwards Seneca encodes Renaissance theatre. Editions of Seneca's dramatic corpus circulated as early as the thirteenth century and abounded in the centuries which followed.[2] From the late fifteenth century his plays were performed regularly in European theatres, in universities, schools and Inns of Court.[3] In non-Latin tragedy Seneca's informing paradigm was acknowledged by dramatist and critic alike: Cinthio's *Orbecche* (1541) and *Discorsi* (1543), Sackville and Norton's *Gorboduc* (1561–2), Sidney's *Apologie* (1595) underscore the position of Seneca within contemporary theatrical thinking.[4] The Newton translations of 1581, which appeared shortly after the opening of the public theatres and reprinted translations published separately between 1559 and 1567 (with one exception),[5] were both index and product of a theatrical ideology in which Seneca had a primary position. Polonius' famous instruction to *Hamlet*'s internal Players: 'Seneca cannot be too heavy, nor Plautus too light' (*Hamlet* 2.2.396f.), despite its baldness and boldness, embodied a cultural truth.

This century's Renaissance scholarship has witnessed a substantial attempt to achieve some precision on the issue of 'Senecan influence', especially as pertains to English drama of the Elizabethan and Jacobean periods. The

confident and crude cataloguing of parallel passages and of formal, structural and thematic debts, exhibited by the scholarship of the earlier part of
this century, soon yielded to a more cautious approach, which both
emphasised the melting-pot of potential determinants in the evolution of
Elizabethan drama and drew attention to the importance of Renaissance
chronicles and of the medieval and Christian traditions (especially *De Casibus*
narratives, biblical 'cycles' and morality plays).[6] More recently this scepticism
in turn has been replaced by an awareness of Seneca's inextricability from
the medieval tradition itself,[7] and by a fuller and more refined understanding
of Seneca's shaping of Renaissance theatre, the latter's 'penetration' (in
Eliot's phrase) by a profoundly 'Senecan sensibility',[8] manifested in features
as disparate as the ideology of heroism and 'the rhetoric and psychology
of power'.[9] The present consensus seems in favour of greater, not lesser,
Senecan impact on sixteenth- and seventeenth-century drama.[10] Indeed it
has recently been argued that Shakespeare's early plays not only display clear
familiarity with Seneca's Latin text (as opposed to the 'anthologised Seneca'),
but that his whole concept of the tragic initially owed much to the Latin
dramatist.[11]

Of course the notions of 'debt', 'influence', and 'source' are themselves
problematic, and can signify a number of relationships both direct and
indirect between author and author, text and text, and text and tradition. The
following three chapters employ the flexible and wide-ranging notion of
influence evident in more recent criticism.[12] This notion embraces everything
from direct quotation and allusion through thematic, imagistic and rhetorical
patterns to generic representation and inversion. The aim throughout is not
to 'prove' causal hypotheses of influence (although in several cases such
proof seems incontrovertible), but to describe the Renaissance achievement
in such a way as to expose the lines of a Senecan tradition. The main area of
attention will be English Renaissance tragedy, although attention will also be
given to sixteenth-century Italian tragedy and seventeenth-century French
tragedy (in the latter case primarily to Corneille and Racine). Occasional
reference will be made to tragicomedy and even to comedy. The focus will be
on dramatic devices, strategies, conventions, and themes; on the use of
quotation and allusion and the rewriting of the Senecan text; on conceptual-
ising tragic experience and the tragic self; and on metatheatre, on the exhibition of theatre as self-reflective and as cultural mirror. The purpose of these
concluding chapters is not to rehearse previous scholarship, but to pursue
some of the ramifications of Part I of this book in an endeavour to further
the understanding of European drama's originating Senecanism.

It should be noted at the outset that Italian and French neo-classical
tragedy imitated Senecan dramaturgy far more closely than English tragedy
did. Both frame themselves around a sequence of declamations, Senecanesque interchanges and (in some cases) choral odes, and maintain their neo-
Senecan form throughout the sixteenth and seventeenth centuries. In France

Buchanan, Muret, Jodelle, Jean de la Taille, Garnier, Hardy, Montchrétien, Rotrou, Crébillon and, most famously, Corneille and Racine revelled in what is often regarded as a drama of the word, in which there is a distinctive and pervasive sense of the value, authority and behavioural force of human speech: 'là *Parler*, c'est *Agir*'.[13] This verbal drama combines with an overtly Senecan predilection for spectacle and horror in such Italian dramatists as Cinthio, Speroni, Dolce and Groto. In England early Renaissance dramatists of the Inns of Court, such as Sackville and Norton, Wilmot, Hughes, and the later 'French Senecans' or closet dramatists of the Countess of Pembroke's circle, attempted close Senecan imitation,[14] but, after the opening of the public theatres in 1576, the dramaturgical response, although extensive, was more indirect, complex and creative.

ALLUSION

One of the most obvious marks of Senecan influence in Elizabethan and Jacobean tragedy is the redeployment of lines from Seneca's dramatic text. In Kyd's *The Spanish Tragedy*, Shakespeare's *Titus Andronicus* and *Richard III*, Marlowe's *Edward II*, Tourneur/Middleton's *The Revenger's Tragedy* and several plays of Marston, Senecan lines make a telling re-appearance.[15] Among the most interesting of these Senecan replays is Hieronimo's soliloquy in *The Spanish Tragedy* 3.13, as he formulates his intention to avenge the death of his son, Horatio. Hieronimo enters with a book in his hand. It is possibly a *florilegium* filled with miscellaneous quotations but more probably a copy of Seneca's tragedies, from which all the Latin quotations come (except the first, perhaps remembered rather than read).

> *Vindicta mihi!*
> Ay, heaven will be reveng'd of every ill,
> Nor will they suffer murder unrepaid.
> Then stay, Hieronimo, attend their will,
> For mortal men may not appoint their time.
> [*Reading*] '*Per scelus semper tutum est sceleribus iter.*'
> Strike, and strike home, where wrong is offer'd thee,
> For evils unto ills conductors be,
> And death's the worst of resolution:
> For he that thinks with patience to contend
> To quiet life, his life shall easily end.
> [*Reading again*] '*Fata si miseros juvant, habes salutem;*
> *Fata si vitam negant, habes sepulchrum.*'
> If destiny thy miseries do ease,
> Then hast thou health, and happy shalt thou be:
> If destiny deny thee life, Hieronimo,
> Yet shalt thou be assured of a tomb:

If neither, yet let this thy comfort be,
Heaven covereth him that hath no burial.
And to conclude, I will revenge his death!
(*Spanish Tragedy* 3.13.1–20)

Lines 6 and 12f. are quotations from Seneca's *Agamemnon* (115) and *Troades* (510–12) respectively. What is striking about this passage is not only the familiarity with the Senecan text which Kyd expects from his audience,[16] but the way that text is used dramatically, to afford a transition from the Christian view of vengeance, represented by the opening allusion to *Romans* 12.19 ('Vengeance is mine; I will repay, saith the Lord'), to a non-Christian, more primitive code of 'justice', the private execution of revenge. The passages and the copy of Seneca's tragedies in Hieronimo's hand underscore this transition by reminding the audience of the Senecan dramatic world of violence, vengeance and the imperatives of private blood. In formulating his strategy of deceptive ignorance he again quotes from Seneca:

> For ignorance, I wot, and well they know,
> *Remedium malorum iners est.*
> (*Spanish Tragedy* 3.13.34f.)

The quotation is from Seneca's *Oedipus* (515), and, although the Senecan context is quite different from this scene, it keeps the Senecan world firmly in the audience's mind.

Specific relevancies are evident too in Marston's Senecan insertions. In *Antonio and Mellida* Piero quotes Atreus' outbursts at *Thyestes* 888 and 911 and, in so doing, exhibits himself as a manic Senecan tyrant, another Tantalid revenge-beast:

> Pish! *Dimitto superos, summa uotorum attigi.*
> Alberto, hast thou yielded up our fix'd decree
> Unto the Genoan ambassador?
> Are they content, if that their Duke return,
> To send his and his son Antonio's head,
> As pledges steep'd in blood, to gain their peace? . . .
> Why then: *O me coelitum excelsissimum!*
> The intestine malice and inveterate hate
> I always bore to that Andrugio
> Glories in triumph o'er his misery;
> Nor shall that carpet-boy, Antonio,
> Match with my daughter, sweet-cheek'd Mellida.
> No, the public power makes my faction strong . . .
> Pish! I prosecute my family's revenge,
> Which I'll pursue with such a burning chase
> Till I have dried up all Andrugio's blood.
> (*Antonio and Mellida* 1.1.59–64, 77–83, 87–9)

144

In Marston's sequel, *Antonio's Revenge*, Latin quotations from Seneca's plays create analogies between Piero and *Agamemnon*'s Clytemnestra (2.5.49), between Andrugio's Ghost and both *Thyestes'* Atreus (3.1.51) and *Octavia*'s Ghost of Agrippina (5.1.1ff.), and between Antonio and *Thyestes'* Ghost of Tantalus, urging vengeance (3.2.15ff.), and Atreus himself (3.3.7f.). Like Kyd's Hieronimo, Antonio even enters at one point (2.3) holding a copy of Seneca, from which he reads (2.3.45ff.); it is, however, a copy of the philosophical works, or at least of *De Providentia*, the Stoic imperative of which he instantly rejects. Equally telling but somewhat more complicated is Shakespeare's use of Seneca's *Phaedra* in *Titus Andronicus* to preface the rape and mutilation of Lavinia (*Per Stygia, per manes uehor*, *Titus* 1.1.635; cf. *Phaedra* 1180) and to express the ineffable pain of Titus on reading the names of those who committed the outrage:

> Magni dominator poli,
> Tam lentus audis scelera, tam lentus uides?
>
> (*Titus Andronicus* 4.1.81f.)

Titus' outburst fuses Hippolytus' cry of 'Magne regnator deum, tam lentus ... uides?' (*Phaedra* 672f.) with the 'philosophical' Seneca's famous statement of Stoic endurance at *Epistle* 107.12:[17]

> Duc, o parens celsique dominator poli,
> Quocumque placuit.
>
> Lead me, father and ruler of the soaring world,
> Wherever you have wished.

The double allusion not only conveys the cosmic dimension of Titus' outrage within a Senecanesque world of cosmic neglect of human suffering, but anticipates the inner strength, the steely indifference to pain and calamity, that will be the hallmark of Titus' response.[18]

More frequent, however, in Elizabethan and Jacobean drama and in Renaissance tragedy generally are vernacular adaptations of the Senecan text, pointed reworkings of scenes and speeches from Seneca's plays. In *Antonio and Mellida*, for example, Andrugio constructs his resolve against the paradigms of Andromache and Medea (cf. 3.1.82–6 with *Medea* 164–7 and *Troades* 507f.), while his speech at 4.1.46–66 rewrites the kingship chorus of *Thyestes* (esp. 344ff.) to set up a model of human behaviour which proves triumphant in the play and, as Piero divests himself of his Atrean robes and transforms his vengeance into love, apparently inverts the action of the Senecan model. 'Apparently' is important, for Marston's sequel, *Antonio's Revenge*, will reveal Piero's transformation to have been an Atrean 'pretence of love' (*Antonio's Revenge* 1.1.62). And the second play's reworkings of both Seneca's philosophical works and his tragedies, especially *Thyestes*,[19] not only sharpen the play's focus on the conflict between Stoic values and the passion for

145

vengeance, but underscore the latter's inevitable triumph. As a diptych the two Antonio plays replay both the action of *Thyestes* (conflict to apparent reconciliation to revenge and a pedophagic finale) and its critique of the Stoic world-view. Two points of detail are illustrative. In Act 2.2 Marston confirms Piero as a new Atreus by creating a scene between him and the Stoic Pandulpho which overtly replays the 'kingship' discussion between Atreus and his attendant at *Thyestes* 204ff. But Piero is not the only Atreus in the play. And in the torture scene of the final act the movement of the Atrean model from Piero to the Stoic Pandulpho is finely encapsulated in the latter's Englishing of Atreus' manic triumphalism at the moment of total satisfaction:

> He weeps! Now do I glorify my hands.
> I had no vengeance if I had no tears.
>
> (*Antonio's Revenge* 5.5.44f.)

The Senecan allusion could hardly have been more pointed:

> Nunc meas laudo manus,
> nunc parta uera est palma. perdideram scelus,
> nisi sic dolores.
>
> (*Thyestes* 1096–8)

> Now do I glorify my hands.
> Now the true palm's won. I had wasted the crime,
> If you weren't in such pain.

The subsequent dwelling on the parentage of the slain child continues the Thyestean replay (cf. *Antonio's Revenge* 5.5.61–4, *Thyestes* 1100–2). Provocatively the Senecan subtext changes to *Hercules Furens* for the drama's final scene (*Antonio's Revenge* 5.6.1f., 12f., 37).[20] Other plays by Marston (*The Malcontent* most especially) similarly appropriate Seneca's texts both to heighten the tragic register and to frame and comment on the dramatic action.

Marston is by no means exceptional. Senecan transformations punctuate the plays of Kyd, Marlowe, Fulke Greville, Chapman, Webster and Jonson.[21] In Jonson's *Sejanus*, Sejanus concludes the first act with lines borrowed from Seneca's *Medea* (*Medea* 151–4 = *Sejanus* 1.576–9), formulates his revenge on Drusus in Act 2 in conspicuously Atrean terms (cf. esp. *Sejanus*. 2.151ff., *Thyestes* 192ff.), and begins the final act with clear mimicry of Atreus' *aequalis astris gradior* soliloquy, which opens *Thyestes*' own final act (*Thyestes* 885ff.). *Hercules Oetaeus* was also considered a Senecan play in the Renaissance, and Chapman's *Bussy d'Ambois* not only models its ending on that of the 'Senecan' text, but signals the fact openly:

> Farewell, brave relics of a complete man,
> Look up and see thy spirit made a star;
> Join flames with Hercules, and when thou sett'st
> Thy radiant forehead in the firmament,

Make the vast crystal crack with thy receipt;
Spread to a world of fire, and the aged sky
Cheer with new sparks of old humanity.
(*Bussy d'Ambois* 5.4.147–53)

No Senecan transformation, however, is more famous than Tamburlaine's manic echo of the raging Hercules' impious claim (*2 Tamburlaine* 4.1.116–220; cf. *Hercules Furens* 958–61) or the metamorphosis of *Medea superest* (*Medea* 166) into the great riposte of Webster's heroine:

I am Duchess of Malfi still.
(*Duchess of Malfi*, 4.2.142)

Indeed Webster's Duchess seems to combine the overt sexuality of Seneca's Phaedra with Medea's sense of her own authoritative existence, and like the latter she annexes the universe in the expression of her rage:

I could curse the stars . . .
And those three smiling seasons of the year
Into a Russian winter, nay the world
To its first chaos.

(*Malfi* 4.1.96ff.)

More crudely imitative is Wilmot and company's remodelling of the *Thyestes'* messenger scene in *Gismond of Salerne* (5.1), or Thomas Hughes' *The Misfortunes of Arthur*, a play constituted, as Cunliffe shows,[22] out of Senecan adaptations linked together sometimes by only a handful of 'original' lines. And then there is Shakespeare, whose plays rewrite Senecan scenes and speeches constantly.[23] Lady Macbeth's transformation of *Medea*'s prologue is well known (1.5.40ff.). Less often observed are *Hamlet*'s debts to *Thyestes* especially in the use and inversion of the fatal banquet motif ('*Hamlet* is *Thyestes* inverted'),[24] or the transfusion of Atreus' entrance monologue (*Thyestes* 176ff.) into Hamlet's 'dull and muddy-mettled rascal' soliloquy at 2.2.550ff. *Agamemnon* too makes its way into *Hamlet* in the remodelling of the Clytemnestra–Electra exchange at *Agamemnon* 953ff. into that between Hamlet and his mother at 3.4.7ff.; so too *Hercules Furens* (see 970–3) in Laertes' outburst at 5.1.244–7. *Hercules Furens* acts as a subtext in *King Lear* too, the great speech of pain that follows Hercules' discovery of his *scelus* (1202ff.) providing the model for Lear's *Schreirede* on the Heath (3.2.1ff.). Other texts discerned in *King Lear* include *Thyestes, Agamemnon* and *Troades*. Nor was Shakespeare's indebtedness confined to his mature tragedies. Tragicomedies such as *The Tempest* and comedies such as *Midsummer Night's Dream* display several Senecan pointers. The latter replays motifs from Seneca's *Phaedra*;[25] while Hercules' *tibi tela frangam nostra* speech ('For you I'll break my shafts . . . ', *Hercules Furens* 1231ff.) reappears at the climax of Prospero's abjuration of his art to indicate his victory over 'fury':

> I'll break my staff,
> Bury it certain fadoms in the earth,
> And deeper than did ever plummet sound
> I'll drown my book.
>
> (*Tempest* 5.1.54–7)

Two of Shakespeare's most Senecan plays are among his earliest, *Titus Andronicus* and *Richard III*. The former's use of *Phaedra* was noted above. But to *Phaedra* too it may be indebted for its cyclical structure,[26] as it most certainly is for its ending (5.3.190–9): a series of funeral instructions, in which honourable burial is to be given to Saturninus, Titus and Lavinia, but refused to Tamora, whose life was 'devoid of pity' (5.3.198), as Phaedra's was of *pietas* (*impio capiti*, *Phaedra* 1280). Shakespeare's debts to Ovid's *Metamorphoses* are even more self-consciously paraded.[27] But relevant too is *Troades*, especially for its powerful use of the tomb in the stage-setting, although there are presumably debts here also to religious drama. Most important is *Thyestes*, whose dissolution of the opposition between civilisation and savagery is a pervasive motif of Shakespeare's play (e.g. 1.1.124ff., 3.1.53ff.), and, as in Seneca, is reflected in imagery of sacrifice, eating and animality,[28] which climaxes in a sacrificial slaying of children and a revenge banquet of their cooked bodies. Significantly Atreus' ghoulish ironies (*Thyestes* 976ff., 998) are replayed by both Aaron (3.1.201f.) and Titus (5.3.59ff.).

In *Richard III*, formally perhaps the most Senecanesque of Shakespeare's plays in its single action (there is no sub-plot), style and tone (apart from Richard's fiendish wit there is little comic relief),[29] several characters and scenes seem variations of Senecan models, *Troades* especially looms large, influencing the dramatisation of the drama's royal female figures, especially in the so-called 'scenes of the wailing queens' (2.2, 4.4),[30] where parallels can be discerned between Elizabeth, Anne and Margaret, on the one hand, and Andromache, Polyxena and Helen, on the other.[31] Particularly telling is the role of Richard's mother, the Duchess of York, as a kind of Hecuba figure, who reformulates Hecuba's 'universal grief' speech of *Troades*' final act (*Troades* 1060–2):

> Alas, I am the mother of these griefs:
> Their woes are parcell'd, mine is general.
>
> (*Richard III* 2.2.80f.)

and is castigated by others as the source of all disaster through giving birth:

> From forth the kennel of thy womb hath crept
> A hell-hound that doth hunt us all to death . . .
> That foul defacer of God's handiwork
> Thy womb let loose to chase us to our graves.
>
> (*Richard III* 4.4.47f., 53f.)

Senecan tyrant paradigms betray themselves in Richard, Atreus most obviously, who, like Richard (1.2.71), outbestialises the beasts (*Thyestes* 749ff.), and whose penchant for psychological revelation and word-play is reflected in Shakespeare's Richard from the start. Appropriately Richard's greeting of his brother, Clarence (1.1.42f.), resonates with Atrean hypocrisy (*Thyestes* 508). Lycus too figures prominently, and nowhere more than in Richard's outrageous wooing of Lady Anne (1.2), which remodels and improves upon Lycus' wooing of Megara in *Hercules Furens* (332ff.). Like Richard, Lycus had killed the previous king, and attempted to win over the old king's daughter (imminent daughter-in-law in Shakespeare); Lycus had also killed Megara's brothers, as Richard had killed Anne's future husband. Both wooings are motivated by political rather than 'amatory intent', and both attempt to remove responsibility for the respective slayings from the wooers themselves. But whereas Lycus notoriously fails, Richard succeeds and does so by transfering the responsibility for her future husband's death to Anne's own beauty, and by climaxing his wooing with the combination of a theatrical move (the threatened sword-thrust) borrowed from *Hercules Furens*' final act (1306ff.) and a Senecanesque contest of wits and words, an antilabic exchange in which the verbal victor takes all.

> *Richard* Then bid me kill myself, and I will do it.
> *Anne* I have already.
> *Rich.* That was in thy rage:
> Speak it again, and even with the word,
> This hand, which for thy love did kill thy love,
> Shall for thy love kill a far truer love:
> To both their deaths shalt thou be accessary.
> *Anne* I would I knew your heart.
> *Rich.* 'Tis figur'd in my tongue.
> *Anne* I fear me both are false.
> *Rich.* Then never was man true.
> *Anne* Well, well, put up your sword.
> *Rich.* Say then my peace is made.
> *Anne* That shalt thou know hereafter.
> *Rich.* But shall I live in hope?
> *Anne* All men, I hope, live so.
> *Rich.* Vouchsafe to wear this ring.
> *Anne* To take is not to give.
> *Rich.* Look how my ring encompasseth thy finger:
> Even so thy breast encloseth my poor heart;
> Wear both of them, for both of them are thine.
> (*Richard III* 1.2.190–209)

Senecan form underscores Shakespeare's indebtedness and his transcendence in arguably 'one of the greatest scenes written by Shakespeare and one of the greatest ever written'.[32] Marston's imitation (*Antonio's Revenge* 2.4.28ff.) justly flatters.

Senecan allusion is not of course confined to English drama. In Italian tragedy it is constant and overt. The opening appeal to the Furies by Dolce's Marianna (*Marianna* 1.1) replays Medea's prologue even more self-consciously than the invocation of Lady Macbeth (*Macbeth* 1.5.40ff.); so too Berenice's analogous invocation in Groto's *Dalida* (2.3). Berenice's subsequent revenge in Acts 4 and 5 of *Dalida* replays that of Atreus in Acts 4 and 5 of *Thyestes* and, compounding feast, sacrifice, funeral, wedding and murder, fuses it with the vengeance of Medea. At her moment of triumph Berenice echoes the cry of satisfaction of both her models (*Thyestes* 1096–9, *Medea* 982–6):

> Hor son donna, hor son forte, hor son Reina,
> Meritamente hor la corona porto.
> Si fa cosi a ribatter con fortezza
> Da se l'ingiurie. Imparino i mariti
> Ad esser fidi a le lor fide spose.
>
> (*Dalida* 4.3)

> Now I'm a woman, now I'm strong, now I'm Queen,
> Meritoriously now I wear the crown.
> This is the way in which the strong reply
> To injuries suffered. Let husbands learn
> Fidelity towards their faithful wives.

Cinthio's *Orbecche* replays many scenes and speeches from *Thyestes*, echoing (*inter alia*) the star chorus in the speech of the Furies in Act 1, the *satelles*-Atreus scene in Act 3, the Messenger's horror-filled narrative in Act 4, the *Schreirede* of Thyestes in Orbecche's outcry in Act 5:

> O Sol, che solo il mondo orni et illustri,
> Perchè nonti fuggisti allor dal Cielo,
> Che quest fier Tiran, ch' or per me giace,
> Commise così sozzo e orribil atto?
>
> (*Orbecche* 5.3)

> O Sun, who alone adorns and lights the world,
> Why did you not flee from the heavens then,
> When this fierce tyrant, who lies here because of me,
> Committed so foul and dreadful an act?

The *Tiran* is Orbecche's father, Sulmone, who like most Italian tyrants (e.g. Berenice in Groto's *Dalida*) is a remodelling of Atreus, although other Senecan tyrant figures are also apparent. For like Aegisthus (*Agamemnon* 994f.), Lycus (*Hercules Furens* 511ff.), as well as Atreus (*Thyestes* 246f.), Sulmone knows:

D'ogni morte è via più grave sempre
Una infelice e miserabil vita.

(*Orbecche* 3.3)

A worse road than any death always is
An unhappy and miserable life.

There is no 'Lycus–Megara scene' in *Orbecche*, but the model finds itself played out not only in non-Shakespearean English drama (e.g. the anonymous *Locrine*: Locrine and Estrildis; Marston's *Antonio's Revenge* and *The Malcontent*: Piero and Maria, Mendoza and Maria), but also in Garnier's *Porcie* (Arée and Octave). Indeed many of the famous Senecan lines reformulated in English drama are reformulated too into French dramatic verse. Macbeth's repoeticisation of *Phaedra* 715–18 (see also *Hercules Furens* 1323–9) is famous:[33]

> Will all great Neptune's ocean wash this blood
> Clean from my hand? No, this my hand will rather
> The multitudinous seas incarnadine,
> Making the green one red.
>
> (*Macbeth* 2.2.59–62)

Less known is Hérode's version in Tristan l'Hermite's *La Mariane* 5.2/ 1563f.:[34]

> Quel fleuve, ou quelle mer sera jamais capable
> D'effacer la noirceur de ce crime execrable?
>
> What river, or what ocean can ever wash
> Away the blackness of this cursed crime.

French dramatists rework Seneca constantly, whatever they may say in their *Préfaces*. The prologue spoken by Junon in Rotrou's *Les Sosies* (1636) models itself closely on Juno's prologue to *Hercules Furens*. Corneille's last play, *Suréna* (1674), reworks the ending of *Thyestes*, taking over its concluding appeal to the gods for vengeance in its last lines. His *Médée* (1635) reworks many Senecan lines and scenes, none more famously than the first Medea–Nutrix scene:

> *Nutrix*   Abiere Colchi, coniugis nulla est fides
> nihilque superest opibus e tantis tibi.
> *Medea*   Medea superest: hic mare et terras uides
> ferrumque et ignes et deos et fulmina.
>
> (*Medea* 164–7)

> *Nurse*   The Colchians are gone; your husband's vows are nothing.
> Nothing is left of all your wondrous wealth.
> *Medea*   Medea's left. Here you see ocean and earth,
> Iron and fire, gods and thunderbolts.

151

In Corneille the Nurse is Nérine:

> *Nérine* Votre pays vous hait, votre époux est sans foi:
> Dans un si grand revers que vous reste-t-il?
> *Médée* Moi,
> Moi, dis-je, et c'est assez.
> *Nérine* Quoi! vous seule, madame?
> *Médée* Oui, tu vois en moi seule et le fer et la flamme,
> Et la terre, et la mer, et l'enfer, et les cieux,
> Et le sceptre des rois, et le foudre des dieux.
> (*Médée* 1.5/319–24)

> *Nérine* Your country hates you, your husband's faithless:
> In this collapse of fortune, what's left?
> *Medea* Me,
> Me, I say, and that's enough.
> *Nérine* What! You alone, my lady?
> *Medea* Yes, you see in me alone iron and fire,
> And earth and ocean, and hell and heaven,
> The sceptre of kings and thunderbolts of gods.

Less often observed is Corneille's black humour in adapting Medea's 'I nunc, superbe, virginum thalamos pete' ('Go now, proud man, hunt down virginal beds', *Medea* 1007) as:

> Heureux père et mari, ma fuite et leur tombeau
> Laissent la place vide à ton hymen nouveau.
> Rejouis-t'en, Jason, va posséder Créuse.
> (*Médée* 5.6/1543–5)

> Happy father and husband, my flight and their tomb
> Empty the place for your new marriage.
> Rejoice now, Jason, go possess Créuse.

The last line is delivered to Jason as the dead Créuse's flesh-dissolving corpse lies on stage before him. Racine was never so ghoulish, although he too sometimes out-Senecas Seneca. His *Phèdre* rewrites many passages from Seneca's *Phaedra*, often surpassing Seneca's own descriptions, as in the effect of the monstrous bull from the sea, which in Racine embroils sky, air and sea, as well as earth (cf. *Phèdre* 5.6/1522ff., *Phaedra* 1050ff.). Other Senecan plays inform *Phèdre*, *Hercules Furens* most especially (cf. *Hercules Furens* 1329ff., *Phèdre* 5.7/1607ff.). But even after Racine the reworking of Seneca is apparent. Crébillon's *Atrée et Thyeste* (1707) attempts to soften, i.e. de-Senecanise, the horror of the original, but cannot really do so, and is forced to return to the Latin dramatist for some of his most powerful lines, as at the moment of revelation:

Atreus	natos ecquid agnoscis tuos?
Thyestes	Agnosco fratrem.

(Thyestes 1005f.)

Atreus	Do you recognise your sons?
Thyestes	I recognise my brother.

Crébillon:

Atrée	Méconnois-tu ce sang?
Thyeste	Je reconnois mon frère.

(Atrée et Thyeste 5.6.11)[35]

Atreus	Not recognize this blood?
Thyestes	I recognize my brother.

The Senecan paradigm re*presents* itself.

FORMS OF PLAYING

It is sometimes argued that the five-act structure of Renaissance drama derives from commentaries on Terence.[36] Such claims are difficult to prove. At the very least Senecan tragedy confirmed this structure and acted as a major paradigm for European dramatic forms. Indeed some have argued that playwrights such as Corneille owed to Seneca the whole 'art of building the dramatic development around a few, essential, properly distributed scenes'.[37] Italian and English revenge tragedies especially seem to follow a tripartite Senecan model: the appearance of a revenge spirit (ghost or fury), the formation of an avenger, the vengeance (including the all-important revelation to the victim).[38] The prime archetype is *Thyestes*, which had an immense impact on Italian and English Renaissance tragedy, influencing the dramatisation of vengeance in such plays as Corraro's *Progne*, Cinthio's *Orbecche*, Groto's *Dalida*, Decio's *Acripanda*, Kyd's *The Spanish Tragedy*, Tourneur/Middleton's *The Revenger's Tragedy* and, as was observed above, Shakespeare's *Titus Andronicus*.

From *Thyestes* and *Agamemnon* comes the Renaissance revenge ghost, revenge spirit or Fury, often opening the play as in Cinthio's *Orbecche* (*Nemesi Dea* and *Furie infernali*), Speroni's *Canace* (the Ghost of Canace's Child), Groto's *Dalida* (the Ghost of Moleonte and Death), Kyd's *The Spanish Tragedy* (the Ghost of Andrea and Revenge), Hughes's *The Misfortunes of Arthur* (Ghost of Gorlois), and Jonson's *Catiline* (Ghost of Sylla), but appearing too in Muret, Jodelle, Grévin, Garnier ('l'ombre d'Égée' in *Hippolyte*), Marston, Chapman – and Shakespeare.[39] The Ghost of Sylla in the prologue of Jonson's *Catiline* resurrects the language of *Thyestes'* Tantalus, but the more complex ghosts of Hamlet's father and Marston's Andrugio owe much to both *Thyestes* and *Agamemnon*, the Senecan spirit's *respice ad patrem* (*Agamemnon* 52) reappearing 1550 years later as the seminal 'Remember me' (*Hamlet*

1.5.91) and as Marston's 'Remember this' (*Antonio's Revenge* 3.1.50). To secure the Senecan connection Marston not only has Andrugio's Ghost follow his imperative with a Latin quotation from *Thyestes*, but even has the son Antonio quote extensively in Latin from the Ghost of Tantalus' despairing address to the inhabitants of Hades (*Antonio's Revenge* 3.2.15ff. = *Thyestes* 13–15, 75–79, 80f.). Normally however, as in Seneca, it is the ghost who catalogues the horrors of the underworld, and the catalogues are themselves often intentionally Senecanesque. Thus the Ghost of Andrea in *The Spanish Tragedy*:

> Then, sweet Revenge, do this at my request,
> Let me be judge, and doom them to unrest.
> Let loose poor Tityus from the vulture's gripe,
> And let Don Cyprian supply his room:
> Place Don Lorenzo on Ixion's wheel,
> And let the lover's endless pains surcease
> (Juno forgets old wrath and grants him ease):
> Hang Balthasar about Chimaera's neck,
> And let him there bewail his bloody love,
> Repining at our joys that are above:
> Let Serberine go roll the fatal stone,
> And take from Sisyphus his endless moan:
> False Pedringano, for his treachery,
> Let him be dragg'd through boiling Acheron,
> And there live, dying still in endless flames,
> Blaspheming gods and all their holy names.
> *(Spanish Tragedy* 4.5.29–44)

The passage's fusion of the Roman ghost's traditional underworld description (including the triad of Tityus, Ixion and Sisyphus: see *Agamemnon* 15ff., *Thyestes* 6ff.) with the demand for extraordinary punishment articulated elsewhere by Seneca's Theseus (*Phaedra* 1229ff.) provides fitting climax to Kyd's Senecanesque play. Sometimes the atmosphere of infernal horror, sought in Renaissance tragedy by dramatists as distinct as Peele (*The Battle of Alcazar*) and Shakespeare (*Macbeth*), is provided by such 'Senecan' devices as witches (Medea is important here), prophecies, oracles, the description of unnatural events, or the impassioned address to the Furies or the powers of hell. But the ghost remained an Elizabethan addiction, and even gave rise to parody:

> A filthie whining ghost,
> Lapt in some fowle sheet, or a leather pelch,
> Comes skreaming like a pigge half stickt,
> And cries *Vindicta*, revenge, revenge.
> *(A Warning for Fair Women*, Induction 54–7)

The addiction was not confined to vernacular plays. William Alabaster begins his neo-Latin *Roxana* (acted *c*.1592) with a revenge ghost (of Moleon), and Matthew Gwinne's *Nero* (printed 1603) has five different revenge ghosts, each opening a separate act. Even Seneca's own plays were rewritten to include ghost scenes that were never there. William Gager's 1591/2 Oxford production of Seneca's *Hippolytus* (i.e. *Phaedra*) in Latin expands Seneca's text to include a ghost scene.[40] So too does the translation which preceded and in part caused the explosion of English Senecanism in the 1560s, Heywood's *Troas*. The Ghost of Achilles in Seneca's *Troades* neither appears on stage nor cries for vengeance; in Heywood's 1559 'translation' it does:

> Vengeance and bloud doth Orcus pit require,
> To quench the fires of Achilles yre.

The first Senecan revenge ghost to enter English drama ironically was not Seneca's.

But it was not only the Senecan ghost that was taken over by Renaissance dramatists. So too the Senecan messenger, often as in Seneca contributing a moment of high spectacle (the *Nuntio* in Cinthio's *Orbecche* was played by the great actor Sebastiano Montefalco) or providing a moral frame for the action. In Corneille and Racine the messenger is often a major character; less so in Elizabethan drama, where, however, they multiply: four in *Richard III*, for example, two in *Macbeth*, where, as in *Troades* (168ff., 1118ff.), a conventional messenger's speech (1.2.7ff.) is later contrasted with one redolent with moral feeling (4.2.64ff.). The Senecan chorus is also transformed. Choruses occur quite frequently in Renaissance drama. They can be found, for example, in Norton and Sackville's *Gorboduc*, Wilmot's *Gismond of Salerne*, Hughes's *The Misfortunes of Arthur*, Marlowe's *Dr Faustus*, Daniel's *Cleopatra*, Peele's *David and Bethsabe*, Kyd's *Cornelia*, Shakespeare's *Romeo and Juliet*, *2 Henry IV* (Rumour), *Henry V*, *Pericles* (Gower), *The Winter's Tale* (Time), and *Henry VIII*, Jonson's *Catiline*, Cinthio's *Orbecche*, Dolce's *Marianna*, Groto's *Dalida*, Jodelle's *Cléopâtre captive*, Corneille's *Andromède*, Racine's *Esther* and *Athalie*. Influence of the Greek tragic chorus is also apparent, but it is noticeable that in several plays (e.g. *Orbecche*, *Gorboduc*, *Henry V*, *Alaham*, *Athalie*) the chorus is not only used, as in Seneca, to divide the acts, but is also, as in Seneca, not present continuously on the stage after the first entrance. It enters and exits like other characters. In *Athalie* it is even instructed by a non-choric figure what to sing (1.3/310), and, as at *Oedipus* 402, told to praise a god.

Sometimes Senecan choruses are reshaped into the meditations of a character. The *libera mors* chorus of *Agamemnon* (see esp. 589–604) is reshaped into Titus' funereal tribute to his dead sons (*Titus Andronicus* 1.1.153–9) and subsequently into Macbeth's ironic comments on the dead Duncan's enviable state ('After life's fitful fever he sleeps well . . . ' *Macbeth* 3.2.23–6).[41] Act 3 of *The Spanish Tragedy* commences with a remodelling of *Agamemnon*'s opening chorus on *fallax fortuna* (57ff.). The speaker is the Viceroy of Portingale:

> Infortunate condition of kings,
> Seated amidst so many helpless doubts!
> First we are plac'd upon extremest height,
> And oft supplanted with exceeding heat,
> But ever subject to the wheel of chance:
> And at our highest never joy we so,
> As we both doubt and dread our overthrow.
> So striveth not the waves with sundry winds
> As fortune toileth in the affairs of kings,
> That would be fear'd, yet fear to be belov'd,
> Sith fear or love to kings is flattery:
> For instance lordings, look upon your king,
> By hate deprived of his dearest son,
> The only hope of our successive line.
>
> (*Spanish Tragedy* 3.1.1–14)

Many of the soliloquies of Elizabethan drama are essentially choric reflections on existential, social or moral questions: so Hieronimo at *The Spanish Tragedy* 3.2.1ff., the King at *2 Henry IV* 3.1.4ff., *Henry V* 4.1.227ff., or the recurrent meditations on death, as at *Macbeth* 5.5.19ff. or *Hamlet* 3.1.56ff., which bear comparison with the *post mortem nihil* chorus of *Troades* (371ff.). Sometimes in Shakespeare a whole scene might have a choric function, as, for example, the closing scenes of Acts 2 and 3 of *Macbeth* (2.4 and 3.6), which construct from the discourse of minor characters a moral commentary on the events of the preceding act. Sometimes too a main character in Shakespeare and others operates as a recurrent chorus. Arruntius in Jonson's *Sejanus* falls into this category, as do Malevole in *The Malcontent* and Edgar in *King Lear*. They talk in choric maxims throughout the play, and in *Sejanus* and *Lear* close it in a choric fashion (*Sejanus* 5.901–7, *Lear* 5.3.322–5) avoided by Seneca himself, but reminiscent of *Octavia* and *Hercules Oetaeus*. Edgar's closing 'choric' commentary at *King Lear* 3.6.101ff. merits attention for its replay of the sentiments of the opening lines of the final chorus of *Troades*:

> When we our betters see bearing our woes,
> We scarcely think our miseries our foes.
> Who alone suffers suffers most i' th' mind,
> Leaving free things and happy shows behind;
> But then the mind much sufferance doth o'erskip,
> When grief hath mates, and bearing fellowship.
>
> (*King Lear* 3.6.100–5)

The Renaissance meditative soliloquy is not always choric. But even when it is not, despite some inheritance from the *psychomachia* of the medieval tradition (itself not without Senecan influence), it is principally indebted to Seneca for its psychological focus and its self-presentational mode. Much has

156

been made of the 'new' modes of perception of self and others displayed by
the Renaissance soliloquy, too little of their relationship to Senecan tragedy's
own interiority.[42] The Senecan self-questioning, self-addressing monologue is
everywhere in Renaissance drama, and used structurally as one of the
building-blocks of the play. In Cinthio's *Cleopatra* it is *the* building-block,
accounting for fifteen of the play's thirty-seven scenes.[43] It is the basis of
Corneille's dramaturgy.[44] Sometimes fairly clear Senecan relations seem
involved. Richard III's staccato wrestling with identity and past crimes on the
night before Bosworth Field (*Richard III* 5.3.180ff.) seems to climb out of
Medea's soliloquies in Seneca's play, especially her final introspection at
Medea 895ff., which seems clearly to have influenced other famous theatrical
moments (e.g. Hermione's turbulent soliloquy at the opening of Act 5 of
Racine's *Andromaque*. 5.1/1393ff.). Not infrequently in the soliloquies the
characteristically Roman and Senecan technique of having the speaker
address his or her own passions or parts of body is found:

> Heart, wilt not break? And thou, abhorred life,
> Wilt thou still breathe in my enraged blood?
> Veins, sinews, arteries, why crack ye not,
> Burst and divuls'd with anguish of my grief?
> (*Antonio and Mellida* 1.1.1–4)

Thus Marston's Antonio, addressing his body. 'Silence, amour, silence', says
Corneille's Lyse, addressing her passion in the vengeance soliloquy at *L'Illusion comique* 3.6.855. These modes of address are found even in dialogue-
turned-monologue, as in Émilie's address to her *passion* at *Cinna* 1.2/125:
'Tout beau, ma passion, deviens un peu moins forte'; or in Othello's, Lear's
and Antony's open expressions of pain: 'Yield up, O love, thy crown and
hearted throne | To tyrannous hate. Swell, bosom . . . ' (*Othello* 3.3.455f.);
'Down, thy climbing sorrow' (*Lear* 2.4.55); 'O, me! my heart, my rising heart!
but, down!' (*Lear* 2.4.118); 'O, cleave, my sides! | Heart, once be stronger than
thy continent; | Crack thy frail case!' (*Antony and Cleopatra* 4.14.40–2). They are
all versions of the Senecan *age, anime,* formula, and the various apostrophes of
dolor, ira, amor, pudor, pectus and *manus,* which mark his tragic discourse.

Émilie's address comes from the concluding moments of one of the
many confidant(e) scenes that permeate Renaissance drama, French tragedy
most especially. And this too seems a Senecan inheritance. Important here
are the many so-called 'passion-restraint' scenes in which, as in *Phaedra,
Medea, Agamemnon,* and *Thyestes,* a subordinate figure/confidant(e) attempts to
restrain the passion of a social superior. Such, for example, are the scenes in
Corneille's *Le Cid* between L'Infante and Léonor (1.2, 2.5) and Chimène and
Elvire (3.3); in *Cinna* between Émilie and Fulvie (1.2), and Auguste and Livie
(4.3); in Racine's *Iphigénie* between Ériphile and Doris (2.1, 4.1), and in *Phèdre*
between Phèdre and Oenone (3.1). With these may be compared the third
act of Cinthio's *Orbecche* (3.2), where the counsellor Malecche tries to control

the rage of the tyrant Sulmone, or of his *Altile* (3.5), where Naina attempts to control her tyrannical brother's fury; or the third and fourth acts respectively of Dolce's *Marianna* (3.2) and Speroni's *Canace* (4.2), where royal counsellors vainly attempt to restrain their raging monarchs (Herod and Eolo). Examples in Shakespeare include the scenes where Marcus attempts to restrain Titus (*Titus* 3.1.215ff.), where Kent vainly tries to restrain the enraged Lear (*Lear* 1.1.119ff.) or Camillo the jealous Leontes (*Winter's Tale* 1.2.235ff.), where Ariel prompts Prospero to tenderness (*Tempest* 5.1.1ff.), and the various exchanges in *Hamlet* between Horatio and the prince. Other influences inevitably are often at work, and it would be vain to classify every 'advice scene' as Senecan. But the line of inheritance seems there, even in its non-Senecan mutations. For Shakespeare is just as likely to invert the Senecan paradigm and have the protagonist urge passion on the confidant, as in the dialogue between Richard and Buckingham in the post-coronation scene of *Richard III* (4.2.1ff.), or have the confidante attempt to impassion a protagonist as Lady Macbeth attempts to impassion her husband in *Macbeth*'s opening act (1.7.28–82).

Pervasive throughout these scenes and throughout Renaissance drama as a whole is tragic rhetoricity, the Senecan high style of tragic speech, essential to French tragedy of the sixteenth and seventeenth centuries, which relies so much on *declamatio* to articulate its drama of the word and will. Typical are the verbal outbursts of Corneille's Chimène at *Le Cid* 2.8/659ff., Cinna at *Cinna* 3.4/1049ff., Cléopâtre at *Rodogune* 5.1/1515ff., or the extraordinary declamation of Camille just before her death at the hands of her brother, Horace:

> Rome, l'unique objet de mon ressentiment!
> Rome, à qui vient ton bras d'immoler mon amant!
> Rome, qui t'a vu naître, et que ton coeur adore!
> Rome enfin que je hais parce qu'elle t'honore!
> Puissent tous ses voisins ensemble conjurés
> Saper ses fondements encor mal assurés!
> Et si ce n'est assez de toute l'Italie,
> Que l'Orient contre elle à l'Occident s'allie;
> Que cent peuples unis des bouts de l'univers
> Passent pour la détruire et les monts et les mers!
> Qu'elle-même sur soi renverse ses murailles,
> Et de ses propres mains déchire ses entrailles;
> Que le courroux du ciel allumé par mes voeux
> Fasse pleuvoir sur elle un déluge de feux!
> Puissé-je de mes yeux y voir tomber ce foudre,
> Voir ses maisons en cendre, et tes lauriers en poudre,
> Voir le dernier Romain à son dernier soupir,
> Moi seule en être cause, et mourir de plaisir!
>
> (*Horace* 4.5/1301–18)

Rome, the sole object of my resentment,
Rome, for whom your arm just slew my lover,
Rome, who saw your birth, whom your heart adores,
Rome, whom I hate because she honours you.
Let all her neighbours conspire together
To sap her foundations even now infirm.
And if all Italy is insufficient,
Let East and West ally themselves against her;
Let one hundred nations unite from the world's end
Crossing mountains and seas for her destruction;
Let her pull down her ramparts on herself,
And with her own hands tear out her bowels;
Let the wrath of heaven kindled by my prayers
Rain down upon her a deluge of flame.
Would that my eyes could see the thunderbolt crash,
See her houses ash and your laurels dust,
See the last Roman at his final breath,
Myself alone the cause, and die of pleasure.

The indebtedness of Corneille's lofty style to Seneca is widely acknowledged, and finds paradigmatic realisation in the grand narrations that are the hallmark of his drama. Some readers of Corneille even attribute to Seneca 'the best devices of his style' *simpliciter*.[45] But in Racine too, renowned for his greater naturalness of tone and more sparing theatricality, in which overt dramatic gesticulation is kept to a minimum, declamatory force has its role, as in the Iphigénie, Agamemnon, Clytemnestre confrontation in *Iphigénie* 4.4, or the bombast of Clytemnestre's *Schreirede* against Eriphile and the Greeks later in the play (5.4/1675ff.), which replays the curse of Seneca's Hecuba (cf. 5.4/1679ff. with *Troades* 1005ff.).

The French were not alone. English Renaissance audiences, like the Roman aristocracy of the imperial period, were the product of an education system with a strong emphasis on training in classical rhetoric. The *Progymnasmata* of the fourth century CE sophist Aphthonius was 'almost the standard grammar-school textbook of composition'.[46] The result was a culture, for which, like that of ancient Rome, truth was more often a function of disputation than of experiment. It was a culture not simply able to respond to rhetorical drama, but determinant of it. Here is Gorboduc's one sentence statement of his own wretchedness that opens the third act:

O cruel fates, O mindful wrath of gods,
Whose vengeance neither Simois' stained streams
Flowing with blood of Trojan princes slain,
Nor Phrygian fields made rank with corpses dead
Of Asian kings and lords, can yet appease;
Ne slaughter of unhappy Priam's race,

> Nor Ilion's fall made level with the soil
> Can yet suffice; but still continu'd rage
> Pursues our lives, and from the farthest seas
> Doth chase the issues of destroyed Troy.
> (*Gorboduc* 3.1.1–10)

Here is Othello using the world to image his desire for vengence:

> Like to the Pontic sea,
> Whose icy current and compulsive course
> Ne'er feels retiring ebb, but keeps due on
> To the Propontic and the Hellespont,
> Even so my bloody thoughts, with violent pace,
> Shall ne'er look back, ne'er ebb to humble love,
> Till that a capable and wide revenge
> Swallow them up.
> (*Othello* 3.3.460–7)

For English declamatory verse, as for French, Seneca constituted not the only model (one must not neglect the speeches of classical epic), but the principal and 'most immediate' classical one.[47] Bombast can be overdone, as in the hyper-Senecan conceit of D'Amville in *The Atheist's Tragedy*:

> Drop out
> Mine eye-balls, and let envious Fortune play
> At tennis with 'em.
> (*Atheist's Tragedy* 2.4.27–9)

It did however establish itself as an appropriate mode for tragic narration and not only in Corneille (see the speech of the 'bleeding Captain' at *Macbeth* 1.2.7ff.). In English tragedy, where a host of Senecan rhetorical *topoi* (*dehisce tellus*, the sinners/monsters of hell, the punishments of hell, the wish for universal annhilation, etc.)[48] may be found, bombast is used, as in Seneca, not only to express the inexpressible, to give the control of rhetorical form to unbridled passion and pain, but to construct tragic character out of the very grandiosity and cosmic dimensions of the language used. Titus, Macbeth, Othello, Lear are cases in point; but so too are Gorboduc, Faustus and, most especially, Tamburlaine, whose competitive immenseness and matchless power are verbal as much as anything and remain undiminished even in the language of his dying speech:

> Now, eyes, enjoy your latest benefit,
> And when my soul hath virtue of your sight,
> Pierce through the coffin and the sheet of gold
> And glut your longings with a heaven of joy.
> So, reign, my son, scourge and control those slaves,
> Guiding thy chariot with thy father's hand.

As precious is the charge thou undertakest
As that which Clymen's brain-sick son did guide
When wandering Phoebe's ivory cheeks were scorched,
And all the earth, like Aetna, breathing fire.
Be warned by him, then, learn with awful eye
To sway a throne as dangerous as his:
For if thy body thrive not full of thoughts
As pure and fiery as Phyteus' beams,
The nature of these proud rebelling jades
Will take occasion by the slenderest hair
And draw thee piecemeal like Hippolytus
Through rocks more steep and sharp than Caspian clifts.
The nature of thy chariot will not bear
A guide of baser temper than myself,
More than heaven's coach the pride of Phaeton.
Farewell, my boys, my dearest friends farewell,
My body feels, my soul doth weep to see
Your sweet desires deprived my company,
For Tamburlaine, the scourge of God, must die.

(2 Tamburlaine 5.3.224–48)

The verbal onslaught is impressive; so too the decasyllablic verse-form, which began in English with Surrey's translations of Virgil's *Aeneid* (*c.*1540), but its establishment as the canonic form for English drama dates from the Senecan *Gorboduc* (1561–2) and is in part attributed by Eliot to the impact of Seneca's sonorous iambic line.[49] Sonority and bombast were, however, also parodied. Feliche's response to Matzagente's manner of speech in Marston's *Antonio and Mellida* (Induction 86f.) is illustrative:

Rampum scrampum, mount tufty Tamburlaine! What rattling thunder-clap breaks from his lips?

So prevalent is this bombast on the Elizabethan and Jacobean stage that parody and non-parody commonly exist in uneasy conjunction, jostling for the audience's attention.

What bombast is also often linked to is the 'attitude of self-dramatisation', informing the speech of so many Renaissance dramatic figures, and heralded by Eliot as one of Seneca's greatest legacies to Elizabethan tragedy.[50] Particularly important here is a character's own onomastic play, their concern to rhetoricise their name, to give it the force of argument. Notice how the final line of Tamburlaine's final speech focuses on his name; how in Racine's *Mithridate* (5.5) the dying king's last word is his name; how the Duchess of Malfi in her moment of greatest vulnerability relies on her name (4.2.142). Self-signalling of this kind is ubiquitous in Renaissance drama: thus Dolce's Edippo in Act 5 of *Giocasta*: 'io sarò sempre Edippo';

161

his Medea in her opening speech: 'Ecco Medea'; Cinthio's queen in Act 5 of *Cleopatra*: 'et che s'hai vinto | L'Egitto, non hai vinta Cleopatra'; Garnier's triumvir in Act 3 of *Marc Antoine* (1030f.): 'Son empire asseuré jamais ne pensera | Tandis que Marc Antoine en ce monde sera'; and Corneille's Pulchérie: 'Je suis impératrice, et j'étais Pulchérie' (*Pulchérie* 3.1/754). Such onomastic rhetoric derives clearly from Senecan tragedy, in which characters regularly play with and upon their names, none more dramatically than Medea, whose *Medea superest* (166) and *Medea nunc sum* (910) seem to have provided the model for many rhetorical moments: 'Know I am Hieronimo' (*Spanish Tragedy* 4.4.83); 'Richard loves Richard, that is, I am I' (*Richard III* 5.3.184); 'This is I, | Hamlet the Dane' (*Hamlet* 5.1.250f.); 'Were I the Moor, I would not be Iago' (*Othello* 1.1.57); ''Tis I, 'tis Vindice, 'tis I!' (*Revenger's Tragedy* 3.5.165); 'I am | Antony yet' (*Antony and Cleopatra* 3.13.97f.). The paradigm is inverted in Lear's: 'This is not Lear' (1.4.223). The assumed correlation of name and personal and social identity is questioned by Shakespeare's young lovers ('What's in a name?' *Romeo and Juliet* 2.2.43) and problematised in the great tragedy of name, *Coriolanus* (see, e.g., *Coriolanus* 5.1.11ff.). Famously Corneille's Médée avoids the onomastic play of her Senecan prescript.

Other Senecan rhetorical influences may be seen in Renaissance drama's use of epic similes (*1 Tamburlaine* 3.2.76ff., *Richard II* 3.2.106ff., Cinthio *passim*),[51] its predilection for scenes of moral and political debate (*Gorboduc* 1.2, *Richard II* 1.1, *Cinna* 2.1), its ironic and punning use of language (for Seneca, see, e.g., *Thyestes* 525ff., 970ff.), and, most obviously, its sententious style, its deployment of gnomic sayings, epigram, *sententiae*: 'Sorrow doth dark the judgement of the wit' (*Gorboduc* 3.1.140); 'Sorrow concealed, like an oven stopped, | Doth burn the heart to cinders where it is' (*Titus* 2.3.36f.);[52] 'Fairer than nature's fair is foulest vice' (*Antonio's Revenge* 1.3.56); 'He does his vantage know | That makes it home, and gives the foremost blow' (*Sejanus* 4.91f.); 'Things bad begun make strong themselves by ill' (*Macbeth* 3.2.55);[53] 'Qui ne craint point la mort ne craint point les menaces' (*Le Cid* 2.1/393); 'Qui méprise sa vie est maître de la sienne' (*Cinna* 1.2/130). There are occasions too where the Senecan use of such commonplaces to de-individualise the speaker (they often cluster in the speeches of social subordinates such as Nurses or Attendants) is clearly at work, and even extended to major figures. In Marlowe's *The Jew of Malta*, for example, Barabas often seems to construct himself out of proverbs and *sententiae*, sometimes overtly and ironically Christian ('Faith is not to be held with heretics', 2.3.316).[54] Similarly Senecan-derived seems the occasional use of antilabic or stichomythic exchanges in the construction of dialogue:

> *Richard* Should dying men flatter with those that live?
> *Gaunt* No, no, men living flatter those that die.
> *Richard* Thou now a-dying sayest thou flatterest me.

162

Gaunt   Oh no, thou diest, though I the sicker be.
Richard I am in health, I breathe, and see thee ill.
Gaunt   Now He that made me knows I see thee ill.
(*Richard II* 2.1.88–93)

What is particularly telling here, as elsewhere in Shakespearean and other English drama (e.g., *Spanish Tragedy* 1.4.77ff., *Hamlet* 3.4.8ff., *Richard III* 4.4.343ff.), is the employment of Seneca's *Stichworttechnik*, his construction of stichomythic exchanges around a repetition of keywords and concomitant creation of what is essentially a tournament of words. This 'verbal contest' aspect is a clear Senecan inheritance and sets this kind of dialogue apart from the one-line exchanges of medieval drama. The French dramatists employed this technique too, including Corneille (e.g. *Le Cid* 1.3./215ff., *Cinna* 2.2/647ff.) and Racine, who constructs a Senecanesque verbal duel between Néron and Britannicus at *Britannicus* 3.8/1051ff.

The verbal violence of the Renaissance *Schreirede* also owes much to Seneca, the cries of indignation against the inactivity of heaven which become commonplace especially in English tragedy.[55] Typical is Malevole's speech closing Act 3 scene 3 of Marston's *The Malcontent*:

> O heaven, didst hear
> Such devilish mischief? Sufferest thou the world
> Carouse damnation even with greedy swallow,
> And still dost wink, still does thy vengeance slumber?
> If now thy brows are clear, when will they thunder?
> (*Malcontent* 3.3.119–23)

Worth quoting also is the outburst of Vindice in the aftermath of his own (disguised) enlistment of his mother in the seduction of his sister.

> Oh more uncivil, more unnatural
> Than those base-titled creatures that look downward,
> Why does not heaven turn black, or with a frown
> Undo the world? Why does not earth start up
> And strike the sins that tread upon it? Oh,
> Were't not for gold and women there would be no damnation,
> Hell would look like a lord's great kitchen without fire in't;
> But 'twas decreed before the world began
> That they should be the hooks to catch at man.
> (*Revenger's Tragedy* 2.1.249–57)

Comparisons with Seneca lie not only in the forms of language. For here Tourneur/Middleton has fused Hippolytus' great speech of cosmic outrage at *Phaedra* 671ff. with the Hippolytan misogynistic analysis of human sin at *Phaedra* 540–64. Hippolytus' *lucrum* (540) and *femina* (560) reappear as Vindice's 'gold and women'. Vindice constructs himself as the Hippolito his brother is.

163

The Renaissance passion for *Schreirede* was an aspect of its passion for theatricality and spectacle, and for their use in structuring or climaxing the dramatic action. Italian drama revelled in *lo spettacolo*; Cinthio's own dramas and critical writings proclaim its importance, as well as that of 'tutto l'apparecchio della scena' and *la maraviglia*. *Orbecche*, for example, from its opening infernal scenes onwards implements an urge for dramatic spectacle which at the level of scenic design was to become a major preoccupation of Italian painters and architects (notably Serlio and Palladio) in the sixteenth and seventeenth centuries. French tragedy too deserves notice here. The pervasive spectacle, for example, of Racine's last play, *Athalie*, with its mass processions of worshippers, exotic and evocative background (Solomon's Temple), its stirring music and large chorus of maidens, its sophisticated stage-machines, its multitude of extras, is reminiscent of such visually powerful Senecan plays as *Medea* and *Agamemnon*. The turning-point of the action is itself a piece of theatrical spectacle. As the curtain is drawn to reveal Joas, the young king: 'Ici le fond du théâtre s'ouvre. On voit dedans du temple, et les lévites armés sortent de tous côtés sur la scène.'

Renaissance tragedy abounds with spectacular scenes: the presentation of the head of Oronte in *Orbecche* (which caused the actor's lover to collapse 'come morta');[56] Tamburlaine's chariot drawn by the captive kings; the death-banquet at the end of *Hamlet*; the royal suicide closing *Antony and Cleopatra*; the arraignment of Vittoria Corombona at the central point of *The White Devil*; the end of Act 5 scene 1 of *The Atheist's Tragedy*, with its theatrical juxtaposition of the biers of Rousard and Sebastian with D'Amville's pile of gold; Médée's magic scene in Corneille. Corneille of course made his interest in spectacle overt in his introductory remarks to *Andromède*: 'Mon principal but ici a été de satisfaire la vue par l'éclat et la diversité du spectacle, et non pas de toucher l'esprit par la force du raissonnement, ou le coeur par la délicatesse des passions.' And, however untypical such 'machine plays' as *Andromède* or *La Toison d'or* may be claimed to be, they represent an interest in spectacle apparent in all Corneille's plays.

Many of the theatrical high spots of Senecan tragedy are characterised by violence: the revelation of the children's heads in *Thyestes*, the dismembered corpse of Hippolytus in *Phaedra*, the deaths on stage in *Medea*, *Oedipus*, *Hercules Furens*. Renaissance spectacle is often similarly characterised. Visual display of dismemberment and death permeates English and Italian tragedy, influenced in part (at least in England) by the mystery plays but also in substantial part by Seneca: the bloody flayings, executions, and murders of Preston's *Cambises*; the decapitation of Virginia and the exhibition of her head in *Appius and Virginia*; the 'spectacle' of Horatio's dead body revealed alongside the other four corpses in *The Spanish Tragedy*; the amputation of Titus' left hand in the third act of *Titus Andronicus*, or the filicide and banquet of the dead at the climax of that play; Bajazeth and Zabina dashing their brains out on the bars of Tamburlaine's cage; the mutilations, amputations

and decapitations of *Henry VI*, *Macbeth*, and *Antonio's Revenge*; the blinding
of Gloucester in *King Lear*; the severed hand, the torture and strangling of
the Duchess in Act 4 of *The Duchess of Malfi*; the stabbing of Alonzo, the
severing of his finger and its subsequent display in Middleton's and Rowley's
The Changeling; Giovanni's entrance in Ford's *'Tis Pity She's A Whore* with his
sister's heart upon his dagger. In Cinthio's *Orbecche* the audience is treated to
many images of bodily dismemberment, including the severing of the hero's
hands and the presentation of his head on stage to Orbecche herself,
together with the bodies of their slain children still pierced by the fatal
daggers. The heads of Dalida and her children are similarly presented on
stage in *Dalida*'s final act, this time on a golden platter.

Even in French drama, which is notoriously stringent in its prohibition of
violence from the stage, the occasional, theatrical use of violence is evident.
The ending of Corneille's *Suréna* follows the verbal description of Suréna's
murder with Eurydice's death on stage; the final act of his *Médée* surpasses
Seneca in its violence, through the introduction of Jason's suicide and its
innovative treatment of Créon and Créuse, who appear on stage in agony, as
their flesh comes apart, and commit suicide or die in full dramatic view. In
Corneille's *Clitandre* the audience witnesses an attempted rape followed by
the gouging of the would-be rapist's eye with *un poinçon*.

The murder of childen prominent in Senecan tragedy (*Hercules Furens*,
Troades, *Medea*, *Thyestes*) is especially common: *Orbecche*, *Canace*, *Dalida*, *Gorbo-*
duc, *Tamburlaine*, *The Jew of Malta*, *Titus Andronicus*, *Richard III*, *Sejanus*, *Macbeth*,
Rodogune, *Phèdre* are but some examples. Also as in Seneca visual violence is
sometimes accompanied, sometimes replaced, by verbal violence. The dismemberment of Sejanus, for example, like that of Hippolytus in *Phaedra* to
which it seems indebted, is reported, not shown (*Sejanus* 5.815–42). At times
there seems a competition of verbal horror of a quasi-Atrean dimension.
Thus Tamburlaine to Almeda:

> Go, villain, cast thee headlong from a rock,
> Or rip thy bowels and rend out thy heart
> T'appease my wrath, or else I'll torture thee,
> Searing thy hateful flesh with burning irons
> And drops of scalding lead, while all thy joints
> Be racked and beat asunder with the wheel:
> For if thou livest, not any element
> Shall shroud thee from the wrath of Tamburlaine.
>
> (*2 Tamburlaine* 3.5.120–7)

Or Ferdinand on the Duchess of Malfi and her lover:

> I would have their bodies
> Burnt in a coal-pit, with the ventage stopp'd,
> That their curs'd smoke might not ascend to heaven:

165

Or dip the sheets they lie in, in pitch or sulphur,
Wrap them in't, and then light them like a match;
Or else to boil their bastard to a cullis,
And give't his lecherous father, to renew
The sin of his back.

(Malfi 2.5.66–73)

This competition of horror is especially prominent in Italian neo-Senecan tragedies, in which the tragic effect is not one of pity and fear but 'horrore e compassione',[57] the aim being to outdo even the violence and horror of Seneca himself. As Berenice explains in Groto's *Dalida*,[58] in response to the chorus' question, 'E perche tanto mal?' (And why so much evil?'):

Perche le mense
Di Tantalo, di Tereo, e di Thieste,
Rispetto à questa dispietata cena,
Possan quei, che verran, nomar pietose –
Per far del mio dolor degna vendetta.

(Dalida 4.3)

That the banquets
Of Tantalus, Tereus and Thyestes,
In comparison with this impious feast,
May be called pious by posterity –
To create a vengeance matching my grief.

Indeed one of the great contemporary appeals of Senecan and Renaissance drama is precisely its use of violence as a dramatic mode. Late twentieth-century cinema revels in the spectacular effects of violence. Allegorical narratives such as Tarantino's *Pulp Fiction* (USA 1994) and Stone's *Natural Born Killers* (USA 1994), historical dramas such as Chéreau's *La Reine Margot* (France 1994) – with its bloody reproduction of the St Bartholomew's Day massacre of Protestants in Paris of 1572, followed by court intrigue, lust, adultery, incest and murder worthy of a Jacobean tragedy, complete with the lover's severed head – and Jarman's film of Marlowe's *Edward II* (UK 1991), are paradigm cases. But it should be observed that, in the late twentieth century, audiences are likely to regard violent death less as a generic necessity appropriate to the tragic form, more as 'an historical necessity, or as something altogether natural'.[59] I suspect that some of the Elizabethans might have agreed. Seneca's Romans certainly would have.

8

IDEOLOGY AND MEANING

So that the right vse of Comedy will (I thinke) by no body be blamed, and
much lesse of the high and excellent Tragedy, that openeth the greatest
wounds, and sheweth forth the Vlcers that are couered with Tissue; that
maketh Kinges feare to be Tyrants, and Tyrants manifest their tirannical
humors; that, with sturring the affects of admiration and commiseration,
teacheth the vncertainety of this world, and vpon how weake foundations
guilden roofes are builded; that maketh vs knowe,

> Qui sceptra saeuus duro imperio regit,
> Timet timentes, metus in auctorem redit. [Seneca Oedipus 705f.]

Sir Philip Sidney, An Apologie for Poetrie (1595)[1]

The Senecanism of Renaissance tragedy extended beyond allusion, action
and form. It encompassed thought, idea and meaning. Central ideas structuring Renaissance playmaking before sixteenth- and seventeenth-century
audiences seem derived directly or indirectly from the Roman dramatist.
Although most obviously revealed in plays which go overtly to Senecan
material (Corneille's Médée, Rotrou's L'Hercule mourant, La Pinelière's
Hippolyte, Racine's Phèdre) and rewrite that material to reflect contemporary
concerns,[2] ideological indebtedness is apparent throughout the whole of
Renaissance tragedy. This chapter restricts itself to four areas of such
indebtedness.

MODES OF POWER

Renaissance tragedy is filled with speeches on kingship and power, replaying
many of the ideas articulated in Senecan drama. Thus the Countess of
Cambrai in Chapman's The Revenge of Bussy D'Ambois, re-expressing the
Senecan notion of the interdependence of power's stability and its justice
(Troades 258f., Medea 196, Thyestes 215ff.):

> Will kings make treason lawful? Is society
> (To keep which only kings were first ordained)

167

Less broke in breaking faith 'twixt friend and friend
Than 'twixt the king and subject? Let them fear.
Kings' precedents in license lack no danger.
Kings are compar'd to gods and should be like them,
Full in all right, in naught superfluous,
Nor nothing straining past right for their right:
Reign justly and reign safely.

> *(Revenge of Bussy D'Ambois* 4.3.41–9)

Similarly Senecanesque, even Thyestean (*Thyestes* 446ff.), discussions of the vanities of power may be found in the mouth of Henry V (*Henry V* 4.1.226ff.) and Corneille's Auguste (*Cinna* 2.1/371ff.), or statements of power's inversion of moral values in the mouth of Shakespeare's Edward:

But for a kingdom any oath may be broken:
I would break a thousand oaths to reign one year.

> *(3 Henry VI* 1.2.16f.)

Or Jonson's Sejanus:

Sejanus   Whom hatred frights,
                Let him not dream on sov'reignty.
Tiberius   Are rites
            Of faith, love, piety, to be trod down?
            Forgotten? And made vain?
Sejanus   All for a crown.

> *(Sejanus* 2.174–7)

Or Chapman's Baligny:

            Your Highness knows
        I will be honest, and betray for you
        Brother and father; for I know, my lord,
        Treachery for kings is truest loyalty,
        Nor is to bear the name of treachery,
        But grave, deep policy.

> *(Revenge of Bussy D'Ambois* 2.1.29–34)

Or Massinger's Parthenius:

        Monarchs that dare not do unlawfull things,
        Yet bare them out, are Constables, not Kings.

> *(Roman Actor* 1.2.86f.)

Other sources for discussions of kingship were available to Renaissance dramatists, most famously Machiavelli's *Il Principe* (completed 1513; published 1532), itself indebted to Seneca for its representation of power.[3] Another source is the great epic of Seneca's nephew, Lucan, whose speech of Pothinus (*Bellum Ciuile* 8.484ff.) became a model for the opening of Corneille's *Pompée*. Seneca's influence, however, seems foundational. The so-called 'Machiavellianism' of the passages quoted above is a replay of the positions of Oedipus (*Oedipus* 703f.), Eteocles (*Phoenissae* 653f.), and Atreus (*Thyestes* 215ff.). It pervades the Senecan *Gorboduc* (1.2.261ff., 2.1.140ff., 3.1.170ff.), and becomes a commonplace of English tragedy from that point onwards.[4]

Indeed Seneca's tyrant figures, most especially that of Atreus, provide influential models for Renaissance drama's figuring of power, in which, almost ubiquitously, 'Power and wealth move to tyranny, not bounty' (*Revenge of Bussy D'Ambois* 4.2.26). The tyrant's resort to torture (*Spanish Tragedy* 4.4.183ff.) and predilection for the murder of children have their origins in Atreus, and realise themselves in Mussato's Ezzelino, Cinthio's Sulmone, Speroni's Eolo, Marlowe's Tamburlaine and Barabas, Richard III, Marston's Piero and Antonio, Macbeth, the 'jealous tyrant' Leontes (in part), Corneille's Cléopâtre (who fuses Atreus and Medea), Grimoald and Phocas. The Herod figure of the medieval mystery plays must not be overlooked in the Renaissance construction of tyranny, but it is clear that even in the dramatisation of Hérode in Tristan l'Hermite's *La Mariane* Senecan paradigms are involved. Atrean insatiability and monomania are readily adopted and adapted – together with the self-consuming will to power that defines Lycus, Eteocles and in part Atreus, albeit Atreus is not consumed.

Although Atreus was perhaps the single most important model for Renaissance tyranny, influencing even the wit, irony and speech-style of figures such as Shakespeare's Richard III, Seneca's Hercules was also significant and supplies the major paradigm for Shakespeare's Coriolanus and, more conspicuously, for Marlowe's Tamburlaine.[5] Like Hercules before he slays his children, Tamburlaine, as he readies himself to slay his own son Calyphas, impiously pits his power into and against the heavens:

> Here, Jove, receive his fainting soul again,
> A form not meet to give that subject essence
> Whose matter is the flesh of Tamburlaine,
> Wherein an incorporeal spirit moves,
> Made of the mould whereof thyself consists,
> Which makes me valiant, proud, ambitious,
> Ready to levy power against thy throne,
> That I might move the turning spheres of heaven!
> For earth and all this airy region
> Cannot contain the state of Tamburlaine.
>
> (*2 Tamburlaine* 4.1.111–20)

There is ironic allusion here. Hercules was insane when he made his impious verbal assault on the heavens (*non capit terra Herculem*, 'earth does not contain

Hercules', *Hercules Furens* 960) and then killed his sons. Tamburlaine is fully conscious.[6] Marlowe has taken from Seneca the tyrant's monomaniacal drive to annex the universe and placed it in a fully cognisant brain.

Marlowe's examination of power in *Tamburlaine* borrows other Senecan things. Noticeable, as in *Hercules Furens*, is the preoccupation with 'virtue' in the play, in the sense of the Latin *uirtus*, 'manliness', and its relationship to power.[7] For Tamburlaine, although 'virtue is the fount whence honour springs' (*1 Tamburlaine* 4.4.131) and 'solely is the sum of glory' (5.1.189), that 'glory' and 'honour' 'consists in shedding blood' (5.1.478) until he himself reaches 'The sweet fruition of an earthly crown' (2.7.29) and hangs his 'weapons on Alcides' post' (5.1.529). Tamburlaine's glorification of kingly power could have come from Eteocles (*Phoenissae* 664):

> A god is not so glorious as a king.
> I think the pleasure they enjoy in heaven
> Cannot compare with kingly joys on earth.
> To wear a crown enchas'd with pearl and gold,
> Whose virtues carry with it life and death;
> To ask and have, command and be obeyed.
>
> (*1 Tamburlaine* 2.5.57–62)

Like a typically Senecan figure, he is deaf to appeals for mercy or compassion (5.1.80ff.). He views his own being in metaphysical terms:

> They have refused the offer of their lives,
> And know my customs are as peremptory
> As wrathful planets, death, or destiny.
>
> (*1 Tamburlaine* 5.1.126–8)

And like Medea, he sees himself as co-extensive with the cosmos:

> No, strike the drums, and, in revenge of this,
> Come, let us charge our spears and pierce his breast
> Whose shoulders bear the axis of the world,
> That if I perish, heaven and earth may fade.
>
> (*2 Tamburlaine* 5.3.57–60)

Unlike Medea his construction of himself in language transpires to be an illusion. His death, though self-dramatising, does not consume the universe. The trick for Seneca's Colchian princess was that her control of language mirrored her control of the world:

> sternam et euertam omnia.
> . . . inuadam deos
> et cuncta quatiam . . .
> sola est quies,

mecum ruina cuncta si uideo obruta:
mecum omnia abeant. trahere, cum pereas, libet.
(Medea 414, 424f., 426–8)

I'll destroy and raze everything.
. . . I'll attack the gods
And shake the universe . . .
The only calm is to see
The universe collapse in ruin with me:
Let all die with me. To take to the grave is sweet.

Tamburlaine is no magician, nor is he the offspring of the Sun. Medea is both and destroys the Corinthian universe without dying. But neither play offers its audience moral comfort. The world which allows the mass killings and tortures of a Tamburlaine and witnesses his death after his burning of the Koran is as morally perplexing as the one which witnesses the mass-murderess' departure in the chariot of the Sun.

Shakespeare's *Coriolanus* plays with and against the Herculean paradigm, preoccupied throughout with 'virtue' and 'valour', but inverting the Herculean slaughter of kin to allow the living wife, child and mother to turn the tragic hero from his city to 'a world elsewhere' which, rather than cleanse or renew, kills its own 'god' (4.6.91, 5.4.24). Shakespeare's use of Atreus is obviously more widespread, as it is complex. Sometimes, as in *Titus Andronicus* and *Macbeth*, tyrannical characteristics are split between characters to allow for greater complexity of audience response. Aaron's Atrean qualities allow more sympathy to move to Titus,[8] as Macbeth's 'fiend-like Queen' creates space for a more profound and subtle protagonist. Macbeth also brings to his Atrean portrait the properties of a Christian sinner and one with the most extraordinary poetic imagination, whose guilt like that of a Thyestes or a Theseus affects the entire cosmos:

And Pity, like a naked new-born babe,
Striding the blast, or heaven's Cherubins, hors'd
Upon the sightless couriers of the air,
Shall blow the horrid deed in every eye,
That tears shall drown the wind.
(Macbeth 1.7.21–5)

Filled initially with moral anguish, horror, and all the linguistic registers of remorse, Macbeth becomes incarcerated by his own evil, and ends his life not in Christian repentance but in poetic despair. The articulation of that despair and his self-consciously heroic death problematise not only the play's treatment of heroism but any simple response to its protagonist.

In *Macbeth* too the issue of power and its illusion is also brought home through Shakespeare's use of another Senecan strategy, the destabilising of male power, hierarchy and status by the behaviour and language of women.

The ambiguous prophecies and discourse of the marginalised witches, even if not directly indebted to Seneca, in a larger sense replay those of Cassandra in *Agamemnon* and Medea in *Medea*, marginalised female figures with super-natural powers, who similarly expose the fictions underlying the narratives of male order.[9] So too the language, body and desire of Phaedra anticipate those of Cleopatra, similarly pitted against the assumptions of male power:

> o dure Theseu semper, o numquam tuis
> tuto reuerse: gnatus et genitor nece
> reditus tuos luere; peruertis domum
> amore semper coniugum aut odio nocens.
>
>   Hippolyte, tales intuor uultus tuos
> talesque feci? . . .
>
>   heu me, quo tuus fugit decor
> oculique nostrum sidus? exanimis iaces?
> ades parumper, uerbaque exaudi mea.
>   (*Phaedra* 1164–75)

> Ever brutal Theseus, never returning
> To kin without harm. Your son's and sire's death
> Paid for your returns. You destroy your house
> Through love of wife or hate, baneful always.
>
>   Hippolytus, is this your face I see,
> This what I made it? . . .
>
>   O, where has your beauty fled
> And eyes that were my stars? Do you lie dead?
> Come back a little while and hear my words.

>   Noblest of men, woo't die?
> Hast thou no care of me? Shall I abide
> In this dull world, which in thy absence is
> No better than a sty? O see, my women,
> The crown o'th'earth doth melt. My lord!
>   (*Antony and Cleopatra* 4.15.61–5)

> My desolation does begin to make
> A better life. 'Tis paltry to be Caesar.
>   (*Antony and Cleopatra* 5.2.1f.)

Both queens are acculturations of 'nature', and with the latter they are espe-cially associated (*Phaedra* 352, *Antony and Cleopatra* 1.2.153ff., 2.2.201ff.). It is 'nature' in the form of female desire and physicality that in one case destroys, in the other ideologically undermines, the traditional social order of male tyranny and power. In Seneca the tyrant demands annihilation before his male offspring's dismembered corpse, and casts Phaedra into the earth. Shakespeare's Caesar politicises the woman's dead body, literally incorporat-

172

ing it into the rituals of power; but that body and its desire cannot be so easily refigured.

It is noticeable that after the death of Elizabeth the English stage witnesseses an upsurge in female tragic protagonists (Webster's heroines are prime cases), the *locus*, as in Seneca, of male anxieties about control, death, mutability and power. It is noticeable too that in the tragicomedies of this period Shakespeare's approach to the tyrant figure changes. Either he has the tyrant repent (Leontes in *The Winter's Tale*; cf. Lamano in Cinthio's *Altile*), or sets up anti-tyrant, anti-*furor* figures such as Pericles (in successful opposition to the incestuous tyrant Antiochus) or Prospero. Although Prospero displays tyrannical features throughout much of *The Tempest* (to Caliban he is simply 'the tyrant', 2.2.162, 3.2.40), he overcomes anger and the temptations to *furor* and revenge, and, in clear opposition to such potential tyrant figures as the usurper Antonio and the would-be ursurper Sebastian, manifests at the end an anti-Atrean mode of power. But if the Senecan concept of the true king ('He's a king who's banished fear | And the evils of a dreadful heart', *Thyestes* 348f.), articulated only to be undermined in *Thyestes*, is hinted at in figures such as Prospero, it is even more substantially realised in the Auguste of Corneille's *Cinna* – a play itself built upon a Senecan text, *De Clementia*. Corneille's *Cinna* is especially interesting because of its reflection of the contemporary political milieu. Its support of absolute monarchy has been seen to accord with the policies of Richelieu, Corneille's ambivalent patron, who was attempting to transform the French feudal system into a centralised monarchy. Like his *Horace*, which received its first performance at Richelieu's home, *Cinna* met with the cardinal's enthusiastic approval. But one should observe that the issue of power's legitimacy (one never explored by Seneca *tragicus*)[10] marks several of Corneille's plays (his *Oedipe* is a case in point) and that in *Cinna* the approval of absolutism is tempered by a more liberal conception of a clement monarchy.

A return to Senecan tyranny is evident in Racine. He lives in the same world as Corneille, but, while he occasionally articulates criteria for the true or wise king, *un roi sage* (*Athalie* 4.2/1278ff., cf. 4.3/1381ff.), and most of his plays explore the whole issue of the legitimacy of rule, his rulers tend to be tyrannical figures (Néron, Thésée, Amurat, Mithridate, Athalie), even if complex ones. Criticism of the world of power and of the dangers of tyranny abounds (even in *Athalie*: see Joad's speech when crowning Joas at 4.3/1387ff.), and, as in Seneca, insistence on fate and the imperatives of the past underscore both power's illusion and history's determinism.

THE SENECAN SELF

What Racine's tragic representations (and not merely those of rulers) have in common with those of Corneille centres on the concept of personal consciousness and force, the sense of self. Seneca's 'autarchic style of selfhood',[11] one defined by its own will, sufficiency, empowerment, and its drive towards actualisation of that power, was an important legacy to French and Renaissance drama. Such selfhood manifests itself in (among other things) the contempt for life and death displayed almost ubiquitously by both Senecan and Renaissance tragic figures. It realises some of its finest dramatic moments in death-scenes architected to show an assertion of the dying figure's identity and will.

Clytemnestra Furiosa morere.
Cassandra Veniet et uobis furor.
(*Agamemnon* 1012)

Clytemnestra Die raging.
Cassandra To you too will rage come.

Theridamas and Tamburlaine, I die:
And fearful vengeance light upon you both.
(*1 Tamburlaine* 2.7.51f.)

haud frangit animum uanus hic terror meum:
nam mihi paternus uincere est tauros labor.
(*Phaedra* 1066f.)

This idle terror does not break my spirit;
For to vanquish bulls is my father's trade.

I will not yield,
To kiss the ground before young Malcolm's feet,
And to be baited with the rabble's curse.
(*Macbeth* 5.8.27–9)

o mors amoris una sedamen mali,
o mors pudoris maximum laesi decus,
confugimus ad te: pande placatos sinus.
(*Phaedra* 1188–90)

O death, sole remedy of wicked love,
O death, great ornament of blighted shame,
We fly to you; spread your merciful arms.

Come violent death,
Serve for mandragora to make me sleep.
(*Malfi* 4.2.234f.)

Et la mort, à mes yeux dérobant la clarté,
Rend au jour, qu'ils souillaient, toute sa pureté.
(*Phèdre* 5.7/1643f.)

And death, robbing my eyes of light, restores
To the polluted day all its purity.

This autarchic selfhood manifests itself ubiquitously and conspicuously in the ability of characters to construct their identity and their domination of the world in language. Marlowe's Tamburlaine was quoted above. All of Shakespeare's great tragic figures are in some sense Tamburlaine, that is to say, Hercules, Medea, Hippolytus, Theseus, Oedipus, Atreus, Thyestes. They create a linguistic world with their self as its referential centre:

> 'Tis now the very witching time of night,
> When churchyards yawn and hell itself breathes out
> Contagion to the world. Now could I drink hot blood,
> And do such bitter business as the day
> Would quake to look on.
>
> (*Hamlet* 3.2.379–83)

> No, you unnatural hags,
> I will have such revenges on you both
> That all the world shall – I will do such things,
> What they are, yet I know not, but they shall be
> The terrors of the earth.
>
> (*Lear* 2.4.276–80)

> Come, seeling Night,
> Scarf up the tender eye of pitiful Day,
> And, with thy bloody and invisible hand,
> Cancel, and tear to pieces, that great bond
> Which keeps me pale.
>
> (*Macbeth* 3.2.46–50)

The self's drive towards dominance and actualisation is evident in Renaissance tragedy from Mussato's Ezzelino onwards, who was primarily modelled on Atreus. From Atreus too, but most especially from Medea, seems derived the existential function of violence in a number of tragedies, its use in the construction and fixing of the self: *Medea nunc sum*, 'Now I am Medea' (*Medea* 910). Obvious examples again are Marlowe's heroes, especially Tamburlaine and Barabas. Medea is perhaps also, even more than Atreus, the Senecan paradigm of the linguistic base of the Renaissance self, its foundation on the ability to construct and fix itself through and in language. It is no accident that Seneca's *Medea* was a prominent subtext throughout the Renaissance and was itself rewritten several times, e.g. in La Péruse's *La Médée* (1556), Dolce's *Medea* (1558 – based admittedly on both Euripides and Seneca), Fulke Greville's *Alaham* (1600). Significantly Corneille's first real attempt at tragedy was his *Médée* (1635).

In the French tradition this selfhood, expressed in set speeches and verbal declamation, shows a marked concern with *honneur*. So Cléopâtre's last words in Jodelle's *Cléopâtre captive* (4/1361f.), where Senecan onomastic rhetoric highlights the preoccupation with *honneur*:

> L'honneur que je te fais l'honneur dernier sera
> Qu'à son Antoine mort Cléopâtre fera.

> The honour I do you will be the last honour
> Cleopatra will do for her dead Antony.

Or Chimène in Corneille's *Le Cid* (3.3/821):

> Je cours sans balancer où mon honneur m'oblige.

> I rush unwavering where my honour calls.

This *honneur* is, especially in Corneille, often the moral centre of a character's emotional solipsism, not simply a categorical imperative but the linchpin of identity. It is an ideological development not as distant from the Senecan paradigm as it may appear. Certainly for some Senecan figures 'shame', 'moral integrity', 'honour' are defining aspects of their self. Thus Hercules:

> non sic furore cessit extinctus pudor,
> populos ut omnes impio aspectu fugem.
> > (*Hercules Furens* 1240f.)

> Madness hasn't so extinguished my honour
> To have the world flee at my unholy sight.

Thus Phaedra:

> Hippolyte, nunc me compotem uoti facis:
> sanas furentem. maius hoc uoto meo est,
> saluo ut pudore manibus immoriar tuis.
> > (*Phaedra* 710–12)

> Hippolytus, you now fulfil my prayer:
> You heal my passion. This transcends my prayer:
> At your hands to die with my honour safe.

What Phaedra and Hercules also share is *furor*: passion, rage, madness. A defining feature of such major figures as Atreus, Thyestes, Medea, Oedipus, Cassandra, *furor* is a central ingredient of what the Renaissance received as the Senecan tragic self.

Furor was well known to Renaissance poets. Spenser's personification of it as a 'mad man' and 'monster', defeated and bound by the knight Guyon, is justly famous:

> With hundred yron chaines he did him bind,
> And hundred knots that did him sore constraine:

176

> Yet his great yron teeth he still did grind,
> And grimly gnash, threatning reuenge in vaine;
> His burning eyen, whom bloudie strakes did staine,
> Stared full wide, and threw forth sparkes of fire,
> And more for ranck despight, then for great paine,
> Shakt his long lockes, coulourd like copper-wire,
> And bit his tawny beard to shew his raging ire.
>
> *(The Faerie Queen* 2.4.15)

Furor was especially well known to Renaissance dramatists, who were some-times drawn to Seneca precisely because of his ability to dramatise violent emotions or *affetti* (so Cinthio). The presentation of *furor* in *Hercules Furens* and the non-Senecan *Hercules Oetaeus* was particularly influential. Jean de la Taille's *Saül Le Furieux*, Garnier's *Porcie*, Norton and Sackville's *Gorboduc*, Tristan l'Hermite's *La Mariane* are among the plays most obviously indebted. *Medea* too looms large in this regard. In Corneille's plays we find the Colchian princess' rage manipulated from Médée herself into Marcelle in *Théodore* and Cléopâtre in *Rodogune*. In Shakespeare *furor* – rage, passion, lust, ambition or anger verging on madness – is the central psychological issue in such plays as *Richard III, Macbeth, King Lear* and *Othello*. In *Othello* even the post-*furor* recog-nition of guilt that marks Seneca's treatment in *Hercules Furens* and *Phaedra* is re-dramatised; while the sleep that follows Hercules' rage and restores the tragic figure to sanity finds itself replayed in Marston's *Antonio* plays and Greene's *Orlando Furioso*.[12] The motif is used enigmatically at the end of Racine's *Andromaque*, where the post-madness sleep descends on Oreste, but the play ends in uncertainty before he awakes.

Racine makes much of *fureur*, not only in the case of the madness of Oreste. It is to Racine especially that one should turn for *furor* in the sense of the *amor* or erotic passion which drives men and women (primarily the latter) to tragic action. Brilliantly articulated in Seneca's *Phaedra*, it is rearticulated by Racine not only in his *Phèdre*, where, however, the extraordinary fusion of moral sensibility and debasing *amor-furor*, which defines Seneca's heroine, is reproduced with theatrical force:

> Mon époux est vivant, et moi je brûle encore!
> Pour qui? Quel est le coeur où prétendent mes voeux?
> Chaque mot sur mon front fait dresser mes cheveux.
> Mes crimes désormais ont comblé la mesure.
> Je respire à la fois l'inceste et l'imposture.
>
> *(Phèdre* 4.6/1266–70)

> My husband is alive and yet I burn!
> For whom? Whose is the heart which my prayers claim?
> Each word makes the hair bristle on my brow.
> My crimes henceforth have filled their measure.
> I now breathe out both incest and deceit.

177

In Racine's secular tragedies as a whole love seems the prime motor of the tragic action. It is almost always unreciprocated. Described by both Phèdre and Hippolyte as *un mal*, both sickness and evil, it seems more akin to hate in the actions it produces. Characters such as Hermione and Oreste in *Andromaque*, Roxane in *Bajazet*, Eriphile in *Iphigénie* oscillate between love and hate, sometimes quite self-consciously. It is Eriphile herself who describes the transformation of her passion for Achille into hatred of Iphigénie as the *triste effet* of her own *fureurs* (*Iphigénie* 2.1/505). *Andromaque*'s Oreste comments on the opposite movement, from hate to love (of Hermione):

> Je sentis que ma haine allait finir son cours,
> Ou plutôt je sentis que je l'aimais toujours.
> (*Andromaque* 1.1/87f.)

> I felt that my hatred had run its course;
> Or rather I felt that I loved her always.

Oreste, like Phèdre, evidences considerable moral sensibility and turmoil under the onslaught of passion (*Andromaque* 3.1/771–84, 4.3/1173ff., 5.4/1565ff.). But more often *fureur* is accompanied by little moral feeling; generally, the objects of passion are scantly regarded. Racine's debts are in part (and a most important part) Euripidean, but in the background too seems Seneca's Medea, the supreme moral and emotional solipsist, who at the end of Seneca's play divests herself of all human ties.

Opposed to *furor* in Senecan tragedy is *ratio*, reason. In the cases of Thyestes and Phaedra, they struggle for control of the human self:

> quid ratio possit? uicit ac regnat furor,
> potensque tota mente dominatur deus.
> (*Phaedra* 184f.)

> What can reason do? Passion's conquered and reigns,
> And a potent god commands my whole heart.

Compare this confidant scene between Pylade and Oreste in *Andromaque*:

> *Pylade* Modérez donc, Seigneur, cette fureur extrême.
> Je ne vous connais plus: vous n'êtes plus vous-même.
> Souffrez . . .
> *Oreste*   Non, tes conseils ne sont plus de saison,
> Pylade, je suis las d'écouter la raison.
> (*Andromaque* 3.1/709–12)

> *Pylade* Restrain then, my lord, this excessive rage.
> I don't know you: you're no longer yourself.
> Allow . . .
> *Oreste*   No, your advice is out of order,
> Pylades, I'm tired of listening to reason.

Always in Seneca, generally in Racine, *furor/fureur* proves triumphant. Although *Hercules Furens* may offer some hope for personal recovery after the onset of *furor*, when the latter is faced with a confrontation with reason or knowledge, in Seneca it wins. The prime example is Thyestes, whose Stoic knowledge and rational understanding yield to what his brother terms *uetus regni furor*, his 'inveterate passion for power' (*Thyestes* 302). Similarly, in Marston's *Antonio* plays, Stoicism gives way to Atrean passion in both Antonio and Pandulpho, while in Chapman's *The Revenge of Bussy D'Ambois* Clermont, the 'Senecal man',[13] voices standard Stoic positions from Seneca's prose works and from Epictetus, but displays naivety in his handling of the world. Informed of the plot against himself and aware of the suspicious behaviour of Maillard, Clermont still yields to him (*Revenge of Bussy D'Ambois* 3.2). The Messenger's comment on the vanity of 'men's foreknowledges of things' (3.2.243) could have come from a Senecan tragic text. Of course Thyestes is not the Stoic hero that Clermont is. There are no Stoic heroes in Senecan tragedy. Neither Clermont nor Shakespeare's Brutus have any real counterpart in the Senecan plays, in which such allegedly Stoic heroes as Thyestes or Hippolytus are either self-deceived pathological idealists or have their intellectual credo immediately inverted by their own burgeoning passion. The Stoicism of Elizabethan and Jacobean drama, if Senecan, is from the prose works or from the tragedies, eclectically construed. And against *furor*'s triumphant presentation in tragedy should be set its treatment in Shakespeare's tragicomedies. *Pericles* shows the eventual victory of an anti-*furor* protagonist; while *Cymbeline*, *The Winter's Tale* and *The Tempest* construct an essentially un-Senecan, even anti-Senecan world, in which *furor* or anger is the mainspring of the action but dissolves by the action's end, where what is celebrated is not the triumph of evil in the human soul but forgiveness, even redemption, and social community. The fact that these were among the last plays which Shakespeare wrote argues for a final distance from Seneca's presentation of the self.

REVENGE

> Impatients désirs d'une illustre vengeance
> Dont la mort de mon père a formé la naissance,
> Enfants impétueux de mon ressentiment,
> Que ma douleur séduite embrasse aveuglément,
> Vous prenez sur mon âme un trop puissant empire.
> (*Cinna* 1.1/1–5)

> Impatient desires for illustrious revenge,
> To which my father's death has given birth,
> Impetuous children of my resentment,

179

Which my sorrow, seduced, blindly grasps,
You hold too great a sway over my soul.

So Émilie opens Corneille's *Cinna*. Though the play is a study of monarchic clemency, revenge drives the action. Similarly in *Le Cid* and elsewhere in Corneille's tragedies the imperatives of vengeance are emphatic. Not accidentally his *Médée* inaugurated his tragedic career. From Seneca's *Medea*, in rewriting which, according to one critic,[14] Corneille 'a découvert . . . la nature de son propre tragique', the French dramatist derived the centrality of vengeance to tragic action. He was not alone. Revenge dominates Renaissance tragedy from its inception: Corraro's *Progne*, Cinthio's *Orbecche*, Groto's *Dalida*, Kyd's *The Spanish Tragedy*, Shakespeare's *Titus Andronicus* and *Hamlet*, Tourneur/Middleton's *The Revenger's Tragedy*, Racine's *Andromaque* and *Iphigénie* . . . the list could go on – almost endlessly. In Racine's case not only characters like Eriphile and Hermione are driven by vengeance, but even in such a religious play as *Athalie* both unbeliever (Athalie) and believer (Joad) are motivated by vengeance, and the Hebrew God is proclaimed 'le Dieu jaloux . . . le Dieu des vengeances' (4.6/1470f., 1488f.). Often there is a plurality of revengers: in *Titus Andronicus* there are three revengers, as in *The Spanish Tragedy*; in *Hamlet* and Marston's *The Malcontent* there are two, and in the latter of very different kind: Mendoza, who becomes a tyrant, and Malevole, who foregoes his vengeance and turns to mercy. Even Seneca's own treatment of revenge is multiplied by mistranslations,[15] or by additional final speeches, as in Heywood's *Thyestes* and Studley's *Agamemnon*, heralding the vengeance to come. Almost always the revenger is a complex figure, none more so than Webster's Bosola, spy and assassin, who becomes a 'heroic' multiple avenger in *The Duchess of Malfi*'s final act. Sometimes Revenge or Vengeance becomes (unlike in Seneca) a *dramatis persona* appearing onstage: so *Orbecche* and *The Spanish Tragedy*; or is addressed (also unlike in Seneca) by the play's characters: so Vindice in *The Revenger's Tragedy* 1.1.39ff., Tamyra in *The Revenge of Bussy D'Ambois* 1.2.1ff. Sometimes Revenge is impersonated:

> I am Revenge, sent from th'infernal kingdom
> To ease the gnawing vulture of thy mind
> By working wreakful vengeance on thy foes.
> Come down and welcome me to this world's light,
> Confer with me of murder and of death.
> There's not a hollow cave or lurking place,
> No vast obscurity or misty vale
> Where bloody murder or detested rape
> Can couch for fear, but I will find them out,
> And in their ears tell them my dreadful name,
> Revenge, which makes the foul offender quake.
>
> (*Titus* 5.2.30–40)

Thus Tamora to Titus, whose 'lunacy' she mistakes and to whose vengeance she succumbs. Nor is it only in tragedy that the preoccupation with vengeance is apparent. In Shakespeare's tragicomedies, for example, the impulse to vengeance is almost as emphatic as in his tragedies, but in the tragicomedies it is dissolved by the opposite imperatives of repentance and forgiveness. *The Tempest* has even been called a 'revenge comedy',[16] a play which sets up the possibility for revenge and then substitutes forgiveness:

> Though with their high wrongs I am struck to th' quick,
> Yet with my noble reason 'gainst my fury
> Do I take part: the rarer action is
> In virtue than in vengeance.
>
> (*Tempest* 5.1.25–8)

At the end of Seneca's *Medea* the Colchian's magic implements the most savage vengeance and she herself departs the world in apotheotic flight. In *The Tempest*'s concluding display of its protagonist's 'tender affections', Prospero the magician inverts Seneca's ending: abjuring his magic, he replaces vengeance with virtue and compassion, and returns to the social world from which he had been expelled. In emphasising his forgiveness of the brother who had wronged him ('I do forgive thee', | Unnatural though thou art', *Tempest* 5.1.78f.; I do forgive | Thy rankest fault', 5.1.131f.), Prospero inverts the ending of *Thyestes* too.[17] Self-conscious avoidance of either Senecan conclusion underscores the absent paradigm.

There are cultural reasons for this preoccupation with revenge in English and European Renaissance drama. In England, France and Europe at large the aristocracy was in a situation of crisis arising from the loss of its traditional powers before an increasingly centralised monarchy. Revenge, Bacon's 'wild justice', was the aristocracy's traditional manner and right of settling 'injustices', but one which the central organs of government were endeavouring to control. Despite its stigmatisation by the law, however, revenge exerted both social and moral claims, and not only because of its relationship to aristocratic concepts of status and honour. There was also the problem of justice within an entrenched social hierarchy. Access to justice was often a function of patronage and of rhetorical skill. For social inferiors revenge was often the only means of 'righting' a wrong perpetrated by superiors; but, in order to do so, the revenger had to shatter central rules of social and moral behaviour. The dramatisation of revenge thus afforded the Renaissance playwright an opportunity to examine issues of morality, justice, power and social status specific to his world and to expose, even negotiate, their intrinsic contradictions.

Hence the popularity of Seneca, to whom Renaissance playwrights seem substantially indebted for the literary construction of vengeance. The Revenger's 'hesitation', for example – Hamlet, Hieronimo (*Spanish Tragedy* 3.2.37ff., etc.), Antonio (*Antonio's Revenge* 3.3.88ff.), Clermont (*Revenge of*

181

SENECA AND RENAISSANCE DRAMA

Bussy D'Ambois 3.2.107ff.) – seems a transformation of the *dubitatio* of Senecan figures, especially Clytemnestra, Aegisthus and Medea. Hamlet (see below) and Hieronimo even have to work themselves up to the task with Senecanesque soliloquies. So Hieronimo, recalling Medea's use of past wrongs to motivate her final vengeance (*Medea* 895ff.):

> Bethink thyself, Hieronimo,
> Recall thy wits, recompt thy former wrongs
> Thou has receiv'd by murder of thy son,
> And lastly, not least, how Isabel,
> Once his mother and thy dearest wife,
> All woe-begone for him, hath slain herself.
> Behoves thee then, Hieronimo, to be reveng'd:
> The plot is laid of dire revenge:
> On then, Hieronimo, pursue revenge,
> For nothing wants but acting of revenge.
>> (*Spanish Tragedy* 4.3.21–30)

Similarly Senecan is the revenger's insistence on the victim's full consciousness of the revenge while it is being enacted. Racine's Hermione in apparently Atrean mode (*Thyestes* 1066ff.):

> Ma vengeance est perdue
> S'il ignore en mourant que c'est moi qui le tue.
>> (*Andromaque* 4.4/1269f.)

> My vengeance is lost
> Unless he knows, dying, it's *I* who kill him.

Senecan too is the fusion of revenge and passion:

> What would he do
> Had he the motive and the cue for passion
> That I have? He would drown the stage with tears,
> And cleave the general ear with horrid speech,
> Make mad the guilty and appal the free,
> Confound the ignorant, and amaze indeed
> The very faculties of eyes and ears.
> Yet I,
> A dull and muddy-mettled rascal, peak
> Like John-a-dreams, unpregnant of my cause,
> And can say nothing . . .
>> (*Hamlet* 2.2.554–64)

So Shakespeare's most famous revenger, reformulating Atreus' opening speech (*Thyestes* 176ff.);[18] so too Cinthio's Sulmone, Marston's Piero, Marlowe's Barabas. For some Renaissance revengers the passion becomes an obsession verging on madness:

And art thou come, Horatio, from the depth,
To ask for justice in this upper earth?
(*Spanish Tragedy* 3.13.133f.)

The words are those of Hieronimo, 'mistaking' an old man for his dead son. For others the insatiability of the passion is an issue: e.g. Aaron (*Titus* 5.1.141ff.), Clifford (*3 Henry VI* 1.3.25ff.), Othello (*Othello* 3.3.449f., 5.2.75f.). But, although it is an issue derived from Seneca,[19] the suggestion of revenge's intrinsic inability to satisfy is far from the Roman dramatist's vision. Part of the discomfort generated by *Medea* and *Thyestes* is that at the end of their respective plays Medea and Atreus are triumphant and satisfied, and proclaim both states in speeches of remarkable theatrical power (*Medea* 982ff., 1018ff.; *Thyestes* 1096ff.). The issue of insatiability is raised to be contradicted by the revenger's satisfaction.

Vindice's proclaimed satisfaction at the end of *The Revenger's Tragedy* is thus entirely Senecan:

> We have enough –
> I' faith we're well – our mother turned, our sister true,
> We die after a nest of dukes! Adieu.
> (*Revenger's Tragedy* 5.3.124–6)

What is not Senecan about this ending (other than the tone) is that Vindice is punished for his vengeance. In Seneca's *Medea* and *Thyestes* the revenger is unpunished (and known to remain so in the myth), even though the revenge is out of all proportion to the offence. In Renaissance drama the Christian morality play tradition and the requirements of both monarchic pressure and the legal code often assert themselves at the end: the revenger is punished or killed. Andrea is consigned to hell; Orbecche, Hieronimo, Clermont, Marcelle and Hermione suicide; Sulmone, (Groto's) Berenice, Barabas, Hamlet and Bosola are slain; Vindice is taken away to be executed; Oreste is driven mad. In Marston's *Antonio's Revenge* the revengers Antonio and Pandulpho are not punished as such, but vow to become 'most constant votaries' (5.3.153); in Tourneur's *The Atheist's Tragedy* the revenger Charlemont survives and triumphs by not being a revenger at all. The Christian ideology of *Orbecche* is proclaimed from the start:

> Come'l mal non è senza la pena,
> Così non è senza mercede il bene.
> (*Orbecche* 1.1)

> As evil is not without punishment,
> So good is not without reward.

That of *The Atheist's Tragedy* is articulated at the end:

183

Only to Heav'n I attribute the work,
Whose gracious motives made me still forbear
To be mine own revenger. Now I see
That *patience is the honest man's revenge.*
(*Atheist's Tragedy* 5.2.275–8)

Not all plays are so overt. But it is noticeable that even with Seneca's own *oeuvre* (see Studley's *Medea* and Heywood's *Thyestes*) translators felt a need to change the ending. This move towards moral order and social reintegration in revenge tragedy indicates a concern (sometimes as in *The Revenger's Tragedy* almost self-parodic) to return the audience to the more comforting world of conventional morality and law. It is essentially unSenecan. *Hercules Furens* is no exception to this, because the acts for which the protagonist has to atone in that play are not those of a revenger and are committed after the onset of madness. The kind of new beginning that Shakespeare provides at the end of *Titus Andronicus*, as all the revengers lie dead or in chains, signals something other than the permanent dislocation which closes all but two of the extant Senecan tragedies:

You sad-faced men, people and sons of Rome,
By uproars severed, as a flight of fowl
Scattered by winds and high tempestuous gusts,
O let me teach you how to knit again
This scattered corn into one mutual sheaf,
These broken limbs again into one body.
(*Titus* 5.3.66–71)

The very last lines of *Titus Andronicus* (5.3.190–9) replay Theseus' final speech in *Phaedra* (1273–80) only to point up the difference from Seneca's dismembered world.

But though Renaissance drama does not allow the revenger to be unpunished or untransformed, it problematises the act itself. Not all revengers are of the Cornwall type in *King Lear*, where the revenge on Gloucester is of the Atrean manner, including appropriately shocking witticisms: 'Out, vile jelly! | Where is thy lustre now?' (*Lear* 3.7.81f.). Many revengers have at least in part the audience's sympathy, however complex and ambiguous the audience's overall response: so for example, Hieronimo, Titus, Vindice, Hamlet, Phèdre and Orbecche. Orbecche is an interesting case because her revenge, like Hamlet's, is unpremeditated and approved by those who witness it, and yet she dies anyway. As Sulmone displays the bodies of Orbecche's children before her, she takes the knives from their bodies and kills Sulmone himself. The chorus are stunned but approve because she has slain an evil tyrant. Her act, like Hamlet's, can be seen as 'public revenge':

Public revenges are for the most part fortunate: as that for the death of

Caesar, for the death of Pertinax, for the Death of Henry the Third of France, and many more. But in private revenges this is not so. Nay rather, vindictive persons live the life of witches, who, as they are mischievous, so end they infortunate.

(Francis Bacon, 'Of Revenge')

How representative Bacon's views are is debatable. And even Bacon regards private revenge as 'tolerable' if the wrong to which it responds cannot be set right by law (although the revenge itself should not then breach the law).[20] The whole area is clearly problematised in Renaissance drama, which, contrary to what is sometimes argued,[21] only superficially condemns the revenger. The latter's conduct and the wrong that conduct seeks to 'right' frequently display the inadequacy not only of the law but of the world.

> O Sol, che solo il mondo orni et illustri,
> Perchè nonti fuggisti allor dal Cielo,
> Che quest fier Tiran, ch' or per me giace,
> Commise così sozzo e orribil atto?
>
> (*Orbecche* 5.3)

> O Sun, who alone adorns and lights the world,
> Why did you not flee from the heavens then,
> When this fierce tyrant, who lies here because of me,
> Committed so foul and dreadful an act?

Here Orbecche alludes to Thyestes' cry of outrage (*Thyestes* 1035ff.) in order to complain of cosmic indifference. She has revenged herself on the revenger, but the world is wanting. Even in *Titus Andronicus*, whose ending signals a re*membered* Rome (5.3.71), the moral vacuum of the drama has been such that Justice has abandoned the earth (*Terras Astraea reliquit*, 4.3.4), employed apparently in heaven, leaving as the only possibility for redressive action 'Revenge from hell' (4.3.39f.). There was nowhere for Titus to go but where he did. His death complicates rather than resolves the audience's disquiet.

There is also another matter. Both Renaissance Europe and Neronian Rome were societies that prominently institutionalised violence. The violence of the Roman arena was matched in spectacle, if not in numbers, by the Renaissance theatre of public execution: the beheadings, hangings, disembowellings, drawings, quarterings which constituted society's vengeance on those it sought to punish. The ritualising of the revenger's violence in Renaissance drama is not simply the indulgence of decadent contemporary taste, but a self-conscious reflection of and on the ritualised, legally sanctioned violence of the culture, exposing that violence as itself a theatre of power. A signal ingredient of this reflection on violence is its focus on the subjectivity of the victim. Those Senecan-derived cries of pain from the mouths of Orbecche, Lear, Thésée and others have more than rhetorical function. Like Hieronimo's address to the Viceroy of Portingale in the final scene of *The Spanish Tragedy*, they attempt to generate a new evaluation of violence by looking at both the commonality and the irreducibility of the pain it inflicts:

> There merciless they butcher'd up my boy,
> In black dark night, to pale dim cruel death . . .
> And griev'd I, think you, at this spectacle?
> Speak, Portuguese, whose loss resembles mine:
> If thou canst weep upon thy Balthazar,
> 'Tis like I wailed for my Horatio.
> And you, my lord, whose reconciled son
> Marched in a net, and thought himself unseen . . .
> How can you brook our play's catastrophe?
>
> (*Spanish Tragedy* 4.4.106ff.)

THE TRAGIC FRAME

The problematisation of vengeance extends to the moral structure of the world in which it takes place. The moral universe of Renaissance tragedy is anything other than consistently Christian. It shows more affinity to Seneca's tragic world than to any Christian theistic construct, generally projecting itself as hostile, morally perplexing if not amoral or perverse, sometimes, as in *Orbecche*, *Canace*, *Dalida*, *The Spanish Tragedy*, *Titus Andronicus*, *The Duchess of Malfi*, *Andromaque* and *Phèdre*, even irretrievably flawed. Plays such as Tourneur's *The Atheist's Tragedy*, in which a beneficent deity observes and punishes wrongdoing (there is even appropriate thunder and lightning after Montferrers' murder: 2.4.140), are the exception, not the rule. More typical in its implications is Chapman's *Bussy D'Ambois*, whose hero's proclaimed Herculean demise follows a movement from poverty to royal court and knowledge to corruption reminiscent of Seneca's *Thyestes*,[22] and whose first line proclaims an anti-providential, anti-Christian (and anti-Stoic) stance:

> Fortune, not Reason, rules the state of things.
>
> (*Bussy D'Ambois* 1.1.1)

Or, rather more subtly, *The Revenger's Tragedy*, in which the notion of divine intervention and justice is parodied and the universe at best seems morally obscure.[23] At its extreme, this Renaissance universe replays the existential blackness of Seneca's *Phaedra*, where life and sin were for Phaedra inseparable (*Phaedra* 879f.), hell was where she was.

> Hell hath no limits, nor is circumscrib'd
> In one self place, but where we are is hell,
> And where hell is, there must we ever be.
>
> (*Faustus* 5.122–5)

Thus Mephistophilis in Marlowe's *Dr Faustus*, at the end of which Senecan language and motifs cluster (19.135ff.) to focus the indifference of the natural universe to Faustus' suffering. Even in Dolce's *Marianna*, where the tyrant ends in remorse, the moral repugnance of what has transpired in the play, underscored by the failure of the chorus' repeated appeals for divine intervention, is hardly lessened by the concluding choric wisdom that 'l'ira è cagione | D'incomparabil mali'. Whether one agrees that an 'inimical universe' was 'from a philosophical point of view at least . . . Seneca's most important contribution' to Renaissance tragedy, it was certainly a signal one.[24]

At the heart of Renaissance and Senecan pessimism is the impotence of reason. The pointed irrelevance of the extensive moral debate between Pyrrhus and Agamemnon in Seneca's *Troades*, between the Nurse and Hippolytus in *Phaedra*, between Thyestes and his son in *Thyestes*, is mirrored time and again in Renaissance drama: the arguments of Malecche to Sulmone (*Orbecche* 3.2), the prolonged discussion of Gorboduc's counsellors (*Gorboduc* 1.2), the unsuccessful speeches of Antony in Lodge's *The Wounds of Civil War*, of York in *Richard II* (2.1.186ff.), of Hippolyte in Racine's *Phèdre* (esp. 4.2/1087ff.) have no effect on the dramatic action. But they have an effect on the audience. Product of Renaissance rhetorical training and its celebrated skill in arguing 'on either side' (*in utramque partem*), such failed speeches reflect too the dramatists' concern to complicate the moral and human dimension of their plays through engaging the audience, as Seneca did, in a variety of involving perspectives.[25] Often in such debates – again as in Seneca – central ideas of the plays are focused upon in a manner which reveals their ambiguity or polyvalence (compare the disputatious use of 'nature' in *Gorboduc* or *King Lear* with that of *natura* in *Phaedra*),[26] and the uncertainties attending their employment in human discourse and human life. What results is not simply an airing of moral or political issues, but an increasing complexity in the audience's dramatic experience and a correspondingly complex and problematic tragic frame.

It should be observed, however, that Seneca's universe on the whole is determined in a way that that of Renaissance drama is often not. In Cinthio, for example, the focus is on fortune rather than fate, both *Orbecche* and *Didone* concluding with short choric statements on the transience of human happiness or fortune's instability. A similar choric commonplace on life's uncertainty closes Groto's *Dalida*. Speroni's *Canace* does draw some attention to past causes, citing Venus' hatred of Eolo, and it concludes with the latter's curse on the descendants of Aeneas. But the sense of history's determinism is slight. In English tragedy such Senecanesque plays as *Gorboduc*, *Gismond of Salerne*, and *The Misfortunes of Arthur* project a surface fatalism, sometimes simply appropriating Seneca's own text. Hughes borrows *Oedipus* 987f. for:

All things are rulde in constant course: No Fate
But is foreset: The first daie leades the last.

(Arthur 2.3.127f.)

Shakespeare's presentation of fate is more complex. Fate is certainly strong in the history plays: 'What fates impose, that men must needs abide' (*3 Henry VI* 4.3.58). Here the notion of a hereditary curse affecting a dynasty is often conspicuous, and the 'grand machine' of the Senecan universe plays itself out through the repetitive rise and fall of kings, the cycle of murders in the service of power, the iteration of the cries of mothers:

> *Margaret* I had an Edward, till a Richard kill'd him;
> I had a husband, till a Richard kill'd him;
> Thou hadst an Edward, till a Richard kill'd him;
> Thou hadst a Richard, till a Richard kill'd him.
> *Duchess* I had a Richard too, and thou didst kill him;
> I had a Rutland too: thou holp'st to kill him.
> *Margaret* Thou hadst a Clarence too, and Richard kill'd him.
>
> *(Richard III* 4.4.40–6)

In the tragedies fate seems less strong. Hamlet's talk of 'a divinity that shapes our end' (5.2.10) and 'providence in the fall of the sparrow' (5.2.215f.) is not sustained by the dramatic action, which seems more appropriately described by the 'accidental judgements, casual slaughters' and 'purposes mistook' of Horatio's concluding commentary (5.2.385ff.). Similarly in *The Revenge of Bussy D'Ambois* the 'Senecal' Clermont's proclamation of indifference to 'Fortune' (3.4.159ff.) and subservience to 'Necessity' (4.5.4ff.) prefaces a denouement marked by fortune's incomprehensible triumph (5.5.211ff.). Compare the ending of Jonson's *Sejanus* (5.898ff.). More Senecan are the existential implications of *The Spanish Tragedy* in that, while the determinism of the past is not stressed in the play and there is a marked concern with fortune (see esp. 1.2.1ff., 3.1.1ff.), the sense of human life as pre-scripted is strong, underscored by the drama's preternatural frame and commentary. Notably Webster's implied universe, 'the skull beneath the skin',[27] is one of doomed men and women, living and dying in a world fundamentally evil and unprovidential:

> We are merely the stars' tennis balls, struck and banded
> Which way please them.
>
> *(Malfi* 5.4.54f.)

> O, this gloomy world!
> In what a shadow, or deep pit of darkness,
> Doth womanish and fearful mankind live!
>
> *(Malfi* 5.5.100–2)

As in Seneca, evil flowers where it should wither – in the family; and the cry of 'Mercy', the Duchess' final word (in *Troades* Astyanax' all but only word: 792)[28] echoed by her brother Cardinal in the final act (4.2.353, 5.5.41), is unanswered.

There is of course strong opposition to the Senecan universe in the more providential world of tragicomedy, especially English tragicomedy, where wickedness is punished, adversities overcome, and plays end in repentance, forgiveness, restoration, reunion, self-knowledge, and apparent felicity, even if qualified, for the virtuous.[29] In the epilogue to *Pericles* the felicity requires no qualification:

> In Antiochus and his daughter you have heard
> Of monstrous lust the due and just reward.
> In Pericles, his queen and daughter, seen,
> Although assail'd with fortune fierce and keen,
> Virtue preserv'd from fell destruction's blast,
> Led on by heaven, and crown'd with joy at last.
>
> (*Pericles* Ep. 1–6)

There is also opposition to Senecan nihilism in the tragedies of Corneille, where the action implies on the whole a theistic universe in which justice is affirmed, albeit sometimes artificially. Seneca's *Medea* ends with Jason questioning the very existence of the gods, but in the final lines of Corneille's *Médée* Jason asserts the justice of the gods, 'dont le pouvoir égale la justice' (5.7/1625), even as he suicides to rejoin Créuse, leaving Médée to divine retribution. Indeed optimistic endings are common in Corneille, who often concludes his plays with providential claims about 'le juste ciel' (*Rodogune* 5.4/ 1832) or 'la main d'Exupère' and 'la céleste puissance' (*Héraclius* 5.6/1832, 5.7/1914). In the tragedies *Cinna* and *Nicomède* the ending is one of almost total reconciliation at the human level and a revivified harmony with the gods. Even in *Oedipe*, where Oedipe is revealed as a victim of unjust fate and of the gods and attains truly tragic stature, the play concludes with the moralising of Thésée ('le ciel fait assez voir | Que le sang de Laïus a rempli son devoir', 5.9/2003f.) and the (naive) theistic confidence of Dircé: 'Et remettons aux Dieux à disposer du reste' (5.9/2010). According to one critic, 'the whole of Corneille's theatre has the same metaphysical background: man faces fate, but in so doing he obeys a higher intelligence which demands a sacrifice the purpose of which he does not understand at first.'[30] Whatever the apparently incomprehensible adversities of life, in Corneille they are all subject to a controlling providence.

A more Senecan universe is that of Racine. His plays observe the social conventions and proprieties but assume a world by no means moral. Good is not normally rewarded or the wicked punished; providence does not watch over the hero or heroine. There are gods, but they seem vicious, arbitrary, cruel. Thus Jocaste in *La Thébaïde*, Racine's first performed play:

Voilà de ces grands Dieux la suprême justice!
Jusques au bord du crime ils conduisent nos pas,
Ils nous le font commettre, et ne l'excusent pas!
(*Thébaide* 3.2/608–10)

Behold the high justice of the mighty gods.
To the edge of crime they conduct our steps,
They make us commit it and pardon us not.

Connaissez mieux du ciel la vengeance fatale:
Toujours à ma douleur il met quelque intervalle.
Mais, hélas! quand sa main semble me secourir,
C'est alors qu'il s'apprête à me faire périr.
(*Thébaide* 3.3/675–8)

Recognise well heaven's fateful vengeance:
Always it gives my suffering a respite.
But, alas!, when its hand seems to help me,
It is then that it prepares to make me die.

Though extreme, her words are not only borne out in this play but provide a paradigm for the tragic worlds to come. Observe Oreste in *Andromaque*:

Je ne sais de tout temps quelle injuste puissance
Laisse le crime en paix, et poursuit l'innocence.
De quelque part sur moi que je tourne les yeux,
Je ne vois que malheurs qui condamnent les Dieux.
(*Andromaque* 3.1/773–6)

I can never understand what unjust power
Leaves crime in peace, and persecutes innocence.
Wherever around me I turn my eyes
I see only misery condemning the gods.

If the patterned mayhem of the ending of *Andromaque* (see below) provides slight grounds for qualification, the triumph of evil at the end of *Britannicus* provides none. Even in *Iphigénie*, which Racine has self-consciously moralised to end providentially (the final lines, spoken by Clytemnestre, are even a thanksgiving to heaven: 5.6/1791f.),[31] the gods are still arbitrary in their malice. And the Jansenist play *Athalie* paradoxically presents a victim of divine wrath, who emphatically draws the audience's sympathy, and a Hebrew god unmerciful, obscure, inaccessible, a god of vengeance rather than of justice, whose main instrument of victory, Joad, is an unattractive mixture of self-righteousness, deviousness, ruthlessness and cruelty. Athalie's outburst on the god who drove her to destruction hits home:

Impitoyable Dieu, toi seul as tout conduit!
(*Athalie* 5.6/1774)

Pitiless God, your hand alone guided all!

Though ostensibly providential *Athalie*'s world seems little different from that of Racine's last secular play and his finest tragedy, *Phèdre*, in which the gods drive the action, motivated by their own obscure hate to make Hippolyte inspire a passion in the queen's heart because of no fault in her. The condemnation of the gods in *Phèdre* and its Senecan model is the same (cf. Seneca *Phaedra* 1207, 1242f., Racine *Phèdre* 5.6/1572, 5.7/1612ff.).

In Racine too fate and history's determinism permeate the tragic action. *Andromaque*, for example, like Seneca's *Agamemnon*, dramatises the deaths of the present as a repetition of those of the past: Pyrrhus dies on an altar like Priam at Troy (5.3/1520), Hermione replays Polyxène (5.5/1610ff.), the *ruisseaux de sang* encompassing Oreste (5.5/1628) recall those of Troy's bloody fall (4.5/1337). In other plays the issue of heredity is prominent, derived from the Old Testament as well as from Seneca. Thus Racine's first non-secular play, *Esther*:

> Nos pères ont péché, nos pères ne sont plus,
> Et nous portons la peine de leurs crimes.
> (*Esther* 1.5/334f.)

Our fathers sinned, our fathers are no more,
And we are punished for their crimes.

The idea pervades Racine's work from *La Thébaïde* onwards. In *Britannicus* there is great emphasis on the forebears of Néron, just as there is later on those of Phèdre, who speaks painfully, as in Seneca (cf. *Phaedra* 113f., 124–8, 698f.), of the cursed history of her family and the gods' role in that history:

> Objet infortuné des vengeances célestes,
> Je m'abhorre encor plus que tu ne me détestes.
> Les dieux m'en sont témoins, ces dieux qui dans mon flanc
> Ont allumé le feu fatal à tout mon sang;
> Ces dieux qui se sont fait une gloire cruelle
> De séduire le coeur d'une faible mortelle.
> (*Phèdre* 2.5/677–83)

A misfortuned victim of heaven's vengeance,
I loathe myself still more than you detest me.
The gods are witness, those gods who in my flesh
Have lit the fire fatal to all of my blood;
Those gods to whom belongs the cruel glory
Of seducing a feeble mortal's heart.

191

In *Athalie* too blood will out. One of the brilliant aspects of Athalie's final speech is precisely her concluding prophecy (5.6/1783ff.) that the blood of Ahab will triumph over that of David in Joas' veins and overthrow all that Joad had worked for. The distance between the Senecan world of *Phèdre* and the Jansenist world of *Athalie* is not substantial. Nor was the distance of Seneca's own world from Racine's.

9

THE METATHEATRICAL MIND

No Renaissance stage is forgetful of the metaphorical possibilities of its own condition, but no country devotes as much energy as England does to the special reliteralization of that metaphor.
Gordon Braden, *Renaissance Tragedy and the Senecan Tradition* (1985)

The metatheatrical nature of Senecan tragedy, its fusion of illusionism and self-reflection, its self-conscious display of its own theatrical construction, conventions and form, were analysed above. Renaissance tragedy, English drama most especially, revels in a parade of its own dramatic artifice which seems to owe its origins in part to Seneca, but develops an explicitness, even an obsessive focus, which goes beyond the Latin playwright. Kyd's *The Spanish Tragedy* again proves exemplary. Manifesting its Senecan indebtedness in quotation and structure, dramaturgical devices, dialogue and theme, it imitates too *Thyestes* and *Medea* in creating a revenge drama produced and directed by the revenger himself. The theatrical metaphor, though more explicit, is substantially the same. After demonstrating Hieronimo's theatrical expertise in the masque of the first act (the audience for which is Kyd's Elizabethan playgoer as much as the Spanish court), Kyd unleashes Hieronimo as *bravura* actor-playwright-director in the final act's production of *Soliman and Perseda*, which Hieronimo has not only written but produces, laying the groundwork in 4.1 and 4.3 for the play's performance in 4.4, casting and assigning appropriate 'parts', attending to wardrobe and to make-up, giving instructions on dialogue, title-boards and place-labels, directing what Hieronimo calls his '*Tragedia cothurnata*' (4.1.160). In the performance itself (4.4) Hieronimo imposes his own revenge 'plot' on that of his play. And in the play's finale, like Medea and Atreus, he wants recognition:

> No, princes, know I am Hieronimo,
> The hopeless father of a hapless son ...
> And princes, now behold Hieronimo,

193

Author and actor in this tragedy,
Bearing his latest fortune in his fist:
And will as resolute conclude his part
As any of the actors gone before.
(*Spanish Tragedy* 4.4.83ff.)

What Hieronimo does not realise is that his own fusion of reality and play is itself a play before the audience of Andrea's Ghost and Revenge, who frame and punctuate the whole drama (they probably remain on stage throughout, watching from an upper level or balcony), and 'serve for Chorus in this tragedy' (1.1.91). Like the 'spectating' Tantalus in Seneca's *Thyestes*, Revenge and its accompanying Ghost view a sequence of events already prescripted.

The precise date of the first performance of *The Spanish Tragedy* is disputed, but, if the 1587 date is accepted, it is possible that it was the first English tragedy to contain its own play-within-play. English metatheatre of course predates Kyd. Theatrical framing devices are apparent at the very start of secular drama in England (Medwall's *Fulgens and Lucrece*, 1497), and, from the commencement of so-called 'regular tragedy', the prominent use of the dumbshow (*Gorboduc*, Gascoine's *Jocasta*, *Gismond of Salerne*, *The Misfortunes of Arthur*) advertises a play's theatricality. Greene and Peele also employed metatheatrical devices. Kyd's practice proved especially influential.[1] *Titus Andronicus*, for example, plays with its own theatricality in a manner reminiscent of both Kyd and Seneca. Like Hieronimo in Kyd, Tamora receives her theatrical training early in the play when she creates the tragedy of *The Murder of Bassianus*, through arranging a few props and writing part of the script, the letter she hands to Saturninus:

Then all too late I bring this fatal writ,
The complot of this timeless tragedy,
And wonder greatly that man's face can fold
In pleasing smiles such murderous tyranny.
(*Titus* 2.2.264–7)

Tamora's main theatrical performance is in Act 5, where as actor-playwright-director she acts out her role as Revenge, dressed apparently to look like a Fury:[2]

Know thou, sad man, I am not Tamora:
She is thy enemy and I thy friend.
I am Revenge, sent from th'infernal kingdom
To ease the gnawing vulture of thy mind
By working wreakful vengeance on thy foes.
(*Titus* 5.2.28–32)

She is accompanied by her sons Chiron and Demetrius, whom she casts as Rape and Murder. Her audience is Titus, who sees through the performance and imposes upon them his own plot, in which he acknowledges his debts to Ovid (the myth of 'Progne') and Roman history (Verginius), but for which he is indebted too, most conspicuously, to Seneca. The description of the preparation of the children for the play's pedophagic banquet recalls the Messenger's description in Seneca's *Thyestes*, although this time it is not Atreus but Titus who 'plays' the cook (5.2.204). Like Atreus, Titus directs the performance of his revenge before his enemies as both audience and uncomprehending cast-members.

Shakespeare's preoccupation with metatheatre permeates his dramatic corpus. It operates in both implicit and explicit modes. The former is apparent throughout the history plays, most overtly in the climax of the first tetralogy, *Richard III*, in which the dissembling Richard scripts and acts his bloody path to power.

> Plots have I laid, inductions dangerous,
> By drunken prophecies, libels, and dreams,
> To set my brother Clarence and the King
> In deadly hate, the one against the other.
> (*Richard III* 1.1.32–5)

Richard's questions to Buckingham in Act 3 are those of director to actor:

Richard	Come, cousin, canst thou quake and change thy colour,
	Murder thy breath in middle of a word,
	And then again begin, and stop again,
	As if thou were distraught and mad with terror?
Buckingham	Tut, I can counterfeit the deep tragedian,
	Speak, and look back, and pry on every side,
	Tremble and start at wagging of a straw,
	Intending deep suspicion. Ghastly looks
	Are at my service like enforced smiles,
	And both are ready in their offices
	At any time to grace my stratagems.
	(*Richard III* 3.5.1–11)

Two scenes later it is Buckingham's turn to direct Richard in his crown-winning performance before the Mayor of London: 'Play the maid's part: still answer nay, and take it' (3.7.50).[3] In the Henriad, theatricality is represented not simply as an instrument of manic ambition, but as inseparable from statecraft and monarchy. Machiavellian theory triumphs; more importantly, kingship is demystified. The right to rule is shown to depend less on blood than on performance, as the crown passes to Bolingbroke, the superior performer and playmaker. The deposition scene in *Richard II* functions not only as public spectacle –

Fetch hither Richard, that in common view
He may surrender

(*Richard II* 4.1.155f.)

– but also as a play-within-play, in which Bolingbroke assigns parts to both Richard and Northumberland and directs the whole performance, literally staging the transfer of power despite the recalcitrant king's attempts to modify Bolingbroke's script. When it is the latter's turn to perform, his triumphant entrance into London is that of 'a well-grac'd actor' (5.2.24) before the city's 'desiring eyes' (5.2.14). Bolingbroke's son learns well – nor only from his father. In the Boar's Head Tavern in Eastcheap the future victor of Agincourt in a mock drama before Mistress Quickly and the others plays Hal to Falstaff's king and king to Falstaff's Hal (*1 Henry IV* 2.4.368ff.). He replays the selfsame kingly role in the rejection scene following his coronation (*2 Henry IV* 5.5.47ff.), in preparation for the continuous theatrics of successful monarchy in *Henry V*, where the reduction of kingship to performance is highlighted by the performer's own incisive commentary (*Henry V* 4.1.235ff.). It is not only Falstaff who resembles 'one of these harlotry players' (*1 Henry IV* 2.4.390f.). Hal's whole behaviour throughout the *Henry* trilogy is self-scripted mime (*1 Henry IV* 1.2.190–212).[4]

The tragedies and comedies have their own representations of theatrical practice. *Antony and Cleopatra*'s long final scene transforms itself (5.2.110ff.) into a mini-drama controlled by Cleopatra, who plays suppliant queen to the conquering Caesar and then arranges the props, costume, stage-set and audience for her own apotheotic death. *The Winter's Tale* similarly concludes (5.3) with a mini-drama (a version of 'Pygmalion'), but this time it stars one woman (Hermione) and is produced and directed by another (Paulina). In *King Lear* two main characters, Kent and Edgar, are constrained by circumstances to become self-scripting actors in their own plays, adopting the roles of servant and 'poor Tom' respectively. In contrast, Edgar's bastard brother is a willing and accomplished theatricalist, who plots his way to power through a series of 'lying' scripts and self-and-other directed performances. A similar counterpoint between good and evil theatricality is apparent in the 'dramatic productions' of Don Pedro and his illegitimate brother in *Much Ado About Nothing*. In *Othello* it is the master role-player Iago who, as a dark representation of the playwright himself, fashions his tragic plot from the psychic structures of those he manipulates. Overt metatheatre is evident in the plays-within-play of works such as *Love's Labour's Lost*, *Midsummer Night's Dream* and *Hamlet*. In the two comedies the playmaking within the final act offers ironic commentary on the ludicity and histrionic self-obsession of the spectating 'lovers'. In *Hamlet* the central playlet, *The Murder of Gonzago*, stages constituents of *Hamlet*'s own plot,[5] in a way which not only signals the main play's status as theatre, but locates that play within a theatrical tradition whose origins are in Seneca.[6] Pointers in this regard are the murderer's Latin name (Lucianus), Ophelia's description of Hamlet as 'chorus' (3.2.240), and the rhetoric and style of the speeches themselves, which are self-consciously 'Senecan':

> Thoughts black, hands apt, drugs fit, and time agreeing,
> Confederate season, else no creature seeing,
> Thou mixture rank, of midnight weeds collected,
> With Hecate's ban thrice blasted, thrice infected,
> Thy natural magic and dire property
> On wholesome life usurps immediately.
>
> (*Hamlet* 3.2.249–54)

Underscoring the Senecan aetiology: Hamlet's promptings to the Player cast as Lucianus, which reveal the playlet's primary focus:

> Begin, murderer. Leave thy damnable faces and begin,
> Come, the croaking raven doth bellow for revenge.
>
> (*Hamlet* 3.2.246–8)

The prince's Senecan revenge drama mirrors and reflects upon *Hamlet* itself. It also sets up a model of Hamlet as failed actor-director in the action of the play at large, in contrast both with Hamlet's own players whose acting accords with 'the motive and the cue for passion' (2.2.555) precisely as Hamlet's does not, and with such successful revenge models as Atreus and Medea.[7]

Of course Medea had an advantage over Hamlet; as a sorceress she could direct the world and does. Her successor in Shakespearean metatheatre is Prospero, who creates the action of *The Tempest* from the storm onwards,[8] controlling and manipulating play and players both human and divine. The Jacobean masque of Act 4 is a transparent manifestation of his theatrical power throughout the play. Prospero's success inverts the failure of Marlowe's Faustus, who claims for magic the same 'world of profit and delight' (*Faustus* 1.52) assigned traditionally to dramatic poetry, but cannot create through trivial and insubstantial theatrics a transformation of his world. If Prospero reflects Shakespeare's creative power, Faustus is Marlowe's dark, menacing glass.[9]

In French drama Medea's metatheatrical successor is the *grand Mage*, Alcandre, in Corneille's *L'Illusion comique*, written immediately after his *Médée*, from which he clearly derived the notion of magician-director. Like Seneca's Colchian princess Alcandre has the power to create reality through language. The whole structure of *L'Illusion* is metatheatrical. Alcandre and Pridamant set the scene in Act 1 as director and audience for the plays-within-play which will occupy Acts 2 to 5, and punctuate the action thereafter, framing Act 2 and Act 5, and concluding Acts 3 and 4. Especially striking is the play-within-play of Act 5, which features (unbeknown to Pridamant) players playing players and parades the illusionism of theatre through the illusionism of theatre. It is Corneille's most self-reflective play, more overtly so than the Senecan *Medea* which seems to lie behind it. It ends appropriately in Alcandre's extraordinary panegyric of theatre, which, if true of Corneille's Paris, was also true of imperial Rome, even if the concept of *le théâtre* needed further explication:

> À présent le théâtre
> Est en un point si haut que chacun l'idolâtre;
> Et ce que votre temps voyait avec mépris
> Est aujourd'hui l'amour de tous les bons esprits,
> L'entretien de Paris, le souhait des provinces,
> Le divertissement le plus doux de nos princes,
> Les délices du peuple, et le plaisir des grands.
> (*Illusion* 5.5/1645–51)

> At present the theatre
> Is at so high a point that all worship it;
> And what your age used to view with contempt
> Is today the love of all good natured people,
> The talk of Paris, the provinces' desire,
> The sweetest diversion of our princes,
> The people's delight and pleasure of the great.

French metatheatre is on the whole less explicit than that evident in *L'Illusion comique*, and more akin to Seneca in its implied quality. Racine, for example, focuses on the joys of spectating in the presentation of Roxane's vengeance in *Bajazet*; her pleasure derives from watching her victims watching each other's death:

> Ma rivale est ici: Suis-moi sans différer;
> Dans les mains des muets viens la voir expirer.
> (*Bajazet* 5.4/1544f.)

> My rival's here: Follow me without delay.
> Come and see her die in the hands of the mutes.

Elsewhere he theatricalises manipulative power, as in *Britannicus* when Néron becomes director/audience to Junie, to whom he assigns a very specific role in 2.3/2.4 with equally specific directions (coldness towards Britannicus, whom she loves), and whom he observes perform that role in 2.6. Junie is not allowed to forget the presence of Néron as audience:

> Caché près de ces lieux, je vous verrai, Madame.
> Renfermez votre amour dans le fond de votre âme.
> Vous n'aurez point pour moi de langages secrets:
> J'entendrai des regards que vous croirez muets . . .

Sa fortune dépend de vous plus que de moi.
Madame, en le voyant, songez que je vous voi.
(Britannicus 2.3/679ff.)

Hidden nearby, I shall see you, lady.
Lock up your love in the depths of your soul.
You cannot engage in secret language:
I'll intercept looks you believe voiceless . . .
His fortune depends on you more than me.
Lady, seeing him, remember I see you.

Italian metatheatre is similarly implicit, but, as is to be expected given Italian drama's greater dependence on the Roman tragedian, sometimes operates in a more obviously Senecan mode. Sulmone in *Orbecche*, for example, creates a revenge play modelled on that of Atreus in *Thyestes*, playing the role of forgiving father to Orbecche and Oronte, butchering the latter and his children, and casting his daughter as spectator to the climax of his vengeance. Less Senecan is the prologue to Dolce's *Marianna*, in which Tragedia itself appears to state its theatrical field and suggest the relative worth of the play.

In English drama metatheatre maintains, even increases its overtness. Masques, dumbshows, and plays-within-play are found in playwrights as diverse as Marlowe, Chapman, Marston, Middleton, Beaumont, Fletcher, Tourneur, Webster and Massinger. In Chettle's or Munday's *The Tragedy of Hoffman* Kyd's revenge play-within-play has been transformed into a curtained alcove near the cave of the revenger, where the skeleton of the revenger's father, 'prologue to a tragedy' (1.3.407), is soon joined by the victim's corpse. Marston is particularly fond of advertising his own theatricality. In *Antonio's Revenge*, Acts 2, 3 and 5 commence with dumb-shows underscoring his drama as 'play'. In the final scene of Act 2, as he whips himself into a frenzy of revenge-*furor*, Piero presents himself as an actor in a Senecan tragedy:

> Swell plump, bold heart,
> For now thy tide of vengeance rolleth in.
> O now *Tragoedia Cothurnata* mounts;
> Piero's thoughts are fixed on dire exploits;
> Pell mell! Confusion and black murder guides
> The organs of my spirit – shrink not, heart;
> *Capienda rebus in malis praeceps uia est.*
> (*Antonio's Revenge* 2.5.43–9)

Jonson attacked this passage for its language (*Poetaster* 5.3.281). As metatheatre it works, its effect sharpened by the concluding quotation from Seneca's *Agamemnon* (154) and the elaborate dumb-show which begins Act 3. An analogous effect is achieved by Pandulpho's theatrical metaphors at several crucial junctures of the play. At the death of his son Feliche Pandulpho replays the Shakespearean Titus' 'Ha, ha, ha' (*Antonio's Revenge* 1.5.58), and then sits down with his nephew Alberto (1.5.62ff.) to 'talk as chorus to the tragedy', avoiding 'mimic action' and 'player-like' gestures. Just before the dumb-show of the final act Pandulpho weeps over his son's body:

> Man will break out, despite philosophy.
> Why, all this while I ha' but played a part,
> Like to some boy that acts a tragedy,
> Speaks burly words and raves out passion;
> But when he thinks upon his infant weakness,
> He droops his eye.
>
> (*Antonio's Revenge* 4.5.46–51)

Since this play was performed by the boys of St Paul's, Pandulpho's simile is pointedly self-reflective and appropriate preparation for the metatheatre of Act 5, whose opening dumb-show is followed by the entry of a Senecan ghost quoting lines from *Octavia*, and supplying in Tantalus fashion details of the plot to be played out before him. The theatrical language is undisguised:

> Now down looks providence
> T'attend the last act of my son's revenge.
> Be gracious, Observation, to our scene;
> For now the plot unites his scattered limbs
> Close in contracted bands.
>
> (*Antonio's Revenge* 5.1.10–14)

Appropriately the revenge itself is enacted through a fusion of Senecan allusion and overt playmaking (Antonio's masque), performed before the Ghost of Andrugio as audience, a Kydian/Senecan 'spectator of revenge' (*Antonio's Revenge* 5.5.22). The focus on the Ghost's spectatorial pleasures is explicit: 'I taste the joys of heaven, | Viewing my son triumph in his black blood' (5.5.36f.). The play's final speech not only closes 'the last act' (5.6.55) of Antonio's vengeance, but, transforming Antonio into an Epilogue, brings to the fore the relationship between 'tragedy' and the 'pen'.[10]

The analogy between the theatre and life pervades high Renaissance English drama. Marston's Antonio and Pandulpho belong to an entire group of characters in the plays of this period (Bussy, Malevole, Vindice, Flamineo, Bosola) who seem designed to function as extra-theatrical commentators on the play of which they are a constitutive part, dissolving the boundaries between theatre and life, as they signal the former's artifice. Even in his dying words Webster's Bosola puns on his own role as 'an actor' in the whole catastrophe and wittily theatricalises the manner of Antonio's death:

> In a mist: I know not how –
> Such a mistake as I have often seen
> In a play.
>
> (*Malfi* 5.5.94–6)

Compare Shakespeare's Fabian on the deception of Malvolio in *Twelfth Night*: 'If this were played upon a stage now, I could condemn it as an improbable fiction' (3.4.128f.); or Bussy's Ghost in Chapman's *Revenge of Bussy d'Ambois*: 'Clermont must author this just tragedy' (*Revenge of Bussy d'Ambois* 5.3.46); or Brutus to his fellow conspirators: 'Let not our looks put on our purposes, | But bear it as our Roman actors do' (*Julius Caesar* 2.1.225f.), Coriolanus to his mother: 'I play | The man I am' (*Coriolanus*.3.2.15f.); or Domitilla to Paris, both playing parts in a play within Massinger's own play, *The Roman Actor*: 'I shall look on your tragedy unmov'd, | Peradventure laugh at it, for it will prove | A comedy to me' (3.2.266–8); or King Henry in Ford's Caroline drama, *Perkin Warbeck*: 'The player's on the stage still, 'tis his part; | 'A does but act' (5.2.68f.). The tradition, begun by Kyd, of the climactic revenge masque or play, which overtly theatricalises the revenge itself and collapses the stage–life distinction, becomes commonplace by the time of Middleton's *Women Beware Women*, in whose finale failed 'plots' and fatal performances crowd in upon each other in patently comic excess. But even earlier the metatheatrical idiom is so common that it often seems intentionally ironic, as in Arruntius' triple-edged comment on Tiberius in Jonson's *Sejanus*: 'Well acted, Caesar' (3.105), or Delio's humorous commentary on the unreality of theatrical time in *The Duchess of Malfi* (3.1.8ff.). Sometimes it is self-parodic. Thus Vindice's exposure of the artifice of the Renaissance *Schreirede* and its concomitant Hippolytan outrage:

> Is there no thunder left, or is't kept up
> In stock for heavier vengeance? [*Thunder*] There it goes!
> (*Revenger's Tragedy* 4.2.196f.)

Indeed *The Revenger's Tragedy* is permeated with references to itself as tragedy, often of an overtly humorous nature: 'When the bad bleeds, then is the tragedy good' (3.5.198); 'When thunder claps, heaven likes the tragedy' (5.3.47). It projects itself from the start as a paradigm of revenge tragedy (1.1.39f.) and then deploys the genre's conventions in a self-consciously caricaturist fashion: the skull of the victim, poisoned and dressed as an attractive woman, used in a bizarre form of vengeance ('Now to my tragic business . . .', 3.5.99ff.); identity confusion with severed heads; the revenger's punishment arranged artificially through Vindice's unnecessary confession; the open presentation of revenge as theatre through the doubling of the revenge-masque. In Tourneur/Middleton's classic play the metatheatrical idiom of Renaissance drama has become part of the dramatic subject-matter.

But there is a socio-cultural dimension too, transcending the *theatrum mundi* commonplace embodied even in the name of Shakespeare's Southwark theatre[11] – and its roots are in Seneca: the representation of human life as *essentially* theatrical, human behaviour as role-play, human social relations as constructs of self-scripted duplicity, justice, law, monarchy and authority

as a ritualised theatre of power. The implications of this world-view are, as in
Seneca, both precise and generally cheerless:

> This wide and universal theatre
> Presents more woeful pageants than the scene
> Wherein we play in.
>
> *(As You Like It* 2.7.137–9)

> When we are born, we cry that we are come
> To this great stage of fools.
>
> *(Lear* 4.6.180f.)

> Life's but a walking shadow; a poor player,
> That struts and frets his hour upon the stage,
> And then is heard no more: it is a tale
> Told by an idiot, full of sound and fury,
> Signifying nothing.
>
> *(Macbeth* 5.5.24–8)

Macbeth's sentiments are echoed by a more innocent tragic figure, Webster's
Duchess:

> I account this world a tedious theatre,
> For I do play a part in't 'gainst my will.
>
> *(Malfi* 4.1.84f.)

For Vindice, Gloriana's unmasked, rotting skull is the reality of human life,
female beauty mere duplicity: 'See, ladies, with false forms | You deceive
men, but cannot deceive worms' *(Revenger's Tragedy* 3.5.96f.). In Massinger's
The Roman Actor the boundaries between the theatre and the world completely dissolve in the drama's final play-within-play, *The False Servant*, in
which the actor Paris plays the role which the emperor Domitian thinks he
has performed in life and Domitian himself plays 'the injur'd Lord' and
executes his 'false servant'. Similarly for Kyd's Hieronimo theatre and reality
are inseparable: theatrical vengeance becomes real vengeance, theatrical
death real death; the climactic 'spectacle' and 'show' *(Spanish Tragedy* 4.4.89)
are his son Horatio's body 'through-girt with wounds'. For Seneca the climactic theatrical spectacle are the murdered children of Jason, the heads of
Thyestes' devoured sons, the sacrificial, marital slaying of an innocent virgin,
'the final act of Troy's collapse' performed in a landscape translated into
theatre *(theatri more, Troades* 1125).

    If the Roman imperial theatre of public execution and amphitheatrical
slaughter and its authorisation of law and power are mirrored in Senecan
tragedy, their counterparts in Renaissance England are similarly entexted.
The following judicial sentence, passed on an English nobleman in 1589,
could function as the plot of a contemporary tragedy's final act. The

audience for this theatricalised event would have been the same as for Kyd's
The Spanish Tragedy, performed perhaps in the same year:

> He should be conveyed to the Place from whence he came, and from
> thence to the place of Execution, and there to be hanged until he were
> half dead, his Members to be cut off, his Bowels to be cast into the
> Fire, his Head to be cut off, his Quarters to be divided into four several
> parts, and to be bestowed in four several places.[12]

This is not representational theatre, but reality theatricalised, political and
judicial authority transformed into a ritualised spectacle of power. In
Renaissance England similarly theatrical practices and exemplary displays
were common, and fundamental to the maintenance of monarchic
hegemony and social control. In early imperial Rome public executions
sometimes went further, dissolving the boundary between representation
and reality by a 'fatal charade',[13] in which a criminal's death in the amphitheatre was theatricalised into a representation of a mythic or stage 'death'.
Martial's epigrams *De Spectaculis* or 'On the Games', written to celebrate
the opening of the Colosseum in 80 CE, describe several examples of a
practice that began under Nero. The following execution of a criminal,
dressed as the bandit Laureolus whose death was the climax of a famous
mime, is typical. The translation, by Thomas Pecke, was published in
1659:[14]

> Prometheus to cold Caucasus is chain'd,
> Whilst by his Entrails Vultures are sustain'd.
> Wretched Laureolus a Northern Bear
> Very sincerely did asunder tear.
> Every Vein to weep Bloud was inclin'd:
> Strict search in's Carkass could no Body finde.
> Thus one that stab'd his Master must have dy'd,
> Or Actors of infernal Parricide.
> This Torment is his due, who dares Rome Fire,
> Or who deflowres the Gods most sacred Quire.
> Obsolete Mischiefs, resalute the Stage:
> Fables prove True in this our conscious Age.
>
> (Martial *De Spectaculis* 9)

But English monarchs and Roman emperors not only used spectacle to
validate and implement their power; they were themselves self-conscious
spectacle. Nero performed on the stage, within his private grounds at first,
later in the public theatre. His most famous roles were those which mirrored
his infamous life: Orestes, Oedipus, Hercules – a confusion of modalities
reflected in the emperor's use of dramatic masks modelled to represent his
own features or those of his wife or paramours (Suetonius *Nero* 21.3, Dio
63.9.5).[15] Unlike Nero, neither Elizabeth I nor James I appeared on the

public stage, but they were, nevertheless, self-conscious performers, in the popular imagination –

> Wee all (that's Kings and all) but Players are
> Upon this earthly Stage.
>> (John Davies, *The Scourge of Folly*)

– and in their own: 'A King is as one set on a skaffold, whose smallest actions and gestures all the people gazingly doe behold'.[16] Thus James I in his *Basilicon Doron*, articulating the paradox that kings were also subjects, at least visual ones. Thus too Elizabeth, whose appearance in later years was a masterpiece of costuming, hairpieces and perfumery, to disguise her ageing body: 'We Princes . . . are set on stages, in the sight and view of all the world dulie observed.'[17] Her awareness of the connection between role-play and power was apparent at least as early as her 1559 procession through London, aptly described by a contemporary account as 'a stage wherin was shewed the wonderfull spectacle of a noble hearted princesse toward her most loving people'.[18] Inevitably the focus at court, as Sir John Harington's testimony displays, was on the '*shewe* of love and obedience'.[19] Much of the monarchic spectacle was a secularisation and replacement of the theatrical rituals of medieval Catholicism: the queen's own en*act*ment of the change in cultural authority. As a way of reflecting and maintaining her power relations with both the aristocracy and the people, Elizabeth even appropriated the discourses of pastoral and myth to create highly conventionalised and overtly artificial roles for herself and her subjects to play.[20] During her summer progresses, pastoral and mythological masques and verses were performed in her presence, addressing her or otherwise incorporating her into their fictions; and they were often merely plays-within-play. For highly figurative, theatrical ceremonies generally preceded and followed them – at the boundaries of shire, town and estate – in which Elizabeth was the main performer.[21] At the queen's entry to Sudeley Castle in the 1591 progress, an 'olde Shepheard' spoke:

> If in anything we shall chance to discover our lewdnes, it will be in over boldnesse, in gazinge at you, who fils our harts with joye, and our eies with wonder . . . This lock of wooll, Cotsholdes best fruite, and my poor gifte, I offer to your Highnes; in which nothing is to be esteemed, but the whitenes, virginities colour; nor to be expected but duetye, shephards religion.[22]

Elizabeth's reproofs too theatricalised her power: 'I would not have my sheepe branded with another mans marke; I would not they should follow the whistle of a strange Shepherd'.[23] To Ralegh she was 'Cynthia, Phoebe, Flora, Diana and Aurora'; to courtiers and poets she was Laura, Deborah, Oriana, Astraea, Gloriana.[24] In the midst of a pastoral and mythic theatrics which mediated and embodied her ideology of the sovereign prince, 'Eliza,

Queene of shepheardes', goddess and Virgin Mother, controlled her court and her kingdom. In her private moments, when not theatricalising her power, she translated (in part) Horace's poem on dramatic composition and the *Hercules Oetaeus* attributed to Seneca.[25]

Like her father whose theatricality she inherited,[26] Elizabeth also figured occasionally in court plays. In Peele's *Arraignment of Paris*, for example, Diana awards her the contentious apple; in Jonson's *Every Man Out of His Humour* she receives Macilente's final laudation. In all such cases the monarch represented herself.[27] Her Stuart successor, however, kept aloof from the stage, and even in his entrance into London (itself a self-conscious recreation of 'Rome') presented himself as a distant object of spectacle rather than, as Elizabeth had been at her entrance, a speaking participant. The theatrics were all the more apparent, and were captured in Dekker's description at the spectacle's end of the city of London as 'like an actor on stage, stript of her borrowed Majestie'.[28] From that point onwards James cultivated the role of godlike Roman emperor, England's 'Augustus' or 'Caesar'.[29] Not content, however, with pageants, processions, ceremonies, tableaux and the multiform rituals of monarchy, James' wife, Queen Anne, appeared frequently on the stage itself in the masques that began to occupy the centre of court life. She appeared sometimes with James' only son and heir Charles, who seemed drawn to 'the skaffold', and performed on the court stage both when Prince of Wales and later when King, as did his wife and queen, Henrietta Maria. Indeed Davenant's masque, *Salmacida Spolia*, performed at court twice in 1640 on the eve of civil war, featured both Charles I and his queen as theatricalisations of themselves. Jonson declares in the introductory note to his masque, *Love's Triumph*, performed in 1631: 'All representations, especially those of this nature at court, public spectacles, either have been, or ought to be, the mirrors of man's life.' But self-representation of the kind frequent at the Stuart court fuses sign and signified, makes the man the mirror of himself. Like Nero wearing a mask inscribed with his own features, the Stuart monarchs on the eve of their demise had collapsed the distinction between reality and the stage. The *trompe l'oeil* perspective of Inigo Jones' masque scenery served only to emphasise the collapse.[30] Even the political and theatrical spaces were the same: the Banqueting House at Whitehall served as a site for masques and for the reception of political envoys. The figurative and the literal were one.

As in Julio-Claudian Rome too, this dissolution of theatrical boundaries was often reflected in the audience's own self-conscious performance. Dekker's advice to a 'gallant' visiting a Jacobean playhouse, was to sit on the stage itself, but not before the prologue was finished, when you could 'creep from behind the Arras' 'as though you were one of the properties, or that you dropped out of the Hangings'.[31] In both city and country, but most especially at court, role-players abounded, trained, as in imperial Rome, by a rhetorically based education which taught the arts of 'dazzling improvisations'.[32] Often the object to be dazzled was the monarch. For like Nero (e.g. Dio 63.15.2f.), English Renaissance monarchs were attentive audiences of the performance of others. Failed performances by the Earl of Essex, 'the General of our gracious Empress' (*Henry V* 5.0.30) and people's favourite, lost him Elizabeth's favour, his state offices, and eventually (in 1601) his head. As in Nero's Rome, command performances had to please. Also as in Nero's Rome, there were royal spies everywhere, sometimes even among the playwrights themselves. Marlowe and Jonson seem to have supplemented their income from playmaking precisely by spying for the government. They were also spied upon. Their own performances as playmakers were constantly observed by the court's Master of the Revels, the City Fathers and all kinds of anti-theatricalists. Censorship attempted to control, if somewhat sporadically, what could be performed, and, where it failed to repress, it could punish. Jonson was himself imprisoned twice (in 1597 and 1605) for authoring subversive dramas.[33]

The theatricalisation of political and social life overtly reflects an uneven distribution of power. On the one hand, there are those who have the power to impose their fictions on others and to require from them complicit performance of those fictions. Their gaze ensures that the performances are enacted. On the other hand, there are those who are compelled to perform.[34] But monarchs too must perform, and Shakespeare's history plays subject the performance of English monarchs to the judgement of English subjects. Signally, Essex's rebellion used *Richard II* as its prologue;[35] and, as that play exhibits and Charles I (and Nero) testified, failure in monarchic performance can be fatal. Nor are social inferiors without theatrical power themselves. They can, and in drama often do, use the theatricalisation of human relations to their advantage. From Plautus' *seruus callidus* onwards, social inferiors use theatrical modes to achieve their goals. In *Miles Gloriosus* the slave Palaestrio scripts, directs and acts in a play which completely deceives and overthrows the soldier; compelled to perform in a way that receives his superior's approval, he manipulates that performance to overthrow the superior himself. In Seneca's *Medea* it is the exiled and abandoned wife and mother who performs and directs her path to power. Similarly in *The Spanish Tragedy* Hieronimo's inferior social status is stressed; and it is he who scripts, directs and manipulates the theatrical performances of the aristocrats themselves to achieve his revenge. Marston's Antonio and Pandulpho and Tourneur/ Middleton's Vindice plot their theatrical route to revenge over superiors who cannot control the performances they compel. In *Lear* it is the bastard Edmund whose theatrical practices all but give him the world. The English Renaissance's metatheatrical mind was not simply a reflection of the collapse of the distinctions between reality and the stage; like that of Seneca, it exposed the fragility of social relations and their attendant distribution of power. In this it was aided, as was the Roman stage, by the sociology of the theatre itself. Before their own communities seated according to social rank, actors of low estate, branded as 'infamous' (*infames*) in Rome and as 'Vacabondes' in England,[36] transgressed social class and transformed themselves into princes. In turning life into script and power into theatrical performance, Roman and English metatheatre signalled the transmutability of both. One can be self-written, the other easily shifts: a slave can be king, a Galba or Otho can be Caesar, a Cromwell can rule the 'sceptr'd isle'. 'The Tragick Scaffold' on which England's 'Royal Actor' died was erected by his own audience, who 'Did clap their bloody hands'.[37] Like their Roman predecessor, Elizabethan and Jacobean dramatists presaged imminent political and social collapse when the performances of the powerful became aberrant and the control of the state passed to more competent performers, whose scripts were reified as history.

Epilogue

10

TRAGEDY AND CULTURE

> It is impossible to ignore the extent to which civilization is built up on renunciation of instinctual gratifications, the degree to which the existence of civilization presupposes the non-gratification (suppression, repression, or something else?) of powerful instinctual urgencies. This *cultural privation* dominates the whole field of social relations between human beings.
>
> S. Freud, *Civilization and its Discontents* (1930)

It is commonplace to assert that Senecan and Renaissance drama reflects and refracts contemporary cultural contradictions and stress. Late Julio-Claudian Rome and Renaissance Europe were societies undergoing momentous social change and, in some cases, on the verge of dissolution. Both societies were highly stratified and patronal. The closed social system of interlocking obligations and privileges that bound patron to client in both cultures was showing fractures. New men were emerging: freedmen administrators, non-Italian senators, equestrian entrepreneurs, the merchant class in sixteenth- and seventeenth-century Europe, which began to form a rising bourgeoisie in the wake of an expanding cloth trade and the economic and colonial uses of navigation. In both Seneca's Italy and Shakespeare's England liquidity of social relations attended an increasingly urbanised and commercialising world, in which, even as the boundaries between social classes began to erode, there was a fresh attempt to assert the existing social order. In England afflictions affecting not only the lower classes – plague, famine, land enclosures, economic recession, war levies, religious persecution, the repression of popular assemblies – demythologised the body politic and decentred the political subject. The repressive absolutism of the political and social order, exemplified most clearly by the tyrannical behaviour of emperors, monarchs, dukes, and by the condemnation of contemporary social mobility and its defining *mores* in both ancient and Renaissance texts, became overwhelming and conspicuous. Not accidentally in 'revenge tragedies', including Seneca's *Medea* (a seminal text for the Renaissance),[1] a wrong is

211

often committed by a social superior upon an inferior, who can find no redress within the existing social system. Indeed one of the hallmarks of Senecan and Renaissance tragedy is to function as a site within culture where the inadequacies and contradictions of culture may be contested, an institutional space for the representation of the war between social and instinctual imperatives, between passion, thinking, belief, and their social formation, even repression. It is a cultural site which exposes the constructedness and fragility of culture itself, and the abiding strength and ineradicable force of instinct.

> The bitter truth . . . is that men are not gentle, friendly creatures wishing for love, who simply defend themselves if they are attacked, but that a powerful measure of desire for aggression has to be reckoned as part of their instinctual endowments. The result is that their neighbour is to them not only a possible helper or sexual object, but also a temptation to them to gratify their aggressiveness on him, to exploit his capacity for work without recompense, to use him sexually without his consent, to seize his possessions, to humiliate him, to cause him pain, to torture and kill him. *Homo homini lupus.*
>
> (*Civilization and its Discontents*)[2]

Tragedies such as *Thyestes, Orbecche, Titus Andronicus, Richard III, King Lear, Rodogune*, exemplify without explication Freud's thesis of 'men as savage beasts to whom the thought of sparing their own kind is alien.'[3] But what Freud obfuscates through his theory of the sublimation of instinct by culture is the degree to which instincts are hardly sublimated at all, but operate fully within the structures of civilization, concealed behind the theatricality of role play. This theatricality appears most obvious at times of great social stress, when an increased self-consciousness may develop about social relations as 'a manipulable, artful process',[4] and an increased, almost neurotic, concern attach itself to strategies of self-representation, to learning how an aspirant to social success, in the words of Richard Taverner's 1539 tract, 'must . . . fashion himself to the manners of men.'[5] At two such sites of social stress, late Julio-Claudian Rome and Elizabethan-Jacobean England, tragedy combined its representational and metatheatrical energies to advertise its own form as the fundamental structure of social power, and to exhibit itself at times nakedly as the tragedy of culture.

SENECAN CHRONOLOGY

Political events	Dates BCE	Literary and other events
Renewal of the first triumvirate (56 BCE). Dedication of first stone theatre in Rome, Theatre of Pompey (55 BCE).	57–54	Attested productions of Accius' *Eurysaces, Brutus, Clytmnestra, Astyanax*. Catullus *Poems*. Lucretius *De Rerum Natura*.
Assassination of Julius Caesar.	44	Production of Accius' *Tereus*.
Octavian's Triple Triumph.	29	Varius' *Thyestes* performed. Virgil recites *Georgics*.
Second 'Augustan Settlement'.	23	Horace *Odes* 1–3 published.
Augustan marriage ordinances (18 BCE). *Ludi Saeculares* ('Centennial Games': 17 BCE).	20–15	Virgil *Aeneid* published. Horace *Epistles* 1, *Carmen Saeculare*. Ovid *Amores* (1st edn), *Heroides* 1–14 (?).
Theatres of Balbus and Marcellus dedicated. Augustus made *pontifex maximus* (12 BCE). Tiberius marries Augustus' daughter, Julia (11 BCE).	13–10	Ovid's *Medea* (?). Horace *Odes* 4, *Epistle to Augustus, Ars Poetica*.
Ara Pacis Augustae dedicated.	9	
Augustus made *pater patriae*; daughter Julia exiled; opening of Forum of Augustus (2 BCE).	2–1	Ovid *Amores* (2nd edn), *Ars Amatoria*. Lucius Annaeus Seneca ('Younger Seneca') future tragedian, philosopher and imperial minister, born c.1 BCE at Cordoba in Spain, second of three sons to equestrian scholar Lucius (?) Annaeus Seneca ('Elder Seneca', c.55 BCE–c.41 CE).

Political events	Dates CE	Literary and other events
Dynastic intrigue. Augustus adopts Tiberius (4 CE).	1–8	Ovid *Metamorphoses, Fasti*. Seneca brought to Rome.
Augustus' grandson Agrippa Postumus (7 CE) and granddaughter Julia (8 CE) exiled.	7–8	Ovid exiled to Tomis on the Black Sea (8 CE).
Augustus' death and execution of Agrippa Postumus (14 CE). Reign of Tiberius (14–37 CE). Sejanus praetorian prefect (–31 CE).	9–17	Ovid's exile: *Tristia, Epistulae Ex Ponto, Fasti*. Manilius' *Astronomica*. Death of Livy (17 CE) and Ovid (*c.*17 CE). Seneca experiments with an ascetic form of Stoic-Pythagoreanism, from which his father dissuades him.
Deaths of Tiberius' adopted son and heir, Germanicus (19 CE), and natural son, Drusus (23 CE).	19–23	
Pontius Pilate governor of Judaea (26 CE)	25–6	Cremutius Cordus, historian, prosecuted for treason, commits suicide (25 CE); his works burnt.
	25–40	Phaedrus *Fables* 1–4.
Death of Livia, widow of Augustus and mother of Tiberius (29 CE). Elder Agrippina exiled (29 CE). Nerva born (30 CE). Fall of Sejanus (31 CE). Macro praetorian prefect.	29–31	Velleius Paterculus, *Historiae Romanae*. Seneca, who suffered from a tubercular condition, convalesces in Egypt with his aunt. Returns to Rome (31 CE).
Seneca and elder brother Gallio enter senate. Seneca holds quaestorship, aedileship, and tribunate of people. Tiberian treason trials and executions (32–7 CE).	31–41	Elder Seneca, *Controversiae, Suasoriae*, and Seneca, *Ad Marciam* (*c.*37–41 CE). Seneca achieves fame as orator; arouses Caligula's jealousy. Suicide of tragedian Scaurus; birth of Persius (34 CE).
Death of Tiberius and succession of Gaius 'Caligula' (–41). Birth of Nero to Younger Agrippina, sister of Caligula, and Gnaeus Domitius Ahenobarbus.	37	
Agrippina and her sister Julia Livilla exiled.	39	Birth of Lucan, Seneca's nephew and future epicist.
Gnaeus Domitius dies. Octavia born to Claudius and his young wife, Messalina.	40	Martial born.

Date	Events	Literary and related
41	Caligula assassinated. Succession of Claudius (–54). Claudius' son Britannicus born. Seneca accused by Messalina of adultery with Julia Livilla and exiled to Corsica.	
41–9	Seneca's exile. Pleas for clemency.	Senecan Stoic 'Dialogues', *Ad Polybium*, *Ad Helviam Matrem*, *De Ira* 1–2; and *Epigrams* on Exile. Birth of Statius (*c*.45 CE).
47	*Ludi Saeculares* held. Nero and Britannicus participate in the *Troiae Lusus* ('Troy Game'). Imperial edict curbing unruly behaviour in the theatre.	Pomponius Secundus' plays hissed from the stage.
48	Messalina executed.	
49	Seneca recalled to Rome through agency of younger Agrippina, Claudius' new wife. Appointed tutor to her son, Nero.	
49–65	Seneca at the centre of Roman power.	Seneca *Tragedies* (?); *De Ira* 3 (by 52 CE), *De Brevitate Vitae* (by 55 CE), *De Constantia Sapientis*, *De Tranquillitate Animi*, *De Otio*, *De Providentia* (?).
50–3	Seneca holds praetorship; Nero adopted by Claudius (50 CE). Burrus made praetorian prefect (51 CE). Vespasian consul (51 CE). Gallio proconsul in Achaea (51–2 CE). Nero marries Octavia; speaks on behalf of the people of Ilium (53 CE).	Debate between Seneca and Pomponius Secundus on tragic diction (51–53 CE?): remembered by Quintilian (8.3.31).
54	Death of Claudius. Succession of Nero (–68). Parthian war begins.	Seneca *Apocolocyntosis*.
54–62	Seneca and praetorian prefect, Burrus, chief ministers and counsellors of Nero.	Seneca *De Clementia*, *De Vita Beata*, *De Beneficiis*.
54–9	'Golden Age of Nero' (*Quinquennium Neronis*). Nero's murder of Claudius' son, Britannicus (55 CE); Seneca's consulship (56 CE); Nero orders participation of senators and knights in the games (57 CE). Poppaea Nero's mistress (58 CE).	Calpurnius Siculus *Eclogues* (58 CE?). Birth of Juvenal and Tacitus (*c*.55 CE).

Political events	Dates CE	Literary and other events
Nero's murder of his mother Agrippina.	59	Nero's literary circle founded. Seneca *De Vita Beata*. Nero *Attis* and short poems.
Massive building programme by Nero, esp. two palaces: *Domus Transitoria* (burnt by fire) and *Domus Aurea* (Golden House: begun 64 CE). Revolt of Boudicca in Britain (61–3 CE). End of Parthian war (63 CE).	59–65	Literary and musical activity fostered through new public contests: *Ludi Iuvenales* (59 CE), *Neronia* (60 and 65 CE). Imperial claques formed (*Augustiani*) to applaud Nero's performances. Lucan's epic *The Civil War*; Persius *Satires*; Petronius' *Satyricon*. Seneca *Quaestiones Naturales*, *Epistulae Morales*. Fourth-style Romano-Campanian wall painting.
Death of Burrus and retirement of Seneca. Tigellinus and Faenius Rufus made praetorian prefects. Octavia divorced, exiled and murdered. Nero marries Poppaea. Other Neronian executions.	62	Death of the satirist, Persius.
Nero appears on public stage in Naples. Great Fire of Rome. Persecution of Christians. Nero rebuilds Rome.	64	Lucan banned from publication. Nero's epic on fall of Troy: *Troica*. Epigrammatist Martial arrives in Rome.
Pisonian conspiracy to kill Nero fails: many executions. Lucan and Seneca ordered to commit suicide. Poppaea dies.	65	Suicides of Lucan and Seneca. Stoic philosopher Annaeus Cornutus exiled.
Further executions. Nero tours and performs in Greece (66–7 CE). Nero dethroned and commits suicide (68 CE); Galba succeeds.	66–8	Suicides of Petronius and Stoic Thrasea Paetus (66 CE).
The Year of the Four Emperors: Galba, succeeded by Otho, Vitellius, and Vespasian, who reigns until 79 CE.	69	

NOTES

1 THE ROMAN THEATRE

1 On the ambivalence of the theatre in Rome's definition of itself see the excellent discussion of Edwards (1993), 98–136. Useful accounts of the origins and history of the Roman theatre may be found in Bieber (1961), Beare (1964), and, most recently, Beacham (1992), to all of which I am indebted. See also the valuable introduction to Jocelyn (1969).

2 See Slater (1985), 168–78, and Williams (1993).

3 'Verbal violence' comes from Beacham (1992), 124: 'Accius' plays were admired for their flamboyance and energy; they also contained much verbal violence and descriptive gore: Thyestes dining upon his sons; Philomel raped by Tereus who cuts out her tongue to avoid detection; Medea's murder of her children. Accius probed his mythic material to bring forth its most intense pathos and horror.'

4 *Ludi Romani* (September) and *Ludi Plebeii* (November) in honour of Jupiter; *Ludi Apollinares* (July) for Apollo; *Ludi Megalenses* (April) for the Great Mother; *Ludi Florales* (April–May) for Flora; *Ludi Ceriales* (April) for Ceres.

5 Seventeen is the figure of Hunter (1985), 14; Gratwick (1982), 81, opts for fourteen days. The number of days devoted to *ludi scaenici* increased substantially during the empire. It had reached a hundred by 354 CE. See Bieber (1961), 227.

6 Naevius' *Clastidium* must have dramatised the battle of 222 BCE, in which M. Claudius Marcellus defeated the Gallic chieftain in single combat. However Naevius treated the event, there were bound to be social and political ramifications.

7 The issue of the legal rights and restrictions of the acting profession at different periods is a complex one. See Edwards (1993), 123–26.

8 This difficult question is discussed by Beare (1964), 267–74.

9 The following may be cited as typical: (i) 59 BCE, at the *Ludi Apollinares*, Pompey the 'Great', seated in the audience, has the line 'Through our misery you are Great' (*nostra miseria tu es magnus*) hurled at him from the stage; the actor is applauded (Cicero *Ad Atticum* 39.3). (ii) 57 BCE, at a performance of Accius' *Brutus*, the line describing Servius Tullius, an early king of Rome – 'Tullius, who set the citizens' freedom on safe ground' – was encored countless times in reference to another Tullius, Cicero, recently exiled; in July of 57 the Senate recalled Cicero from exile, and, when the news reached the theatre, the great tragic actor Aesopus turned his own performance in Accius' *Eurysaces* into a defence of Cicero (Cicero *Pro Sestio* 120ff.). (iii) About 45 BCE, Laberius, a member of the equestrian order who had written mimes critical of Julius Caesar and was forced by him to go on to the stage, laments in his own prologue the humiliation he suffered at the hands of 'him to whom the gods have been able to deny nothing'

(Macrobius *Saturnalia* 2.7.3). (iv) About 60 CE, an actor of Atellane farce sings the line, 'Farewell father, farewell mother', accompanied by imitations of the murders of Claudius (drinking) and Agrippina (swimming); the actor is banished (Suetonius *Nero* 39.3). In the empire the theatre was also a place where citizens might petition the emperor, and his favour or disfavour be publicly seen. See further Edwards (1993), esp. 121–36.

10 Abortive attempts were made to build a stone theatre in Rome in 179, 174 and 154 BCE (see Livy 40.51.3, 41.27.5, *Periocha* 48). In 151 BCE the stone theatre commissioned by the censors three years earlier was torn down by order of a decree of the senate on the motion of the consul, Publius Cornelius Nasica. The grounds were 'inexpediency and the likelihood of damage to public morals' (*inutile et nociturum publicis moribus*, *Periocha* 48). It would be a hundred years before the next (and successful) attempt was made.

11 For Quintus, see Cicero *Ad Quintum Fratrem* 3.5, 6.7; for Julius Caesar and Augustus, see Suetonius: *Iulius* 56.7, *Augustus* 85.2.

12 Cf. also Tacitus *Dialogus* 12.5.

13 On mime see Fantham (1989).

14 See, e.g. Seneca *Epistle* 80.7f., Quintilian *Institutio Oratoria* 11.3.73f., 112, 178ff., Juvenal *Satire* 6.67–75, Suetonius *Nero* 11, *Historia Augusta: Hadrian* 19.6, 26.4. See also Bieber (1961), 227ff.; Jocelyn (1969), 47ff.

15 See also Pliny *Epistles* 7.17.11.

16 The date of this debate is uncertain, but probably after 51 CE. See Fantham (1982a), 7f.

17 See Suetonius *Domitian* 7.1; cf. Seneca *Naturales Quaestiones* 7.32. For the Marius evidence, Sallust *Jugurtha* 85.13.

18 *Oedipus* is certainly a six-act play; for *Phaedra* see my edition (1987), 134, and p. 227, n. 45 below.

19 Extended asides: e.g. *Troades* 607ff., *Phaedra* 424ff., 592ff.; entrance monologue-asides: e.g. *Hercules Furens* 332ff., *Troades* 861ff., *Medea* 177ff.

20 There is evidence from Delphi that in the late third century BCE the chorus consisted of only seven or four members: see Gomme and Sandbach (1973), 12 n. 1. Independently of this, Calder (1975), 32ff., argues for a Senecan chorus of between three and seven members, as against the twelve or fifteen member choruses of the fifth-century Attic tragedians. A smaller chorus allowed for greater flexibility in the matter of choral entrances and exits and in the number of choruses employed.

21 In Hellenistic, as in Attic drama, the choral odes were still delivered or sung away from the stage in the semi circular space, the *orchestra*, which lay in front of it. This enabled the chorus to function as a bridge between audience and stage or as an overtly theatrical 'frame' for the dramatic action. In the Roman theatre by Vitruvius' day, the 'orchestral' area had been given over to senatorial seating and the chorus performed on the large stage or *pulpitum*, occupying the same theatrical space as the actors themselves.

22 For 'reading' see Fantham (1982a), 34–49; for 'recitation' see Zwierlein (1966). The dramatic realisability of Senecan drama is strongly advocated by (among others) Calder (1983) 184, Dupont (1995), Herington (1966), 444, Sutton (1986), Walker (1969).

23 One piece of epigraphic evidence, however, is suggestive: the opening words of *Agamemnon* 730 (*idai cernu nemura*, 'I see the groves of Ida'), taken from the theatrically powerful clairvoyant speech of Cassandra, are inscribed on a wall in Pompeii (perhaps together with a few words from *Agamemnon* 693: Lebek (1985): *Corpus Inscriptionum Latinarum* iv. Suppl. 2.6698). This only 'proves' that Seneca's

Agamemnon was known, not that it had been performed. But the possibility that a performance (of some kind) influenced the graffito is tempting.

24 It is customary to cite performances of Senecan tragedy in Renaissance Europe and Tudor England. More interesting is the fact that Seneca has been and is regularly performed in modern Italy, France and Switzerland. In the English-speaking world four recent performances may perhaps be mentioned: Seneca's *Oedipus* (adapted by Ted Hughes) at the Old Vic Theatre, London, March 1968; *Phaedra* (my translation) at the Sydney Opera House, July 1987; *Troades* (also my translation) at the Alexander Theatre, Melbourne, September–October 1988; *Thyestes* (translated by Caryl Churchill) at the Royal Court Theatre, London, June 1994.

25 So Corneille had several of his plays read in public prior to performance: *Polyeucte* (1641) was read at the Hôtel de Rambouillet while still in rehearsal, and *Pulchérie* (1672) was read at the homes of the Duc de la Rochefoucauld and of the Cardinal de Retz before its unsuccessful performance by the Marais company. The plays of Corneille, Racine and other Renaissance dramatists were also some-times performed *intra domum*: so the former's *Horace* (1640), at the home of Cardinal Richelieu, and the latter's *Andromaque* (1667) in the Queen's apartment at the Louvre. This is not even to mention Versailles – or the Tudor and Stuart courts.

26 Among the more obvious problems for *recitatio*: dialogue–speaker identification; setting identification; chorus identification; referential content of personal and deictic pronouns (e.g. *hanc, Troades* 924, *hic, Phoenissae* 498, *te, Phoenissae* 652); rapid exchanges in stichomythia and *antilabai*; extensive attention to the behaviour of other characters, especially mutes (see e.g. *Troades* Act 4); only *occasional* stage directions for soliloquies, the entrances and exits of characters, etc.; a multiplicity of vocal registers, as in *Medea* Act 4 (Nurse describing Medea, Nurse quoting Medea, Medea herself speaking). Several of the above undermine the 'only for reading' hypothesis also. Most importantly, the very randomness of textual stage directions firmly indicates that Seneca was not relying solely on textual or verbal means for his dramas' realisation. Stage performance alone clarifies and realises his text.

27 See most esp. Sutton (1986), 28ff., 43ff., who comments on the 'sound dramaturgic principles' involved in Seneca's stage practice. On stage-setting see Seidensticker (1969), 145; on props (in *Phaedra*), see Segal (1986), 152f. For an occasionally aberrant account of implicit stage directions in *Phaedra* see Fortey and Glucker (1975), 699–715. On identification cues it should be observed that recitation drama requires all characters to be identified verbally at their first appearance. This does not happen in Seneca, who uses some verbal identification cues but relies in several cases on context and visual identification. Similarly Seneca's use of mutes (e.g. Polyxena and Pyrrhus in *Troades* Act 4, Orestes and Pylades in *Agamemnon* Act 5) and textually unidentified extras is 'redolent of the stage' (Sutton, p. 35). Disappointingly, Seneca's most recent editor reverts to the misdescriptions and worn-out prejudices of the earlier part of this century: 'The lack of internal cohesion, the absence of constructive dialogue (as opposed to stichomythic point-scoring), the long monologues, the declamatory extravagance of the language – none of these makes for good stage drama' (Frank (1995), 42).

28 The point is made with clarity and humour by Herington (1966), 444f.

29 Calder (1975), 32ff., favours private performance of Seneca's tragedies, and cites other passages attesting the practice: for tragedy (Plutarch *Crassus* 33); for comedy (Pliny *Epistles* 1.15.2, 3.1.9).

30 Cinthio, *Scritti critici*, Crocetti (1973), 184. The English quotation is from Charlton (1946), lxxx n. 6.

31 The translator of *Oedipus* (1563, reprinted in Newton 1581), expressly mentions Seneca's 'tragicall and Pompous showe upon Stage'.

32 Eliot (1951a), 70. Something else from this Eliot essay merits quotation: 'What is "dramatic"? . . . Whether a writer expected his play to be played or not is irrelevant, the point is whether it is playable' (p. 75). Since actuality entails potentiality, the history of Senecan productions entails the playability of the tragedies and thus (according to Eliot's own criteria) their 'dramatic' nature.

2 THE DECLAMATORY STYLE

1 Such are the titles of the plays in the E branch of the MS tradition, except for *Hercules Furens* which is simply *Hercules*. In the A branch *Hercules* is given the augmented title *Hercules Furens*, *Troades* is called *Tros*, *Phaedra* is called *Hippolytus* (*Phaedra* is also the title used by the sixth-century grammarian Priscian, quoting *Phaedra* 710), and *Phoenissae*, which possesses no choral odes and is generally regarded as incomplete, is called *Thebais*. A ninth play, *Hercules Oetaeus*, is almost twice as long as the average Senecan play and is generally agreed to be (at least in its present form) non-Senecan. A tenth play, the *fabula praetexta* or historical drama, *Octavia*, in which Seneca appears as a character and which seems to refer to events after Seneca's death, is missing from A and is certainly not by Seneca. On the non-Senecan authorship of *Hercules Oetaeus* and *Octavia* see Axelson (1967); Friedrich (1954); Helm (1934), 283–347; and Sutton (1983). More recently Nisbet (1987) has defended the authenticity of *HO*, dating the play to the very end of Seneca's life, but acknowledges in his 1990 essay the problems posed for his thesis by the stylometric dating of Fitch (1981).

2 See Chapter 1, n. 23.

3 Fitch (1981), 289–307. One should also mention that some commentators maintain a *terminus ante quem* of 54 CE for *Hercules Furens* on the ground that the *Apocolocyntosis* (securely dated to 54 CE) seems to parody it. But this is by no means certain. See Fitch (1987a), 51–3.

4 It is a regular Senecan technique to structure such exchanges around keywords; Seidensticker (1969), 44, terms it Seneca's 'Stichworttechnik'. For other instances, see, e.g., *Hercules Furens* 422ff., *Troades* 301ff., *Medea* 490ff., *Phaedra* 218ff.

5 Herington (1966), 423.

6 Eliot (1951a), 91.

7 The Renaissance most especially. For the dramatic response, see Chapters 7–9 below. For critics, note Julius Caesar Scaliger: 'I regard Seneca as inferior to none of the Greeks in majesty (*maiestas*), greater even than Euripides in ornamentation (*cultus*) and splendour (*nitor*). The plots are theirs; but the majesty (*maiestas*), sound (*sonus*), spirit (*spiritus*) of the poetry are his' (*Poetices Libri Septem*, Lyons (1561), 323). See further Binns (1974), 230, who quotes the Scaliger passage and analyses similar responses from Justus Lipsius and Bartolomeo Ricci.

8 See Williams (1978), *passim*.

9 For other victims see *Tacitus Annals* 3.49ff., Seneca Rhetor *Controuersiae* 10 Preface 3 and 5ff., Dio *Roman History* 57.22.5.

10 E.g. Persius *Satire* 1.13ff., Tacitus *Dialogus* 9, Juvenal *Satire* 1.1ff.

11 See Tarrant (1985), ad loc.

12 See the excellent note of Tarrant (1985), ad loc: 'The choice of *pati* is revealing . . . Thyestes shows that he . . . regards power as a positive good.'

13 Some asides: *Troades* 607ff., 623f., 625f., 642ff., *Medea* 549f., *Phaedra* 136ff., 424ff., 580ff., 592ff., 634f. On both entrance monologues and asides in Senecan tragedy

see Tarrant (1978) 231–46. Tarrant's observation (p. 243) is telling: 'No scene of fifth-century tragedy has been shown to contain an aside in pure form.'

14 E.g. *Hercules Furens* 332ff., *Troades* 1ff., 861ff., *Medea* 1ff., 179ff., 431ff., *Phaedra* 835ff., *Oedipus* 1ff., *Agamemnon* 226ff., *Thyestes* 404ff., 491ff., 885ff.

15 The greater interiority of Senecan (and Roman) tragedy – as opposed to Greek – may be profitably related to differences in dramatic space. Certainly the Roman imperial theatre was far more of an enclosed, interior space than the theatre of classical Greece; and, as noted above (p. 10), Roman plays were also performed in private houses. On Roman tragedy's focus on emotional expressiveness, see Henry and Walker (1985), 3ff., who however make far too much of the contrast between Roman *pathos* tragedy and Greek *praxis* tragedy, the latter tightly structured, the former expositional.

16 On Cassandra see Calder (1976), 32ff. and Boyle (1983b), esp. 206ff.; on Helen see Wilson (1983), 38f., (1985), 314ff., and Boyle (1994), 30f., 207f.; on Hippolytus see Boyle (1985), 1305–10, Segal (1986), *passim*, and Skovgaard-Hansen (1968), 92–123, esp. 106f.; on Medea see Henry and Walker (1967), *passim*, Fyfe (1983), *passim*, and further above p. 122–33.

17 Thus e.g. Coffey (1960) 16ff., Motto and Clark (1972) 69–77, esp. 70, and Herington (1966) 448, 456. The adverse remarks of Eliot (1951a), 70 – 'The characters of Seneca's plays have no subtlety and no "private life"' – had their predictable effect.

18 Seneca's dramatisation of Phaedra is discussed by me in detail (1985) 1326–34, and (1987), 30–3. Excellent comments may be found in Tobin (1966), 66ff., Garton (1972), 197, Fitch (1974), 19ff., and Segal (1986), *passim*. The comments of Hermann (1924), 413–15, are still worth attention.

19 Cf. Racine's remark upon his own Phèdre: 'La seule pensée du crime y est regardée avec autant d'horreur que le crime même' (*Préface* to *Phèdre*).

20 A perspective wrongly claimed by the influential Hunter (1974), 170, to be 'quite absent from Seneca'.

21 The phrase is that of Braden (1985), 62.

22 Herington (1966), 423.

3 IDEAS MADE FLESH

1 Calder (1983), 184.

2 Herington (1966), 429.

3 For Seneca and Nero see especially Tacitus *Annals* 13–14; for the *post factum* justification of Nero's murder of Agrippina, see *Ann.* 14.11.

4 'Die Negation der Philosophie' is J. Dingel's judgement on the tragedies (1974), 72.

5 Failure to recognise these differences underlies many of Hunter's comments (1974) on the relationship between Seneca and English tragedy.

6 On *Agamemnon* see esp. Calder (1976), Lefèvre (1972b), Shelton (1983). On *Thyestes* see esp. Calder (1983), Hine (1981), Poe (1969), Schiesaro (1994), Steidle (1972b). On both see Tarrant's editions (1976 and 1985), and Boyle (1983b), which this chapter rewrites.

7 For other motifs common to *Agamemnon* and *Thyestes* see p. 227, n. 1 below.

8 Verse dialogue, lyric metre, prologue integration, interrelation between chorus and act, the choral *persona*, the structuring and unfolding of dramatic language and imagery, the messenger's speech, dramatic structure, movement and tempo are handled very differently in each play. Even the number of actors and choruses differ. For details see Boyle (1983b), 224 n.1.

9 'Probably' is important. Opinion is divided on the relative dating of the two plays. Both Herzog (1928) and Calder (1976), 28–30, place *Agamemnon* after *Thyestes*, the

former on the grounds of *Ag.*'s increased metrical complexity, the latter on the grounds of prologue integration (superior in *Thy.*) with subsequent dramatic action. Leo (1878–79), 133, on the other hand, sees *Ag.* as a youthful experiment in lyric, while Shelton (1977), 39, uses Calder's own thesis – that *Ag.*'s prologue is less well integrated with its context – to argue that it is the earlier play. Tarrant (1976), 7, also regards the early dating of *Ag.* as 'inherently plausible'. Certainly there are aspects of *Ag.* which seem to indicate dramatic immaturity: see Boyle (1983b), 223 and nn. The stylometric criteria of Fitch (1981) locate *Ag.* in the earliest group of plays (with *Oedipus* and *Phaedra*), and *Thy.* in the latest group (with *Phoenissae*).

10 See Boyle (1985), 1312–20.

11 As, e.g., at 162ff., 226ff., 292ff., 907ff., 984f.

12 As stated in the 'Textual Note', the text of *Agamemnon*, unless otherwise indicated, is taken from Tarrant's edition (1976).

13 Despite Tarrant (1976), ad loc, *alterno* does not *mean* 'retributive', although it may be *used of* retributive situations. It means 'alternating', 'answering', 'reciprocal', etc.: see *Oxford Latin Dictionary*.

14 Other references: 465ff., 512, 594f.

15 On the development of the association of sea-storm and fortune in *Agamemnon* see Pratt (1963), 225f.

16 The only tolerable explanation of 239–309: so Croisille (1964a), 466–9, and Calder (1976), 31f. The need for Clytemnestra's testing of Aegisthus has been dramatically prepared for (48–52, 226–33). Contrast Tarrant (1976), 217 and 230.

17 See Anliker (1960), 98ff.; Calder (1976), 31ff; Lefèvre (1972b), 470ff.; Lohikoski (1966), 63ff.; Seidensticker (1969), 119ff.

18 Aegisthus and Paris: 730ff., 884, 890; Clytemnestra and Helen: 124f., 162, 220ff., 234, 306, 736, 795, 897, 907; Agamemnon and Priam: 514, 794, 879f.; Argos and Troy: 644f., 728ff., 791f., 875ff.; the Argive chorus and deluded Trojan 'youth' and their 'festive mothers': 310ff., 638ff.

19 Treachery and guile: 612–26, 732, 887ff., 1009; festal day or feast: 311f., 644ff., 780, 791, 875ff.; adultery: 109ff., 273ff., 1009; fatal gift: 628, 1009.

20 For the strongest case (too strong) in support of Agamemnon's guilt see Lefèvre (1973b), 64–91. Agamemnon's guilt has, however, to be understood within the context of history's determinism.

21 Thyestean *cena*: 37ff., 875ff.; Greek sack of Troy, etc.: 612–58, 793f., 869ff., 1005ff.; sacrifice of Iphigenia, etc.: 165ff., 869ff., 1007ff., 175ff.

22 Note the emphasis on this: 204ff., 356ff., 395af., 778f., 783ff., 802ff.

23 'Ambiguous' is a necessary qualification. What is alluded to is a *Choephori*, or *Electra* or even an *Orestes*, in which the justice to be meted out to the regicides will at the very least involve matricide.

24 The relationship between human responsibility and history's determinism was a notorious difficulty in Stoic philosophy. For an intelligent discussion see Long (1971), 173–99. Long notes (p. 187) that while character to the Stoics was a proximate cause of action, and good and bad men were 'men who deliberately in consequence of their characters choose actions meriting praise or blame', an 'individual's character' was itself 'determined since it follows from his particular nature *and* upbringing', 'the fully developed disposition' being 'a necessary consequence of heredity . . . and environment'. See also Sandbach (1975), 101ff.: 'the determining causes' of action (assent, impulse, character, the condition of the *psyche)* 'are themselves determined'; 'Fate . . . determines what he [a man] is' (p. 103).

25 Of heredity: 48ff., 165, 906f.; or the past behaviour of others: 162ff., 226ff.

26 As in the prose works where nature, god, fate command, and man perforce obeys: *ducunt uolentem fata, nolentem trahunt (Epistle* 107.11). On the interchangeability of the

names, *fatum, fortuna, deus, natura, Iuppiter,* for the controlling force of the universe, see *De Beneficiis* 4.7–8, *Ep.* 107.7ff.

27 For the 'tragischen Ironie' of this ode, see Seidensticker (1969), 131, n. 163.

28 For Roman triumphal protocol, see Silius Italicus, *Punica* 17. 629ff. (triumph of Scipio Africanus), Plutarch, *Aemilius Paullus* 31–5 (triumph of Paullus).

29 The chorus' sentiment should not be confused with the commonplace familiar in Attic tragedy and voiced even by Frankenstein in Mary Shelley's Gothic novel: 'How strange is that clinging love we have of life even in the excess of misery' (*Frankenstein, or, The Modern Prometheus,* University of California edn, p. 185). Seneca *tragicus* presents such 'love' not as curious but perverse, based on nothing but delusion. Compare Seneca's analogous treatment in *De Brevitate Vitae* 11.

30 He seems to have read the same handbook as Atreus (*Thyestes* 247f.) and Lycus (*Hercules Furens* 511f.).

31 There is no need to punctuate with a comma after *furiosa,* as in Tarrant (1976) and others. Even so the epithet *furiosa* seems more plausibly construed as Clytemnestra's description of Cassandra's present behaviour rather than some general reference to Cassandra's experience of prophetic *furor* (as Tarrant).

32 As Calder (1976), 36, astutely observes: '*Furor* picks up *furiosa* and means "what you call madness, the desire for death, will in time come upon you both". In the Senecan manner the *metus* of the regicides will teach them in time the meaning of *mors libera.*' Cf. Anliker (1960), 99ff. Of course Cassandra's death-wish is not the 'unreflecting tendency towards death' (*ad moriendum inconsulta animi inclinatio*) criticised in *Epistle* 24.25. What the latter passage suggests, however, which both Petronius and Tacitus confirm, is that the death-wish, though a debating topic in the schools (Seneca Rhetor *Controuersiae* 9.6.2), was also index of an age. See Boyle (1985), 1335ff.; Barton (1993), *passim.*

33 See n. 23 above.

34 Other references: 64f., 97f., 103, 119.

35 The Tantalus figure is of course a negation of the *De Ira* image of man as by nature inclined towards kindness, harmony, mutual love and succour (see, e.g., Seneca *De Ira* 1.5.2–3). Certainly there are those kinds of impulses in Tantalus (90–5), but they prove useless before the constraints of *fames infixa.* Against those who would see the prologue's ghost as an emblem in the play of 'unnatural man' along the lines of *De Ira,* the dominant association of Tantalus' and Atreus' *furor* with natural human appetites, fixed and, in Atreus' case, inherited, seems telling, as does Tantalus' status as proto-man (hence his association in certain contexts with Prometheus: e.g. Horace *Odes* 2.13.37f., 2.18.35ff.) and *each* protagonist's instantiation of the Tantalus paradigm. *Aeterna fames* and *aeterna sitis* (149f.) seem presented in the play not as human aberration but as the defining attributes of the species.

36 Zwierlein prefers Axelson's conjecture *uorantur* to the universal manuscript reading *seruantur.* Tarrant (1985), ad loc., conjectures *scinduntur.*

37 The view, for example, of Detienne (1972), 71–113. Cf. also Segal (1977), 104: 'Sacrifice creates a series of mediations between god and beast and god and man and thereby asserts an orderly distinction of these planes of existence in the biological and alimentary codes.'

38 There is another matter. Poe (1969), 364f.: 'The very length of the description of Atreus' *furor* shows that Seneca sees in it not just a matter of individual wickedness to be condemned objectively or modified upon, but an instinct which he to some degree shares and which he expects his audience to share.'

39 The beast's triumph would not surprise Freud. See especially *Civilization and its Discontents* (1930), 40, cited below in Chapter 10.

40 The Satellite's remark at 334f. means precisely the opposite of what it says. As

Calder (1976/7), 8f., notes, a slight pause before the delivery of the final word, *fides*, would make it clear that it is the other word, *timor*, which is meant.

41 He is not the 'stoischer *sophos*' of Gigon (1938), 176ff., nor the noble Stoic of Herington (1966), 458ff., nor the 'wandering ascetic sage' of Poe (1969), 360. His Stoic attitudes are product of his circumstances, not index of his nature: the past which he acknowledges (513ff., 1103), the present which he displays (404ff.), the future which he reveals (520ff., 780ff., 909ff., 948, 1110f.) testify to that. The 'momentary lapse' theory of Seidensticker (1969), 104ff., similarly misleads.

42 See p. 24.

43 So at the end of the play Thyestes does not deny his earlier *scelus* (1103).

44 Significantly, perhaps, Thyestes' behaviour dramatises the futility of Seneca's own advice at *Epistle* 8.3: *ad omne fortuitum bonum suspiciosi pauidique subsistite; et fera et piscis spe aliqua oblectante decipitur. munera ista fortunae putatis? insidiae sunt.* ('Halt before every good that chance brings with suspicion and fear; wild beasts and fish are tricked by tempting hopes. Think these things fortune's gifts? They are traps.') Thyestes knows all this (see esp. 472: *errat hic aliquis dolus*, 'some trick strays hereabouts') and more. It affects his behaviour not a jot. He becomes the beast in the trap (*plagis . . . fera*, 491). If it is true, as Marti (1945), 240, claims, that 'his suffering in exile has taught him much', it is also true that such teaching has no significant effect on Thyestes' actions and behaviour.

45 For which see Poe (1969), 369.

46 On the play as 'contest' see Braden (1970), 30ff.

47 Note the ironic verbal counterpoint here with the prologue: *arceat . . . scelerum* recall Tantalus' futile *arcebo scelus* (95): *alternae . . . ne . . . uices* recall the Fury's prophetic command, *alterna uice . . . (25)*. The counterpoint points up the naivety of the choric prayer.

48 The text here is that of Costa (1973).

49 As the fulfilment of Medea's prayers and the relation of Jason's suffering to 'cosmic crime' attest. What happens in *Medea* is carefully positioned within a complex, quasi-moral scheme of cause and effect, both cosmic and human. See pp. 125ff.

50 See 507ff., 717f., 972, 1024; cf. 215ff.

51 For cosmic imagery, see 48–51, 120f., 262–5, 47, 82, 577–95, 613f., 636–8, 678f., 699f., 776–8, 784–7. On Seneca's transformation of 'celestial commonplace' into 'dramatic symbol' in *Thyestes* see the intelligent remarks of Owen (1968), 296–300.

52 I retain the manuscript reading. Zwierlein prints Leo's conjecture *cingens*.

53 An interpretation articulated in the Stoic doctrine of *sympatheia tōn holōn*.

54 The reaction of nature is dramatically underscored by Seneca's presentation of the sun's disappearance through four separate experiences of it, that of the Messenger, the Chorus, Atreus and Thyestes: see Owen (1968), 297. In each case the reaction is all. Nothing follows.

55 Note too how Atreus' *cape* of 982 picks up the *cape* of the persuasion scene (525). The play on *capio* and *caput* (525–45) is repeated in this scene, as what Thyestes' former 'capitulation' has led to is revealed.

56 With *Thyestes* 313f. cf. especially the emphasis on the imperatives of Aegisthus' birth at *Agamemnon* 48 and 233. Cf. also Phaedra's enigmatic *quod uiuo* ('That I live') reply to Theseus' question at *Phaedra* 879f., on which see Boyle (1985), 1335ff., (1987), 33ff.

57 See, e.g., 18–20, 26–32, 41f., 133–5. Note Poe (1969), 366f. Relevant here is the Thracian *nefas* motif. As Tantalus' crime is regenerated with increased horror, so Thracian *nefas* is re-enacted with greater number (*maiore numero*, 55f.; cf. 272ff.).

58 Of the endings of extant Senecan plays that of *Medea* is closest, but still not close.

Its theatrical closure and assertion of at least ambivalent 'cosmic' or 'moral' order contrast with *Thyestes'* end. Noticeably too Medea triumphs at the cost of her humanity; Atreus triumphs *because* of his.

4 THE BODY OF THE PLAY

1 For example: *Medea* 28ff., 56ff., 439f., 531ff., 595ff., 668f., 740ff., 874ff., 1002.
2 *Medea* 56ff., 75ff., 166ff., 207ff., 319, 335ff., 365, 401ff., 531ff., 570ff., 577f., 579ff., 605f., 614f., 670ff., 684ff., 705ff., 752ff., 787ff., 817ff., 835ff., 863ff., 874ff.)
3 For further discussion of the verbal and ideological texture of *Phaedra* see Boyle (1985); also Davis (1983); Henry and Walker (1966), and Segal (1986) *passim*.
4 Chief among these: master/slave, conqueror/conquered, agent/victim, Greek/ Trojan, marriage-maker/marriage-breaker, truth/falsehood, justice/injustice, joy/sorrow, past/present, life/death, survival-in-death/annihilation-in-death, sacrifice/murder, ritual/barbarism, civilisation/savagery.
5 See Chapter 3.
6 Legal imagery: e.g. *Oedipus* 24f., 371, 416, 875f., 916ff., 942ff., 1026; the fate/ fortune motif: e.g. *Oed.* 11, 28, 72ff., 412, 709ff., 882ff., 980ff., 1042ff.
7 For example: *Agamemnon* 11, 43, 63ff., 98, 138ff., 188, 219, 465ff., 580, 875., 898ff.
8 See Boyle (1983b), 228 n. 60.
9 For example: *Hercules Furens* 122, 882ff., 918f., 1192.
10 The structural and thematic dimensions of such analogies are explored by Calder (1976).
11 *Medea* 2f., 118ff., 225ff., 447ff.
12 Esp. *Medea* 185, 294, 579ff., 849ff.
13 *Medea* 118ff., 238ff., 272ff., 447ff., 486ff.
14 For a fuller discussion of the function of the Argonautic choruses in *Medea*, see Chapter 6.
15 On *Medea*'s finale see Chapter 6.
16 Phaedra and Pasiphae: esp. 112ff., 169ff., 242, 688ff., 698f.; Hippolytus and Pasiphae's bull: cf. esp. 116–18 with 413–17, and note the sustained application of 'wild animal' epithets to Hippolytus (231, 240, 272f., 414, 416. 798, 1064); the Minotaur and the bull from the sea: cf. 122, 171ff., 649f., 688ff., 1067, with 1015ff.
17 *Phaedra* 276, 309, 330, 337, 338, 355.
18 See my commentary (1987) ad loc.
19 *Troades* 15ff., 84ff., 171ff., 371ff., 409ff., 478ff., 634ff., 766ff., 806ff., 888ff., 1042ff., 1084ff., 1106ff., 1148ff.
20 Dirge/laudation: 142ff.; wedding/funeral: 195ff., 287ff., 361ff., 938ff., 1132ff.; burial/salvation: 500ff.; sacrifice/murder: 44ff., 255, 289, 1155ff.
21 'Perhaps' is important. Polyxena's conduct in Act 4 (945ff.) and her reported behaviour facing death in Act 5 (1148ff.) display her welcoming death presumably as annihilation and not a state of marriage with the dead Achilles. The Messenger's report of her anger as she falls problematises this: see my comment (1994) on *Troades* 1158–63.
22 See Wilson (1983), 41, and Boyle (1994), 176.
23 See Chapter 2.
24 See Chapter 2.
25 *Troades* 250ff., 349ff., 524ff., 605ff., 736ff., 1056ff., 1178ff.
26 I am drawn again to the incisive phrase of Herington (1966), 423. The death-chorus attracted important translators in Restoration and Augustan England: the Earl of Rochester (1680) and Matthew Prior (1708).

27 Cf., e.g., *Phaedra* 273 with 274, *Medea* 114f. with 116ff., *Thyestes* 401–3 with 404ff. On the linking between chorus and act in *Thyestes* see pp. 81f.

28 See Boyle (1994), 144f., 219f.

29 The closest in length is *Phaedra*'s third act (358–735), also a mini-drama.

30 The most obvious linguistic pick-up is in the first line of the first choral ode – *Diua non miti generata ponto* ('Goddess born of ungentle sea') – where *non miti* picks up *immitis* of the last line of the preceding act: *mentemque saeuam flectere immitis uiri* (lit. 'And to bend the savage will of the ungentle man'). There are many similar linguistic echoes in this and in the other choral odes: for details see my essay (1985), 1323, n. 76.

31 Cf. esp. *Phaedra* 542–9 with 31–80; 498f., 547f., with 706–9.

32 See Chapter 2.

33 The 'canonic' version of the Lucretia-Tarquin story is Livy 1.57–60. But see also Ovid's 'elegiac' version at *Fasti* 2.685–852.

34 See, e.g., Coffey (1960), 16: 'Seneca's choruses ... are self-contained and undramatic'; or Ogilvie (1980), 211: 'His [Seneca's] choruses, mere literary interludes, sometimes contain moralizing of a philosophical kind ... but for the most part they are mere padding, indulging in mythological and similar decoration for its own sake.'

35 Crown: *Thyestes* 544f.; altar and sword *Phaedra* 54ff., 406ff., 706ff.,896ff.,1154ff.

36 See Chapter 3.

37 Eliot (1951a), 73: 'In the verbal *coup de théâtre* no one has ever excelled him. The final cry of Jason to Medea departing in her car is unique; I can think of no other play which reserves such a shock for the last word.' For the endings of *Agamemnon* and *Medea* see Chapters 3 and 6.

38 Wilson (1985), 72f., argues strongly against the assumption 'that the similarities between the plays [of Seneca] are greater or more important than the differences'.

39 Compare the following variations in prologue design: *Hercules Furens, Troades, Medea, Agamemnon*: trimeter monologue; *Oedipus, Thyestes*: trimeter monologue leading to dialogue; *Phoenissae*: trimeter dialogue throughout; *Phaedra*: anapaestic monody. In *HF, Thy.* and *Ag.* the preternatural *Aussenprolog* is complemented by a *Binnenprolog* (opening monologue of Act 2); in *Med., Oed.* and *Tro.* the opening (in part) expository monologue thrusts the reader *in medias res*, but less so than *Phaedra*'s lyric opening which is in no sense expository. On variation in prologue integration compare *Thy.'s* greater thematic and imagistic integration of prologue and play with that of *Ag.*: see Boyle (1983b), 228 n. 60; Calder (1976), 29f.; Shelton (1977), 33ff.

40 Compare *Troades* with its long kommos (67–163) followed by three short choral odes (371–408, 814–60, 1009–65), *Medea* with its long Argonautic odes (301–79, 579–669) in the centre of the play flanked by two shorter ones (56–115, 849–79), *Phaedra* with two long choral odes (274–357, 736–823) followed by two short ones (959–88b, 1123–53), *Oedipus* with two long choral odes (110–201, 403–508) followed by three short ones diminishing in size (709–63, 882–914, 980–97), *Thyestes* in which there is a gradual increase in choral length until the climactic star chorus (122–75, 336–403, 546–622, 789–884) and *Hercules Furens* in which the four choral odes are of similar size (125–201, 524–91, 830–94, 1054–137).

41 Explicit self-identification by the chorus is common in the parodos of fifth-century Attic tragedy, more rare in Seneca (*Troades* 67ff., *Oedipus* 124ff.). Senecan choruses sometimes identify themselves (e.g. *Agamemnon* 310ff.) or are identified by others later in the plays (e.g. *Hercules Furens* 827ff., *Ag* 586ff., *Oed.* 401f.), or identify themselves implicitly as in *Medea* and *Thyestes*. In performance the identity of the chorus is of course generally unproblematic.

42 Note, however, that as at *Medea* 56ff, the *persona* of the chorus in *Thyestes* is established implicitly by the context and dramatic function of their opening song.

43 Although in *Agamemnon* there is, strictly speaking, only one Messenger's speech, that of Eurybates in Act 3 (421ff.), Cassandra's 'vision' in Act 5 (867ff.) also serves several of the functions of such a speech.

44 See Fitch (1981), 289ff.

45 Heldmann (1974), 71, advocates a six act division of *Phaedra*, arguing that the two prologues of the play (one by Hippolytus, 1–84, one by Phaedra, 85–128) correspond to first and second act prologues (one 'external', one 'internal': *Aussenprolog/Binnenprolog*) in *Hercules Furens*, *Agamemnon*, *Thyestes*. He suggests that the absence of a parodos in *Phaedra* is compensated for by the lyric form given to Hippolytus' monologue. I adopt a six-act division in my 1987 edition of *Phaedra*.

46 See, e.g., Tarrant (1978), 229f., who, however, considers *Phoenissae* to be complete: 'It seems best to regard *Phoenissae* as an essay in a distinct subgenre of tragedy.' Tarrant compares *Pho.* to Ezechiel's *Exagoge*. Recently Sutton (1986), 16 and 57, noted an important dramaturgical difference between *Pho.* and the other (genuine) Senecan plays, namely a paucity of implicit stage-directions ('pervasive absence' according to Sutton). Whether this difference justifies a hypothesis of dramaturgical incompleteness (so Sutton) is debatable. But even if justified, the hypothesis would leave the issue of whether *Pho.* was intentionally unchorused largely unaffected.

47 Discussed by Segal (1986), 203f.

48 Some scholars question the authenticity of several Euripidean choric endings and suspect interpolation. The argument is unaffected. Such interpolations would already have occurred by Seneca's day, and would be part of the available 'Euripidean' texts.

5 THE PALIMPSESTIC CODE

1 Cycle of crime: *Agamemnon* 77, *Thyestes* 133; contest of crime: *Ag.* 169, *Thy.* 195f.; fortune's wheel: *Ag.* 72, *Thy.* 618; the 'freedom of death', etc.: *Ag.* 202, 589ff., 611; *Thy.* 367f., 883f.; birth as destiny: *Ag.* 48, 233; *Thy.* 42, 314; beast in the net: *Ag.* 892ff., *Thy.* 491ff.; catastrophic clothing: *Ag.* 887ff., *Thy.* 524ff.; Tantalid auspices: *Ag.* 8f., *Thy.* 657; bloody decapitation: *Ag.* 901ff., *Thy.* 727ff.; fear of universal chaos: *Ag.* 486f., *Thy.* 830ff.; Thyestean eclipse: *Ag.* 36, 295ff., 909; *Thy.* 776ff., 789., etc.; Thyestean crime against children: *Ag.* 26ff., *Thy.* 1112; 'king of kings': *Ag.* 39, 291; *Thy.* 912; mingling of blood and wine: *Ag.* 886, *Thy.* 65, 1914f.; underworld triad: *Ag.* 15–18, *Thy.* 6–12; lion, 'vanquisher of beasts': *Ag.* 738ff., *Thy.* 732ff.; 'feast-day': *Ag.* 791ff., *Thy.* 970; cf. *Ag.* 311, 644f., 780, *Thy.* 902, 919; palm of victory: *Ag.* 919, 938; *Thy.* 410, 1096f.; sacrifice and feast: *Ag.* 11, 21, 43, 48, 165ff., 875ff., 898ff., etc., *Thy.* 62ff., 93ff., 449ff., 682ff., 885ff., etc.; morality–power incompatibility: *Ag.* 79ff., *Thy.* 215ff.; true kingship, etc.: *Ag.* 610, *Thy.* 348ff.; ship–oar–waves analogy for psychological struggle: *Ag.* 141ff., *Thy.* 437ff.; advice against staining altars with impious blood: *Ag.* 219, *Thy.* 93ff.

2 On the relationship of *Agamemnon* to *Troades* see Fantham (1982a); on *Phoenissae*'s relationship to *Oedipus* see pp. 103ff.

3 The semiotic function of which is most profitably interpreted as a critical placement of the latter by the former. Contrast, for example, the providential attitude to the gods in *De Ira* 2.27.1 and the attitude evident in *Phaedra*, *Thyestes*, *Medea* and *Oedipus* (see esp. *Pha.* 1242f., *Thy.* 1020f., *Med.* 1027, *Oed.* 1042ff.). Certainly attempts by such critics as Knoche (1972) and Marti (1945) to regard the dramatic

works as 'philosophical propaganda-plays' (Marti, 219) are ill-founded. But see Dingel quoted above at ch. 3, n. 4.

4　See Boyle (1987) ad loc. For the remodeling of Ovid (and of Virgil) elsewhere in *Phaedra* see that edition *passim*. See also Segal (1984) and Fantham (1975).

5　'Rewriting' is important. Attempts such as that of Snell (1964), 23ff., to dismiss many of Seneca's dramatic innovations in *Phaedra* as essentially derivative (generally from Euripides' lost *Hippolytos Kalyptomenos*) are now discredited. What needs stressing too in connection with this whole issue is that Seneca could expect an audience (or at least a significant part of it) to respond to the interplay between his own plays and those of the Attic tragedians. Greek literature was still an active and formative ingredient in Roman culture (see, e.g., the authors whom Statius' father, a *grammaticus*, was teaching in the second half of the first century CE – Statius *Siluae* 5.3.146ff.).

6　*Phaedra* 113ff., 124ff., 174., 242, 688.

7　Cf. esp. *Phaedra* 330–57 with *Georgics* 3. 209–83.

8　Relevant here is the important association of Venus with the sea (*Phaedra* 274).

9　Racine's indebtedness to Seneca's *Phaedra* is not of course confined to the Messenger's speech. The French tragedian models, for example, Phèdre's revelation speech (*Phd.* 2.5/634ff.) upon *Pha.* 646ff. and develops Seneca's focus on the tragic implications of the hereditary curse (*Phd.* 1.3/249f., 257f., 277f., 306; 2.5/679f.; 4.6/1289). For other intertextual connections between the two plays see the Index to Boyle (1987).

10　With *Phaedra* 1256 ff. cf. Agaue's actions in the lost part of Euripides' *Bacchae* (reconstructed by Dodds (1960), 234). See also Segal (1986), 215. For self-reflective ramifications of this scene see Chapter 6.

11　See p. 80.

12　See Boyle (1994) on *Troades* 360.

13　Albeit one with large cultural ramifications. Note too that, although the wedding–sacrifice conflation is not central to Euripides' dramatisation of Polyxena's death, a wedding metaphor is used (ironically) by Hecuba of Polyxena's death after it has occurred: *Hecuba* 612.

14　See Boyle (1994), 185, 208.

15　This is no isolated occurrence. From Ennius onwards the connection between Assaracus, Rome and the Julian family is frequently rehearsed. For references see Boyle (1994) on *Troades* 17.

16　For Caligula: Suetonius *Gaius* 18.3, Dio *Roman History* 59.7.4, 59.11.1; for Claudius: Tacitus *Annals* 11.11, Suetonius *Claudius* 21.3.

17　Post-Neronian writers are equally insistent on the Troy–Rome identity: e.g. Valerius Flaccus *Argonautica* 1.9, Silius Italicus *Punica* 1.2, 14, 106 and *passim*, Juvenal *Satire* 1.100, 4.60f.

18　Tacitus *Annals* 15.39, Suetonius *Nero* 38.2, Dio *Roman History* 62.18.1; see also *RH* 62.29.1 for other 'Trojan recitations'.

19　See Henry and Walker (1983), 135, who refer with approval to Paratore (1956), who describes the deformities in the entrails 'as striking the keynote, *l'accordo tonale*, of the whole play'. For analysis of the precise symbolism of the different aspects of the extispicy see Davis (1991), 158f.

20　Elsewhere Seneca's norm through both the manipulation of choral odes and the dramatisation of pain is to draw some pity from his audience for human suffering. Contrary to Henry and Walker (1983), 130, this pity is not 'almost exclusively evoked for children'. In *Phaedra*, for example, the first, second and fourth choral odes are designed to move the audience's sympathy in the direction of Phaedra, Hippolytus and Theseus respectively. Theseus' final words (1279f.) move the sympathy back to Phaedra. See Boyle (1987), 33ff.

21 Accius did, however, write a *Phoenissae*, dealing with the conflict between Oedipus' sons.

22 On air imagery in *Oedipus* see Henry and Walker (1983), 132f.

23 On the play as a tragedy of fate, see especially Davis (1991), Giancotti (1953), Müller (1953), Paratore (1956), Poe (1983) and Schetter (1972).

24 In the first ode (110ff.) *fatum* is pestilence, plague, death, Theban 'deathstiny' (to use John Henderson's term, 1988); in the second ode (403ff.) Bacchus is addressed as potential nullifier of death and 'fate's greed' (*auidum fatum*, 410). The third ode is a theodicy of Theban fate (709ff.), the fourth a moral fantasy 'if fate could be shaped by will' (882ff.).

25 Stoicism evaluated the morality of an action by the intention of the actor. For a discussion of this issue in *Oedipus* and its relation to Oedipus' own guilt see Poe (1983) and Davis (1991). For the latter *Oed.* is 'a tragedy of fate . . . the protagonist is truly guilty and . . . no contradiction is entailed' (p. 150): 'guilt is assigned on the basis of an action's inherent quality, not the doer's mind or intention' (p. 163). For Poe 'Oedipus has accomplished evil intending good because he is bound to a universe whose process is destructive' (p. 150).

26 Suetonius *Nero* 21.3, 46.3; Dio *Roman History* 62.9.4, 63.22.6, 63.28.5.

27 Kragelund (1982), 53ff., argues for a date in 68 CE itself, the year of Nero's death.

28 At Ashland, Oregon, 1996, in the premiere performance of Rita Dove's transference of the Oedipus myth to antebellum South Carolina (*The Darker Face of the Earth*), the Jocasta-figure, Amalia, on discovering that her lover was her son, plunged the knife into her womb (Act 2, sc. 8). Despite the obvious references to Greek tragedy in the production, the death was pure Seneca – and Roman.

29 Tarrant (1978), 229f., quoted at Chapter 4, n. 46.

30 'Una severa scarnificazione' is Barchiesi's description of this rewriting: Barchiesi (1988), 17.

31 See Zeitlin (1990) and Henderson (1993), 167ff.

32 A similar reversion to Sophocles – this time to *Oedipus at Colonus* – may be seen in the opening of the play and in the positioning of Oedipus' curse on his sons after their dissension, rather than prior to it and thus in some sense its cause. Statius follows Euripides in making Oedipus' curse a cause of the brothers' strife.

33 Even at so-called *columbaria*, large collective tombs financed by funeral clubs, where the ashes of unrelated persons were interred in small niches in the tomb's walls, both space and facilities were generally provided for the annual feast.

34 The phrase is that of Hopkins (1983), 202, to whose work on this issue I am indebted.

35 The neck or throat is the standard body part involved in the killing of women in Greek tragedy. A notable exception is the suicide of Deianira in Sophocles' *Trachiniae*, where the sword penetrates 'the side below the liver' (*Tr.* 931). Loraux (1987), 50ff., associates the female neck's vulnerability and beauty with its status as the prime place of tragic death in Greek drama.

36 See, e.g., Barchiesi (1988), 36.

37 I print the *A* manuscript reading, *dispone*, in preference to Axelson's conjecture, *compone*, favoured by Zwierlein.

38 For details see Fitch (1987a), 44–50.

39 See Fitch (1987a), ad loc.

40 For example: *Hercules Furens* 58, 114, 122, 247, 254, 566.

41 The phrase is that of Fitch (1987a), 30. See generally his excellent discussion (24ff.) of Hercules' 'obsessive' psychology and its proximity to madness. This focus on 'the *psychological* causation of madness' Fitch sees as absent from Euripides and 'original to Seneca' (p. 31).

42 In contrast to their earlier, more global view of Heracles: *Heracles* 348–450.
43 For details see Lawall (1983), 6ff.
44 Hadas (1939) discusses the amphitheatrical modelling of the scene at *Hercules Furens* 939ff., where Hercules kills his wife and children.
45 In *Aeneid* 8 both Aeneas and Augustus are presented as successors of Hercules. In *Aen.* 6 (791–803) a comparison with Hercules as universal civiliser immediately follows Anchises' panegyric of Augustus. See also Horace *Odes* 3.3.9ff.
46 See, e.g., Virgil *Aeneid* 6.791ff., Calpurnius Siculus *Eclogue* 1.33ff., 4.5ff.
47 Suetonius *Nero* 21.3; cf. Dio *Roman History* 63.9.4. Much of the evidence for Nero's association with Hercules points to an identification with Hercules at the end of his principate after his return from Greece, when according to Dio (*RH* 62.20.5) he was hailed as Nero Hercules and Nero Apollo, and according to Suetonius (*Nero* 53) planned to 'imitate the exploits of Hercules' (*imitari et Herculis facta*) at the next Olympic Games. The coins inscribed *Herculi Augusto* were also late. Nero's fascination with Hercules, however, clearly predates the Greek tour. Note also that Dio (*RH* 59.26.5ff.) reports that Caligula sometimes 'impersonated' Hercules, appearing with club and lion-skin (and indeed impersonated all the gods). Fitch (1987a), 18f., 39f., wedded to the belief that *Hercules Furens* predates Nero's accession, takes a more sceptical view of the Neronian evidence.
48 Virgilian allusions dominate Theseus' whole description of the underworld, and are clearly detectable in the passage quoted (cf. esp. *Hercules Furens* 735 and *Aeneid* 6.743). This makes it more surprising that Theseus' account of the judgement of the dead differs so markedly from the Sibylline description in Virgil (*Aen.* 6.608ff.), where a considerable variety of contemporary crimes is mentioned and tyranny receives less than a line (621).
49 Hercules as civiliser: Pindar, *Isthmian* 4.57, Virgil *Aeneid* 6.802f.; as thug: Homer *Iliad* 5.403, *Odyssey* 21.28, Sophodes *Trachiniae*. It should be noted that Virgil's overall treatment of Hercules in his *Aen.* is ambivalent: see Boyle (forthcoming).
50 Augustus *Res Gestae* 13; Seneca *De Clementia* 1.2; Calpurnius *Eclogue* 1.42ff.
51 Fitch (1987a), 35–8, offers an original but (to my mind) quite unconvincing interpretation of the final act, aligning it with the other endings of Seneca's tragedies. No Senecan play ends as this one with the promise of purification and moral restoration for the sinner. The ironies involved in transferring this promise to the world of Seneca's audience are discussed below.

6 THE THEATRICALISED WOR(L)D

1 Bloom (1973).
2 Segal (1986), 218, interprets Theseus' failure differently: 'Tragedy is about suffering whose parts refuse to be entirely accounted for, justified, and laid to rest either by the social forms of ritual (burial) or the rationalised logic of moral explanation (justice and law).' The generalisation, however, misses the specific relevance of Theseus' failure and of *Phaedra's* ending to Senecan tragedy as such.
3 On the history of the reception of Seneca see, e.g., Enk (1957), 282–307, esp. 288–90.
4 Useful remarks on Senecan metatheatre may be found in Curley (1986).
5 Artaud, Gallimard edn (1964) of *Oeuvres complètes*, vol. 4, 39.
6 Nor are the *spectatores* of the dramatic action/spectacle confined to the living: *Agamemnon* 758 (the Trojan dead), *Thyestes* 66 (Ghost of Tantalus).
7 It will be apparent that my use of the term 'metatheatre' to mean theatrically self-conscious theatre, theatre which itself represents theatrical practices, is in line with current usage. Like Abel, whose 1963 book is foundational to modern treatments,

I also see metatheatre as a function of a theatrical ideology of social relations. Unlike Abel, however, I do not see it as a practice or mentality which originated in the Renaissance. For Renaissance metatheatre and its debts to Seneca, see Chapter 9.

8 See, e.g., also *Epistles* 74.7, 76.31, 115.14ff. On Stoicism and self-dramatisation, see Rosenmeyer (1989), 47ff.

9 Terms used by the sociologist Lerner (1964), quoted by Greenblatt (1980), 224ff., in his detailed discussion of the Renaissance capacity for 'improvisation'.

10 See Bartsch (1994), 2ff.

11 Strabo *Geography* 6.2.6, Suetonius *Gaius* 35.2, *Nero* 11.2, 12.2, Martial *De Spectaculis* 7, 8, *Epigrams* 8.30, Dio *Roman History* 59.10.3.

12 *Spectare*: see, e.g., Cicero *De Oratore* 1.18, Horace *Epistles* 2.1.203; *spectatores*: see also Horace *Epistles* 2.1.178, 215, etc..

13 For a different reading of the metadramatic nature of *Thyestes'* prologue, see Schiesaro (1994).

14 *Troades* 4, 95f., 371, 614, 715, 860, 870f., 884, 1055, 1067, 1075ff., 1087, 1125, 1129, 1131, 1147f. On all these passages see Boyle (1994).

15 See Boyle (1994), on *Troades* 360.

16 See Boyle (1994), ad loc.

17 See, e.g., Seneca *De Tranquillitate Animi* 11.4f., *Epistles* 30.8, 70.20–7.

18 Aristotle *Poetics* 1449b21–8: 'Tragedy, therefore, is a representation (*mimēsis*) of serious action . . . achieving by means of pity (*eleos*) and fear (*phobos*) the purification (*katharsis*) of those emotions'; cf. *Poetics* 1452a1ff. Tragic wonder (*to thaumaston*, cf. 'marvel', *mirantur*, *Troades* 1148) is also associated by Aristotle with the production of pity and fear (*Poetics* 1452a4ff.). Important too is 'spectacle' (*opsis*), regarded by Aristotle as one of the six parts of tragedy (*Poetics* 1450a7ff.), but, though psychologically powerful, seen as least pertaining to the poet's art (*Poetics* 1450b17ff.). Indeed Aristotle considered the arousing of pity and fear by spectacle as indicating an inferior poet (*Poetics* 1453b1ff.). No Roman tragedian could have agreed. Spectacle informed Roman tragedy, as it informed Roman culture. Further disagreement with Aristotle's prescriptions (*Poetics* 1449b24ff.) is evident in Seneca's generation of pity and fear at the conclusion of *Troades* through 'narrative' (*apaggelia*) rather than through 'action' (*drōntōn*).

19 Representation of 'la fermeté des grands coeurs' in *Nicomède* succeeds according to Corneille in exciting 'l'admiration dans l'âme du spectateur' but not 'la compassion' normally produced by tragedy (*Nicomède, Examen*).

20 *Préface* to *Bérénice* (1670).

21 This is not to suggest that Hamlet's views of the purpose of 'playing' are 'coterminous' with those of Shakespeare, but rather part of the latter's more 'capacious' perspective. For an incisive discussion, see Montrose (1996), 42–4.

22 On *Medea* see esp. Fyfe (1983), Henderson (1983), Henry and Walker (1967) and Lawall (1979).

23 See Chapter 4.

24 Indeed rare in extant Greek tragedy: only at Euripides *Troades* 307–40 and *Phaethon* (fr. 781.14ff. Nauck). Aristophanes sometimes parodied the genre in his comedies: *Birds* 1725ff., *Peace* 1333ff.

25 *Fugitiua* is the reading of the Codex Etruscus. Zwierlein prints the Heinsius conjecture, *furtiua*.

26 The 'barbarian' nature of Medea is underscored throughout Ovid's treatment in *Metamorphoses* 7. At *Met.* 7.144 the narrator himself even addresses Medea as *barbara*.

27 See p. 62 above.

28 See Catullus 64, Virgil *Eclogue* 4.31ff., 6.42ff., Horace *Epode* 16.57ff.
29 I print Gronovius' correction of the manuscript reading, *litori*, accepted by Zwierlein.
30 Wilamowitz-Moellendorff (1919), III, 162.
31 The only comparable set of openings are those to Acts 3 and 4 of *Phaedra*, where Act 3 commences with an extensive description by the Nurse of Phaedra's passion (*Pha.* 360–86) and Act 4 commences with a very brief description by the Chorus of Phaedra's behaviour as she attempts to incriminate Hippolytus (*Pha.* 824–8).
32 Seneca here remodels considerably Ovid *Heroides* 12.160, where Medea offers her personal desolation as 'grave-offerings' (*inferiae*) to her brother's spirit.
33 For the gladiatorial language, see *Agamemnon* 901, *Oedipus* 998; cf. *Medea* 550.
34 The appearance of *Medea*'s final choric lines (1416–19) at the conclusions of *Alcestis, Andromache, Helen* and *Bacchae* has cast doubt on the authenticity of this 'Euripidean' ending. It was presumably, however, the ending known to Seneca.
35 Eliot (1951a), 73, quoted at Chapter 4, n. 37.
36 See pp. 104f. above.
37 For the view that all the murders take place offstage, see Fitch (1987a), 351f.
38 Suetonius *Gaius* 57.4, Josephus 19.94. The matter is discussed by Sutton (1986), 63–7.
39 See Beacham's account of Accius' 'descriptive gore', p. 217, n. 3 above. For Roman 'descriptive gore' (plentiful) outside drama: see, e.g., Ovid *Metamorphoses* 6.387–91 (the flaying of Marsyas), Lucan *Bellum Ciuile* 2.174ff. (the torture and death of Marius Gratidianus), Statius *Thebaid* 8.751–66 (the cannibalism of Tydeus).
40 See Rosenmeyer (1989), 118ff.
41 See, e.g., *Hercules Furens* 624f., *Troades* 83ff., *Phaedra* 640ff., 829–33, *Phoenissae* 245f.
42 'Murderous games' is Hopkins' phrase (1983), 1, whose opening chapter (1–30) contains an excellent discussion of this issue.
43 Gibbon, vol. 2 (1781), ch. XXX, n. 59.
44 Plutarch recounts (*Pelopidas* 29) how the tyrant Alexander of Pherae (fourth century BCE) murdered without pity many of his citizens but wept at a performance of Euripides' *Troades* to see the sufferings of Hecuba and Andromache. The story is used by Sidney in his *Apologie* to defend the moral value of 'the sweet violence of a Tragedie': Smith (1904), vol. 1, 178.

7 SENECA INSCRIPTVS

1 *Ecerinis*' most famous successors were Loschi's *Achilles* (c.1390) and Corraro's *Progne* (1429). The latter was not printed until over a century later (Venice 1558) and was revived shortly afterwards in 1566 for a performance at Oxford before Elizabeth I. Other performances in England in the mid-sixteenth century included a *Medea* and a *Dido* in Cambridge. At the same time in France Montaigne was performing in Muret's *Julius Caesar* (pub. 1553) and Buchanan's *Baptistes* (pub. 1576) and *Jephthes* (pub. 1554). Later in the century Thomas Legge's *Richardus Tertius* was performed at Cambridge in 1573 and repeated in 1579 and 1582. William Gager's neo-Latin tragedies, *Meleager, Dido* and *Ulysses Redux*, were written and performed at Oxford in the 1580s and 1590s, and William Alabaster's *Roxana* was performed in Cambridge c.1592. In 1624 Nicolas de Vernulz' *Henricus Octavus* was performed in Louvain. On *Ecerinis* and its aftermath see Braden (1985), 99ff.
2 By the end of the sixteenth century approximately thirty editions of the collected plays had been published in five countries alone: Italy, Germany, France, Holland

and England. Erasmus himself was involved in both the Ascensius Paris edition of 1514 and the Avantius Aldine edition (Venice) of 1517.

3 Noted productions were those of *Phaedra* by Pomponius Laetus in Rome in the mid-1480s, and in England by Alexander Nowell at Westminster School in the mid-1540s. In 1551–2 *Troades* was produced at Trinity College, Cambridge, and at the same college in 1559–61 *Oedipus, Medea*, and (probably twice) *Troades* again. For other performances in England see Binns (1974), 206, Charlton (1946), cxliii.

4 For Cinthio, see p. 12 above; for Sidney, see his praise of *Gorboduc* in *An Apologie for Poetrie* (pub. 1595) as 'clyming to the height of *Seneca* his stile, and as full of notable moralitie, which it doth most delightfully teach, and so obtayne the very end of Poesie' (quoted from Smith (1904), vol. 1, 197). For further testimony see Cunliffe (1893), 9–12.

5 The exception was *Thebais* (= *Phoenissae*), done especially for the collection by Newton himself. Charlton (1946), cxlf., regards Heywood's translations of *Troas* (1559 and reprinted twice by 1562), *Thyestes* (1560) and *Hercules Furens* (1561) as themselves inaugurating the Senecan dramatic fashion realised in the first vernacular English tragedy, *Gorboduc*, acted before Elizabeth I at Christchurch, Oxford, in 1562. Worth mentioning too is the survival of a manuscript fragment of a translation of *Hercules Oetaeus* by Elizabeth I (Bradner, 1964, 16ff.) – not in rhyming fourteeners (the main verse form of the 1581 translators), but in blank verse. Testimony to Seneca's continuing influence on English dramatic culture after 1581 is provided by the second wave of translations in the middle of the next century: *Medea* (1648), *Troades* (1679), *Phaedra* (not printed until 1701) by Sir Edward Sherburne, *Phaedra* (1651) by Edmund Prestwich, *Troades* (1660) by Samuel Pordage, *Thyestes* (1674) by John Wright.

6 Particularly important are the *De Casibus* narratives of writers such as Boccaccio (*De Casibus Virorum Illustrium*, c.1360–74) and John Lydgate (*The Fall of Princes*, c.1431–9), which culminated in the influential *A Mirror for Magistrates* (1559). The most significant contributor to *A Mirror for Magistrates* was Thomas Sackville, co-author of the Senecanesque *Gorboduc* (1562). The medieval dramatic tradition in both its 'mystery' and 'morality' dimensions is more complex, more varied, and itself more impregnated with Senecan ideas and practices than is often assumed (see next note). Other manifest influences on Elizabethan drama include Italian and French theatre, Plutarch, Tudor historians, especially Holinshed, the Italian *novella* (and the ancient Greek novel), Montaigne, and (pervasively) Ovid. On Shakespeare and Ovid see Bate (1993).

7 The traditional *psychomachia* of the morality play, for example, is an allegorical descendant of the Senecan meditative soliloquy. Cassandra's pre-death expression of joy and admonition to her slayer, which conclude *Agamemnon*, anticipate those of Hrotsvitha's martyr Irena at the end of *Dulcitius*. The *Carmina Burana* seem filled with Senecanesque *topoi*. On Seneca's influence on the medieval construction of Medea, see Morse (1996).

8 Eliot (1951b), 140.

9 The phrase is taken from Braden (1970), whose later book (1985) discusses the notion fully within the context of Senecan and Renaissance drama.

10 For a clear, well-documented account of the vagaries of this century's scholarship on the issue, see Miola (1992), 1–6.

11 Bullough (1964), 196. See also Jones (1977), 268: 'It seems likely in fact that not only Shakespeare but many of his contemporaries had a subtler and more inward appreciation of the minutiae of Seneca's style than most classical authors have nowadays.' Both authors are cited by Miola (1992), 5 and 9.

12 For details, see Miola (1992), esp. 8f.

13 D'Aubignac, *Pratique du théâtre*, 4.11. See Braden (1985), 128.

14 The Countess of Pembroke's *Antonius: A Tragedie* (1592), reprinted (1595) as *The Tragedie of Antonie*, 'translates' Garnier's *Marc Antoine* (1578) and reproduces the self-conscious Senecanism of its model. It influenced (among others) Kyd's *Cornelia* and Daniel's *The Tragedie of Cleopatra* and *Philotas*. For a sympathetic account of the Countess' achievement in *Antonius*, see Freer (1987).

15 For details see Cunliffe (1893), 127–9.

16 Familiarity with Lucan too: *Spanish Tragedy* 3.13.19 translates Lucan *Bellum Ciuile* 7.819: *caelo tegitur qui non habet urnam*.

17 The verses are part of a translation by Seneca of Cleanthes' *Hymn to Zeus*. They are quoted by Augustine at *Civitas Dei* 5.8 as Seneca's own.

18 See further J. Bate's introduction to the 1995 Arden edition of *Titus Andronicus* p. 30.

19 See, e.g., *Antonio's Revenge* 1.5.99ff., 2.2.56ff., 89ff., 3.130, 4.5.11ff., 74ff., 5.5.44f. (refs to Gair's edition, 1978).

20 For the counterpoint with *Hercules Furens*, see Altman (1978), 300–2.

21 Some examples: cf. Kyd *Spanish Tragedy* 4.4.180f. with *Oedipus* 523f., Greville *Alaham* 5.3.99ff. with *Hercules Furens* 1138ff., Chapman *The Conspiracy and Tragedy of Charles Duke of Byron* 4.2.166ff. with *Oed.* 504ff., 5.4.69ff. with *HF* 1258ff., Jonson *Catiline* 1.1.11ff. with *Thyestes* 87ff., 3.1.179 with *Thy.* 883f. See also Cunliffe (1893), *passim*.

22 Cunliffe (1893), 130–55.

23 On Seneca's influence on Shakespeare see the excellent account in Miola (1992), to which I am much indebted in this and the following chapters.

24 Daalder (1982), xxxiii.

25 See Miola (1992), 177–87.

26 On the cyclical structure of *Titus Andronicus*, see J. Bates' shrewd observations in the introduction to his Arden edition (1995), 15.

27 E.g. at 2.3.38ff., 4.1.42ff., 5.2.194f. For a discussion of the Ovidianism of *Titus* see Bate (1993), 100–17, who however (103, n. 33) underestimates the Senecan indebtedness. What is often ignored is that Seneca's *Thyestes* itself self-consciously (56f., 272–7) incorporates and rewrites Ovid's Tereus–Procne–Philomela narrative.

28 See, e.g., *Titus* 1.1.99ff., 2.2.142ff., 3.1.56ff., 5.3.194ff.

29 See A. Hammond's introduction to the Arden edition (1994), 98. Hammond (p. 82) also argues against Shakespeare's Senecanism being derived from Legge's Senecanesque *Richardus Tertius*, which was performed three times in Cambridge between 1573 and 1582, but was not printed nor recorded as performed in London. Apart from *Titus Andronicus*, the main rival to *Richard III* for Senecan honours is perhaps *Macbeth* with its 'heated rhetoric, the brooding sense of evil, the pre-occupation with power, the obsessive introspection, the claustrophobic images of cosmic destruction . . . and an unusually high number of passages which seem to derive from his [Seneca's] plays' (Martindale, 1990, 37).

30 The phrase is from Hammond (n. 29 above), 80.

31 For details see Brooks (1980). Margaret also doubles as a Senecan Fury: 'Foul wrinkled witch' is how Richard greets her unheralded appearance at 1.3.164.

32 Kott (1974), 42. Aspects of the Richard–Anne scene are replayed in the attempted wooing of the young Elizabeth through her mother in Act 4.4. See especially the stichomythia at 4.4.418ff.

33 Cf. Marston's *Antonio's Revenge* 4.3.32–6, which combines *Phaedra* 715ff. and 682f.

34 Noted by Braden (1985), 159.

35 I use the *Répertoire général du théâtre français* text of 1818 (Paris).

36 See Baldwin (1947). Also important is Horace's *Ars Poetica*.

37 Stegmann (1965), 171.

38 See Mercer (1987), ch. 2.

39 As Hunter (1974), 179f., notes, ghosts appear too in *A Mirror for Magistrates* (1559), which had considerable impact on English tragedy. But even that influence was probably in part 'Senecan'. Its chief contributor was Sackville (see n. 6 above).

40 On neo-Latin Elizabethan tragedy, see Binns (1974).

41 See J. Bate's Arden edition of *Titus Andronicus* (1995), 31.

42 See, e.g., Williams (1981), 142, who regards the soliloquy as a 'discovery, *in dramatic form*, of new and altered social relationships, perceptions of self and others, complex alternatives of private and public thought'.

43 See Herrick (1965), 109.

44 Moretti (1982), 31f.

45 Stegmann (1965), 188: 'Seneca gave to Corneille the best devices of his style: the lofty but not bombastic style, the antithetic reply, the irony, the simple images, the use of sentences (*sententiae*), certain unusual associations of words which give new freshness to a term.' As the Camille speech shows, however, Corneille's lofty Senecan style included bombast.

46 McDonald (1966), 75.

47 Martindale (1990), 33. See further Clemen (1961), 25 (cited also by Martindale), who argues for Senecan tragedy's reinforcement of an 'already existing tendency [in English drama] to express whatever has emotional potentialities in speeches of a heightened poetic quality'.

48 Some examples: *dehisce tellus*: *1 Tamburlaine* 5.1.243, *Richard III* 1.2.65, 4.4.75, Greene's *Alphonsus* 1627ff.; sinners/monsters of hell, *Gorboduc* 2.1.16ff., *Spanish Tragedy* 4.5.31ff.; punishments in hell, *Othello* 5.2.278ff.; wish for universal annihilation, Greene's *Orlando Furioso* 1420ff.

49 Eliot (1951a), 85: 'The establishment of blank verse as the vehicle for drama, instead of the old fourteener, or the heroic couplet, ... received considerable support from its being obviously the nearest equivalent to the solemnity and weight of the Senecan iambic.'

50 Eliot (1951b), 129.

51 Epic similes are pervasive in Senecan tragedy but absent from Greek tragedy, and even rare in speeches in epic.

52 Or as a variation of this at *Macbeth* 4.3.209f.: 'the grief, that does not speak, | Whispers the o'erfraught heart, and bids it break', which exposes the dependence on *Phaedra* 607: 'Curae leues loquuntur, ingentes stupent', quoted with slight alteration at *Revenger's Tragedy* 1.4.24. Several reformulations of this *sententia* may be found, including Webster, *White Devil* 2.1.277: 'Those are the killing griefs which dare not speak'; Ford, *Broken Heart* 5.3.75: 'They are the silent griefs which cut the heartstrings'; and Racine, *Andromaque* 3.3/834: 'La douleur qui se tait n'en est que plus funeste'. Cf. also *Antonio's Revenge* 2.3.4–6: 'Pigmy cares | Can shelter under patience' shield, but giant griefs | Will burst all covert', which replays the similar *sententia* at *Medea* 155f.

53 A reformulation of *Agamemnon* 115: *per scelera semper sceleribus tutum est iter* ('The safe passageway for sin is always sin'). The line is replayed by Hughes, Marston, Jonson, Webster and Massinger, as well as Shakespeare. Webster's version is typically trenchant: 'Small mischiefs are by greater made secure' (*White Devil* 2.1.317). See Cunliffe (1893), 24f.

54 See Greenblatt (1980), 207ff.

55 Examples occur at *Antonio's Revenge* 1.5.32f., *Sejanus* 4.259ff., *Othello* 5.2.235f., *Atheist's Tragedy* 4.3.162ff., *Revenger's Tragedy* 4.2.156, Anon. *King Leir* 1649–52, Greene's *Alphonsus* 211–14, Shakespeare's *Pericles* 1.1.73ff., Massinger's *Roman Actor* 3.1.106f.

56 Charlton (1946), lxxiii, n. 1.
57 Cinthio in Charlton (1946), lvi.
58 See Braden (1985), 117, who also cites this passage.
59 Kott (1974), 5.

8 IDEOLOGY AND MEANING

1 Quoted from Smith (1904), vol. 1, 177.
2 Note the focus in *Médée* on *raisons d'état* as motivators of action and a concern with the privileges due to a king.
3 Most notably to Seneca's *De Clementia*: see Skinner and Price (1988), xvff. But cf. *Il Principe*, ch. 17: 'It is much safer to be feared than loved'; and *Phoenissae* 659: 'qui uult amari, languida regnat manu' ('who wants to be loved reigns with drooping hand'); *Oedipus* 704: 'regna custodit metus' ('fear protects kingdoms').
4 For echoes (esp.) of the *Thyestes* discussion in English tragedy, see Cunliffe (1893). A close imitation is that of Greene in *Selimus* (Cunliffe, 63ff.).
5 See Waith (1962), 60ff., 121ff.
6 See Braden (1985), 186f.
7 For Tamburlaine as 'an embodiment of Renaissance "virtù"', see the edition of J. D. Jump (Lincoln, Nebr., 1967), xixff.
8 For Aaron's 'Atrean qualities', note the ghoulish ironies and jubilation attending his removal of Titus' hand: *Titus* 3.1.201–6. The witticisms continue in Aaron's revelation speeches at *Titus* 5.1.89ff., where they are conjoined with a (similarly Atrean) limitless capacity for evil: *Titus* 5.1.124–44.
9 A similar function in Senecan drama can be given to less powerful female figures, such as Hecuba and Andromache in *Troades*, or Phaedra.
10 Seneca examines, in the Lycus scene of *Hercules Furens* and the final act of *Agamemnon*, for example, the issue of usurped power. But the legitimacy of the system of absolute monarchy is not explored.
11 Miola (1992), 6, describing the thesis of Braden (1985).
12 For these and other examples see Soellner (1958) and Miola (1992), 123f.
13 Braden (1985), 75: 'perhaps the most self-conscious Stoic on the Renaissance stage.'
14 Stegmann (1964), 125.
15 See above p. 155.
16 So Miola (1992), 211, building on the work of Black (1986).
17 It is true that Prospero leaves open the possibility of one day revealing Antonio and Sebastian's plot ('at this time | I will tell no tales', 5.1.128f.); but this is not dwelt upon and hardly qualifies the focus on forgiveness.
18 On Hamlet's 'passion', see Miola (1992), 55f.
19 See esp. *Medea* 897ff., 1009ff., *Thyestes* 890ff., 1052ff.
20 See Bates's introduction to the Arden edition (1995) of *Titus Andronicus*, 26, where the Bacon essay is discussed.
21 As by Bowers (1940).
22 On Bussy as 'Herculean hero overcome by fate' see Waith (1962), 88–111, who ignores the additional paradigm of Thyestes. It is of some importance too that Bussy's Herculean valedictory is delivered by a corrupt cleric.
23 Dollimore (1984), 139–43, sees the play's 'parody of the providential viewpoint' as pervasive.
24 The quotations, cited by Miola (1992), 31, are from Smith (1988), 244, whose claim is restricted to Elizabethan tragedy.
25 For this in early English Renaissance tragedy, see Altman (1978), 249ff.

26 On 'nature' in *Lear* see Greer (1986), 92ff.; on *natura* in *Phaedra* see above, pp. 60ff.

27 T. S. Eliot, 'Whispers of Immortality':

> Webster was much possessed by death
> And saw the skull beneath the skin.

28 For the 'mercy' motif elsewhere in Senecan tragedy, see *Troades* 694, 703, *Phaedra* 623, 636, 671, *Hercules Furens* 1192, *Medea* 482, 1018. See Boyle (1994), on *Troades* 694.

29 At the end of *The Winter's Tale* Mamillius and Antigonus remain dead, and the renaissant Hermione speaks no word to Leontes; in *The Tempest* Prospero's intention is to retire to 'Milan, where | Every third thought shall be my grave' (*Tempest* 5.1.310f.). Such qualify but do not erase the emphasis on reconciliation and felicity, associated in each case with a promised wedding or weddings, at the end of those plays.

30 Stegmann (1965), 183.

31 For Racine's self-conscious moralisation of the ending, see his remarks in his *Préface*: 'Quelle apparence que j'eusse souillé la scène par le meurtre horrible d'une personne aussi vertueuse et aussi aimable qu'il fallait représenter Iphigénie.'

9 THE METATHEATRICAL MIND

1 See Braunmuller in Braunmuller and Hattaway (1990), 81.

2 See Bates' introduction to the new Arden edition (1995), 22.

3 The theatricality of this scene is precociously underscored in Ian McKellen's 1995 film, by having two makeup women work on Richard before the scene with the Mayor and citizens.

4 On the theatrics of the Henriad see the fine discussion of Montrose (1996), 82–5, 94–8, to which I am indebted.

5 Claudius' murder of Hamlet's father and Hamlet's murderous intentions towards his uncle are rival 'meanings' of Hamlet's play.

6 See Miola (1992), 46f.

7 Other playmakers in *Hamlet* include notoriously Polonius, who gets his daughter to draw Hamlet into a play staged before the concealed audience of Claudius and Gertrude (3.1), and arranges for himself to be the hidden audience to the scene played by Gertrude with her son (3.4), who kills the rival playmaker as he too will be killed.

8 The metatheatricality of the opening storm is complex and ironic: the audience is asked to believe that theatrically manufactured noises are a storm, only to be told that they were created by one of the stage figures as a manufactured storm in the play's world. See the excellent discussion in Greer (1986), 28ff., who observes that Prospero's island 'like the stage itself, has two principal resources, costume and script'.

9 See Altman (1978), 374ff.

10 Altman (1978), 293–5, notes the 'heavy theatricalism' of *Antonio's Revenge*, and suggests that Marston 'was very much interested in how men tend to assume imaginative postures as a way of dealing with the evil in which they find themselves, and that "parody" may be a character's most appropriate mode of expression'. The parody point seems to me to mislead. Nor need Marston's interest in theatrical behaviour be limited to situations of evil. There are larger social and cultural ramifications of theatricalism, as discussed below.

11 The Globe, the metaphoric implications of which are reflected in its motto: *totus mundus agit histrionem*, 'All the world's an actor'.

12 'The Tryal of Philip Howard, Earl of Arundel, the 18th day of April, 1589, and in the 31st Year of the Reign of Queen Elizabeth', in *State Trials*, 1.140–44. The passage is quoted in Bates's Arden edition of *Titus Andronicus* (1995), 23f.

13 The phrase is taken from Coleman (1990), who discusses these executions-cum-theatre in detail.

14 Thomas Pecke, *Parnassi Puerperium* (London 1659).

15 On Nero's theatrical behaviour on and off the stage, see Bartsch (1994), *passim*.

16 I am again indebted to Bates's *Titus Andronicus* for this quotation.

17 Holinshed's *Chronicles of England, Scotland, and Ireland* (1587), quoted by Montrose (1996), 76; also Neale (1965), 2:119. On theatricality and the Elizabethan monarchy see Montrose (1980a and 1996).

18 Montrose (1996), 26, who labels this account an 'authorized record'. On the procession see Goldberg (1983), 29ff., esp. 30: 'She acted out her conformity to the script her citizens presented her with.'

19 From a letter to Robert Markham (1606). The italics are mine.

20 See Greenblatt (1980), 165–9.

21 See Montrose (1980a), esp. 168ff., and the analysis of the ceremonies and entertainments at Sudeley during Elizabeth's progress in 1591. See also Howard (1994), 154.

22 From *Speeches Delivered to Her Majestie this Last Progresse*, etc. (Oxford 1592); cited by Montrose (1980a), 171.

23 William Camden, *Annales or the History of the most Renowned and Victorious Princesse Elizabeth*, tr. R. N., 3rd edn (London 1635), 469. Cited by Montrose (1980a), 159.

24 See Greenblatt (1980), 168 and n. 25.

25 Elizabeth's translation of *Hercules Oetaeus* may be found in the Bodleian Library, Oxford.

26 See Greenblatt (1980), 28ff. for a detailed description of the 'theatricalization of public life' by Henry VIII, whose 'taste for lavish dress, ceremonial banquets, pageantry, masque, and festivity astonished his contemporaries and profoundly affected their conception of power' (p. 28).

27 For obvious reasons: to mime authority was to undermine it. The notorious exception of the miming of the queen in the Globe performances of *Every Man out of his Humour* was widely regarded as overstepping the mark, 'making the monarch subject to the whim of the playwright' (Orgel (1982), 45). Shakespeare's *Henry VIII* (performed ten years after Elizabeth's death in 1613) had the effect in the eyes of one member of its original audience, Sir Henry Wotten, of making 'greatness very familiar, if not ridiculous' (Orgel (1982), 47). The furore in 1608 emanating from the representation of the current French monarchy in Chapman's Byron plays, which included an order (later rescinded) by James I to close the London theatres completely (Gurr (1992), 54), indicated how politically and socially damaging the dramatic representation of monarchy was taken to be.

28 Nichols (1828), 1.374.

29 See Goldberg (1983), 33ff. The title of Henry Petowe's panegyric is *England's Caesar*; in Jonson's *Hymenaei* (1606) James is Augustus. Others, less flatteringly, compared him 'to Tiberius for Dissimulation' (Wilson quoted in Goldberg, 164).

30 Among the masques featuring the Stuart monarchs designed by Inigo Jones were Townshend's *Tempe Restored* (1632), Carew's *Coelum Britannicum* (1634), and Davenant's *Salmacida Spolia* (1640) noted above.

31 *The Gull's Hornbook* (1609), ch. 6. Similarly in the French theatre nobles frequently sat on the stage, where they both watched and were the spectacle. Molière even

complains of one marquis placing himself between actors and audience and blocking the latter's view (*Les Fâcheux* 1.1.32).

32 Greenblatt (1980), 231, who cites both Altman (1978) and Cope (1973). Of especial importance in Renaissance education is the *argumentum in utramque partem*, which, like the Roman *controuersia* and *suasoria*, trained students to rhetoricise different moral and intellectual positions; i.e. it taught them how to act.

33 See Gurr (1992), 22ff.

34 On social 'performances' in power relations see Scott (1990), esp. 28ff.

35 A revival of the play, commissioned by members of the Essex circle and attended by eleven of them, was performed at the Globe on the eve of the attempted coup. For a discussion of this and of Elizabeth's reported complaint that 'this tragedy was played 40tie times in open streets and houses', see Montrose (1996), 66–75. A connection between Essex' theatricality and that of Seneca may be found in the publication in the same year as his execution (1601) of Sir William Cornwallis' *Discourses upon Seneca the Tragedian*. Cornwallis served with Essex in Ireland. In his *Essayes* of 1600 Cornwallis writes (Allen, 1946, 193): 'Among poets, *Seneca*'s Tragedies fit well the hands of a statesman; for upon that supposed stage are brought many actions and fitting the stage of life.'

36 They are included in the 1572 *Acte for the punishement of Vacabondes and for Releif of the Poore & Impotent.*

37 The quoted phrases in this sentence are from Marvell's *An Horatian Ode upon Cromwel's Return from Ireland.*

10 TRAGEDY AND CULTURE

1 One of the many distinguishing features of Seneca's, as opposed to Euripides', *Medea*, is that in Seneca's play Medea achieves her triumphant vengeance without the help of any social superior; in Euripides' play she asks for, and receives, the assistance of King Aegeus.

2 Freud (1930), 40.

3 Ibid.

4 See Greenblatt (1980), 2, whose comment, however, refers to sixteenth-century attitudes to 'the fashioning of human identity'. Taverner is also quoted by Greenblatt.

5 Richard Taverner, *Garden of Wisdom* (1539), p. Bviii[v].

BIBLIOGRAPHY

SENECAN EDITIONS, TRANSLATIONS, COMMENTARIES

Ahl, F. (1986) *Seneca Medea, Phaedra, Trojan Women*. Ithaca, NY.

Barchiesi, A. (1988) *Seneca: Le Fenicie*, Venice.

Boyle, A. J. (1987) *Seneca's Phaedra*, Liverpool (repr. Leeds 1992).

—— (1994) *Seneca's Troades*, Leeds.

Caviglia, F. (1979) *L. Anneo Seneca: Il Furore di Ercole*, Rome.

—— (1981) *L. Anneo Seneca: Le Troiane*, Rome.

Coffey, M. and Mayer, R. (1990) *Seneca Phaedra*, Cambridge.

Costa, C. D. N. (1973) *Seneca Medea*, Oxford.

Daalder, J. (1982) *'Thyestes', Lucius Annaeus Seneca, translated by Jasper Heywood (1560)*, London.

Fantham, E. (1982a) *Seneca's Troades: A Literary Commentary*, Princeton, NJ.

Fitch, J. G. (1987a) *Seneca's Hercules Furens*, Ithaca, NY.

Frank, M. (1995) *Seneca's Phoenissae: Introduction and Commentary*, Leiden.

Giardina, G. C. (1966) *L. Annaei Senecae Tragoediae*, Bologna.

Giomini, R. (1955a) *Senecae Phaedra*, Rome.

—— (1956) *Senecae Agamemnon*, Rome.

Grimal, P. (1965) *L. Annaei Senecae Phaedra*, Paris.

Häuptli, B. (1983) *Seneca Oedipus*, Frauenfeld.

Hirschberg, T. (1989) *Senecas Phoenissen: Einleitung und Kommentar*, Berlin and New York.

Hughes, T. (1969) *Seneca's Oedipus*, London.

Kingery, H. M. (1908) *Three Tragedies of Seneca: Hercules Furens, Troades, Medea,* New York (repr. Norman, Okla., 1966).

Lawall, G. (with Lawall, S. and Kunkel, G.) (1976) *The Hippolytus or Phaedra of Seneca*, Amherst, Mass.

Leo, F. (1878–9). *L. Annaei Senecae Tragoediae*, Berlin.

Miller, F. J. (1917) *Seneca: Tragedies*, London and Cambridge, Mass.

Moricca, U. (1917–23) *L. Annaei Senecae Tragoediae*, Turin (2nd edn, 1947).

Newton, T. (1581) *Seneca: His Tenne Tragedies*, London (repr. 1927).

Peiper, R. and Richter, G. (1902) *L. Annaei Senecae Tragoediae*, Leipzig.

Tarrant, R. J. (1976) *Seneca: Agamemnon*, Cambridge.

—— (1985) *Seneca's Thyestes*, Atlanta, Ga.

Viansino, G. (1965) *L. Annaei Senecae Tragoediae*, Turin.

—— (1993) *Seneca Teatro*, 2 vols, Rome.

Watling, E. F. (1966) *Seneca: Four Tragedies and Octavia*, Harmondsworth.

Zwierlein, O. (1986) *L. Annaei Senecae Tragoediae*, Oxford.

OTHER EDITIONS AND COMMENTARIES

For the plays of William Shakespeare I have used the Arden editions, published 1951–95, London.

Ayres, P. J. (1990) *Ben Jonson: Sejanus His Fall*, Manchester and New York.

Barlow, S. A. (1986) *Euripides: Trojan Women*, Warminster.

Barrett, W. S. (1964) *Euripides Hippolytos*, Oxford.

Bowers, F. (1981) *Christopher Marlowe: The Complete Works*, 2 vols, 2nd edn, Cambridge.

Brown, J. R. (1964) *John Webster: The Duchess of Malfi*, London.

Bullough, G. (1945) *Poems and Dramas of Fulke Greville*, Oxford.

Cauthen, I. B., Jr. (1970) *Sackville and Norton: Gorboduc, or, Ferrex and Porrex*, Lincoln, Nebr.

Cinthio, Giraldi (1583) *Tragedie*, Venice.

Couton, G. (1971) *Théâtre complet de Corneille*, 3 vols, Paris.

Craik, E. (1988) *Euripides: Phoenician Women*, Warminster.

Crocetti, C. G. (1973), *Giambattista Cinthio Giraldi: Scritti critici*, Milan.

Cunningham, J. S. (1981) *Christopher Marlowe: Tamburlaine the Great*, Manchester and Baltimore, Md.

Dodds, E. R. (1960) *Euripides Bacchae*, 2nd edn, Oxford.

Edwards, P. (1959) *Thomas Kyd: The Spanish Tragedy*, Cambridge, Mass.

Edwards, P. and Gibson, C. (1976) *The Plays and Poems of Philip Massinger*, 3 vols, Oxford.

Gair, W. R. (1978) *John Marston: Antonio's Revenge*, Baltimore, Md.

Gibbons, B. (1967) *Cyril Tourneur: The Revenger's Tragedy*, New York.

Groto, Luigi (1572) *La Dalida tragedia nova*, Venice.

Grumbine, H. C. (1900) *Thomas Hughes and Others: The Misfortunes of Arthur*, Berlin.

Harris, B. (1967) *John Marston: The Malcontent*, London.

Hunter, G. K. (1965) *John Marston: Antonio and Mellida*, Lincoln, Nebr.

Jocelyn, H. D. (ed.) (1969) *The Tragedies of Ennius*, Cambridge.

Lee, K. H. (1976) *Euripides Troades*, London.

Mastronarde, D. J. (1994) *Euripides Phoenissae*, Cambridge.

Maurens, J. (1980) *Pierre Corneille:Théâtre*, vol 2, Paris.

Morel, J. and Viala, A. (1980) *Racine: Théâtre complet*, Paris.

Morris, B. (1968) *John Ford: 'Tis Pity She's A Whore*, New York.

Mulryne, J. R. (1969) *John Webster: The White Devil*, Lincoln, Nebr.

Parrott, T. M. (1961) *The Plays of George Chapman: The Tragedies*, 2 vols, New York.

Ribner, I. (1964) *Cyril Tourneur: The Atheist's Tragedy*, London.

Skinner, Q. and Price, R. (1988) *Machiavelli: The Prince*, Cambridge.

Spencer, T. J. B. (1980) *John Ford: The Broken Heart*, Manchester and Baltimore, Md.

Ure, P. (1968) *John Ford: The Chronicle History of Perkin Warbeck*, London.

Vahlen, I. (1928) *Ennianae Poesis Reliquiae*, 3rd edn, Leipzig.

Warmington, E. H. (1936) *Remains of Old Latin* II, London and Cambridge, Mass.

WORKS OF REFERENCE AND CRITICISM

Abel, L. (1963) *Metatheatre*, New York.

Abraham, C. (1972) *Pierre Corneille*, New York.

—— (1977) *Jean Racine*, Boston, Mass.

Ahl, F. M. (1984) 'The Rider and the Horse: Politics and Power in Roman Poetry from Horace to Statius', *Aufstieg und Niedergang der römischen Welt* II.32.1: 40–124.

Allen, D. C. (ed.) (1946) *Essayes by Sir William Cornwallis the Younger*, Baltimore, Md.

Altman, J. B. (1978) *The Tudor Play of Mind: Rhetorical Inquiry and the Development of Elizabethan Drama*, Berkeley, Calif.

Amoroso, F. (1984) *Seneca uomo di teatro? Le Troiane e lo spectacolo*, Palermo.

—— (1981) 'Les Troyennes de Sénèque: dramaturgie et théâtralité', in Zehnacker (1981): 81–96.

Anliker, K. (1960) *Prologe und Akteinteilung in Senecas Tragödien*, Bern.

Argenio, R. (1969) 'La vita e la morte nei drammi di Seneca', *Rivista di studi classici* 17: 339–48.

Axelson, B. (1967) *Korruptelenkult: Studien zur Textkritik der unechten Seneca-Tragödie Hercules Oetaeus*, Lund.

Baldwin, T. W. (1947) *Shakespeare's Five-Act Structure*, Urbana, Ill.

Barton, C. A. (1993) *The Sorrows of the Ancient Romans: The Gladiator and the Monster*, Princeton, NJ.

Bartsch, S. (1994) *Actors in the Audience: Theatricality and Doublespeak from Nero to Hadrian*, Cambridge, Mass.

Bate, J. (1993) *Shakespeare and Ovid*, Oxford.

Beacham, R. C. (1992) *The Roman Theatre and its Audience*, Cambridge, Mass.

Beare, W. (1964) *The Roman Stage*, 3rd rev. edn, London.

Bettini, M. (1983) 'L'arcobaleno, l'incesto, e l'enigma', *Dioniso* NS 54: 137ff.

—— (1984) 'Lettura divinatoria di un incesto', *Materiali e Discussioni* 12: 145ff.

—— (1991) *Anthropology and Roman Culture*, tr. J. Van Sickle, Baltimore, Md.

Bieber, M. (1961) *The History of the Greek and Roman Theatre*, 2nd edn, Princeton, NJ.

Billerbeck, M. (1988) *Seneca Tragödien*, Leiden.

Binns, J. W. (1974) 'Seneca and Neo-Latin Tragedy in England', in Costa (1974a): 215–24.

Bishop, J. D. (1965) 'The Choral Odes of Seneca's *Medea*', *Classical Journal* 60: 313–16.

—— (1966) 'Seneca's *Hercules Furens*: Tragedy from *Modus Vitae*', *Classica et Mediaevalia* 27: 216–24.

—— (1968) 'The Meaning of the Choral Meters in Senecan Tragedy', *Rheinisches Museum für Philologie* 111: 197–219.

—— (1972) 'Seneca's *Troades*: Dissolution of a Way of Life', *Rheinisches Museum für Philologie* 115: 329–37.

Black, J. (1986) 'Shakespeare and the Comedy of Revenge', in D. Beecher and M. Ciavolella (eds), *Comparative Critical Approaches to Renaissance Comedy*: 137–51, Ottawa.

Bloom, H. (1973) *The Anxiety of Influence: A theory of Poetry*, Oxford.

Boas, F. S. (1914) *University Drama in the Tudor Age*, Oxford.

—— (1932) 'University Plays', in A. W. Ward and A. R. Walker (eds), *The Cambridge History of English Literature*, VI: 293–327, Cambridge.

Boella, U. (1979) 'Osservazioni sulle Troiane di Seneca', *Rivista di studi classici* 27: 66–79.

Bonnelli, G. (1978) 'Il carattere retorico delle tragedie di Seneca', *Latomus* 37: 395–418.

Bonner, S. F. (1949) *Roman Declamation*, Berkeley, Calif.

Bowers, F. B. (1940) *Elizabethan Revenge Tragedy*, Princeton, NJ.

Boyle, A. J. (ed.) (1983a) *Seneca Tragicus. Ramus Essays on Senecan Drama*, Berwick, Vic.

—— (1983b) '*Hic Epulis Locus*: the Tragic Worlds of Seneca's *Agamemnon* and *Thyestes*', in Boyle (1983a): 199–228.

—— (1985) 'In Nature's Bonds: a Study of Seneca's *Phaedra*', *Aufstieg und Niedergang der römischen Welt* II.32.2: 1284–347.

—— (ed.) (1988a) *The Imperial Muse*, vol. I, *To Juvenal Through Ovid*, Berwick, Vic.

—— (1988b) 'Senecan Tragedy: Twelve Propositions', in Boyle (1988a): 78–101.

—— (1992) A review of Rosenmeyer 1989, *American Journal of Philology* 113: 122–25.

—— (ed.) (1993) *Roman Epic*, London.

—— (forthcoming) 'Aeneid 8: Images of Rome', in C. Perkell (ed.) Reading Vergil's Aeneid, Norman, Okla.

—— and Sullivan, J. P. (eds) (1991), Roman Poets of the Early Empire, Harmondsworth.

Braden, G. (1970) 'The Rhetoric and Psychology of Power in the Dramas of Seneca', Arion 9: 5–41.

—— (1984) 'Senecan Tragedy and the Renaissance', Illinois Classical Studies 9: 277–92.

—— (1985) Renaissance Tragedy and the Senecan Tradition: Anger's Privilege, New Haven, Conn.

Bradner, L. (ed.) (1964) The Poems of Queen Elizabeth, Providence, RI.

Braginton, M. V. (1933) The Supernatural in Seneca's Tragedies, Menasha, Wis.

Brandt, J. (1986) Argumentative Struktur in Senecas Tragödien, Hildesheim.

Braunmuller, A. R. and Hattaway, M. (eds) (1990) The Cambridge Companion to English Renaissance Drama, Cambridge.

Brooks, H. F. (1979) 'Richard III: Antecedents of Clarence's Dream', Shakespeare Survey 32: 145–50.

—— (1980) 'Richard III, Unhistorical Amplifications: the Women's Scenes and Seneca', Modern Language Review 75: 721–37.

Brooks, P. (1976) The Melodramatic Imagination, New Haven, Conn.

Brower, R. A. (1971) Hero and Saint: Shakespeare and the Graeco-Roman Heroic Tradition, Oxford.

Bullough, G. (1957–75) Narrative and Dramatic Sources of Shakespeare, 8 vols, London.

—— (1964) 'Sénèque, Greville et le jeune Shakespeare', in Jacquot (1964): 189–201.

Burck, E. (1971) Vom römischen Manierismus, Darmstadt.

Busa, R. and Zampolli, A. (1975) Concordantiae Senecanae, Hildesheim.

Calder, W. M. (1970) 'Originality in Seneca's Troades', Classical Philology 65: 75–82.

—— (1975) 'The Size of the Chorus in Seneca's Agamemnon', Classical Philology 70: 32–35.

—— (1976) 'Seneca's Agamemnon', Classical Philology 71: 27–36.

—— (1976/7) 'Seneca, Tragedian of Imperial Rome', Classical Journal 72: 1–11.

—— (1983) 'Secreti loquimur: an Interpretation of Seneca's Thyestes', in Boyle (1983a): 184–98.

Canter, H.V. (1925) Rhetorical Elements in the Tragedies of Seneca, Urbana, Ill. (repr. Hildesheim, 1970).

Carbone, H. V. (1977) 'The Octavia: Structure, Date and Authenticity', Phoenix 31: 48–67.

Cattin, A. (1963) Les thèmes lyriques dans les tragédies de Sénèque, Neuchâtel.

Charlton, H. B. (1946) The Senecan Tradition in Renaissance Tragedy, Manchester.

Cizek, E. (1972) 'L'Époque de Néron et ses controverses idéologiques', Roma Aeterna 4: 255–62, Leiden.

Cleasby, H. (1907) 'The Medea of Seneca', Harvard Studies in Classical Philology 18: 39–71.

Clemen, W. (1961) English Tragedy before Shakespeare: the Development of Dramatic Speech, tr. T. S. Dorsch, London.

Coffey, M. (1957) 'Seneca: Tragedies: Report for the Years 1922–1955', Lustrum 2: 113–86.

—— (1960) 'Seneca and his Tragedies', Proceedings of the African Classical Association 3: 14–20.

Cole, J. I. (1973) The Theater and the Dream: From Metaphor to Form in Renaissance Drama, Baltimore, Md.

Coleman, K. M. (1990) 'Fatal Charades: Roman Executions Staged as Mythological Enactments', Journal of Roman Studies 80: 44–73.

Colie, R. (1966) Paradoxia Epidemica, Princeton, NJ.

Cope, J. (1973) *The Theatre and the Dream: from Metaphor to Form in Renaissance Drama*, Baltimore, Md.

Cornwallis, W. (1601) *Discourses upon Seneca the Tragedian*, London.

Costa, C. D. N. (ed.) (1974a) *Seneca*, London.

—— (1974b) 'The Tragedies', in Costa (1974a): 96–115.

Croisille, J. M. (1964a) 'Le personnage de Clytemnestre dans l'*Agamemnon* de Sénèque', *Latomus* 23: 464–72.

—— (1964b) 'Lieux communs, *sententiae* et intentions philosophiques dans la *Phèdre* de Sénèque', *Revue des Études Latines* 42: 276–301.

Cunliffe, J. W. (1893) *The Influence of Seneca on Elizabethan Tragedy*, London (repr. New York, 1965).

Curley, T. F. (1986) *The Nature of Senecan Drama*, Rome.

Davis, P. J. (1983) '*Vindicat omnes natura sibi*: a Reading of Seneca's *Phaedra*', in Boyle (1983a): 114–27.

—— (1989) 'Death and Emotion in Seneca's *Trojan Women*', in C. Deroux (ed.), *Studies in Latin Literature and Roman History* V: 305–16, Brussels.

—— (1991) 'Fate and Human Responsibility in Seneca's *Oedipus*', *Latomus* 50: 150–63.

—— (1993) *Shifting Song: the Chorus in Seneca's Tragedies*, Hildesheim.

Denooz, J. (1980) *Lucius Annaeus Seneca Tragoediae Index Verborum*, Hildesheim.

Detienne, M. (1972) *Les Jardins d'Adonis*, Paris.

Dingel, J. (1974) *Seneca und die Dichtung*, Heidelberg.

Dollimore, J. (1984) *Radical Tragedy*, Chicago, Ill.

Doran, M. (1954) *Endeavours of Art: a Study of Form in Elizabethan Drama*, Madison, Wis.

Dorey, T. A. and Dudley, D. R. (eds) (1965) *Roman Drama*, London.

Dupont, F. (1985) *L'Acteur-roi, ou le théâtre dans la Rome antique*, Paris.

—— (1995) *Les monstres de Sénèque*, Paris.

Eagleton, T. (1986) *William Shakespeare*, Oxford.

Eliot, T. S. (1951a) 'Seneca in Elizabethan Translation', *Selected Essays*, 3rd edn: 65–105, London.

—— (1951b) 'Shakespeare and the Stoicism of Seneca', *Selected Essays*, 3rd edn: 126–40, London.

Edwards, C. (1993) *The Politics of Immorality in Ancient Rome*, Cambridge.

Enk, P. J. (1957) 'Roman Tragedy', *Neophilologus* 41: 282–307.

Evans, E. C. (1950) 'A Stoic Aspect of Senecan Drama: Portraiture', *Transactions and Proceedings of the American Philological Association* 81: 169–84.

Fantham, E. (1975) 'Virgil's Dido and Seneca's Tragic Heroines', *Greece and Rome* NS 22: 1–10.

—— (1982b) 'Seneca's *Troades* and *Agamemnon*: Continuity and Sequence', *Classical Journal* 77: 118–29.

—— (1983) '*Nihil iam iura naturae ualent*: Incest and Fratricide in Seneca's *Phoenissae*', in Boyle (1983a): 61–76.

—— (1989) 'Mime: The Missing Link in Roman Literary History', *Classical World* 82: 153–63.

Ferruci, F. (1980) *The Poetics of Disguise: the Autobiography of the Work in Homer, Dante and Shakespeare*, tr. A. Dunnigan, Ithaca, NY.

Fitch, J. G. (1974) 'Character in Senecan Tragedy', Ph.D. dissertation, Cornell University.

—— (1981) 'Sense-pauses and Relative Dating in Seneca, Sophocles and Shakespeare', *American Journal of Philology* 102: 289–307.

—— (1987b) *Seneca's Anapaests: Metre, Colometry, Text and Artistry in the Anapaests of Seneca's Tragedies*, Atlanta, Ga.

Fortey, S. and Glucker, J. (1975) 'Actus Tragicus: Seneca on the Stage', *Latomus* 34: 699–715.

Freer, C. (1987) 'Mary Sidney: Countess of Pembroke', in K. M. Wilson (ed.), *Women Writers of the Renaissance and Reformation*: 481–521, Athens and London.

Freud, S. (1930) *Civilization and its Discontents*, tr. J. Rivière, Dover edn, London (repr. New York 1994).

Friedrich, W.-H. (1933) *Untersuchungen zu Senecas dramatischer Technik*, Borna-Leipzig.

—— (1954) 'Sprache und Stil des Hercules Oetaeus', *Hermes* 82: 51–84.

Fyfe, H. (1983) 'An Analysis of Seneca's *Medea*', in Boyle (1983a): 77–93.

Galinsky, G. K. (1972) *The Herakles Theme*, Oxford.

Garton, C. (1972) *Personal Aspects of the Roman Theatre*, Toronto.

Giancotti, F. (1953) *Saggio sulle tragedie di Seneca*, Rome.

Giardina, G. C. (1964) 'Per un inquadramento del teatro di Seneca nella cultura e nella società del suo tempo', *Rivista di cultura classica e medievalia* 6: 171–80.

Gigon, O. (1938) 'Bemerkungen zu Senecas Thyestes', *Philologus* 93: 176–83.

Gilbert, A. H. (ed.) (1940) *Literary Criticism: Plato to Dryden*, Detroit, Mich.

Giomini, R. (1955b) *Saggio sulla Fedra di Seneca*, Rome.

Goldberg, J. (1983) *James I and the Politics of Literature: Jonson, Shakespeare, Donne, and their Contemporaries*, Baltimore, Md.

Gomme, A. W. and Sandbach, F. H. (eds) (1973) *Menander: a Commentary*, Oxford.

Gratwick, A. S. (1982) 'Drama', in E. Kenney and W. Clausen (eds), *The Cambridge History of Classical Literature*, II: *Latin Literature*: 77–137, Cambridge.

Greenblatt, S. (1980) *Renaissance Self-Fashioning: From More to Shakespeare*, Chicago, Ill.

—— (ed.) (1982) *The Power of Forms in the English Renaissance*, Norman, Okla.

Greer, G. (1986) *Shakespeare*, Oxford.

Griffin, M. T. (1974) 'Imago Vitae Suae' in Costa (1974a): 1–38.

—— (1976) *Seneca: a Philosopher in Politics*, Oxford.

—— (1984) *Nero: the End of a Dynasty*, London.

Grimal, P. (1963) 'L'originalité de Sénèque dans la tragédie de *Phèdre*', *Revue des Études Latines* 41: 297–314.

—— (1964) 'Les tragédies de Sénèque', in Jacquot (1964): 1–10.

Gurr, A. (1992) *The Shakespearean Stage 1574–1642*, 3rd edn, Cambridge.

Hadas, M. (1939) 'The Roman Stamp of Seneca's Tragedies', *American Journal of Philology* 60: 220–31.

Hallett, C. A. and E. S. (1980) *The Revenger's Madness: a Study of Revenge Tragedy Motifs*, Lincoln, Nebr.

Hansen, E. H. A. (1934) *Die Stellung der Affektrede in den Tragödien des Seneca*, Berlin.

Haywood, R. M. (1969) 'The Poetry of the Choruses of Seneca's *Troades*', in *Hommages à Marcel Renard*: I. 415–20, Brussels.

Heldmann, K. (1974) *Untersuchungen zu den Tragödien Senecas*, Wiesbaden.

Helm, R. (1934) *Die Praetexta Octavia*, Berlin.

Hempelmann, A. (1960) *Senecas Medea als eigenständiges Kunstwerk*, Kiel.

Henderson, J. (1983) 'Poetic Technique and Amplification: Seneca *Medea* 579–669', in Boyle (1983a): 94–113.

—— (1988) 'Lucan/The Word at War', in Boyle (1988a): 122–64.

—— (1993) 'Form Remade/Statius' *Thebaid*', in Boyle (1993): 162–91.

Henry, D. and Walker, B. (1963a) 'Seneca and the *Agamemnon*: Some Thoughts on Tragic Doom', *Classical Philology* 58: 1–10.

—— (1963b) 'Tacitus and Seneca', *Greece and Rome* NS 10: 98–110.

—— (1965) 'The Futility of Action: a Study of Seneca's *Hercules Furens*', *Classical Philology* 60: 11–22.

—— (1966) 'Phantasmagoria and Idyll: an Element of Seneca's *Phaedra*', *Greece and Rome* NS 13: 223–39.

—— (1967) 'Loss of Identity: *Medea Superest?* A Study of Seneca's *Medea*', *Classical Philology* 62: 169–81.

—— (1983) 'The *Oedipus* of Seneca: an Imperial Tragedy', in Boyle (1983a): 128–39.

—— (1985) *The Mask of Power: Seneca's Tragedies and Imperial Rome*, Warminster.

Henry, E. (1988) 'Seneca's Hecuba', *Bulletin of the Institute of Classical Studies*, Supplement 51: 44–52.

Herington, C. J. (1961) '*Octavia Praetexta*: a Survey', *Classical Quarterly* NS 11: 18–30 (repr. in Lefèvre (1972a): 559–82).

—— (1966) 'Senecan Tragedy', *Arion* 5: 422–71.

—— (1982) 'The Younger Seneca', in E. Kenney and W. Clausen (eds), *The Cambridge History of Classical Literature*, II: *Latin Literature*: 511–32, Cambridge.

Hermann, L. (1924) *Le théâtre de Sénèque*, Paris.

Herrick, M. T. (1955) *Tragicomedy*, Urbana, Ill.

—— (1965) *Italian Tragedy in the Renaissance*, Urbana, Ill.

Herter, H. (1971) 'Phaidra in griechischer und römischer Gestalt', *Rheinisches Museum für Philologie* 114: 14–77.

Herzog, O. (1928) 'Datierung der Tragödien des Seneca', *Rheinisches Museum für Philologie* 77: 51–104.

Hijmans, B. L., Jr. (1966) 'Drama in Seneca's Stoicism', *Transactions and Proceedings of the American Philological Association* 97: 237–51.

Hine, H. (1981) 'The Structure of Seneca's *Thyestes*', in F. Cairns (ed.), *Papers of the Liverpool Latin Seminar* 3: 259–75, Liverpool.

Hopkins, K. (1983) *Death and Renewal*, Cambridge.

Horne, P. R. (1962) *The Tragedies of Giambattista Giraldi*, Oxford.

Howard, J. E. (1994) *The Stage and Social Struggle in Early Modern England*, London and New York.

Hunter, G. K. (1967) 'Seneca and the Elizabethans: a Case-Study in "Influence"', *Shakespeare Survey* 20: 17–26.

—— (1974) 'Seneca and English Tragedy', in Costa (1974a): 166–204.

Hunter, R.L. (1985) *The New Comedy of Greece and Rome*, Cambridge.

Hutchinson, G. O. (1993) *Latin Literature from Seneca to Juvenal: a Critical Study*, Oxford.

Jacquot, J. (ed.) (1964) *Les tragédies de Sénèque et le théâtre de la Renaissance*, Paris.

Jacobson, H. (1981) 'Two Studies on Ezechiel the Tragedian', *Greek, Roman and Byzantine Studies* 22: 167–78.

—— (1983) *The Exagoge of Ezechiel*, Cambridge.

Jakobi, R. (1988) *Der Einfluss Ovids auf den Tragiker Seneca*, Berlin.

Jones, E. (1977) *The Origins of Shakespeare*, Oxford.

Kastan, D. S. (1986) 'Proud Majesty Made a Subject: Shakespeare and the Spectacle of Rule', *Shakespeare Quarterly* 37: 459–75.

Kaufmann, R. J. (1967) 'The Senecan Perspective and the Shakespearean Poetic', *Comparative Drama* 1: 182–98.

Kelly, H. A. (1979) 'Tragedy and the Performance of Tragedy in Late Roman Antiquity', *Traditio* 35: 21–44.

Knoche, U. (1972) 'Senecas Atreus. Ein Beispiel', in Lefèvre (1972a): 477–89. Orig. pub. *Antike* 17 (1941): 60–76.

Kott, J. (1974) *Shakespeare Our Contemporary*, New York and London. Orig. pub. London, 1964.

Kragelund, P. (1982) *Prophecy, Populism, and Propaganda in the 'Octavia'*, Copenhagen.

Kullmann, W. (1970) 'Medeas Entwicklung bei Seneca', in W. Wimmel (ed.), *Forschungen zur römischen Literatur*: 158–67, Wiesbaden.

BIBLIOGRAPHY

Lapp, J. (1964) 'Racine est-il sénéquien?' in Jacquot (1964): 127–38.

Lawall, G. (1979) 'Seneca's *Medea*: the Elusive Triumph of Civilization', in G. Bowersock, W. Burkert, M. Putnam (eds), *Arktouros: Hellenic Studies Presented to B. M. W. Knox*: 419–26, Berlin and New York.

—— (1982) 'Death and Perspective in Seneca's *Troades*', *Classical Journal* 77: 244–52.

—— (1983) '*Virtus* and *Pietas* in Seneca's *Hercules Furens*', in Boyle (1983a): 6–26.

Lebek, W. D. (1985) 'Senecas Agamemnon in Pompeji (CIL iv 6698)', *Zeitschrift für Papyrologie und Epigraphik* 59: 1–6.

Leeman, A. D. (1976) 'Seneca's *Phaedra* as a Stoic Tragedy', in J. M. Bremer, S. L. Radt, and C. J. Ruigh (eds), *Miscellanea Tragica in honorem J. C. Kamerbeek*: 199–212, Amsterdam.

Lefèvre, E. (ed.) (1972a) *Senecas Tragödien*, Darmstadt.

—— (1972b) 'Schicksal und Selbstverschuldung in Senecas *Agamemnon*', in Lefèvre (1972a): 457–76. Orig. pub. *Hermes* 94 (1966): 482–96.

—— (1972c) '*Quid ratio possit*? Senecas *Phaedra* als stoisches Drama', in Lefèvre (1972a): 343–75. Orig. pub. *Wiener Studien* NS 3 (1969): 131–60.

—— (1973a) 'Die Schuld des *Agamemnon*', *Hermes* 101: 64–91.

—— (1973b) 'Die Kinder des Thyestes', *Symbolae Osloenses* 48: 97–108.

—— (ed.) (1978) *Der Einfluss Senecas auf das europäische Drama*, Darmstadt.

—— (1981) 'A Cult without God or the Unfreedom of Freedom in Seneca Tragicus', *Classical Journal* 77: 32–36.

—— (1985) 'Die politische Bedeutung der römischen Tragödie und Senecas "Oedipus"', *Aufstieg und Niedergang der römischen Welt* II.32.2: 1242–62.

Lerner, D. (1964) *The Passing of Traditional Society: Modernizing the Middle East*, rev. edn, New York.

Leo, F. (1897) 'Die Composition der Chorlieder Senecas', *Rheinisches Museum für Philologie* 52: 509–18.

Liebermann, W.-L. (1974) *Studien zu Senecas Tragödien*, Meisenheim am Glan.

Lohikoski, K. K. (1966) 'Der Parallelismus Mykene-Troja in Senecas *Agamemnon*', *Arctos* NS 4: 63–70.

Long, A. A. (1971) *Problems in Stoicism*, London.

—— (1974) *Hellenistic Philosophy*, London (repr. Berkeley and Los Angeles, Calif. 1986).

—— and Sedley, D. N. (1987) *The Hellenistic Philosophers*, Cambridge.

Loraux, N. (1987) *Tragic Ways of Killing a Woman*, Cambridge, Mass. and London.

Lucas, F. L. (1922) *Seneca and Elizabethan Tragedy*, Cambridge.

McDonald, C. O. (1966) *The Rhetoric of Tragedy: Form in Stuart Drama*, Amherst, Mass.

Mader, G. (1990) 'Form and Meaning in Seneca's "Dawn Song" (*HF* 125–201)', *Acta Classica* 33: 1–32.

Marcosignori, A. M. (1960) 'Il concetto di *virtus tragica* nel teatro di Seneca', *Aevum* 34: 217–33.

Marti, B. M. (1945) 'Seneca's Tragedies: a New Interpretation', *Transactions of the American Philological Association* 76: 216–45.

—— (1947) 'The Prototypes of Seneca's Tragedies', *Classical Philology* 42: 1–16.

Martindale C. and M. (1990) *Shakespeare and the Uses of Antiquity*, London and New York.

Marx, W. (1932) *Funktion und Form der Chorlieder in den Seneca-Tragödien*, Heidelberg.

Maskell, D. (1991) *Racine: a Theatrical Reading*, Oxford.

Mastronarde, D. J. (1970) 'Seneca's *Oedipus*: the Drama in the Word', *Transactions and Proceedings of the American Philological Association* 101: 291–315.

Maurach, G. (1972) 'Jason und Medea bei Seneca', in Lefèvre 1972a: 292–320. Orig. pub. *Antike und Abendland* 12 (1966): 125–40.

Mazzoli, G. (1970) *Seneca e la poesia*, Milan.

Mazzoli, L. (1961) 'Umanità e poesia nelle Troiane di Seneca', *Maia* 13: 51–67.

Mendell, C. W. (1941) *Our Seneca*, New Haven, Conn.

Mercer, P. (1987) *'Hamlet' and the Acting of Revenge*, Iowa City, Ia.

Merzlak, R. F. (1983) '*Furor* in Seneca's *Phaedra*', *Collection Latomus* 180: 193–210, Brussels.

Mesk, J. (1915) 'Senecas *Phoenissen*', *Wiener Studien* 37: 298–322.

—— (1942) 'Zu Senecas *Troerinnen*', *Wiener Studien* 60: 93–7.

Mette, H. J. (1966) 'Die Funktion des Löwengleichnisses in Senecas *Hercules Furens*', *Wiener Studien* 79: 477–89.

Miola, R. S. (1992) *Shakespeare and Classical Tragedy: the Influence of Seneca*, Oxford.

Montrose, L. (1980a) '"Eliza, Queene of shepheardes," and the Pastoral of Power', *English Literary Renaissance* 10: 153–82.

—— (1980b) 'The Purpose of Playing: Reflections on a Shakespearean Anthropology', *Helios* 7(2): 51–74.

—— (1996) *The Purpose of Playing: Shakespeare and the Cultural Politics of the Elizabethan Theatre*, Chicago and London.

Moretti, F. (1982) '"A Huge Eclipse": Tragic Form and the Deconsecration of Sovereignty', in Greenblatt (1982): 7–40.

Morse, R. (1996) *The Medieval Medea*, Woodbridge, Suffolk.

Mossman, J. (1995) *Wild Justice: a Study of Euripides' 'Hecuba'*, Oxford.

Motto, A. L. and Clark, J. R. (1972) 'Senecan Tragedy. Patterns of Irony and Art', *Classical Bulletin* 48: 69–77.

—— (1981) '*Maxima Virtus* in Seneca's *Hercules Furens*', *Classical Philology* 76: 101–17.

—— (1985) 'Seneca's *Agamemnon*: Tragedy without a Hero', *Athenaeum* 63: 136–44.

—— (1988) *Senecan Tragedy*, Amsterdam.

Mueller-Goldingen, C. (1995) 'Seneca und Euripides. Zur Rezeptionsgeschichte der Phönissen', *Rheinisches Museum für Philologie* 138: 82–92.

Muir, K. (1978) *The Sources of Shakespeare's Plays*, New Haven, Conn.

Müller, G. (1953) 'Senecas Oedipus als Drama', *Hermes* 81: 447–64 (repr. in Lefèvre (1972a): 376–401).

Neale, J. E. (1965) *Elizabeth I and Her Parliaments, 1584–1601*, 2 vols, London.

Nelson, A. H. (1989) *Records of Early English Drama: Cambridge*, Toronto.

Nelson, R. J. (1958) *Play within a Play*, New Haven, Conn.

Nichols, J. (1828) *The Progresses, Processions, and Magnificent Festivities of King James the First*, 4 vols, London.

Nisbet, R. G. M. (1987) 'The Oak and the Axe: Symbolism in Seneca, *Hercules Oetaeus* 1618ff.', in M. Whitby, P. Hardie, M. Whitby (eds), *Homo Viator: Classical Essays for John Bramble*: 243–51, Bristol.

—— (1990) 'The Dating of Seneca's Tragedies, with Special Reference to *Thyestes*', in F. Cairns (ed.), *Papers of the Leeds International Latin Seminar* 6: 95–114, Leeds.

Nussbaum, M. (1994) 'Serpents in the Soul: a Reading of Seneca's *Medea*', in *The Therapy of Desire: Theory and Practice in Hellenistic Ethics*: 439–83, Princeton, NJ.

Ogilvie, R. M. (1980) *Roman Literature and Society*, Harmondsworth.

Oldfather, W. A., Pease A.S. and Canter H. V. (1918) *Index Verborum Quae In Senecae Fabulis Necnon In Octavia Praetexta Reperiuntur*, Urbana, Ill.

Opelt, I. (1951) *Der Tyrann als Unmensch in den Tragödien des L. Annaeus Senecas*, Freiburg.

—— (1972a) 'Senecas Konzeption des Tragischen', in Lefèvre (1972a): 92–128.

—— (1972b) 'Zu Senecas Phoenissen', in Lefèvre (1972a): 272–85.

Orgel, S. (ed.) (1975) *The Renaissance Imagination*, Berkeley and Los Angeles, Calif.

—— (1982) 'Making Greatness Familiar', in Greenblatt (1982): 41–8.

Owen, W. H. (1968) 'Commonplace and Dramatic Symbol in Seneca's Tragedies', *Transactions and Proceedings of the American Philological Association* 99: 291–313.

—— (1970) 'Time and Event in Seneca's *Troades*', *Wiener Studien* NS 4: 118–37.

Pack, R. A. (1940) 'On Guilt and Error in Senecan Tragedy', *Transactions and Proceedings of the American Philological Association* 71: 360–71.

Paul, A. (1953) *Untersuchungen zur Eigenart von Senecas Phoenissen*, Bonn.

Paratore, E. (1952) 'Sulla "Phaedra" di Seneca', *Dioniso* NS 15: 199–234.

—— (1956) 'La poesia nell' "Oedipus" di Seneca', *Giornale di Istituto di Filologia* 9: 97–132.

—— (1957) 'Originalità del teatro di Seneca', *Dioniso* NS 20 (1957): 53–74.

Pettine, E. (1974) *Studio dei caratteri e poesia nelle tragedie di Seneca*, Salerno.

Plass, P. (1995) *The Game of Death in Ancient Rome: Arena Sport and Political Suicide*, Madison, Wis.

Poe, J. P. (1969) 'An Analysis of Seneca's *Thyestes*', *Transactions and Proceedings of the American Philological Association* 100: 355–76.

—— (1983) 'The Sinful Nature of the Protagonist of Seneca's *Oedipus*', in Boyle (1983a): 140–58.

Pöschl, V. (1977) 'Bemerkungen zum Thyest des Seneca', in H. Bannert and J. Divjak (eds), *Latinität und Alte Kirche: Festschrift für R. Hanslik zum 70. Geburtstag*: 224–34, Vienna.

Pratt, N. T. (1939) *Dramatic Suspense in Seneca and his Greek Predecessors*, Princeton, NJ.

—— (1948) 'The Stoic Base of Senecan Drama', *Transactions of the American Philological Association* 79: 1–11.

—— (1963) 'Major Systems of Figurative Language in Senecan Melodrama', *Transactions of the American Philological Association* 94: 199–234.

—— (1983) *Seneca's Drama*, Chapel Hill, NC and London.

Rambaux, C. (1972) 'Le mythe de Médée d'Euripide à Anouilh ou l'originalité psychologique de la Médée de Sénèque', *Latomus* 31: 1010–36.

Raven, D. (1965) *Latin Metre*, London.

Rees, B. R. (1969) 'English Seneca: a Preamble', *Greece and Rome* NS 16: 119–33.

Regenbogen, O. (1927–28) 'Schmerz und Tod in den Tragödien des Seneca', *Vorträge der Bibliothek Warburg*: 167–218.

Richter, G. (1899) *Kritische Untersuchungen zu Senecas Tragödien*, Jena.

Righter, A. (1962) *Shakespeare and the Idea of the Play*, London.

Rist, J. M. (1969) *Stoic Philosophy*, Cambridge.

Rose, A. (1979/80) 'Seneca's *HF*: a Politico-Didactic Reading', *Classical Journal* 75: 135–42.

Rosenmeyer, T. G. (1989) *Senecan Drama and Stoic Cosmology*, Berkeley, Calif.

Rozelaar, M. (1976) *Seneca: Eine Gesamtdarstellung*, Amsterdam.

Runchina, G. (1960) 'Tecnica drammatica e retorica nelle Tragedie di Seneca', *Annali della Facoltà di Lettere, Filosofia e Magistero della Università di Cagliari* 28: 165–324.

—— (1966) 'Sulla *Phaedra* di Seneca', *Rivista di cultura classica e medievalia* 8: 12–37.

Sandbach, F. H. (1975) *The Stoics*, London.

Schetter, W. (1965) 'Sulla struttura delle Troiane di Seneca', *Rivista di filologia classica* 93: 396–429 (repr. as 'Zum Aufbau von Senecas Troerinnen', in Lefèvre (1972a): 230–71).

—— (1972) 'Senecas Oedipus-Tragödie' in Lefèvre (1972a): 402–49: Orig. pub. as 'Die Prologszene zu Senecas Oedipus', *Der altsprachliche Unterricht* 11 (1968): 23–49, with *Nachtrag* (1970).

Schiesaro, A. (1994) 'Seneca's *Thyestes* and the Morality of Tragic *Furor*', in J. Elsner and J. Masters (eds), *Reflections of Nero: Culture, History and Representation*: 196–210, London.

Scott, J. C. (1990) *Domination and the Arts of Resistance: Hidden Transcripts*, New Haven, Conn.

Segal, C. P. (1977) 'Euripides' *Bacchae*: Conflict and Mediation', *Ramus* 6: 103–20.
—— (1983) 'Boundary Violation and the Landscape of the Self in Senecan Tragedy', *Antike und Abendland* 29: 172–87.
—— (1984) 'Senecan Baroque: the Death of Hippolytus in Seneca, Ovid and Euripides', *Transactions of the American Philological Association* 114: 311–26.
—— (1986) *Language and Desire in Seneca's Phaedra*, Princeton, NJ.
Seidensticker, B. (1969) *Die Gesprächsverdichtung in den Tragödien Senecas*, Heidelberg.
—— and Armstrong, D. (1985) 'Seneca Tragicus 1878–1978 (with Addenda 1979ff.)', *Aufstieg und Niedergang der römischen Welt* II.32.2: 916–68.
Seidler, B. (1955) *Studien zur Wortstellung in den Tragödien Senecas*, Diss. Vienna.
Shelton, J.-A. (1977) 'The Dramatization of Inner Experience: the Opening Scene of Seneca's *Agamemnon*', *Ramus* 6: 33–43.
—— (1978) *Seneca's Hercules Furens: Theme, Structure and Style*, Göttingen.
—— (1983) 'Revenge or Resignation: Seneca's *Agamemnon*', in Boyle (1983a): 159–83.
Simmons, J. L. (1982) 'Shakespeare and the Antique Romans', in P. A. Ramsey (ed.), *Rome in the Renaissance*: 77–92, Binghampton, NY.
Skovgaard-Hansen, M. (1968) 'The Fall of Phaethon: Meaning in Seneca's *Hippolytus*', *Classica et Mediaevalia* 29: 92–123.
Slater, N. (1985) *Plautus in Performance*, Princeton, NJ.
Smereka, J. (1936) 'De Senecae tragici uocabulorum copiae certa quadam lege', in *Munera Philologica L. Cwiklinski Oblata*: 253–61, Posnan.
Smith, B. R. (1988) *Ancient Scripts and Modern Experience on the English Stage 1500–1700*, Princeton, NJ.
Smith, G. Gregory (ed.) (1904) *Elizabethan Critical Essays*, 2 vols. Oxford.
Snell, B. (1964) *Scenes from Greek Drama*, Berkeley and Los Angeles, Calif.
Soellner, R. (1958) 'The Madness of Hercules and the Elizabethans', *Comparative Literature* 10: 309–24.
Specka, A. (1937) *Der hohe Stil der Dichtungen Senecas und Lucans*, Diss. Königsberg.
Stähli-Peter, M. M. (1974) *Die Arie des Hippolytus. Kommentar zu Eingangsmonodie in der Phaedra des Seneca*, Diss. Zurich.
Staley, G. A. 'Ira: Theme and Form in Senecan Tragedy', Ph.D. dissertation, Princeton University.
Stamm, R. (1975) *The Mirror-Technique in Seneca and pre-Shakespearean Tragedy*, Bern.
Steele, R. B. (1922) 'Some Roman Elements in the Tragedies of Seneca', *American Journal of Philology* 43: 1–31.
Stegmann, A. (1964) 'La *Médée* de Corneille', in Jacquot (1964): 113–26.
—— (1965) 'Seneca and Corneille', in Dorey and Dudley (1965): 161–92.
Steidle, W. (1972a) 'Zu Senecas Troerinnen', in Lefèvre (1972a): 210–29. Orig. pub. *Philologus* 94 (1941): 266–84.
—— (1972b) 'Die Gestalt des Thyest', in Lefèvre 1972a: 490–99. Orig. pub. *Philologus* 96 (1943/4): 250–9.
—— (1972c) 'Medeas Racheplan', in Lefèvre (1972a): 286–91. Orig. publ. *Philologus* 96 (1943/4): 259–64.
Steiner, G. (1975) *After Babel*, London.
Sullivan, J. P. (1985) *Literature and Politics in the Age of Nero*, Ithaca, NY and London.
Sutherland, J. M. (1985) 'Shakespeare and Seneca: a Symbolic Language for Tragedy', Ph.D. dissertation, University of Colorado.
Sutton, D. F. (1983) *The Dramaturgy of the Octavia*, Königstein.
—— (1986) *Seneca on the Stage*, Leiden.
Tarrant, R. J. (1978) 'Senecan Drama and its Antecedents', *Harvard Studies in Classical Philology* 82: 213–63.

BIBLIOGRAPHY

Thomson, P. (1983) *Shakespeare's Theatre*, London.

Tobin, R. W. (1966) 'Tragedy and Catastrophe in Seneca's Theatre', *Classical Journal* 62: 64–70.

—— (1971) *Racine and Seneca*, Chapel Hill, NC.

Trabert, K. (1953) *Studien zur Darstellung des Pathologischen in den Tragödien des Seneca*, Diss. Erlangen.

Trillitzsch, W. (1978) 'Seneca tragicus', *Philologus* 122: 120–36.

Tsirpanlis, C. (1970) 'Helena in Seneca's *Troades*', *Platon* 22: 127–44.

Vickers, B. (1970) *Classical Rhetoric in English Poetry*, London.

Waith, E. M. (1957) 'The Metamorphosis of Violence in *Titus Andronicus*', *Shakespeare Survey* 10: 39–49.

—— (1962) *The Herculean Hero in Marlowe, Chapman, Shakespeare and Dryden*, New York and London.

Walker, B. (1969) a review of Zwierlein 1966, *Classical Philology* 64: 183–87.

Walter, S. (1975) *Interpretationen zum römischen in Senecas Tragödien*, Diss. Zurich.

Wanke, C. (1964) *Seneca, Lucan, Corneille: Studien zum Manierismus der römischen Kaiserzeit und der französischen Klassik*, Heidelberg.

Watson, G. (ed.) (1962) *John Dryden, Of Dramatic Poesy and Other Critical Essays*, London.

Wilamowitz-Moellendorff, U. von (1919) *Griechische Tragödie*, Berlin.

Williams, B. (1993) 'Games People Play: Metatheatre as Performance Criticism in Plautus' *Casina*', *Ramus* 22: 33–59.

Williams, G. (1978) *Change and Decline: Roman Literature in the Early Empire*, Berkeley and Los Angeles, Calif.

Williams, R. (1981) *Culture*, London.

Wilson, M. (1983) 'The Tragic Mode of Seneca's *Troades*', in Boyle (1983a): 27–60.

—— (1985) 'Seneca's *Agamemnon* and *Troades*: A Critical Study', Ph.D. dissertation, Monash University.

—— (1990) a review of Fitch 1987b, *Phoenix* 44: 189–94.

Winterbottom, M. (ed.) (1974) *The Elder Seneca: Controuersiae, Suasoriae*, London and Cambridge, Mass.

Wright, J. H. (1974) *Dancing in Chains: the Stylistic Unity of the Comoedia Palliata*, Rome.

Wurnig, V. (1982) *Gestaltung und Funktion von Gefühlsdarstellungen in den Tragödien Senecas*, Frankfurt-am-Main.

Zehnacker, H. (ed.) (1981) *Théâtre et spectacles dans l'Antiquité*, Strasbourg.

Zeitlin, F. I (1990) 'Thebes: Theater of Self and Society in Athenian Drama', in J. J. Winkler and F. Zeitlin (eds), *Nothing To Do with Dionysos? Athenian Drama in its Social Context*, Princeton, NJ.

Zintzen, C. (1961) *Analytisches Hypomnema zu Senecas Phaedra*, Meisenheim am Glan.

—— (1972) '*Alte uirtus animosa cadit*: Gedanken zur Darstellung des Tragischen in Senecas *Hercules Furens*', in Lefèvre (1972a): 149–209.

Zwierlein, O. (1966) *Die Rezitationsdramen Senecas*, Meisenheim am Glan.

—— (1984) *Prolegomena zu einer kritischen Ausgabe der Tragödien Senecas*, Wiesbaden.

GENERAL INDEX

INDEX OF MAIN PASSAGES
DISCUSSED